Beverley Eley has for many years been closely associated with the Australian publishing industry. She was Advertising and Promotions Manager with Angus and Robertson Bookshops, and Marketing Manager with Cassell Australia Collier Macmillan. When she was working as Marketing Manager with the Australian Consumers Association she met Ion Idriess's daughter, Wendy, a market researcher, who persuaded her to write this biography. Beverley Eley lives with her husband on a small holding in northern New South Wales, where she writes, tends her garden and talks to her horses.

An IMPRINT book
Imprint is a division of ETT
83 Victoria St, Potts Point 2011, Australia

Distributed by
HarperCollins *Publishers*
25 Ryde Rd, Pymble, Sydney, NSW 2073, Australia
31 View Rd, Glenfield, Auckland 10, New Zealand
HarperCollins *International*
10 East 53rd St, New York, NY 10022, USA
In de Knipscheer *Uitgeverij*
Singel 450, 1017 Av Amsterdam

First published in Australia by ETT IMPRINT 1995

ISBN 1 875892 08 7

Cover design by Robyn Latimer
Printed in Australia by Griffin Paperbacks, Netley, Adelaide

ION IDRIESS

IMPRINT

ION IDRIESS

Beverley Eley

Sydney Amsterdam New York

To my daughters
Vanessa, Samantha and Nicolla

FOREWORD

Bob Carr
Premier of New South Wales

O VER two generations, in more than forty-seven books, Ion Idriess created a new image of Australia—the Australia of the far out-back, the Centre, the tropical North, the deserts, the mining and pearling towns. He did for this Australia what the previous generation of writers like Henry Lawson and A. B. 'Banjo' Paterson had done for old bush Australia: he wrote it into the national consciousness. For at least three decades from the late 1920s, the Australia of which he wrote reflected and reinforced the image Australians, especially young Australians, had of themselves as pioneers of a vast continent. If homes in the great cities like Sydney possessed any Australian books at all, it was odds-on that an Idriess would be among them—most like-ly, *Lasseter's Last Ride*, *The Cattle King* or *Flynn of the Inland*.

Like Lawson and Paterson, Ion Llewellyn Windeyer Idriess—known to his friends as plain 'Jack'— did most of his writing in Sydney and, like them, first wrote for the *Bulletin* and published with Angus and Robertson. But both the *Bulletin* and Australia of the late 1920s had been transformed from the days of the 'bush balladeers'. The great turning-point had been the First World War; fittingly for this new Australian voice, Idriess saw active service in the crucible of Gallipoli. Idriess worked on a much broader canvas than the old bush writers and he brought to his writings a much richer and diverse personal experience. He was nearly forty when he took up writing full-time. By then he had travelled, fossicked around, explored, surveyed and hunted over more of the continent than any Australian writer before and probably since. It was the vast store of personal knowledge and material that enabled him to produce a book a year for another forty years—a feat which itself transformed Australian publishing. His most popular books went into forty and fifty reprintings.

I am delighted that the rich, adventurous life of a great Australian optimist has now been recorded by Beverley Eley and published by ETT Imprint. At a time when Australia is again undergoing a trans-formation even greater than the one which occurred during his long life of ninety years, I very much hope that the biography will encour-age a new generation to turn again to the books of Ion Idriess and find in them a source of information and inspiration about a country he understood so well and loved so much.

Bob Carr
Sydney, Australia
May 1995

CONTENTS

AUTHOR'S NOTE

L IKE most brilliant detailers and chroniclers Jack Idriess (as Ion was best known) had the ability to remain detached from his written works. The abundance of his printed words made it relatively easy to know where he had been and why he had been there but, apart from his public face, the man himself was rarely revealed.

Like many biographers I came in at the end of a life. By the time I began to research and write this work most of the people who had been close to Ion L. Idriess had died, with the exception of Wendy Idriess his daughter, Wendy's half-sister Mrs Judith Peacock, his nephews Ion and Terence Morrison, his niece Mrs Ildyce Pike (née Morrison), and Mrs MacFarlane the wife of the Reverend MacFarlane who was known also as the 'Wandering Missionary'.

Apart from that of Wendy and Judith the most valuable information from a family member came from Dr Ion Morrison, to whom I will be forever grateful for the long hours he spent recording on to audio tape his memories of the uncle he adored. The sun has gone over the yard-arm for Ion who, like his uncle, enjoyed a tipple or two, and I hope that Jack, wherever he is, finds no fault with Ion's memory of him.

I am indebted to Wendy Idriess, who, sadly, passed away prior to this book being published, for the countless hours she spent talking with me about her father. It was she who gave me the twenty-three wooden Norco butter boxes and three large cardboard cartons which contained diaries, notebooks, receipts—dating from 1911—for mining equipment purchased during his prospecting days on the Cape York Peninsula, the fan mail he had received since 1931 to the early 1970s, together with the pencilled drafts of his letters of reply, drafts of letters relevant to his research, family letters, newspaper cuttings from 1926, photographs and many assorted pieces of memorabilia: in short, almost every piece of paper that had passed through his hands, even his betting tickets!

This priceless collection, much of which had travelled extensively with Jack, was a treasure trove for a biographer.

1

Jealously guarded by Jack and meticulously maintained by Wendy, the boxes survived many changes of address during his lifetime to finally come into my hands in 1984.

To be surrounded by these boxes knowing that the contents contained all that Ion Idriess found impossible to part with was somewhat awesome, in the true meaning of that word. In fact, although the work is finished, I often still find myself standing in awe of that mountain of written and printed material which represented a man's life and much of this country's social history. I still marvel that he hadn't, like many of us who move, thrown much of it away. Perhaps he had it at the back of that active mind of his that some day a biographer should have access to all of it.

Unlike some other authors I find myself unable to extend my deep appreciation to an extensive list of supporters for their help and encouragement. However my heartfelt appreciation goes to my husband John, who, apart from entering most of my massive notes into the computer, kept visitors at bay by generally assuming the role of watchdog. I must also thank him for delivering the odd stinging pep-talk when the Muse and I had parted company while struggling up the back stretch and who, on occasions, performed the ultimate sacrifice—the supermarket shopping!

William Morris Colles and Henry Cresswell, the authors of *Success in Literature* published over eighty years ago, and marked 'Colonial Price 3/3' contend that the biographer and historian 'always have graver reason than any other writer to consider long what his shoulders can bear, and what they cannot'. Colles and Cresswell might well have also questioned the weight-bearing capacity of the shoulders of the biographer's and historian's spouse and immediate family, should he or she have one, for their lot demands much strength and forbearance.

Beverley Eley
April 1995

Chapter One

THE HILL

THE death certificate for Juliette Windeyer Idriess shows the principal cause of death, on 13 January 1908, as Peritonitis Typhoid Fever, the period of the illness as five weeks, and the place of death as Sulphide Street, Broken Hill. Juliette Windeyer Idriess, had died in the house which had been the Idriess home since they came to Broken Hill almost ten years before.

Julia's death certificate also shows that she was forty-two years old and that she was survived by her children Ion (Jack), Ildyce, Esmé and Katie, and her husband Walter Owen Idriess. It is a forlorn scrap of paper which somehow seems to convey, even now, sorrow and finality and bleak winds borne of a vast emptiness; winds that brought with them the end of the close relationship that Jack Idriess shared with his family.

With her death Julia had taken with her much more than her presence; it was the end of the Idriess family group, for Jack would never live under the same roof with his family again.

Jack never forgot his years at Broken Hill: 'During all those wandering years and throughout two world wars the influence of the Silver City has clung to me to the present day.'

The strongest adverse personal observations in reference to any place in his beloved Australia that Jack ever committed to paper are probably contained in *The Silver City*, first published in 1956. His usual charitable disposition did not extend to the 'Hill', as Broken Hill was then known. It is obvious by his various references to the place, the weather and way of life that he found little pleasure in his memories of the Hill.

Ion Idriess's father, Walter Owen Idriess, took up the office of Sheriff and Mines Inspector at Broken Hill in 1899. The trip from Tamworth was quite an adventure for the eleven-year-old Jack; for the family, however, it was expensive and arduous. It seems that Walter had gone ahead of his wife and children, for Jack makes no mention of Walter Owen Idriess accompanying his brood from Tamworth to Sydney, over to Melbourne then to Adelaide, through South Australia to Cockburn and across the border to Broken Hill.

Travelling 1,700 miles alone for days and nights, with two small children and a baby—Jack's sister, Esmé, having been born some months earlier—with only a 'very scanty store of sovereigns' must have tried Julia's endurance to the limit and her first sight of Broken Hill with its heat, dust and fumes must have shocked her beyond belief.

Broken Hill was an assault upon the senses and the psyche. There was the continued roar of the mills, 'the ceaseless sound of millions of tons of stone being crushed, pounding, pounding, pounding, grinding, grinding, grinding, hour by hour, day and night, year by year'. Silence was a signal of disaster in a mine, or of a strike, either of which caused equal distress to those on poverty's edge.

Below ground the miners had a better-than-even chance of being buried alive by a cave-in, or of being trapped in a raging inferno. The prospect of longevity above ground was little better, for many, including the miners' families, died of lead poisoning or from a variety of lung diseases.

The western inland mining town of Broken Hill had none of the raw vitality of the rich coastal Richmond River district or the New England tablelands which the family had left behind. This was four square miles of overwhelming isolation. It was a harsh, arid land where the people sweated out cruel summers frequently punctuated by asphyxiating dust storms which immobilised all activity in the town for several days. Water was invariably desperately short: during periods of drought it had to be transported by train from the South Australian Government tank seventy miles away and was then sold to the miners at an exorbitant price. The recurrent droughts dried up not only Stephens Creek, the town's sole water supply, but also the miners' meagre bank accounts, and compounded their plight by bringing the horror of typhoid epidemics, pneumonia and dysentery.

Life for settlers on the northern New South Wales coast and on the New England tablelands was hard enough, but life at Broken Hill was like serving an apprenticeship in hell.

Times were hard at the Hill in the early 1900s when Walter Owen Idriess and his family arrived. Hopelessness, as heavy as the dust storms, permeated the air. To survive the Hill it was necessary to possess a spine of steel and the ability to live one day at a time.

Many years later Jack recalled, and still clearly experienced, the melancholic despondent atmosphere of Broken Hill in the early 1900s:

The pessimistic idea was that the Hill was yet another mining town, with a possible further life of ten years. A dreadful place to live in, but the money was good if there was no strike on. Living conditions were hard indeed. Almost everyone lived in what were really shacks, with the idea of saving as much as possible to make a start elsewhere immediately the mines worked out. Flies and dust and isolation, the deadening feeling that no one else in the world knew or cared whether we lived or died out there, typhoid, pneumonia, dysentery and lead-poisoning had to be put up with; so did the dirty brown water, so frightfully expensive, that in drought time came rumbling up in water trains from South Australia. When I think of air-conditioning and painless dentistry and hearken back to the memory of those days—what a wonderful story is in the medical, transport, electric, chemical and technical discoveries that have done away with such an ocean of pain and death, that have eased so greatly the heart-breaking slavery of the mother's work, that have banished time and distance and isolation, making life livable in the wildest and most arid places all within the last few, swift years.

These words briefly reflect his lingering, bitter resentment of the Hill. There is also accusation, and a certain sense of having been betrayed by the rest of Australia in that 'no one else in the world knew, or cared if we lived or died out there'—one of his rare personal comments.

The Silver City—apart from the recounting of historical fact— is autobiographical of Jack's teenage years, and unlike most of his other works is not written from his diaries but from memory which is often painful. Throughout the book there are recurring references to appalling scenes of drought, sickness, hardship, loss and death. For a combination of reasons Jack rarely made a personal statement in his books. He wrote to a market which embraced men, women and children and he wasn't prepared to lose any portion of this audience. He understood that too much sentimentality would alienate his male readers and that any bush vulgarity would offend the women and put his books out of the reach of children. In writing *The Silver City* he comes close to revealing the real Jack Idriess but stops short when it comes to disclosing his memories of Julia, his mother, and the hardships that she endured at Broken Hill.

He was mindful of the fact that other women at the Hill had experienced the same if not worse deprivations as Julia and was fearful that if he wrote of how hard life had been for her he might antagonise those women. Whether he would not, or could not, expose his emotions is hard to say. It is my view however—despite the many references to the experiences of women, whom he repeatedly identifies throughout the book as 'mothers' and never as 'my mother'—that he was writing of Julia:

> It was a time when ten shillings would buy two pair of boots and the socks to go with them; when bagging a wallaby, kangaroo or a rabbit meant that a shilling or two could be saved. The shooting of game was sport for the boys and a saving for those women with families to feed, especially those who had husbands coughing away their lives.

Remembering the constant strikes that plagued the Broken Hill mines Jack wrote, 'The isolation of all, the feeling of being so far away from all other interests, of being forgotten and abandoned by the outside world, made these fights between companies and men all the more bitter.' The unions and companies did not unite for the common good until some eight years after Jack left Broken Hill.

Those people who could manage to scrape together a few shillings spent them on precious days of holiday in the south at Port Pirie or Adelaide over the Christmas period. It was a difficult decision for any Broken Hill miner to spend savings on a southern vacation. Strikes in the mines were endemic and regularly reduced the average family's budget and their meagre horde of shillings to a pittance. Under the circumstances of such economic instability taking a holiday was the ultimate expression of faith in the future—or a consummate gamble.

As a 'government man', Walter, whose income was not affected by strikes, usually managed to save enough each year to send Julia and the children to Port Pirie. It was there that many children from the waterless waste—the 'land of the shimmering mirage'—saw the ocean for the first time and experienced the luxury of access to unrationed, clean drinking water.

Many years later Jack wrote:

> We were fascinated by the bustle at the wharf, the loaded wagons creaking on their way to the smelters and refinery and piers, the wagons rolling in over the rutted roads of the back country loaded with wheat for the port, new buildings going up, the carts, the buckboards, the sun-browned horsemen riding into town. And then to watch the schooners, and the fishing vessels sailing down the gulf, gulls circling above them!

6

Drought was not just a possibility, it was searing reality at Broken Hill and throughout the Corner Country. Have you ever breathed under an iron roof suffocatingly hot from a blazing sun, knowing that your muddy drinking water for the day is measured in but spoonfuls, staring away from an agonised wife trying to keep a moaning child cool? I have seen such things. As a lad, when the great rabbit plagues came at the height of a drought, I have seen the parched earth round Stephens Creek a moving mass of rabbits as far as the eye could see. The brown water drying up in the catchment was worth far more than its weight in silver to the humans back in the sweltering town. Time and time again it seemed the rabbits would finish it off before the drought broke, while their countless carcasses everywhere in putrid pools helped bring typhoid yet again.

Jack, who loved Banjo Paterson's poems, reached manhood in a land difficult to equate with Clancy's 'sunlit plains', or as a 'vision splendid'. If—as claimed by Jack—he did not absorb his formal lessons too readily, he did learn the art of hunting and acquired the ability to stalk and hunt birds and animals. His first firearm was an air-gun which, as a solitary child spending hours alone on the sombre flats, he learned to use with deadly accuracy. Later he graduated to using a muzzle-loading rifle. It was at Broken Hill, alone, relentlessly stalking his quarry, that he slowly came to recognise life as a ceaseless struggle against death.

Jack's boyhood came to an abrupt end when he made the near-fatal mistake of drinking water straight from a creek in the November of 1907. One night, returning home after completing his final examination paper for qualification as an assayer, he collapsed with typhoid fever. Julia refused to allow him to go to hospital and insisted on nursing him herself.

A week later Walter and an orderly ran through the streets of Broken Hill pushing the delirious Jack on a canvas-covered stretcher on wheels—the ambulance—to the Big Hospital. Jack fought for his life and was given up for dead three times. He survived but Julia, the mother he adored, contracted typhoid while nursing him and died before his delirium had passed.

In eight years at Broken Hill, between the ages of eleven and nineteen, Jack repeatedly saw the destructive face of nature and the towering endurance of miners, bushmen and their women. He lived with the ever-present threat of death from either sickness or swift accident. He learned that courage wasn't a matter of bravery but rather the end result of having no other choice: cheerfulness was the badge of bravery. He had also suffered deep, personal sorrow intensified by embracing a burden of self-inflicted guilt as the unwitting instrument of Julia's untimely death.

Blooded by a life lived in unforgiving outback districts which had no soft under-belly, and having looked on devastation and needless death, Jack accepted the harsh terms of the lease of the land as laid down by Australia, an exacting landlady.

For Jack and the thousands of boys from the bush who volunteered to fight in a war, of which they had no conception, the 1914–1918 war represented no more than an extrapolation of all the bizarre ugliness which had gone before. Those years spent at Broken Hill hold the key to his cool, dispassionate accounts of that desperate conflict, the theatre of war at Gallipoli and the Middle East he would record in *The Desert Column*.

Arguably it was Jack's years at the Hill, and his experiences there, which founded his basically solitary personality and forged the nature and character of the man who was to become Australia's greatest chronicler.

Chapter Two
THE BOY FROM DOLGELLY AND THE
GIRL FROM CUNNINGER

WALTER Owen Idriess was born 3 March, 1862 in the parish Dolgelly, North Wales. The town of Dolgelly nestles at the foot of Cader Idris, a mountain of myth and legend in the county of Merrioneth.

Dark and forbidding the Cader Idris escarpment, rising some 2,927 feet above sea level, forms a natural border between North Wales and England's industrial south as it blocks the end of the Mawddach Valley. Today it rises out of the pollution of the industrial southern lowlands, while Rio Tinto Zinc claws for copper in its foothills and drills for gold in the shining Mawddach Estuary.

It is not difficult to understand how the myth was born that on these rugged mountains around Dolgelly lived four giants, Idris, Yscydion, Offrwin and Ysbryn, after whom the various mountains were named, and that their chief, Idris, lived on Cader Idris.

It is said that the Cader was named for the Noble Idris of Cader, son of Meririon who was one of the seven sons of Cunedda. The Noble Idris of Cader, being a grandson of Cunedda, was also cousin of the Great Maelgwyn, King of Gwynedd. It was Meririon who gave his name to the County of Meririon, now known as Merioneth.

The mighty General Cunedda, deeming it prudent and ultimately commercially profitable to stay on the right side of the Romans, performed for them (and himself) a favour by roaring down with his sons from a county known as Manaw Gododdin in Wales to drive the Irish out of north-western Wales forever.

Cunedda's shrewd appraisal of the outcome was correct; the Romans, suitably satisfied by his successful campaign, allocated the territory taken from the Irish to Cunedda and his sons. It is said that nearly all the royal medieval Welsh houses are descended from these sons of Cunedda and, further still, that all Welshmen are descended from these kings.

The ancient Welshmen, distrustful of keeping records on something as impermanent and easily destroyed as paper, entrusted the history of their nation to succeeding generations by word of

9

mouth. Even now most Welsh people can accurately rattle off their family's genealogical background from memory. Over the centuries the simplest of happenings became the fabric of myths and legends, the real players assuming the mantles of pixies, goblins, fairies, ogres and giants, not to mention a king or two.

According to Walter there was a fair sprinkling of the little people and kings in the Idriess clan. In fact, in later years at Sunday family gatherings he would declare with a twinkle in his eyes, that all were descended from King Arthur. He told them stories of a pixie that helped one Griffith-ap-Idris by giving him a fat herd of cattle and a baby. He also recounted tales of an Owen Tudor who 'rode down from the Welsh hills, threw his weight about, and married Queen Katherine of England'.

A large percentage of Welshmen claim lineage from or a relationship to Morgan, the pardoned pirate and Governor of Jamaica. There was no blood relationship between Walter and the cut-throat Morgan but this was offset by the knowledge that the boys of the Idris and Morgan clans, who had grown up together on Cader Idris, had sailed under Morgan's 'Jolly Roger'. For Walter it was a matter of pride, rather than shame, that a great number of both clans finished their days dangling from the yard-arm. There is little doubt that the sea, if not blue blood, ran in Walter's veins. A few decades earlier his paternal grandfather, Owen Idriess, fought beside Lord Nelson in the Copenhagen and Nile campaigns.

Walter was proud that his ancestry embraced kings and pixies and that his clansmen were pirates. He often hinted that he knew more stories about the Owen Idris clan. It is doubtful, however, that he knew his forebears had journeyed to his native Wales from Libya, or Lehabim, as it was known, as early as five thousand BC. Over the centuries the nations around the Mediterranean mixed, melded and migrated. Swinging north, west, and ultimately drawn again by the magnet of northern lands, this mix of races from the Middle East, the Celts, found their way to Britain.

From Libya to Wales came the name of Idris, a given name. Over the centuries the name has been spelt many ways, Idrys or Iudrys, Iudris or the earlier Eudris, or Idrisi to Idris to finally become Idriess.

The name in its present form emerged as an anglicised surname during the Reformation in the sixteenth century, when the so-called 'Protestant e' was added. Obviously the Idriesses, wishing to be identified publicly as Protestants, slipped in the e, as did hundreds of other families at that time. Down through the ages, in countries which at first glance seem to be unrelated, an 'Idriess', no matter how the name is spelt, rates a mention and it is usually great press. There is the Great Idris of Alooma of Bornu, a West African State; in the medieval Sudan, a number of the Sayed Idrises, reputed to be related to Mohammed; and the noted nobleman of Andalusia, Edrusi the writer and geographer.

So Walter Owen Idriess, officer in Her Majesty's Navy, perhaps related to kings, noblemen, scholars, a pirate or two and perhaps Mohammed and Idris, the Chief of Cader Idris, brought the Idriess name to Sydney, Australia. The Welsh have a fondness for the expression 'the wheel turns full circle'; the Idriess wheel would turn full circle when Walter's son, Ion Llewellyn Windeyer-Idriess, fought with the ANZACs throughout the 1914–1918 War in the Middle Eastern lands of his ancient forefathers.

◆

WALTER'S certificate of service with the British Navy cites his civilian vocation as a draughtsman, surveyor, and that he took up his naval commission on 22 September 1883 on HMS *Brittannia*. Passionately fond of music and able to play many instruments but most proficient at the piano and the violin, he later became bandmaster on the HMS *Nelson*. The *Nelson* was a fast, smart warship, the last of the British warships to be powered by both sail and steam-driven paddle wheel.

Walter had made port in Sydney many times between 1883 and 1887. He had seen Sydney grow and each time he arrived he marvelled at the changes. The merchant seamen found their pleasure and relaxation in the taverns of the Rocks, while the Seamen's Mission provided solace and succour for those less intent on the riotous experience during their stay in port. Around the corner at Royal Naval House in Grosvenor Street, all was elegance, sweetness and light. The 'well-bred' young ladies of Sydney Town and country stations were there in attendance serving tea and cucumber sandwiches for the officers and gentlemen of Her Majesty's Navy.

It was at Royal Naval House that Walter Owen Idriess met Juliette Windeyer-Edmonds. She was fair-haired and handsome, shy and gentle. Walter was immediately captivated by her slow smile and soft voice. From the moment that he set eyes on Juliette Windeyer-Edmonds, Walter knew that she would be his wife, and that Australia would be his home.

Known to her family and friends as Julia she was the niece, twice removed, of Charles Windeyer and second cousin to Sir William Charles Windeyer, grandson of Charles. Charles Windeyer was an adaptable and prolific gentleman who came to the colony in 1829, landing in Sydney with wife, Ann, and nine children. Later, after the addition of another two children, the Windeyer brood grew to eleven.

Charles and Ann had left a son, Richard, in London, together with two of Charles's younger brothers, John and eleven-year-old Walter, both of whom became officers in the British navy. Archibald, another of Charles's brothers, was to come later to New South Wales.

Although life was not kind to Charles and Ann, they were happy in Sydney. They were optimistic for the future of the colony and urged those members of the family who had remained in England to join them and settle in New South Wales.

Several did. The first to arrive was Charles's brother-in-law, William Puddifoot, who then died in 1833, a year later. Next came his brother John who also died very soon after he arrived. Charles was delighted when his eldest son, Richard, joined the family in Australia together with his wife and baby son, William Charles. In adulthood this child, Julia's second cousin, was to become known as Sir William Charles Windeyer, the possessor of a brilliant legal mind and a political activist.

All his life Charles had been interested in, and involved with, the law and politics. Before coming to the colony he had owned and published a small paper, the *Law Chronicle and Estate Advertiser*. He disposed of his paper in 1819 and soon after joined the *Times* as a legal reporter.

It would seem that Charles had more than a nodding acquaintance with the law. In fact this knowledge, not founded on formal training, was sufficient for Governor Darling in 1830 to call him 'a gentleman of legal education' and to further state that 'he had rendered himself very useful by his knowledge of the law, to which he was bred'. Whether Charles had any recognised legal training is of little importance for, with or without accreditation, he obtained the position of Clerk of the Police Office in Sydney. He was promoted to Second Police Magistrate in 1833 and later became Senior Police Magistrate.

Today there is a bust of Charles Windeyer on the wall of the court room in the Central Court of Petty Sessions in Sydney. Under the bust is the inscription 'First Police Magistrate 1839 to 1855'. This is incorrect. Julia's great-uncle Charles was Senior Police Magistrate rather than First Police Magistrate, although he had the status which belonged to the office and he performed those duties in addition to being responsible for and controlling the police force. The date of the inscription is also in error: Charles retired from the office in 1848, 1855 was the year in which he died.

It was the lure of taking up land in the country that had brought Charles and his family to Australia. During his years in public office he acquired various holdings but, unfortunately, fate deemed that he would never succeed as a pastoralist. For many years he battled to retain a number of interests in several properties that he shared with his children and his brother, Archibald. Two of the most notable properties in which he held grants were Tilligra, and the squatting run Tabulam on the Clarence River.

The Depression of the 1840s hit many pastoralists hard. Like so many others Charles found his financial situation in a sorry state and by 1848 he had lost his properties and was forced by the prevailing circumstances to declare himself bankrupt.

Life was not easy for anyone in the colony in the mid–1800s and the Windeyers were not singled out for any special dispensation; in fact their family history is littered with misadventure, unhappy early deaths, suicide and financial ruin.

From the time of his arrival in New South Wales Charles had urged his brother, John, a purser in the British Navy, to leave England and migrate to Australia. John finally made the decision to do so in March 1832, when the Admiralty issued a statement offering a reduction of monies on the purchase price of land in the British Colonies, North America and Australia to Officers of the Army, Navy and Royal Marines who wished to become settlers. The reductions were pursuant to rank and length of service.

So it was that John, Julia's paternal grandfather, enticed by the offer of land, arrived in Sydney aboard the barque *Ann* on 27 April 1835.

John's dream of becoming a land owner was never to be realised. By the time he arrived in the colony the land regulations had been altered. He wrote to the governor stating that he sold his property in England in order to make a purchase of land in the colony. As he had been unaware of the change in the land regulation at the time he had left England he requested that he be allowed the price reduction. The reply was short and to the point. 'I am to inform you,' wrote the Governor's Secretary, 'that His Excellency has no authority to depart, under any circumstances, from the Regulations now in force, as promulgated by His Majesty's Government.'

Sadly, within a few days of his receipt of this letter dated 20 May 1835, John, aged fifty-six, was dead. He died at the home of his brother, Charles, on 2 June 1835 just five weeks after he set foot in Australia.

John had left the tying up of the loose ends of his estate to his brother's son, Richard, when he sailed for Australia. In his letter to Richard, John Windeyer asked him to pay monies owing to various bodies and for Richard to 'be good enough to pay five shillings annually before the second Monday in January to the Royal Naval Charitable Society' and to collect debts owing to him. The letter further requested that 'any arrears of Half Pay that may be due to me, I shall be obliged by your securing (after balancing your own account against me) in any way you think advisable for the benefit of my son John Windeyer-Edmonds, and his Mother.'

John had arranged for Eleanor and their son, born in Settlebourne in Kent, to follow him to Australia. It seems most unlikely that Eleanor would have known of John's sudden death before she sailed. Her distress at the news of his death would only have been eclipsed by the realisation that she was now unsupported with a child to raise in a struggling society.

In Sydney the Charles Windeyer family received Eleanor and John's son with understanding and kindness. This child, John Windeyer-Edmonds, became a recognised cousin and close friend of the Windeyers.

The year 1835 was a most eventful one for the family. Soon after John's death, Richard Windeyer, son of Charles, joined his father in the colony with his wife and child William Charles.

Both William Charles and John were born in London and it would appear that they were almost the same age. It seems that both boys were educated at W. T. Cape's School in Sydney. William Charles went to The King's School, Parramatta, then to Sydney University. John's education after W. T. Cape's school is untraceable. From this point the only similarity between the families was an abiding interest in the land. Richard, father of William Charles, while incessantly engaged in politics and the law, had bought an estate, Tomago, in the Hunter Valley. He subsequently lost the land. Richard died insolvent but part of Tomago was bought back by his widow.

In 1857 William Charles followed his father into law. He held the position of Solicitor-General in the Martin Ministry in 1870 and later became Attorney-General in the Parks Ministries of 1877 and 1878, resigning in 1879 to join the judiciary of New South Wales. As a judge of the Supreme Court from 1879 to 1896 he found himself in the rare position of being a judge in Queensland as well as in New South Wales. He became most famous for presiding over the Mount Rennie Rape Case and the Dean Trial. William Charles was knighted in 1891. He was a man ardently involved in politics and social reform; amongst other achievements he was responsible for the founding of the Discharged Prisoners' Aid Society.

While William Charles climbed to the top of the legal tree, John Windeyer-Edmonds rose through the ranks of the Scottish Australian Investment Company, then one of the country's biggest pastoral companies. His duties as travelling manager included the buying and management of cattle and sheep properties. The majority of these properties were sheep stations, many of them situated in outback Queensland and northern New South Wales. On horseback he moved from station to station checking on the efficiency of the managers and generally keeping an eye on the company's interests.

Life for John was reasonably secure. For many the 1860s brought unemployment but for John things were different. He was not concerned with the marching processions, the deputations or the growing soup kitchen lines. 1860 was a good year: John married Mary Jane Ballard. The couple took up married life together on Demondrille station near Cootamundra where John, having left the employment of the Scottish Australian Investment Company, was employed as the station's resident superintendent.

John and Mary Jane were still living on Demondrille when the station was held up by the bushranger, Ben Hall, and his gang on 29 August 1863. John was held at gun-point by Gilbert and O'Meally while Hall, Vane and Burke ransacked the homestead.

Their second child Julia was born at Demondrille in 1866. The pastoral life was fine for a single man on his own, but as the Windeyer-Edmonds children grew up it became obvious that they should have the benefits of the right schooling; it was also clear that Julia should acquire the polish befitting a daughter of a respected gentlemen who was now an associate of the squattocracy.

Therefore, with his responsibilities in mind, John resigned his patrol post and took up a position as Government Appraiser with the New South Wales Government and rose to the position of Commissioner of Lands. This enabled him and his family to relocate and permanently reside in Sydney.

In 1880 the suburban sprawl had just begun. The rush was to the suburbs, away from the terrace houses that were clustered around the city. The scrub land and paddocks beyond were being divided for housing development. The advent of the Torrens Title, strong building societies and sophisticated mortgage systems made land ownership a possibility for the average citizen.

Most of the refugees from the city clung to the single-storey building which retained the ever-popular wide-front verandah. The simple plans retained a hall that led straight down through the house and the uninspiring back verandah which had a bathroom at one end and kitchen at the other. John however was not interested in the standard four- or six-room brick buildings. He had seen a number of grand two-storey homes being erected on elevated land on Vickery Street, Waverley, a suburb of Sydney. He bought one of these and named it Tanilbar.

Tanilbar was a very solid, handsome house built of red brick and adorned with ornate cast-iron. It stood opposite Queen's Park, facing Darley Road. Vickery Street was later to be renamed Carrington Road, the name it has to this day. Sadly Tanilbar has since been demolished, as have most of the other homes which once surrounded it. When Julia came to live at Tanilbar she was fourteen. She took her place in Sydney and in Sydney Society. Like most of the other young, well-connected ladies of her age, she frequented Trafalgar House for afternoon tea with officers of the Royal Navy and attended the occasional Naval Ball.

Trafalgar House, once known as Goodenough House and now Royal Naval House, was indeed a bastion of colonialism. It was here that the gentlemen of Her Majesty's Navy gathered when in port in Sydney. There the colony's dowagers and their daughters, dressed in their laces, silks and fine lawns, overtly provided refined female companionship for the men, while creating an atmosphere which was fondly imagined to be 'just like home'; but covertly, it was hoped that this activity would produce a good marriage with a naval officer from the 'homeland'.

The central courtyard at Trafalgar House was an oasis of pleasant tranquillity. People strolling around the balconies could look down on a garden planted with palms and ferns; on fine days the sunlight filtering through the greenery fell in dappled patterns on the paved floor and on trysting couples. Light girlish laughter and snatches of muted conversations could be heard over-riding the sounds of a piano tinkling under the hands of some young lady, probably more decorative than deft, her skill most likely forced upon her by her socially ambitious mother, whose vision of her daughter had been realised by some long-suffering tutor.

It was there among the palms and potted plants, surrounded by heavy furniture, relics of home, and suffocating velvet curtains, that the Welsh bandmaster from the HMS *Nelson*, 'one who truly could coax beautiful melody from any piano and play a nifty fiddle', met the shy girl from Cunninger.

Chapter Three
THE FIRST YEARS OF ION

JULIA was said to have been recognised as one of Sydney's beauties in her day and photographs show this to be true. The rest of the story, as told by Julia's daughter, Ildyce, to her grandchildren, is romantic and typically Welsh. Julia was apparently engaged to be married at the time she and Walter met for the first time at a ball; for both it was love at first sight and they eloped. Walter and Julia were married on 1 December 1888. The couple took up residence at Tanilbar, living with Julia's parents, the Windeyer-Edmonds, for a short period at the beginning of their marriage.

Waverley was still regarded as 'the bush' but city and suburb were rapidly beginning to merge. The heavy steam trams, ancestors of the once-famous Bondi Tram, shouldered the hansom cabs to the kerb-side as they snorted and laboriously lumbered to and from Bondi. At that time the old trams were carrying upwards of five thousand passengers per day.

Tanilbar stood only a block or two from Charing Cross which, up until the advent of the steam tram, had been regarded as the main township of the municipality. Already the area boasted a public school which had been established in 1879, the prestigious St Catherine's School for Girls. The municipality also possessed a council chambers.

Despite Walter's belief in this seemingly affluent country it was difficult for the ex-naval officer to find work, so difficult that, when he was given the opportunity to take up a temporary position dispensing law in northern NSW, he left Julia to have their baby with her parents at Waverley and went post-haste to Tamworth. Bearing in mind John Windeyer-Edmonds' family connection with the Windeyers, who by that time were comfortably entrenched in the embrace of the Sydney legal fraternity, one must assume that they had either arranged for Walter to be appointed to the post, or at least had alerted him to the fact that the position was available.

On 15 May 1889 Walter was appointed as temporary District Court Bailiff, Small Debts Bailiff, and Warden's Bailiff for

Tenterfield and Districts, with the princely sum of one hundred and sixty pounds per annum plus thirty-one pounds and four shillings foraging allowance for his horse. After his official appointment at Tamworth, Walter took up the position in Tenterfield on 1 June 1889—three months before the birth of Ion.

That same year Tenterfield was favoured with two momentous events—the arrival of the small Idriess family and a visit by Henry Parkes. While the Idriess family went unnoticed, Henry Parkes, later Sir Henry Parkes, did not. In fact his now-famous speech in which he called for 'a great National Government for all Australia' was heard not only at Tenterfield but all around Australia. Walter recalled hearing that speech made in a 'grimy little hall before half a dozen bushies'. Parkes had taken the opportunity to take almost literally to the stump and make the speech when returning from Brisbane after having had preliminary discussions with the Queensland Government on the subject of an Australian Commonwealth.

There were some at that time who considered the word 'Commonwealth' somewhat inflammatory and perhaps a little revolutionary. Nonetheless with Australia's population exceeding three million and the country rapidly moving towards nationhood the subject was timely. However, the Commonwealth of Australia did not come into being until 1901—twelve years later.

Baby Ion, or Jack as he was later to be known, did not absorb the tensions that attended the 1890 and 1893 bank crashes. He was too young to comprehend much more than the loving ministrations of his mother and, of necessity, the less frequent attention of his father whose work kept him away from home for much of the time.

The depression of the 1890s was as devastating as was the Great Depression of the 1930s. Families were broken up. In some cases, each member went their separate way, perhaps never to meet again. It was in the midst of this depression that young Ion Llewellyn Windeyer Idriess gained his consciousness. He would have heard, yet not completely understood, the cheerless conversations between Julia and Walter as his father discussed the unpalatable aspects of his work which covered mining disputes, the enforced collection of debts and the eviction of working families from properties they considered to be their own, in favour of a foreclosing bank.

The younger Idriess was scarcely four years of age when Walter's employment caused the family to move to Lismore. This time his employment was permanent. Leaving Julia, Ion, and Ion's baby sister Ildyce with friends at Tenterfield, Walter packed his family's heavier belongings on to a bullock wagon travelling to the Lawrence for stores where he packed what he could into a sulky and set out for Lismore.

Walter took the rough trip past the Richmond Range alone, arriving at Lismore just in time to be the last man to cross the old wooden bridge before the town was marooned by flood.

Several miles along the Nimbin road at North Lismore the family took up residence in a weatherboard iron-roofed cottage with an attic. The cottage overlooked the Richmond River where Ion and Julia often caught fish for breakfast. At the back of the cottage on the river bank grew a huge Moreton Bay fig tree where rafts of cedar would often be tied up waiting to be floated down river for shipping at the turn of the tide. They had only one neighbour, a carpenter with a large family living in a slab cottage just in sight of the Idriess home.

The Richmond River district was true frontier territory and alive with colourful characters. Cowboys wearing leather chaps and spurs clinked and jingled their way around town, while ladies in long skirts and calico bonnets shopped and took the opportunity to indulge in a little gossip. River pirates stole cargoes of cedar and pine from barges coming down the Richmond River waterways. The Aborigines around Lismore were a happy-go-lucky people who were known occasionally to booze it up. At night their campfires ringed Lismore. Young Ion would spend hours looking through the attic window of his parents' weatherboard home watching the flickering flames dancing in the night.

Ion was enrolled at Lower Boorie Provisional School on 6 August 1895 at the age of five years and ten months. He lived in Lismore for approximately eighteen months, moving to Tamworth at the age of seven, yet he remembered clearly the following details about Lismore, the 'Big Scrub' which surrounded Lismore, its people and the movements in the town, which he would recall many years later when he wrote *The Silver City*:

> My memories are of a dusty main street, little low-built shops, mostly gloomy inside, shirt-sleeved townsmen, demure matrons in bonnets and long, quaint dresses, shopping baskets over their arms. Bullock-wagons creaking along, probably loaded with giant logs; slouch-hatted, brown-armed horsemen in open-necked shirts, belts and moleskins, the flash ones wearing polished leggings and long spurs that jingled as they dismounted and strode into the pub for a 'quencher'. Sinewy timber-cutters were there, too—and sometimes, if you stood near these men, you could actually smell their envi-

ronment, the faint, cloying scent of freshly cut timber. For they worked in and truly cut out the heart of the Big Scrub, that magnificent jungle forest, untouched since the dawn of time, that now saturated these surgeons with its spilt juices and saps, its scented chips and sawdust, the lifeblood of countless trees. Noisy raftsmen moved amongst the townsfolk, too, on a market day, and bearded selectors, tough cane-cutters in the cane season, an occasional mounted trooper, and strolling blackfellows with their gins, piccaninnies, and dogs. The sulkies and buggies, of course, the springcarts and drays. But we saw these busy happenings only on an occasional Saturday morning when we jogged along in the sulky 'to town'. But it is the Big Scrub, the mighty logs and the rafts that hold memory most. The straining teams hauling those great logs from somewhere deep within the labyrinths of the Big Scrub, the crack of the whip, the teamster's shouts drawing ever nearer, louder, until the swaying necks of the leaders appear from the scrub edge. Then the long haul down the cleared slope past our little house right down to the river's bank. Then the manoeuvring, the casting off of the team, the skids sloping from the wagon top down towards the bank, the levering, the poling of the great log from the wagon down to and over the bank, and the mighty splash.

In his early years Jack was simply an absorbed, childish observer. In later years he was to become a meticulous chronicler who recorded his life's experiences in a series of diaries.

The family moved, again as a result of Walter's work, to Tamworth in 1897. Walter was employed in the same capacity as before but also as a sheriff with the Mines Department. Jack described Tamworth as a growing bush town. It was here that he, at the age of seven, began school days in earnest. He soon had a collection of mates and formed a strong friendship with one boy called Johnny Allsop. When young Ion had to leave for Broken Hill a few years later he wrote, 'It nearly broke my heart to part with Johnny Allsop'. Jack was never to see Johnny Allsop again—Johnny was killed in France.

Jack and his new-found schoolmates had plenty to keep themselves occupied:

On Saturdays we'd meet 'down at the common' with our dogs. Then 'the mob' would take to 'the bush'. Every bird, wallaby, bandicoot, snake, scorpion, spider, centipede, rat, anything that could move quickly enough, would waste no time in escaping our eyes or the eager noses of the dogs. Under a sheet of bark we'd catch a big centipede, a 'beaut' spider or some other repulsive, vicious fanged brute. Then an elder boy would manoeuvre it into a matchbox until we'd found another as big and hideous. We'd tickle the fiends with straws until they became fighting mad, then tip them together. A fight to the death followed.

In 1899 Walter left the frontier town of Tamworth and took up the position of Sheriff and Mines Inspector at Broken Hill. The family, which now included Jack's two sisters, Ildyce and Esmé, both born in Tamworth, followed yet again.

Chapter Four
SALT WATER TO EUCALYPT

JACK attended several schools at Broken Hill. A shy child, he was dubbed 'Old Stick in the Mud' by one of his school teachers. He claimed to have been a 'dull scholar' and that he received his two, four or six cuts with monotonous regularity. The subjects that appealed to him were history, geography and writing short essays; grammar, algebra, euclid, Latin and arithmetic corroded his sense of humour.

Subsistence wages and strikes had most Broken Hill families battling to keep themselves in food and clothing; pocket money for their children was an unknown luxury. Just as with all other youngsters at the Hill, if Jack was in need of a little money to jingle in his pockets he had to earn it. This was easier said than done, as the prevailing tight monetary conditions presented very few business opportunities for any young hopeful aspiring to become a capitalist. Once a year however the Sturt Desert Pea exploded in a riot of red and black blooms, transforming the drab desert. At this time Jack and his mates would carefully gather the seedlings, pot them in jam tins, and hawk them door to door, selling the plants to women who were starved of colour. The larger plants sold for a shilling, while the smaller brought sixpence, a 'sprat'. This legitimate nursery business supplied plants which, if carefully tended, would briefly set the gardens ablaze with their intensely coloured blooms. There was one serious drawback however—the Sturt Desert Pea season did not last long enough to bring in adequate money to cover the remainder of the year.

In search of a steady income some brilliant young entrepreneur hit on a sure-fire money-generating idea, which, if handled successfully, would have overcome the seasonal deficit. This involved catching and painting sparrows yellow, and then selling them as canaries for a shilling, a 'bob'. Forcing the sparrows to take a bath in 'yeller' water which had been coloured with Joe's sister's watercolours (stolen by the boys of course) was not easy. Getting the paint to cling to the feathers was not easy either, but the inventive group overcame the problems. After prolonged research and development the boys couldn't resist flooding the market with the counterfeit canaries and amassing a small fortune. This profitable operation could have continued for some time had not the little birds exposed the fraud, and their true colour, by indulging in their daily ablutions.

In 1904, sometime between the time of the canary racket and when Jack was driving Mr Williams' grocery cart for a wage of seven shillings and sixpence per week during the Christmas holidays, his youngest and third sister Kate was born, an event which somewhat embarrassed him. After leaving school in 1905 he obtained his first full-time employment at the Broken Hill Medical Hall, Argent Street. His responsibility was to 'sweep the medical shop, wash bottles, and not listen to the doctor's yarns'. His work continued until he joined the junior staff of the Assay Office of the Big Mine—the Broken Hill Proprietary.

The Broken Hill Proprietary employed a number of boys as assayers' assistants. At the end of each day's work these sorcerer's apprentices attended assaying, chemistry and metallurgy courses at the Technical College at the Broken Hill School of Mines. Despite his claim that he was a dull student who had no head for algebra or arithmetic he managed to graduate, with honours, as a qualified assayer. At BHP Jack and his fellow apprentices worked in the company of giants in the field of metallurgy. Those were the days when Bradford, Carmichael, Horwood, Henderson, and Potter—men who became famous throughout the world—were working under the great Dutchman, G.D. Delpratt.

Led by Delpratt, this dedicated team of metallurgists systematically solved, over years, a series of complex ore treatment problems, and developed processes which, until then, had eluded the world's best mining brains. Between them they developed the flotation process by which minerals are extracted from complex ores—particularly sulphides—and the profitable treatment of low-grade ores, which had previously been uneconomical to mine. These Australian discoveries led the world, and established the Australian steel industry.

During Jack's time at Broken Hill very few people overseas had heard of Australia, much less the Silver City—even the citizens of Sydney hardly knew it existed. But mining and steel centres around the globe finally came to know of the Silver City through the great industrial progress achieved there. In a rare bitter comment Jack wrote, 'And even Sydney knew a little.' At the time of this innovative experimentation, Cobb and Co. coaches were still thundering along the rutted tracks west of the Darling.

Jack began work in the Samples Room, crushing and sieving ore samples, cracking coke and building up furnace fires. Then he progressed to the Fire Room, where he was fascinated by the chemical mixtures, which, when applied in precise proportions, and under the vicious heat of the furnaces, melted the hardest rock, forcing it to shed its worthless content, leaving only the pure metal.

It was the Wet Room that held his rapt attention. Here the assayers, wet handkerchiefs tied over their nostrils and mouths to protect their lungs from the poisonous gases, hunched over their delicate balances and beakers, measured acids which bit into the crushed ore, dissolving the metals and worthless gangue to a liquid to reveal the metal the ore contained, metal which could be measured to a finite decimal point.

It was there in the Wet Room for the first time that Jack and his work mates were to breathe gas, 'poisonous, heavy, hideous, yellowish-brownish-greenish chlorines and bromides' which occasionally escaped during certain experiments from beakers, ovens or flues. In the not-so-distant future, those vile fumes in concentrated form would be hurled at some of them on the battlefields of France.

♦

WALTER Idriess's work took him far afield to mines, stations and Afghan camps—whenever it was possible Jack travelled with his father. Many times Jack pressed Walter to tell him tales of the bushrangers but Walter would say nothing. Walter's standard tight-lipped answer was, 'There are some questions that should not be asked, no matter in what country you may be. It's a wise policy to keep your eyes and ears wide open—but your mouth shut.'

It was on one of numerous trips with his father, 'jogging along' behind the old grey pony, that the pair drove into White Cliffs. Perhaps it was the memory of the excitement of this opal mining town that spawned Jack's urge to go gouging for opals. He vividly recalled the raw town:

> White Cliffs—a clump of iron shanties like a mirage under the sun, low-built little stores and pubs that a tall man had to stoop to enter, an army of lean-tos and tents and the children on the hill noodling for the opals missed by the miners down the shafts . . . The hills were pock-marked with thousands upon thousands of holes and cuttings; catacombs topped with innumerable dumps and windlasses, swarming with busy earth-stained men who appeared

to be vanishing like ants within the anthill—all spurred on by the beckoning hand of fortune around the corner.

The most intriguing of all the people at Broken Hill for Jack and his mates were the Afghans, some of whom had brought their personal vendettas all the way from India along with their camels.

Jack knew the 'Ghans well for he met them often when travelling with Walter, or he would visit their camps outside Broken Hill. There he and his friends would wait to see the long lines of camels and the bearded men coming in, or watch them dissolve into the heat haze as they plodded out into the desert heading for 'the Darling, Milparinka, Mount Brown, White Cliffs, Wilcannia, the Cooper, Birdsville, Bedourie, the Lake Eyre sandhills, to distant stations in south western Queensland and the frontier stations on the edge of the Simpson Desert and across the wastes towards Mount Hopeless.'

The strong personalities of the bushy-whiskered, turbaned Afghans fascinated him. There was Roda Singh who went 'looking for blood' when in the grip of the grog. Jack had witnessed Roda's turbaned companions lash him down to stakes driven into the ground, where they would leave him to broil in the sun and be gnawed by flies and bitten by ants until his fury died.

Then there was Cabal the Strong striding ahead of his team, his voluminous trousers like balloons filled with wind; Abdul Kader, 'heading his heavily laden team under the great arc of the sky towards the pine-clad hills of the South Australian border'. And the great Bejah Deverish, a piercing-eyed Afghan dressed in his many folded turban, long garishly decorated jacket, long baggy white trousers, striding out of the mirage ahead of his tall camels. Bejah Deverish was a romantic figure who had played a key role in the opening up of the famous Birdsville Track. He had pioneered track after track and helped the settlers to carve stations far out where wheeled teams could not go. He had saved numerous lives and had been the guide of the Calvert Expedition—Bejah Derverish was the local hero. And there were the leaders: the fierce-eyed Mahomet Ali with the black beard, Abdul Khan and Genghis Khan, Abdul Futabulla and old Valait Sah, the broken-nosed priest who brought Walter a length of emerald green silk to wrap around the Holy Koran on which the 'Ghans took the oath at the Broken Hill Court House.

There were the cattle drovers, Kidman's men, pushing great bellowing mobs across the border from Queensland to feed the hungry people of Broken Hill. The drovers told tales of Aborigines, stampedes, drought, epic drives down the Birdsville Track; of cunning traps set for the equally cunning cattle duffers; and of the no-man's land, a thousand miles to the north west; of dead men's bones in lonely graves, and some not in graves.

Life for the teenage Jack was a mobile feast of sights and experiences. When Jack wasn't listening and watching the passing parade he would be out shooting game. Occasionally his sister Ildyce would accompany him on these hunting trips. The Idriess children appear to have kept themselves happily occupied until Julia's death.

♦

AFTER Julia died Walter made the decision to take Jack, who was still very ill and dangerously depressed, to Waverley and place him in the care of John Windeyer-Edmonds' second wife, Kate Eldershaw, a relative of Charles Windeyer, senior magistrate of New South Wales. John Windeyer-Edmonds had died three years earlier in 1905, aged seventy-two.

The melancholy pair made the last journey that they would share together through the three states by train. The first part of the trip was via the privately-owned Silverton Railway to South Australia, from there by the South Australian Government line to Victoria, passing through Victoria on the Victorian Railway to change once again at the New South Wales border for the final part of the journey to Sydney.

Walter stayed only briefly to settle his son at Tanilbar before he returned home to his distraught daughters at Broken Hill. He attempted to take care of Jack's three sisters, Ildyce now fourteen, Esmé, seven, and the four-year-old Katie, but eventually his hope to keep the family together had to be put aside to give the three young girls a woman's care and good schooling. So the Idriess sisters were also sent to Kate a few years later. They made the journey by train to Adelaide, and completed the trip to Sydney by ship.

A letter from W. J. Gainer to Jack in 1934, recalls Jack's departure from Broken Hill, providing this descriptive gem of the young Jack Idriess:

> Happenings of our earlier days often come to mind and I picture I.L.I. in his regalia: pelts hanging to his belt as well as knife and powder flask, pockets full of paper and the old double barrelled muzzle loader gun across his shoulder. That gun!—praised by Holdsworth, cursed by Idriess.

Life at Tanilbar was clearly light years away from all that Jack had known. No father to ride with, no chatty, lively little sisters to nursemaid, no hunting trips with friends to look forward to—just Kate and his memories for company. Lost in a void of desolate isolation and believing himself to be the instrument of Julia's death he tried to come to terms with the deep sense of guilt that he carried with him for the rest of his life.

Even Wonderland City, the Coney Island of Australia, Tamarama, which had opened just three months before his arrival, offering for a sixpence 'Abundant Opportunities for Merriment', failed to entice him. Inconsolable he endured his convalescence: 'Unhappy days, waiting at gran's for returning strength, longing to get away—anywhere.'

Kate Windeyer-Edmonds, who was to outlive John by ten years, is reported to have been a lively little lady who successfully bought and sold real estate in the Waverley district; profiting some thousands of pounds she secured a comfortable old age for both herself and John. Jack makes light reference to Kate in *Lightning Ridge*, first published in 1940:

> Canny old gran saw here a grand opportunity to train up another man about the place; to pack him off to the office in the morning with his tram-fare and sandwiches for lunch, and see him come back each evening on the minute for supper; then a talk, then bed. To manage his pay envelope, darn his socks, keep his collar clean; in short, to 'look after him'.

Jack had no intention of becoming a pillar of suburban respectability or of being civilised by Kate, as John, his grandfather, 'the giant who drove four in hand and never let the dust catch him', had been; neither could he bring himself to return to Broken Hill.

Thirty-one years would pass before he would set foot in Broken Hill again. At that time he was travelling with Sir Stanley Kidman's property manager, Pratt, researching the material for *The Cattle King*. He wrote to Walter after that visit telling him how much returning there had distressed him. Walter replied, 'None of us have any good memories of that place.' It took Jack fifteen years after that to return again to Broken Hill. *The Barrier Miner* recorded his visit in 1950, and that he signed twelve hundred books in two days.

Driven by the need to escape from both Kate and all that he knew Jack spent days roaming the streets of Sydney, haunting the wharves and docks, finally escaping Kate's clutches by taking a job as a lamp trimmer and bosun's mate on the paddle-wheel steamer the SS *Newcastle*. There is no record of the number of trips that Jack made on the little steamer which plied the waters between Sydney and Newcastle and from Newcastle up the Hunter River to Morpeth. However the change of environment and constant work so soon after the typhoid proved to be too much for his fragile state of health and he was forced by a relapse to return to bed and Kate's ministrations.

♦

KATE was not to have the pleasure of his company for long. Just as soon as he regained his strength Jack was out doing the rounds of the shipping offices and the stock and station agents seeking employment in any field that would take him far away from the city. As determined as he was to get away, Kate was equally as determined that he would stay. In the ensuing game of cat and mouse he managed to elude her constant surveillance and signed to ship out as cabin boy on board a German freighter bound for Hamburg. Fortunately for generations of Australian readers the wily Kate stopped him from leaving the country; had she not intervened his life would probably have taken an entirely different direction.

Still weak from his long illness, Jack found it difficult to convince stock and station employment agents to hire him to work for their clients; they were convinced that life in the bush would kill him.

Kate could only forestall the inevitable. By dint of perseverance he persuaded an agent to hire him for work at a station in the north-west of New South Wales near Narrabri. So desperate was his need to get back to the country that he signed on for six months and accepted a token wage of five shillings a week and a paid fare, although he had previously received wages of thirty shillings a week at the Assay Office at the Hill and thirty-six shillings on the SS *Newcastle*. It seems that his employer did not recognise the arbitration court decision of the previous year to set a basic wage which met 'the normal needs of the average employee regarded as a human being in a civilised community'.

The selection was treeless except for those that lined the creek. As general dogsbody Jack was responsible for keeping the Bathurst Burrs and other pests under control, doing the milking, erecting or repairing the fences, skinning dead stray sheep and killing a sheep for the table when needed. The active life in the outdoors soon restored his good health. He enjoyed the company of the 'gentleman cocky's housekeeper and her little girl' but it seems that he shared an uneasy relationship with his employer. A month before his work contract expired the two came to a confrontation which ended in Jack packing his portmanteau and leaving under cover of darkness without the balance of his wages.

Once he had cleared the property he tipped the contents of the awkward portmanteau on to a blanket and hid the offending article. He then rolled his swag, for what was to be the first of many such times. Life on the track had really begun for Jack.

Writing in *Lightning Ridge*, which is, according to the author's note, autobiographical, Jack manages to convey a picture of a carefree lad travelling the road. Apart from the occasional reference to being hungry or missing human companionship he gives the impression that he enjoyed himself. As the work was written some thirty years later, when the edges of his memory were blurred by harsher days, he probably believed it to be so. However some very old, faded and undated notes made on that first trip north do not record the 'glorious dawn', 'the sun all rosy gold' or the 'birds singing'. Instead the rising sun found him cold and miserable, and grateful for its warmth, but by midday he was hot, dusty, and still miserable. By nightfall he was cold, tired and hungry, not to mention lonely and fearful. In one day he had found that life on the track was not all beer and skittles.

Good fortune does not come very often in the bush but that evening of the first day on his own Jack stumbled into a camp near Moree where a house was being built for a squatter. Not only was he given a meal but he was also given two months' employment as a bush carpenter's labourer—the pay was thirty shillings a week which he collected as a lump sum at the end of his time.

When the house was finished the builder arranged for Jack to work for a 'big cocky', breaking horses on a selection about twenty miles out of Moree. Here Jack and his employer, who bred horses, enjoyed each other's company. Jack took to smoking a pipe and became a first-class horseman—a skill that was to stand him in good stead when he rode with the 5th Light Horse Regiment during the First World War.

The boss was proud of his horses and proud of Jack. Jack was content to break horses until a group of shearers travelling the track rekindled his mining urge by telling stories of the Lightning Ridge opal fields and the fortune that could be made there. He resolved to go to the Ridge when he had saved a few more pounds and chance a turn in nature's underground gaming room.

The time of his departure for the Ridge was unwittingly hastened a week later by the boss who had learned that Jack had 'run away' from his first employer. That man had been angered when Jack had left before his time was up, because he preferred to pay a boy's wages for a man's work and had threatened to have the police bring him back. His second employer offered him protection from the police because he had grown fond of Jack and wanted to keep him by his side. Jack was disgusted with both men for attempting to frighten him with the fear of the police being on his trail. He wasn't sure that he could be forced to go back but he did know that neither man could hold him for whatever reason—the Ridge was calling.

He was walking again, swinging west towards the Gwydir River and Collarenebri, ultimately aiming for Lightning Ridge, which he had been told was about a hundred miles away. He hoped to pick up enough work on the way to increase his small bank to an adequate amount to keep him on the Ridge. In the early afternoon of the following day a rider directed him to where a ring-barking gang was working.

The gang consisted of twenty-three axemen each methodically contributing to the destruction of trees which would have amounted to thousands if calculated across Australia, and each laying bare the land to erosion in years to come. This gang had been drawn together in Moree. It was customary for men to make a town their base where they would become known and subsequently offered bush work, either singly or as a group.

Thousands of men all over Australia found employment in this manner and few were out of work for more than a short time— a 'spell-oh'—between contracts. By the time the ring-barking contract was completed Jack had proved himself able with an axe and a good all-round hand; more importantly he had saved himself a sizeable bank from his thirty-shillings-a-week pay packet. He was accepted and respected by the men who asked him to join the gang and return to Moree but his increasing sense of self-sufficiency and the growing idea that he could continue to find work and travel all over the country prompted him to decline the offer.

Once again he was walking through the bush alone. He had been given directions which would save him a hundred miles by taking him cross-country to the Collarenebri road.

Jack parted company at Collarenebri with a man whom he had met and spent a day with on the track. This cheerful little 'chatterbox', a fox and dingo hunter, was the Pied Piper incarnate. The man possessed an uncanny ability to lure to his side, by mimicking, anything that flew, walked or crawled—even birds in flight would answer his call, wheel, and settle in nearby trees to gossip with him. His was a gift so rare that Jack claimed it would only be found in one out of every five thousand men, but he had one or two problems which counterbalanced his skill—he couldn't shoot straight, keep to one objective, or stop talking. He wanted Jack to join up with him, become his partner, but in only one day his constant chatter had put Jack's nerves on the rack.

At nineteen Jack was already a man who was most content with his own company and was not prepared to suffer anyone who talked non-stop—even if it meant that he had to travel alone:

> Already I knew the secret of bush mateship. If you have a real mate, you are contented. You may be two entirely different kinds of men. But so long as you can like and trust one another, can give and take, you are mates—for a lifetime if fate decrees it. But in great part you must give and take, must understand one another's moods, and set your mood to sympathy if necessary—with the other man. It means only trouble otherwise. When in the bush, you must choose your mate well. If you cannot get on together, separate. Once you have found a good mate you will not want to separate.

Instead of heading straight for the Ridge as he had planned Jack took the Barwon road. The closer he came to the opal fields, the more good-luck stories of big opal finds were realistically balanced by tales of hard luck. Taciturn, but optimistic, though still not entirely secure within his newly found self-sufficiency, Jack determined to look for work and build up his bank before he finally struck out for Lightning Ridge. Turning his back on the track to the Ridge he walked along the road which wound along beside the river between Walgett and Collarenebri.

The river was the sundowner's road. The 'sundowners' were members of the nomadic tribe of travelling bush workers 'who yearly ran the river down', working a month or a week here and there when forced by the pressing need for tobacco or other little luxuries.

There was a distinction between the travelling bush worker and the sundowner. Many references define the sundowner, often identified as a tramp or swagman, as a parasite who arrived at the station or homestead just on sundown, too late to work but in time to receive a handout for his evening meal, a man who would disappear with the morning mists, leaving before the day's work began. However, often well-educated, the sundowner could also be an integral part of a circulating labour force at a time when man-power, due to extreme distance and lack of speedy transport, could not be quickly engaged.

In Jack's time the sundowner and pastoralist were still equally dependent on each other. Generally the pastoralist could not afford to employ permanent labour and work was not always available, while the sundowner only wanted casual work when he needed a little money. Jack, while humping the bluey himself, did not plan on travelling the sundowner's road for long. His one aim was to build a bank, get to Lightning Ridge and try his luck.

At Worrawadian Station on the Barwon Road he was taken on to drive a poison cart. The wage he received was one pound per week and keep—not a princely sum but, under the circumstances, better than nothing. The poison cart which Jack was hired to drive was a light-weight iron contraption on iron wheels with the driver's seat mounted on an iron stake. This horse-drawn cart carried a drum containing poisoned pellets of pollard and bran. Poison carts, combined with traps, guns and hundreds of miles of rabbit fences erected across the country, were part of the pastoralists' armory to reduce the rabbit plague.

There were two poison carts on Woorawadian Station, and both seem to have been kept fully in use. Springless, and virtually indestructible, these perambulating bone shakers could be driven without interruption over the roughest terrain, logs, small stumps, rocks and the stray fallen branch.

Jack and the other employee, a Scot predictably nicknamed Scotty, daily mixed the mash with the white sticks of phosphorus, which were kept in a liquid to prevent them from bursting into flame, as they would if exposed to the air. Jack did not enjoy killing the rabbits, but seeing dead birds, which had also eaten the phosphorus-loaded pellets distressed him more. Phosphorus poisoning brings a cruel and ghastly death. Once the material reaches the stomach it burns and eats away the intestine; naturally the stricken creature goes straight for water which, when swallowed, intensifies the effect of the phosphorus.

It took Scotty a week to realise that Jack was mixing the bran and pollard without the phosphorus. Jack had left it out because he couldn't stand to see the dead birds lying beside the ruts. After that Scotty mixed the bait.

It was also Jack's job to clear the timber-lined pits which were built to trap the rabbits. Positioned at the fence corners the covered pits had a sprung trap-door which the unsuspecting rabbits would activate as they hopped along the fences. Once the animal had fallen into the trap the door would swing shut. The rabbit population was so dense that, by the time Jack came to clear them, the pits would be so tightly packed they could hold no more.

While at Woorawadian Station he found himself assisting with the lamb-marking. Lamb-marking is a somewhat genteel term for what is most ungenteel work. Not only were the lambs marked by snipping a piece out of their ears and having their tails cut off, the males were also neutered and turned into wethers by the undignified method of having the sack split with a sharp knife before their testicles were bitten off.

Jack fast became a jack of all trades. Apart from being the reluctant rabbit exterminator, he rode the boundaries and repaired the fences. Scotty was convinced that he would 'go loony' riding on his own. Scotty however had not known Jack long enough to know that he was a born loner. He enjoyed the days but even so found the nights to be lonely and discovered that he really detested cooking, especially grappling with a damper—while the washing of his clothes tested his humour to the limit. He would throw his clothes into the nearest creek or waterhole, anchor them down with stones, so that they couldn't float away and—if he remembered—fish them out the next day and spread them on the grass to dry in the sun.

By the time the boundary riding was done Jack had saved just on fifty pounds, which he was sure would see him through a season at the Ridge, if he handled the money carefully. Evidently Scotty must have been one of the few men whom Jack felt that he could travel with as a mate for he tried to persuade the reluctant Scot to go with him and try his luck. The mining life however was not for a man suffering from tuberculosis.

Now, at twenty years of age, Jack had served his apprenticeship as a bush worker. He knew that he could rely on himself under most circumstances and he was about to make his first independent step towards self-survival and the freedom of answering to no man—the boy from Broken Hill had come of age.

Chapter Five

LIGHTNING RIDGE

A big flat partly cleared of timber appeared among the low hills, a maze of dumps topped by a forest of windlasses. A few bark huts, tents everywhere, campfires twinkling, the billies boiling, men bending over camp-oven and stores.

THIS was Jack's first impression of Lightning Ridge, the camp settlement sixty miles south of the Queensland border in New South Wales. The first opals had been found there in 1905, and by 1908 when Jack arrived the rush to the Ridge was still relatively new. The Ridge was a town of tents which clustered like mushrooms among the heavy timber. There, in the virgin bush, roughly 1,500 men were gouging holes into the heart of the only black opal field to be found in the world.

New men arrived on the field every day and began the frenzied sinking of shafts almost before they had dumped their swags. At the same time other men, who hadn't struck opal, were leaving to find paying work so that they could save enough money to finance another season on the field. Although the existence of an opal field at Lightning Ridge was only a rumour circulating among shearers and itinerant bushworkers the floating population remained constant, and according to Jack it was mostly comprised of off-season shearers.

If Jack was accurate in his estimation of the number of men on the field, and he correctly identified their trade, we find that in 1909 six per cent of the total Australian population of four million were shearers who listened to rumours and spent their savings and spare time gouging for opal between shearing stints. Arriving at the Ridge Jack had first pitched his tent and then looked about for a likely place to sink a shaft. For the first time since taking to the track Jack was the proud owner of his own tent and tools and he was buying his own food.

It was a bitter-sweet freedom. For a time he kept to himself and sunk his shafts alone, while he assessed the field and the men. Jack was not talkative, but a watcher, and he understood what was demanded in order to be accepted. Jack had learned that a quiet man, one who asked no personal questions, was held in high esteem. He perfected the art of saying little. In years to come it would be said of him: 'as a listener sitting back and taking it in while others do the talking, Ion Idriess is in world-championship class.'

He found that washing the 'snoozer' billy before rolling into the blanket at night, filling the water buckets ready for the following morning without being asked and stoking the night fire—all chores that no one particularly liked—meant a breakfast cuppa and slice of damper which he didn't have to cook.

Already, though still a youngster, he appears to have been self-possessed, insular or perhaps seen by the uncharitable as selfish. In fact his personality was gradually developing into one of conscious separate existence. It was this sense of separatism which would allow him to observe dispassionately a world at war. Jack believed that a person could choose his or her emotions and set them to work in the unconscious. It seems likely he employed this philosophy to relieve the self-acknowledged legacy of guilt that he had experienced from the time of Julia's death, as well as to control and modify the potentially painful emotions of love and hate.

At twenty however, his personality was not quite in place and he responded to the lusty vitality of the life around him. The future was plastic and pregnant with possibilities—and promised opals. He felt bigger, better and happier than a king and best of all he was his own boss!

Nonetheless the impracticality of digging and hauling the mullock from the shaft on his own dictated the need for a mate to work with. This need helped him to overcome his natural inclination to be solitary and, to use the vernacular of the day, he 'went mates' with a New Zealander. Jack was well satisfied with the partnership, for the man was also happy to do the cooking—albeit badly.

Neither man brought luck for the other and the two parted company when the New Zealander was offered the opportunity to work on a better prospect. Jack then joined forces with Tom Peel, who would play a significant role in the saga of the life of Ion Llewellyn Idriess—author. Known as Old Tom Peel, this ex-solicitor from Sydney had managed to drown his own rising star by his enthusiastic use of whisky and in doing so had committed himself to the company of nomads.

Jack acknowledged that he and the forty-five-year-old Tom Peel were an odd pair. No doubt Jack found a certain security in the company of the older man without consciously recognising him as a father figure. Tom also appears to have found fulfilment in the relationship for he assumed the role of Jack's surrogate father, and became his mate and experienced adviser.

There are two stories of how Jack began to write, both of which were told by Jack. The most popular version which was to appear in many newspaper interviews given by Jack in later years told how Tom urged Jack to contribute to the *Bulletin's* 'Aboriginalities' page. He also told how he was advised by the *Bulletin's* editor, via the 'Answers to Correspondents' column, to 'stick to his pick and shovel'.

The other version is that Tom pushed him to write his first effort, an article on Lightning Ridge, which Tom posted to the *Sydney Mail*. The article was subsequently published and Jack received a payment of three guineas.

Jack was born a keen observer, but he compounded this gift by making notes of the things he had seen. Since the time he had slipped away from Kate's grip Jack had been scribbling notes, recording the things around him. He detailed the oddities and rarities of nature, recorded snippets of conversation with characters that he had met, and committed to paper a few of his thoughts. These notes he gave to Tom to read.

When Tom had read Jack's notes by the feeble candle-light at Lightning Ridge in 1909 this educated man recognised Jack's ability to see more than most and realised that he had a raw writing talent. He was convinced that this talent, with a little encouragement and nurturing, would produce articles the daily newspapers would buy, and which city people would want to read.

It was Tom Peel's faith and the *Bulletin's* disdain for his efforts, combined with his own cussedness, which made Jack polish his wordsmithing and fulfil Tom's prediction.

While the *Bulletin* ultimately gave up the unequal task of resisting his doggedness by publishing his 'paras', as he called the fact-packed paragraphs, the Ridge, with equal persistance, refused to give up her opals to him, no matter how many shafts he and Tom sunk.

If a man was almost broke then it was acceptable that he 'noodled'. If a stone that a gouger had missed was found by a noodler then it belonged to him. However, if he did find one that would put tucker back in his bag, the unwritten law of the field demanded that he then walk away from the mullock heaps. Many unsuccessful seekers preferred to pack their swags, leave the field, and take in a shearing season.

Jack and Tom battled on through Jack's first season at the Ridge without striking a single stone. Occasionally, in desperation, they too would noodle, always in the belief that the next day, the next rake of the pick, would be rewarded by the sound of that curious clink of metal on glass which meant they were on opal.

Finally, after eight months of never once sighting a single stone—a 'nobbie'—Jack decided that he would have to roll his swag before he was bankrupt and leave the Ridge to look for work. He swore to Tom that he would come back; nothing would deter him from trying his luck again.

Jack rode away from the Ridge employed as a horse-tailer with a droving outfit travelling through Walgett and Barren Junction to Narrabri. He was responsible for the good condition of the droving outfit's horses. The welfare of the horses took precedence over a mob of travelling cattle or sheep, for without the horses the mob would come to a standstill.

The drover, or the Pony Drover, as Jack referred to him, was the proud owner of a lively team of matched grey horses and whenever it was possible he selected his droving routes to follow the country shows. After making camp outside town the drover would settle the mob and take his troupe of cheeky horses to the town's show ground and enter them in the ring events.

The Pony Drover had a flare for dramatics. He had trained his amenable four-footed troupe to wink, nod, waltz to music and to balance on barrels, and he taught Jack to jump a pony through a flaming hoop. The big paper-covered hoop was smeared with tar to create a breathtaking blaze when ignited. Giving vent to a full-throated yell Jack would come at the gallop, put the pony to the jump, then both would hurtle through the fiery ring. Jack said that he and the pony thoroughly enjoyed the excitement of the fire, sparks and smoke and thrived on the applause of the audience. Occasionally both would emerge scorched. Jack observed that he didn't mind getting scorched eyebrows.

'From Narrabri,' Jack wrote, 'we rode down to Boggabri and soon afterwards the Pony Drover lifted a mob of five thousand wethers from Baan Baa Station. We started crawling north then, the sheep were to be delivered to a station near St George, across the Queensland border.'

The mob followed a Stock Route which passed through well settled country. The coming of the travelling mob set the district on Red Alert. The drovers could be relied upon under any circumstances to steal the cow cockies's grass. It was Jack's job as the horse-tailer to take charge of all the horses at sundown after the men had finished with them and then to take them back to where they could get a good feed of grass at night. At sunrise he had to bring them back, fresh and well fed, ready for the drovers.

Jack, the circus performer, horse-tailer and grass stealer for the 'nuggetty little grey ponies, the hardiest, most intelligent, cutest little team that ever stole a cocky's grass in all the north-west', also had to be on guard against horse thieves. These men would wait until the drovers were asleep and, moving silently in the night shadows, gain the confidence of the horses, slip off their hobbles and bells and be gone with the lot before the horse-tailer had a chance to carry out his own nefarious work.

Jack never lost a horse and his horses were always well fed. He could cut a fence and have the horses fed and back on the track, with the fence mended, well before sunrise. He was modestly proud of his ability. 'I was pretty nippy as a young boy and pretty good at this.'

Every grass-stealer has to meet his Waterloo and Jack met his one morning just before sunrise. A suspicious cocky making a pre-dawn patrol of his boundaries caught him red-handed as he was moving the fat horses out through the cut fence. A furious chase followed and Jack found himself on the business end of a green-hide whip dispensing instant justice. The furious man lashed both Jack and his horse as they tried to out-distance him and his singing whip. A badly cut back and a behind which prevented Jack from sitting in the saddle for a fortnight were enough to convince him that it was time that he went back to Lightning Ridge. Jack finished the drive with a cheque which was enough to stake him at the Ridge for almost a year.

Trudging his way back to Lightning Ridge he found work at Dungelear Station. The shear was in progress and Jack was taken on as a rouseabout and given a beginner's pen of sheep to shear. The pay was thirty shillings a week and tucker, which Jack was happy to receive.

Jack admired the gun shearer's deft speed; he could handle two hundred sheep a day. Despite his best efforts Jack couldn't come close to even the slowest shearer, and before long he found himself equipped with a rifle and ammunition and relegated to the back paddocks to shoot fox and dingo. While his shearing hand was less than spectacular, his sharp eyes and straight aim served him well.

The majority of foxes and dingoes in the district were rela-tively safe; Jack worked only for a few weeks until the shed was cut out. The shearers packed up their plant and headed for another shed and many days of back-ache fifty miles away, while Jack Idriess continued on toward Lightning Ridge.

His road lay past Walgett, a bush town on the banks of the Namoi River. Miles of tree-lined, dusty road stretched ahead. The day was hot, and he had a fifty-mile tramp before him. About midday, he saw a cloud of dust moving rapidly his way, accompanied by blasts from a bull-horn, and as it got close he could hear the sound of voices and a banjo being played hell for leather. It was Cobb and Co.'s coach from Lightning Ridge to Walgett. Cobb and Co. was still king of the road when Jack was twenty.

The first day back on the field Jack bought a tent and tools, set up camp and made straight for an old shaft. At that time there was so much opal still left under the ground that many of the miners only part-worked their claims, taking the most accessible opal and then abandoning the claim. As luck would have it just twelve feet down immediately under the roof was a ledge of steel-hard opal which, much to Jack's delight, yielded three good stones in the first few minutes. He sold the stones as they were for fifteen pounds, a large sum of money in those days.

For the next two years, Jack was hardly ever off opal. Although he never really struck large quantities he did find enough to keep him comfortably and to make a few trips to Sydney to visit his grandmother, Kate Windeyer-Edmonds, and his three sisters who were at boarding school, and enough to make the pilgrimage to the Blue Mountains.

Lightning Ridge had become a little more civilised by this time. Several new stores had opened and a handful of opal cutters had set up business. There were four resident buyers, and visiting buyers regularly came from Europe. Things were looking up, or down, depending on the beholder, for over a dozen women had taken up residence in this previously male-dominated preserve.

After Jack had established more than a nodding acquaintanceship with luck he too acquired a hut. On cold winter nights Jack and his cobbers would yarn by the fire while they drank a little or a lot of black market sly grog, the quantity consumed being controlled by the wherewithal to buy it. Jack was working on Three Mile Field which looked as if a plague of rabbits had descended on it—shafts collared by mullock were everywhere. The field abounded with men from many nations. These colourful characters had literally dug themselves into the Ridge; amongst them was one who claimed to be an Austrian count, Count Hoyst.

According to Hoyst, he had been a guest at Mayerling on that fateful night when Crown Prince Rudolf of Austria and the beautiful Baroness Marie Vetsera committed suicide—or were murdered. Hoyst further implied that he, Count Hoyst, besotted with Marie Vetsera, had left the glittering dinner party that evening in a fit of jealous rage. He also said that it was his own brother who, together with the Prince's valet, had broken down the door to the Prince's apartment and found the pair shot through the head.

Jack checked the story and found that the Count who had burst the door was named Count Hoyos. Perhaps—given the Australian ear for European accents—Hoyos is close enough to Hoyst. Whether or not it was just a good story, which gained the Count of Lightning Ridge plenty of attention, could not be proved but it certainly surpassed the usual tall campfire tales.

Sundowners, cockies, counts, kaisers, remittance men and cow cockies burst from the pages of *Lightning Ridge*. The book is one of the few records of the Ridge as it was in its youth.

♦

A FTER settling in at Lightning Ridge Jack and Tom teamed up once again and worked with an old man they nicknamed 'Dad'. Unhappily Dad had a heart attack and died at the bottom of the shaft they were all working on. Jack was above ground at the time and during the subsequent police investigation it was uncovered that Jack had been in charge of the facing and selling of the opals which the three dug from the claim and further that he had not disclosed to the police the existence of five bar opals which he had left with a cutter. The policeman investigating the case was not entirely convinced that Jack did not have other stones hidden and suspected him of killing the old man.

Although Jack was never directly accused of murder the policeman tried to have the body of the old man exhumed by bringing the facts of the case and Jack before a travelling magistrate. The magistrate refused to grant an exhumation order, dismissing the case without asking Jack a single question.

The old man's death and the tension surrounding the events that followed had soured both the claim and the Ridge for Jack. After leaving 'Dead Man's Claim'—for that became the name of this gloomy and, finally, highly profitable claim—Tom and Jack drifted apart.

Stories which must have come from Jack put the value of the opal taken from Dead Man's Claim at three thousand pounds. It is a story which might just as well be fiction for Jack left Lightning Ridge in 1910 with a only seven hundred pounds for opal which he had dug from another mine near Dead Man's Claim—enough to take him once more to visit Kate and his sisters in Sydney.

Chapter Six
THE PENINSULA

WHEN Jack was just a child travelling with Walter, he had promised himself that he would one day cross that invisible barrier—the Queensland border. Walter's jurisdiction ended at Tweed Heads and Jack had found it difficult at that time to comprehend why they could not cross the Tweed River into Queensland. For years he had nursed the itch to cross the border. The tales told of the wild Cape York Peninsula by gold prospectors who were trying their hands at opal gouging had further whetted his appetite for going to the extreme north of Queensland.

Queensland sounded to him like the promised land. Prospecting was in Jack's blood and minerals were never far from his mind. His ambition was to discover a new gold field just for the thrill of it. Jack used to say that if there was a chance that he could open up a new field in the Antarctic he would lead the rush. Whenever in Sydney Jack visited the Mining Museum. There he spent hours standing before the glass showcases studying mineral specimens which had come from all over Australia and other parts of the world. He particularly concentrated on those specimens he hadn't seen in the bush or while working or studying at Broken Hill. Having determined to head north he decided that now was the hour to put his formal training at Broken Hill School of Mines and his voluntary study into practice.

So Jack took himself to Cairns and from there on to the tiny settlement of Nigger Creek on the Wilde River to search for tin: this was the beginning of his life-long romance with the Cape York Peninsula and points north.

The township of Nigger Creek, as with Lightning Ridge, was largely comprised of tents. There were a few cottages, a store, one of the smallest schools in Queensland and two pubs, the New Pub and the Old Pub. The New Pub had been built to cope with the thirsts brought to town by the men building the line from the railhead at Cairns to Herberton. It was inevitable that a certain amount of animosity existed between the two publicans—dirty looks and dirty words were the order of the day. Jack took up residence at the

New Pub and became firm friends with the schoolmaster, Garnet Aitchison, who boarded in one of the cottages.

Jack described himself as slow and solemn and implied that he was enjoying the exquisite misery of being in love with a girl he had left behind in Sydney, while Garnet with the ready smile who 'couldn't cook an egg unless the hen laid it ready fried' was bursting with energy and eager ambition to achieve a heady position with the Queensland Education Department, an ambition Garnet Aitchison later achieved after serving in the 1914–1918 war. These two were to meet up again some years later under the shadow of Turkish guns at Gaza.

Prospecting for tin at Nigger Creek was vastly different from opal gouging at Lightning Ridge. Here no one anticipated getting a fast fortune and neither was there the excitement of a huge mining field under tents. Now that the railway had passed it by the most excitement the little town saw was Mrs Reynolds, who ran the Old Pub with the help of her two daughters, cracking the skull of some out-of-hand railway navvie with her ironwood shillelagh.

At Deep Drift on the Wilde River Jack spent most of his days hefting a pick and shovel while engaged in alluvial tin mining, sinking shafts and tunnels in search of the tin deposits buried in the ancient river bed. After the dirt was hauled to the surface it was taken by horse and dray to a community sluice box which was put into the river where the swiftly flowing water would divide the tin by the power of gravitation.

Jack didn't make much money from the tin he found, just enough to pay the storekeeper. In fact it was the five shillings that the *Bulletin* paid 'Gouger' or 'Up North' (his *noms de plume* at the time) for the dozen or so 'paras' published each month that kept him an independent man. Even though he was enjoying the success of being a *Bulletin* 'Aboriginalities' man Jack never dreamed that he would ever write a book.

While Jack may not have found great wealth in minerals he found wealth of another kind: the fascinating material which he collected and used when writing *Back O' Cairns*, first published in 1958. In *Back O' Cairns* Jack gives the reader a picture of what life was like when the Peninsula jungle was falling under the settler's axe, his own day-to-day experiences, and the district's historical background. The book is peopled by characters given to polite chiacking and the writing of poetry, and the reading of 'pomes' by the evening campfire. One or two tie on a bender and play the occasional elaborate practical joke. Perhaps the most interesting is the 'Jungle Man' who could scent animals and Aborigines in the scrub before they scented him. He also possessed incredible hearing. He was a strange fellow 'with a cold grey look in his eyes' who took Jack into the rugged mountains and the dense jungle and showed him a primitive world few men had ever seen.

Jack was treading in the tracks of his heroes—the explorers. Stories of the great pathfinders, Mulligan, Doyle, Atherton, and Christy Palmerston were fresh in the minds of men, and were still at that time being recounted around the campfires like the news of the day. Jack never missed an opportunity to call in at the store for a chat with Jack and his partner, Newell. These men had founded the Herberton field and the Great Northern field when the 'blacks were bad'. The two had given up prospecting to become store-keepers at Herberton.

By the time Jack arrived at Nigger Creek the line had passed the town, pushing the railway workers camp of tents and hessian huts deeper into the bush and leaving behind at Nigger Creek only the memory of sleeper haulers, blacksmiths, drays and wagons, fist fights and the two pubs.

Jack marvelled upon the fifteen-mile section of the Barron Gorge railway with its ninety-eight curves blasted round the gorge side, the fifteen tunnels blasted through the spurs and the huge escarpments cut from the mountainside track. So precipitous was this terrain that the track afforded only a one-way foothold. He regarded with awe bridges that had been built, under the worst conditions, over every ravine and water-way, often suspended over drops of hundreds of feet.

Jack looked, listened and made his notes. In *Back O' Cairns* he wrote of the men who had achieved this. 'They only had brains and enterprise and brawn, dogged persistence, horse and tip-dray picks and shovels and wheelbarrow, hammer and drill, gunpowder, and a very carefully shepherded supply of gelignite to work with.'

However hard Jack worked the rich lode seemed to keep side-stepping his pick. In the hills all around Herberton the reef miners were blasting rock in their never-ending search for tinstone. Jack worked with a will, hoping against hope that he might some day be able to have enough capital to buy the equipment to become a reef miner and go after the ore locked in a rock reef.

♦

ALMOST two years after Jack came to Nigger Creek in 1912 he decided that it was time to push deeper into the north. With just enough money to pay his boat fare and to keep him in food for a month he left Cairns for Cooktown.

Cooktown, once the port to the 'land of gold', had been a bustling base, the jumping-off point from which twenty to thirty thousand Chinese and a large number of white prospectors had ridden away, or pushed barrows, or trudged to the Palmer, the 'river of gold'. Historians note that the Chinese outnumbered the Europeans at the Palmer diggings in 1877 by seventeen thousand to fourteen hundred, but old records sighted by Jack at the Cooktown Warden's Office estimated that some twenty thousand Chinese or more had streamed on foot to the Palmer.

Cooktown had its Chinatown. A number of Chinese, survivors of the Golden Palmer days, who had realised that the most reliable source of gold was to be found in trading, had shrewdly become storekeepers. These well-respected members of the Cooktown community now met the boats and hopefuls like Jack who steamed into Endeavour Bay.

The world and his dog, literally, came to town and down to the wharf when the SS *Musgrave* tied up under the shadow of Grassy Hill the day of Jack's arrival. The stinking old boat brought with it passengers, food, and the mail, the latter being the most important part of the cargo to people so far removed from the rest of the continent. Mail day was a social occasion, the crowd in a high spirited, carnival mood. It seemed to Jack that the entire population of Cooktown was assembled on the weather-beaten wharf to meet the steamer. Jack was feeling a little self-conscious and lonely as he leant on the ship's rail and looked down on the milling crowd. A deck-hand gave him a running commentary on who was who among the shirt-sleeved men and the women dressed in cool white cotton dresses.

Among the well-known identities were the local solicitor Charlie Patching, the 'Father of Cooktown' (Jack didn't explain how Charlie earned the title); George Love, the mayor; the local sergeant of police, a man by the name of Bodman, whom the deck-hand described as a 'suspicious man'; Stanfield Samson the chemist, identified by the same deck-hand as a 'good man at mixin' fever mixtures'; the luxuriously black-bearded Captain Dan Moynahan; Mrs Louisa Boyd, a little lady who 'could cut a bullick's throat an' skin 'im' and who was known to lend a hand to 'bury men wot's been speared by the blacks'. On the Peninsula the women were as tough as the men—they had to be.

Beside a group from the Chinese community stood James Dickie and Billy Webb. Both men were prospectors and explorers and had been responsible for putting names on the peninsula map where previously there had been empty spaces. Billy had the double distinction of being the first white miner ever to set foot on shore in the early rush days to the Palmer and the first man to be married there.

Staring back at Jack from the wharf were a few Japanese pearling men from the luggers anchored in the same bay which had in the past provided anchorage for Captain James Cook's *Endeavour*, and Billy Hughes' fishing smack, *The Star of Hope*. There were also Rottermah men, a quieter group of sturdy Malays and coal-black Solomon Islanders wearing their Sunday best 'town' singlets. Around the edges of the crowd a good handful of the local Aborigines were gathered with their giggling, excited piccaninnies and their flea-ridden dogs. The town dogs which had sauntered down to the wharf (just to keep an eye on things) took the opportunity to spice the occasion by snarling at this visiting four-legged contingent.

To the boy from Broken Hill and points sou'west, Cooktown was a strange Australian town. Even in his days of wandering around the wharves of Sydney Harbour he had never seen such an assorted collection of races. Neither had he ever seen Japanese pearling luggers, nor yellow sandalwood, nor smelt anything like the odour wafting from the sacks of smoke-dried bêche-de-mer, the giant sea slug so prized as an aphrodisiac by the Chinese. Both of these curious cargoes mellowing under the hot sun on the weather-greyed wharf would eventually be loaded on some ship with a romantic name like the *Empress of China* and sold in the Orient. In the coming years Jack was to harvest both trepang, and fragrant sandalwood.

Jack had first encountered tropical vegetation at Cairns and in the rain forests at Nigger Creek but Cooktown was an exotic extension of all that was verdant. Huge mango trees—the archetype of lush tropical trees—aggressively healthy and polka-dotted with golden fruit, shaded one side of Charlotte Street. Bungalows sheltered from the sun under glossy-leaved banana palms, paw-paw trees loaded with football-sized yellow fruit, soursop trees and five-fingers. The gardens were vibrant with brilliant flowers and flowering vines, which at night released a vapour of heady fragrance.

At the back edge of Endeavour Bay stood Cooktown's Chinatown. This above-ground, wooden catacomb hid its secrets from European eyes and provided an impenetrable barrier between the West Coast Hotel, the big Joss House and three fan-tan banks which never closed their doors. To get to the fan-tan houses incurable gamblers had to pass through forbidding narrow lanes between rows of wooden shacks. The air was thick with the smell of oriental food and blue incense smoke. To the prejudiced whites the barred doors of the wooden shacks hid opium dens where the lotus eaters dreamed their dreams and practised God only knew what other kinds of unthinkable, tantalising perversions.

Jack enjoyed gambling; like prospecting, it was in his blood. Jack claimed to have spent many hours practising the Chinese game of fan-tan in his room at the West Coast Hotel and after he had perfected it he subsequently broke the bank at the three fan-tan houses. Jack further claimed to have been barred from the game at the three establishments. Just how he managed to outfox the Chinese at their own game he didn't disclose. Whatever he did was enough to convince the Chinese that he had to be kept from playing. He was sure that he should take his act on the road to Hong Kong, and make a killing there—he never realised that dream.

The brigantines, barques, schooners and steamers which had crowded into Endeavour Bay—the last port—had all gone. So had the tent city the gold-crazed passengers had built. Even though the rush had ended, Cooktown was very much alive in Jack's day. The only road out of town ended at the Rossville tin fields in the south, thirty miles away. There was no road to the north, only a track the mailman followed along the Overland Telegraph Line which extended to the tip of Cape of York and across to Thursday Island.

Every day brought hard-bitten characters, tin scratchers and miners, usually in pairs, from places such as Rossville, the Palmer, China Camp, Hell's Gate and Black Mountain. There was usually a good mix of sunburned cattlemen from holdings far up north, such as Silver Plains, Merluna Station or Van Rookah; a handful of gold prospectors from the Ebagoolah and Coen goldfields and perhaps a stray prospector from the Batavia River at the top of the Cape; sandalwood harvesters, pearlers, trepangers and packers were also to be found swapping stories with the locals at the West Coast Hotel.

There was always movement in the town. Pack-horse trains loaded with tin or sandalwood moved through down to the wharf, where goods were off-loaded to be shipped to market. Strings of up to eighty pack-horses creaked through carrying bags of flour, potatoes, sugar and cases of jam, picks and shovels, tents and mining supplies. Similar pack-horse trains could be seen coming into town bringing the government-marked hundredweight canvas bags packed with tin ready for shipping.

Wages had just gone up to ten shillings a day and sandalwood was fetching seven pounds per hundredweight—the same price as tin. (A meal cost a shilling at the West Coast Hotel, as did a bed for the night.) If a man didn't have the money to buy a string of horses and set up a sandalwood outfit for himself and the necessary three mates to take turns at keeping watch at night then he could always look for a job on the tin fields.

The Cape York Peninsula is not what is generally thought of as a peninsula. About five hundred miles long and roughly one hundred and fifty miles wide at its base it was, in Jack's time, still heavily populated with tribes of Aborigines. These people whom he consistently referred to as 'the wild folk' were almost to vanish from the Peninsula after the two Spanish Influenza epidemics which followed the First World War.

The Peninsula offered a variety of ways to die. Gathering sandalwood was fraught with as much danger as prospecting and it was still possible to make the death notices by being speared by the Aborigines. If a man managed to avoid the Aborigines, snakes, crocodiles, or any one of a hundred accidents, the chances were that he would not be missed by the malaria mosquito. Although in terms of violent misfortune Jack led a relatively charmed life, he was not overlooked by the mosquito. His days on the Peninsula were to leave him with repeated, long-lasting attacks of malaria.

Jack had come to Cooktown expecting to strike into the interior and carry on prospecting as he had done at Lightning Ridge—alone. He really had no concept of how dangerous the jungle north of Cooktown could be. He had a vague idea that conditions would be rugged and it would be an exciting adventure with some variation to the challenges that he had faced before. After spending a few hours in Cooktown, however, he reluctantly accepted that, just outside the town limits, especially to the north, the rest of the Peninsula was beyond the pale.

With only six pounds in his pocket, a swag, the trousers and shirt he wore and a half worn-out pair of blucher boots, he was in no financial shape to buy even one horse, much less the saddlery. To buy a tent and equipment, without a mate or two to watch his back in the wilds, would have been a waste of what little money he had. The idea of working for a boss again did not appeal to him but then neither did the alternatives. The Annan River Tin Mining Company at Rossville was just beginning to expand and needed men so Jack swallowed his pride and headed for Rossville.

That first night out of Cooktown he stayed at the Lion's Den near Helensvale. This was a pub run by Mrs Watkin who not only cooked meals which tamed many a wild tin scratcher for miles around but also owned unbelievably comfortable beds, which Jack never forgot. The Lion's Den is still there today, as is the piano on which Jack is said to have played many a tune.

Taking a job at the Annan River Mining Company went right against his grain. Swinging a pick and hefting a shovel wasn't what Jack had in mind at all. He had counted on being given a job that would teach him hydraulic sluicing, and pay him while he was learning to build his own plant. He took the unreasonable view that the management was wasting his time by not teaching him the fundamentals of hydraulic sluicing. The more he was overlooked, the more irritated he became and the less he worked, consciously penalising the company for their ignorance by scarcely doing a fair day's work.

Jack claimed to have been given the nickname of 'Watchell Jacky' which meant 'Cyclone Jack' while he was at the Annan mining camp at Rossville. Just who was responsible for bestowing the name on him is unclear—once again there are two stories, both from Jack. One is that the sharp-eyed Aborigines gave him the name in derision; the other is that his mates gave it to him because he was so slow that it would take a cyclone to move him! Either way he wore his tardiness like a mantle of greatness and claimed, with some pride, that he could be trusted not to make one more blow of the pick than was necessary, or lift one more shovel full of dirt than he had to. Paired with Jack, Freddy, a 'wages man', was kept in a constant state of anxiety because Jack's lack of effort reflected on his own work.

Since his first serious writing attempts at Lightning Ridge Jack continued keeping notes and writing. While he was working at the Annan he established a discipline of committing to paper the day's events each evening. Not because he liked the task—he hated it. Writing, in his own words, was 'sheer drudgery' and it continued to be for the rest of his life.

From Cairns, Nigger Creek, Cooktown, and now from the Annan, he sent his paragraphs to the *Bulletin*. If he was working miles from a post office and unable to post his 'paras', he saved them until he happened across a post office. The *Bulletin*, supplied by Jack with whole batches of 'paras' to select from, usually published several of these in each issue. 'Gouger' and on occasions 'Up North' appeared regularly on the 'Aboriginalities' page.

His attitude towards the *Bulletin* had changed; no longer did he regard their acceptance of his work as 'forcing them to eat crow'. The regular cheques had altered that. Apart from the money, which he was stacking flat with what little he could save from his wages, his ego had responded to seeing his work in print and he was feeling quietly pleased with himself.

When Jack was finally identified as 'Gouger, of the Bullerteen' he was treated by his workmates with surprised respect. When his secret was first disclosed he reacted with some embarrassment; however it wasn't long before his self-consciousness gave way to his greater sense of self. Jack states in *The Tin Scratchers*, written some forty-three years after the event, that his ego was inflated somewhat by the respectful silence that fell when he walked among the men after they had learned that he was not just 'another harmless nit-wit'. This is one of the few personal glimpses of Ion L. Idriess that Jack allows us to see. Jack didn't mind having a laugh at Ion's expense. Ion of course didn't expose himself as readily as Jack. By the time he wrote *The Tin Scratchers*, years of writing for a market which preferred 'Happy Jack' had taught him to sidestep comments which might be considered risqué or nasty; however, intentionally or otherwise, the underlying, remembered hurt and an acknowledgement of his own sense of superiority is evident.

I suspect that Jack's self-effacing honesty in relation to his acclaimed laziness was pure sham. He came from a family background which bordered on the upper-class and, although he had chosen the life he was leading, the truth was he couldn't quite identify with the pick-and-shovel brigade. Unlike the other men working at the Annan, Jack scorned the thought of picking up a regular pay packet for the rest of his life. He used their fear of being fired and unemployed in a country where the only chance of finding another job was to take the boat back to Cairns: 'The harder Freddy toiled, the less I toiled: I knew Freddy couldn't help toiling, but I could.' Like the Chinese coolies, he aspired to become a 'Guild Master' by eventually employing wages men to work his own tin show—when he found it.

At twenty-three Jack had developed an enigmatic yet charismatic personality which he used to manipulate those around him. He was probably better educated than most men on the field; a qualified assayer and metallurgist, a writer and a pianist of better than average skill. He had a high degree of self-discipline and he was fiercely independent—a loner who despised the wages men for their lack of courage. He saw himself mostly as miscast among men who, though good-hearted, were not his equal.

Throughout his life Jack was a traveller in time, dipping into the experiences of the group without ever becoming a part of it. With it and yet not with it...the separatist who didn't quite mesh with his peer group and who really didn't give a 'tinker's cuss' about it.

If Jack didn't care for his peer group, he most certainly didn't give a damn about being fired from the Annan River Tin Mining Company. Jack believed the company to be selfish and never satisfied. After the management pushed him and Freddy to complete a job ahead of schedule, when he and Freddie had sunk sampler's shafts by a method devised by Jack which saved a great deal of digging time, he deliberately 'put the brakes on'.

Then the following week, when three *Bulletins* came in with the mail, he settled down to read the 'Red Rag' and was found by the foreman when he should have been working. There were seven paragraphs of his in one, and four in another, all of which paid a total of fifty shillings, which beat digging holes six days a week for a wage of three pounds. So it was that Jack received the Royal Order of the Boot from the Annan River Tin Mining Company.

Chapter Seven
CHINA CAMP, SCRUB CAMP, JUNGLE CAMP

DESPITE the fact that Jack had been riding for a fall and deserved his marching orders, he believed Fate and the Annan Tin Mining Company had set upon him with malicious intent. He seems not to have recognised that he had unconsciously created circumstances which left him no choice but to go prospecting alone.

Jack had previously scouted the river banks for a likely place to find a patch of alluvial tin which he could work alone without laying out his small capital on equipment. After his dismissal he went straight to a small river beach and began work. By the close of his first day as an unemployed man he had set up camp, improvised a sluice box and manhandled long planks through the bush to the workings. The planks, which belonged to the Annan Tin Company, had been stacked ready for use at the site of some future project. Jack didn't see why he shouldn't borrow them to make a firm track to roll a barrow (also borrowed) filled with pay dirt, across the sand to the sluice.

The site proved to be a great success. At the end of the first week he had mined for himself enough black stream tin to fill one of the hundredweight bags that a passing packer had given him. One hundredweight of tin fetched seven pounds which meant that he had earned that for himself while the 'slaves', as he called the wages men, were bullocking for three pounds a week from the company. Happy by himself he worked hard for three weeks, taking a hundredweight of tin each week, until rain high up in the mountains brought down a 'fresh'—a sudden rush of water—which washed away the rest of the tin deposit.

A couple of the men, working a claim near Mount Finnegan, not far from Rossville, urged Jack to pack up and join them prospecting in their area. Jack was motivated to join them when he realised they were operating a small hydraulic plant and he seized the opportunity to learn all he could about handling the plant with a view to operating his own at some future date.

The plant was amazingly simple, a toy compared to the giant nozzle which operated with two hundred feet of pressure at the

Annan; however, it easily did the work of half a dozen men. More importantly Jack recognised that it was comparatively inexpensive to make and he felt certain that he could make one himself as soon as he had found enough tin to pay for the materials.

The mountains of Finnegan and Finlayson were isolated and the three men had the area to themselves. Mount Finlayson, ravaged by roaring creeks and deeply scarred by tortuous ravines, wore a crown of granite above windswept gorges. All was grey— the scrub, the land, the granite—and shrouded in a grey mist.

Jack managed to pick up just enough tin to keep him in food, and that was the extent of it. The men had done very well but the pay dirt was fast giving way to vast areas of huge granite boulders, which took much valuable time to blast way. Jack recognised that it would not be long before they were only making tucker money.

Jack and the two men would walk the eight miles around the mountain to spend the weekend drinking and dancing at Rossville on Saturday night. The piano, fiddle and concertina made the music, while some little old joker named Bill Sykes sang and played the bones. 'On the Road to Mandalay', 'The Wild Colonial Boy' and 'Danny Boy' topped the charts at Rossville.

Jack left Finnegan to prospect around the Rossville site once more. He had not had much success on his own and his money was dwindling fast so he condescended to accept the offer of a job from the Home Rule Company.

The Home Rule workings (or it seems more appropriate to call them 'washings') were a massive hole among the green timber. This decimated landscape was horribly scarred and bleeding from the inescapable force of water. The water had been brought through the bush from the Home Rule Falls two miles distant. This incredible feat of engineering was undertaken by two men, Big Jack Elliott and Bert Francis, who worked without benefit of sophisticated tools or material. They overcame a number of obstacles. First the territory was accurately surveyed and the fluming—wooden planks which were built into a gutter—constructed to carry the water at an incline of one inch in every twelve feet to deliver a continuous, unvarying volume of rushing water, the weight of which was evenly distributed and the strain equalised along the entire length of the flume.

All of which would have been reasonable, if the path of the construction lay over solid ground; however, this was not so. The line clung to the sides of precipices and ravines with the hand-sawn fluming firmly fixed on hard steel drills hammered into the cliff faces. This wooden pipeline, anchored as it was on rock faces, defied tropical storms, cyclonic winds and the torrential rains of the wet season.

When one considers that the pipeline had been built using the almost primitive tools of the bush engineer—a measuring tape, pick and shovel, block and tackle, axe, hammer and drill and cross-cut saw—it is a monument to the persistence, ingenuity and iron nerve of Jack Elliot who, day after day for months on end, worked from a bosun's chair lowered over the side of the cliff face, winds howling around him, hammering the steel drills into the rock faces. When all this preliminary work had been done, the heavy planks for the flume, which had been cut and sawn from timber growing on site, were lowered by two men using block and tackle over the cliff faces, and Jack Elliot then positioned and secured them on the steel drills with a watertight join between each length.

By the time Jack came to Home Rule the workings were scarcely yielding any tin at all. Elliot had sold out, and every speck of tin was being won by desperate effort.

Jack didn't learn much more than he already knew about the refinements of tin mining at Home Rule but he did discover that in terms of hard yakka he would have been better advised to have stayed with the Annan Tin Mining Company. It was at Home Rule that he claimed to have learnt an 'armful' about manhandling huge logs and stumps with the aid of block and tackle, windlass and wire rope, and scientific use of the fulcrum. When he learned that he was to be detailed to fork stones, he fired himself.

Living at the Rossville pub wasn't all that hard to take—he didn't have to eat his own cooking and the company was good. At the pub he met a young man he had worked with at the Annan. Monty was a hard worker, a point which Jack had noted, resolving to take him in as a mate if ever he left the Annan employ. Indeed Monty threw in his lot gladly with Jack and the two took themselves prospecting along a stream known as Slatey Creek.

Inside a week they were 'blind stabbing' for tin in an icy cold pool. Blind stabbing is probably the most difficult and uncomfortable method of tin scratching. Jack somehow worked his charm and the willing, taller Monty found himself up to his chest in cold water, 'stabbing' his long-handled shovel down to the creek's bedrock and completing the almost impossible task of lifting the shovel to the surface without losing the mud and gravel off its face. Jack claims to have done his bit by shouting praise and encouragement while waiting on the bank for Monty to come up with a show of tin Eventually the shovel came up with a load 'as black as the ace of spades'. Then, and only then, did Jack take to the water.

The tin from the pool was hard won. As well as the icy water, there were leeches and yabbies which were not at all particular about what part of the anatomy they fastened on to. There were also snakes to avoid, and the self-inflicted misery when shins barked against the sharp edges of the shovel hidden under the water. It was an exercise that required the patience of a saint and an angelic temperament—neither of which Jack possessed. Blind stabbing also teaches a man the art of unbridled foul language.

Slatey Creek paid out two one-hundredweight bags of tin each week until a sudden storm washed away the deposit. In a sense both Jack and Monty were relieved to find the hole filled with sand and silt: Jack could then move on.

In the back of Jack's mind was the call of the big mountain country and the elusive north. He had managed to save enough cash to strike out alone. After ordering three months' stores from Cooktown, to be packed up to the mountain summit when the packer made his next trip, Jack struck out from Rossville for Mount Hartley.

The track to Mount Hartley took him through Black Peter's Gully, a strange place still haunted by the mad laugh of the big Negro and the smell of the incense he burned at night behind the locked door of his hut. Black Peter was long gone from the valley but men still claimed to hear his chants in the beat of the night birds' wings. Some even claimed to hear him hurling oaths at some phantom aggressor as he worked the ravine in maniacal fury.

Mount Hartley camp stood on the summit of the mountain and sat on mineral country. Many acres had been cleared in the past but the jungle was fast reclaiming its territory. The dozen or so men who were working the claims dotted around the mountain lived in humpies built a respectable two miles apart.

The day Jack reached the summit he walked straight into an abandoned humpy, immediately took possession and considered himself a king. Apart from the benefits of keeping warm and dry, the humpy meant that a man didn't have to share his shelter with the passing wildlife which also disliked rain and cold. The possessor of a humpy could barricade himself against the goannas, snakes, echidnas, centipedes, dingoes and native cats. But come summer, when the fleas took over, he would have gladly traded his bark humpy for a tent, or a tin suit of armour.

Tin was won at Mount Hartley by one of three ways: dry stacking, hand sluicing (if there was running water), or hydraulic sluicing. Jack found himself a small creek which yielded enough tin to keep him in food.

For a time he seems to have been fairly content with life on Mount Hartley. At last he was in jungle country and many of the men on the mountain were real jungle men. It was here that he met and teamed up with the Baird brothers, Norman and Charlie, nephews of Bill Baird who had founded Mount Romeo, one of the great Peninsula tin fields.

Norman and Charlie had grown up in the Cooktown district. Their father, Robert Baird, together with Christy Palmerston, had pushed one of the first mobs of cattle overland to the Palmer River at the time of the Palmer gold rush. Robert had established the China Camp tin field about fifty miles south of Cooktown, which was still producing pay dirt until the collapse of the world tin market in 1986. Robert was to marry an Aboriginal woman, as many men did, and settle down at China Camp where his sons were born.

The Bairds knew the Aborigines' secret life, that deep inner life, which few white men are privy to, and as adults took their places by the council fires. They had also grown up in the company of such noted bushmen as Palmerston, Hislop and Stucke. Their connection to both worlds had equipped them for the role of intermediary between black and white. In this position they enjoyed the respect of the whites and were accepted by the Aborigines as tribal Wise Men and protectors.

Being with the Bairds surpassed Jack's wildest dreams, to the point that studying hydraulic sluicing took second place to learning all that he could about surviving in the jungle.

Jack's one dream was to find a new goldfield. Hydraulic sluicing for tin was only the means by which to get enough stake money to go further north into country that had not yet fallen to the settler's axe. That golden dream would eventually take him from the east to the west coast and from the north of the continent to the south, and to most of the likely gold-bearing areas in between.

Jack Idriess covers in great detail in *Men of the Jungle* the time that he spent with the Baird brothers seeking gold in the jungles between Cairns and Cooktown. Published in 1946, the book is a treasure house of fascinating information about the beauty and natural wealth of the tropical country around the Bloomfield and Daintree Rivers before the area was destroyed by subsequent generations. Jack powers through *Men of the Jungle*, with breathtaking speed from one startling scene to the next. Neither the jungle nor the men gets star billing—the dramas of each are interlocked and played out with equal ferocity.

Jack didn't have to horde his material when he wrote about his days in the jungle. He commented mildly that 'it was pretty lively place for a young man to be'. It was pretty lively place for anyone to be.

All that lived in that primeval place was exotic, lusty, extravagant and deadly. Everything was eating something and thriving; cannibal flowers flashed their colours and ate insects; insects devoured their mates; crocodiles masquerading as floating gnarled logs snatched the foolish and the thirsty — animal or man — from the banks of the Bloomfield River. The jungle swallowed clearings made by men and the Aborigines swallowed many a hapless man for lunch or dinner. Jack was warned by the Bairds that should he ever see this happening he must not show that he was aware that man was on the menu, otherwise he would meet the same fate. And if snakes, spiders, crocodiles and cannibals were not enough to cope with there were also the wild boars. These ugly creatures with their razor-sharp tusks (said to be the descendants of the domestic pigs released at Cooktown by James Cook) had no sense of humour and seemed to take a fiendish delight in frightening witless both whites and Aborigines.

While hunting one of these boars, a man-killer named 'Rungooma', Jack narrowly escaped death by throwing himself under a log. In its attempt to pry Jack from under the log the monster pounded his ribs with its snout before the Aborigines brought it down with their spears. Jack's ego was as bruised as his ribs, especially when the tribesmen immortalised him in a corroboree in which the Aborigine playing the role of Jack—the great white hunter—dropped everything to roll under an imaginary log. 'The Slaying of Rungooma' brought the house down every time.

Jack and the brothers prospected for tin, silver and gold in the district between Cooktown and Cairns. Together they worked from base camps located at the lonely mining camps of China Camp, Scrub Camp and Jungle Camp.

Life at China Camp and Jungle Camp was usually uneventful but at Scrub Camp there was the occasional feud when humpies were barricaded up and men sniped at each other from behind trees. Water rights were usually the bone of contention but there was also the occasional fight over Aboriginal women. Jack and the brothers managed to keep a neutral position because they were not permanent inhabitants and because gold prospecting did not call for the same intensive use of water as tin scratching.

There had been a change in Jack's values. When he had first arrived at Cooktown he had steadfastly refused all offers of credit, paying his way. Now he did as everyone else and ticked up his provisions with the storekeepers, even the butcher. The generosity extended by the tradespeople to most prospectors was founded on the prospector's drive to strike it rich. They knew that small finds fired the prospector's hope of making the big strike in this mineral-rich area, which in turn guaranteed payment of accounts. The shopkeepers and sly grog merchants had the wit to know that the real pay dirt was to be found in the grubby pockets of ragged work trousers.

Jack had found enough gold to recognise its power. At twenty-four he was ravaged by gold fever. Gold had become a 'devil terrible' to fight against. In camp at night he would handle it, gloat over it, committing its colour and feel to his memory. When he licked a piece to see its colour gleam in the firelight, it left its touch on his tongue. He weighed it, and its weight stayed in his hand. He hid it at night but it left its hiding place to haunt his dreams. With the Baird brothers he worked hard and long—gone were his claims of laziness. In search of the yellow metal they often travelled far into country where no other white man had been. Frequently they ran out of rations and lived off the land or shared the same food as the Aborigines, which wasn't a hardship for either Norman or Charlie.

It was during this period with the Bairds that Jack came into close contact with the Aborigines, particularly those tribes of the Bloomfield and Daintree districts. The brothers explained many customs, beliefs and practices of tribal life to Jack but as they were both 'Group' and 'Blood' to the China Camp and Bloomfield tribes, there were those things which could not be spoken of to a white man—no matter how trusted he was.

China Camp, walled in by mountains, was the end of the world. The only way out to Cooktown and civilisation was to take the track to Pierce's Landing on the Bloomfield River and ford the river, cross Wyalla Plain, then on through Stucke's Gap, and over the Romeo Mountains to Cooktown. This lonely eighty-mile journey covered some of the most beautiful country on the Peninsula. Rare travellers had to ford the Bloomfield River at Pierce's Landing. There Albert Pierce and his brother Arthur bred hundreds of horses and maintained two packing teams to carry supplies to the surrounding mining camps. Jack, Norman and Charlie would converge on the Landing to wait for the supply ship, the *Pearl Queen*, to be towed up river to unload. 'We always stayed at Pierce's Landing, a shed and a slab hut built on a high bank overlooking a southern stretch of the river.'

The few families who settled on the Bloomfield managed to carve homes for themselves in this out-of-the-way place and were virtually self-supporting. These pioneers had survived attacks by Aborigines, floods and the terrible loneliness that comes with isolation. Across the river from Pierce's Landing, on the flat land that merged into the Wyalla Plain, a group of houses hid under the shady protection of huge mango trees, pawpaws, five-fingers, and custard-apple trees. The verandahs were festooned with all types of granadilla passion vines and brightly coloured croton vines from which oil is extracted to produce a drastic purgative. Between these houses and the river grew communal gardens of banana palms, sweet-buk and the cassava, a tuberous plant used to make flour and a dish known as manioc.

The settlement was home to a people whose blood was a cocktail of white, Chinese and unidentifiable eastern races, but the dominating full-bloods were Malayan and Islander, bêche-de-mer fishers and their families. Fishing for the giant sea-slug was a cooperative venture carried out by the men of several families who owned, or shared, a lugger or cutter. During the nine-month season most of the men would be 'outside' at sea, or employed as seamen on pearling luggers in northern waters. For those nine months the families of the fishermen supported themselves through the produce of their lush gardens. For the remainder of the year, the cyclone season, the Bloomfield fishermen brought their craft upstream for the three month lay-up.

The people sailing to Cooktown on the little ships passing the mouth of the Bloomfield River would never have guessed that just a few miles upstream such an enclave was hidden behind the mangroves and palms. A few miles downstream from Pierce's Landing, on a river island, was a large Aboriginal camp alive with the sounds of piccaninnies, the high-pitched chatter of women and the perpetual howling of dogs. Often the muted resonance of a beaten hollow log could be heard, accompanied by the slapping of thighs and the hypnotic rhythm of stamping feet. It was here Jack was given his first basic lessons on tracking by the camp youngsters.

Every four months, depending on the rainy season, cyclones, or strikes on the wharves, the *Pearl Queen*, the supply lugger from Cooktown, would heave-to in the mouth of the Bloomfield. The blast of a conch shell blown by an Aborigine stationed on a headland would announce that the lugger had been sighted at sea. The next day, with her white sails furled and bound she would be towed up the river by rowboats. It would be hard to imagine a more romantic scene than that of the *Pearl Queen* with wings pinioned like a captured butterfly, gliding behind the small boats to the song of the rowers echoing back from the mountains along the river—or the riotous scene at the landing as Arthur and Albert Pierce and their Aboriginal stockmen loaded up the big pack teams with supplies for the two mining camps hungry for 'white-man's tucker'.

Little wonder that Jack loved the Peninsula and Pierce's Landing in particular. Right before his eyes passed a parade of people and scenes that he could not have imagined at the Broken Hill Assay Office, the opal mines of Lightning Ridge, aboard the SS *Newcastle* or while he was swallowing dust behind a mob of sheep in New South Wales.

Waiting for the *Pearl Queen* could be a matter of weeks or months. Jack, Norman and Charlie filled in the time fishing, hunting or helping the Pierces with their cattle. Jack spent the evenings in the homes of the Aborigines, listening to true tales of savage people practising fearsome rites: stories of life on the Malay Archipelago, in the South Seas, of pirates and villages, of fights against the Dutch, of native princes, of courageous shipwrecked whites who had survived against incredible odds, of superstitions and intrigues which many had brought with them to their new home.

Jack didn't spend all his evenings listening to stories and telling a few of his own. On his first visit to the Bloomfield he had met and succumbed to the captivating beauty of Mee-lele. The girl, as Jack tells it, was the product of all that is beautiful from a combination of white, Chinese and Malaysian blood:

> She had warm creamy skin delicately tinged with pink and hair that fell like a caressing black shawl right to her knees...I have never forgotten Mee-lele, lovely little animal, warm little human soul. Her eyes would fairly dance to the smile on her lips. She would give all her heart, or else hate passionately. But she liked thrills too much; trouble was the breath of life to her.

It is impossible to be sure of Mee-lele's true identity. As told in *Men of the Jungle* she is a girl who was educated at a convent on Thursday Island and sold as a child to an old Malay, Assan Rah. Mee-lele had been brought back from Thursday Island to prepare for her wedding to Assan Rah, known to the Bloomfield Aborigines as 'The Killer of Pigs'. She loathed the old man who had a reputation for violence. Jack, however, who had experienced his 'heart's first perfect thrill' when he came upon the girl skinny-dipping, was prepared to chance the wrath of Assan Rah, as was Mee-lele.

She persuaded Jack to meet her by the river on her wedding night, and then surprised him by urging him to run away with her and her Filipino lover who was waiting for her on his cutter. In the closing pages of *Men of the Jungle* Mee-lele reaches the Filipino's cutter, Assan Rah runs amok with his kris and Jack makes his getaway across the Wyalla Plain to Cooktown.

This romantic interlude, apart from that described in *Drums of Mer* published in 1933, was the only one Jack was ever to write about after the 1927 publication of *Madman's Island*—which failed because of its pseudo-romantic plot. It brought him dozens of letters of commiseration from women readers. They were sad for him over the loss of his life's love and begged to know what happened to Mee-lele.

In later years Jack was to say that Mee-lele was Assan Rah's daughter, and that the old Malay, in the role of an irate father, not the bridegroom, had chased him that dark night while brandishing the deadly Malay dagger with the wavy blade. On another occasion Jack was to say that the girl was an island princess, and that she had borne him a son. While it is not possible to confirm Mee-lele's background, a letter dated 1941, telling Jack that her son, Ernie Tim, had either drowned or been taken by a crocodile while crossing the Bloomfield, confirms that she did exist and that she lived on the Bloomfield.

Perhaps there was an element of truth in each of the versions. The Mee-lele Jack wrote about was his princess at the time, she may have been convent educated at Thursday Island, Assan Rah most likely was her father and he did chase Jack for dallying with his daughter, perhaps on her wedding night, and it is possible to conjecture that maybe the letter carrying the news of the death of Mee-lele's son was written because the writer knew that Jack had a personal interest in Ernie Tim's death.

Jack's last visit to Pierce's Landing was extended by the late arrival of the *Pearl Queen*, carrying short supplies. Jack, Norman and Charlie had only enough supplies left for a very short prospecting trip into the mountains. They had won very little gold. This left them with two choices; either to go working for wages tin scratching, or to go south to the Mossman. The cane season had just started at the Mossman and the prospect of doing something different, meeting new people and quickly knocking up a big pay check, before taking a boat back to Cooktown from Cairns, seemed to them to be the best choice.

After trekking for many miles across dangerous gorges and almost impossible spurs, the last trial of nerves came at the crocodile-infested Daintree River. It was a dreadful walk across the river which Jack was never to forget. It had to be a walk because it is impossible for a swimmer to see the snout of a crocodile coming towards him. Jack wished that he had been ten feet tall as he forced his toes to the river bottom, while at the same time frantically stretching his neck to keep his chin above the water. They crossed safely to the other side and counted their blessings, and with good reason for a few days later they witnessed the death of an Aboriginal toddler in the jaws of a crocodile, and the frantic efforts of the child's mother to save it. Frozen in horror they watched the woman dive into the water and, with superhuman strength, turn the monster's huge head again and again to the bank, gouging its bulbous eyes with her thumbs. A few months earlier on the banks of the Bloomfield Jack had seen a crocodile take a filly when it came to drink at the Landing.

At the Daintree they decided to split up and send Norman back beyond China Camp to attempt to drop on gold while Jack and Charlie went on to earn enough cash to buy stores for the three of them to continue their prospecting.

It was a thirty-mile trackless walk along the coast to Port Douglas. Their way lay over flat, grassed country but before long they were faced with travelling through eerie mangrove swamps and fighting, sometimes knee-deep, through the thick blue mud. Crossing creeks, even at low tide, they were dicing with death, for every pool was a potential hiding place for sharks and saltwater crocodiles.

The mangrove swamp not only harboured dangerous wild life, it also hid a camp, which Jack and Charlie stumbled upon by accident. A rude platform floor had been lashed to the mangrove roots above the high water line, and its tent roof was just below the tops of the mangroves. Inside were two folding bunks with mosquito nets, boxes, kerosene tins and a primus.

Jack emptied out one of the boxes and found two silver-mounted hair brushes, stamped envelopes with 'foreign' addresses, a jar of 'foreign' hair oil, some pencils and draughtsmen's accessories, and a handful of military cartridges. On the opposite side of the camp was a channel which led to the river mouth. Along the channel the mangrove roots had been cut to allow a dinghy to pass from camp to ocean.

It was quite clear that the camp was a base for spying and for charting the unguarded coast. Jack conjectured that a seemingly innocent fishing lugger would be at sea charting the channels of the Great Barrier Reef by day, while at night it would slip into the river mouth to pick up information and ferry the men from the hidden camp either up or down the coast. Jack believed that the site, set at the river mouth, only thirty miles from cultivated rural lands, railways and roads, was faultlessly positioned for an invading army to land unseen, mobilise and march on Cairns.

Fearing that the spies might come back and dispose of both himself and Charlie, Jack took some of the articles from the camp and they left in a hurry. Jack posted the evidence to the Naval Department, receipt of which was acknowledged. Many years later Jack was to address naval personnel at Rushcutters Bay in Sydney on the episode. Jack however didn't reveal the nationality of the users of the 'foreign' hairbrushes and hair oil, perhaps because it was considered that to have done so might have started an international incident.

The two managed to get to Port Douglas without further incident, then to Mossman, only to find the cane cutters were on strike. Flat broke, depressed and not really expecting to find anything Jack called at the post office, hoping against hope that there just might be a cheque waiting for him from the *Bulletin*. There was—ten pounds! Of course the next call was the pub. 'Two long beers, a good meal, a pair of strides, a shirt and boots, and a sugar bag for tucker later', they were off on the twenty-mile walk over the range to Mount Molloy: 'We found Mount Molloy to be a closed down copper mine, a good-hearted butcher, a dozen houses, a timber mill, and a handful of the finest chaps in the world.'

At Mount Molloy the rumour was that it was possible to find a little tin on Mount Fraser, so Jack and Charlie pushed on and set up camp there. By damming a small creek on Mount Fraser they were able to sluice for four hours each day, and in no time had enough tin to get on good terms with the storekeeper. Then the water began to dry up and it was not a viable proposition to work with pick and shovel.

The wet season was about to start. Jack knew that given a hydraulic sluicing plant they could win enough tin to finance a gold prospecting epic of ten months' duration, but there was always the problem of getting enough cash to build the plant. After years of never writing to his father he decided that a wire to Walter asking for one hundred pounds might be worth a try, and it was.

At this point Jack and Charlie decided that they needed a fourth man and decided Jack's old mate, Dick Welch of Cooktown, was the man for the job. Jack had met Dick when they were both working for wages at the Annan River Tin Mining Company. After that they had prospected together on various trips. Dick had put together a team of pack horses which Jack and Charlie both agreed would be useful to transport the pipes to Mount Fraser and for taking the tin down to the Mount Molloy township. Working towards this end they sold all the tin they had on hand. Jack left Charlie to take care of the camp while he went to Cooktown to find Dick.

The trip to Cooktown was a pleasant change from Jack's usual travelling mode. He took the Molloy train via Biboohra to Cairns, then from Cairns he sailed to Cooktown aboard the weekly steamer. Wearing new clothes and staying at hotels, eating good meals that he hadn't cooked himself, made him feel like a member of the aristocracy.

Jack looked forward to landing at Cooktown and to seeing Dick but even more he was eagerly anticipating seeing Mee-lele once again. Dick was on the wharf waiting to meet him when the SS *Musgrave* tied up. That night Dick agreed to have the outfit ready to move out a week later when Jack came back from the Bloomfield after the wedding of Mee-lele. They made plans to take the packhorses by the only known horse track which ran behind the mountains and past Mount Carbine and down into Molloy.

It was indeed most fortunate (or a convenient closing chapter for *Men of the Jungle*) that Jack had organised his departure for Molloy in advance. Dick and his team were ready to move out within a few hours of Jack's arrival back in Cooktown after he had outrun Assan Rah and his trusty kris. Fact or fiction? Who can say? As Jack once said in reference to that period, 'It was a happy life ... a romance out of a proper book of romance.'

Chapter Eight
WAR IS DECLARED

THE northernmost tip of the Peninsula drew Jack like a magnet. It was not long before he and Dick parted with the Baird brothers and travelled further north to prospect around the Normanby River where the river's three mouths run into Princess Charlotte Bay.

Travelling through the Peninsula, alone or in company, was fraught with danger. However Dick and Jack, convinced they were invincible, gambled on their ability to survive the hazards and continued to tempt fate by prospecting for gold and gathering sandalwood in hostile territory.

On several occasions the two covered vast tracts of wild country beyond the Kennedy and Normanby Rivers. The Aboriginal tribes in this area were an extended group, or sub-branch, as Jack called them, of the Koko-yimidir and the Bulpoonor. Their tribal lands stretched from the Bloomfield River and the Roaring Meg near China Camp south of Cooktown, through to Cape Bedford and further north along the east coast of the Peninsula, then inland to the Dividing Range. Together Dick and Jack forded rivers, rode the timber flats and crossed the ranges of the Koko-yimidir and Bulpoonor without coming to harm.

Dick could speak a number of Aboriginal dialects and had grown to adulthood with the Aboriginal children around Cooktown. This made it possible for Jack and Dick to watch many of their ceremonial rites, a privilege extended to very few European whites. Jack later noted that the circumcision ceremony practised there was identical to the rite practised in Arabia and along the Nile one thousand years before the birth of Mohammed.

As Dick was not always free to leave Cooktown to go roaming, Jack would pack north with other men. On one of these trips with Jim, Andy, Harry, 'Black Charlie' (an ex-wrestler) and Travers, Jack almost became the subject of a death notice which would have read 'missing believed speared'.

The six men had pooled their resources to buy a team of pack horses. Their plan was to travel far up the Peninsula to the

Coen, primarily to gather sandalwood and do a little prospecting for gold or tin. They were packing approximately six tons of sandalwood deep in unfriendly territory when they came upon an Aboriginal camp of eighty gunyahs, each housing four Aborigines. The Aborginal spears were frightening weapons nine feet long with barbs of jagged kangaroo bone or chipped quartz. An uneasy peace was briefly established until one of the pack horses was speared and eaten. Knowing all the horses would meet the same fate, one by one, and that their own chance of survival was precarious, the six tried to escape through the dense jungle, hoping it would provide them with cover. The Aborigines set fire to the jungle in order to flush out Jack and his companions. The desperate situation was saved by driving the loaded horses into a waterhole and burning a two hundred-yard break between themselves and the fire started by the Aborigines, then making good their escape in the resulting confusion.

Despite such a close call Jack took his share of the profit from the sandalwood sale and together with Bill Younger and Harry Reynolds whom he had known at Lightning Ridge and two other men set off to prospect at Cape Melville, two hundred miles north of Cooktown. Cooktown was, and still is, the end of civilisation on the Cape York Peninsula. Jack and his four mates sailed to Cape Melville on Captain Dan Moynahan's ketch, the *Spray*, and were put ashore on the southern side of the cape.

The tall, luxuriantly black-bearded Daniel Patrick Moynahan was a man Jack admired: 'He was a man who had done things.' Born in Newcastle in 1865, in his early twenties he had gone north where he built and sailed several sailing ships. Dan had spent many of his years fishing for bêche-de-mer in the Coral Sea but at the time Jack became his passenger Dan was trading between Cooktown and Port Stewart carrying passengers and freight. Port Stewart was the jumping-off point, the outlet for the gold-mining centres of the Coen and Ebagoola.

Captain Dan and his mate, Doug Hall, continued on their way north to Port Stewart. From there Dan set sail again back down the coast to Cooktown, the round trip taking approximately three months. It was arranged that Dan would pick up the prospecting party when he made the return supply trip to Port Stewart.

The Cape Melville prospecting trip was ill-conceived. The men with Jack were much older than he was and unable to walk and carry their heavy tools for more than twenty miles a day. The distance was not acceptable to Jack, who felt handicapped both by the age of the men and the lack of horses. The waterhole on the beach, and the need to stay in sight of the sea in the event of Captain Dan returning earlier than expected, dictated their choice of a campsite. Behind them, surrounded by hills, lay a swamp which stretched inland. Jack itched to get to the 'likely looking hills' showing promise of gold, tin or wolfram but it would have been dangerous for him to have attempted to go off on his own since the hills were full of unfriendly Aborigines.

Opposite lay Howick Island. The sight of the island made the men uneasy for it was a constant warning that death could come at any time. Prior to this prospecting trip Jack and his mates had landed on Lizard Island, some fifty miles down the coast. Lizard Island had been the home of the ill-fated Mrs Watson, the wife of a fisherman. This enterprising young couple had established the nucleus of a bêche-de-mer and pearl-shell fishing station on the island. Following his profession, Watson regularly put to sea on his lugger, leaving Mrs Watson alone with her two Chinese servants. On one of these occasions, mainland Aborigines had paddled to the island, attacked the Watson homestead and had killed one Chinese servant and wounded the other.

The courageous woman managed to get the wounded man, her baby and herself into half of an iron tank used for boiling the bêche-de-mer, and set it adrift on a hot summer sea. The cruel tropical sun blazing down on the iron tank quickly took the baby's life. Mrs Watson and the surviving servant floated in the tank to Howick Island some thirty miles away, where, unable to find water, they died.

Little did Jack know that he too would one day be marooned on Howick Island and that the diary he kept there at that time would later become the basis for his first book, *Madman's Island* published in 1927.

Ears of corn, still growing where the Watsons had planted them, could be seen clearly from the mainland campsite set up by Jack and his companions. Knowing that the native tribe which had attacked Mrs Watson had probably come from somewhere behind where they were camped did not foster their sense of security. Neither did the Captain's warning to be on the look-out for 'unfriendliness', or the sound of a tinkling bell which he said was tied around the neck of a horse which had belonged to a prospector who had somehow managed to travel overland from Cooktown to Cape Melville. The man had been speared to death but the horse had escaped and was still outwitting the Aborigines.

The presence of the horse intrigued Jack; why the leather strap around the horse's neck hadn't rotted and, as a consequence, the bell been lost, was one thing; but why the Aborigines hadn't been able to catch and spear the horse was a mystery. Jack never laid claim to seeing the horse, only to hearing the bell. He and his companions knew that there wasn't another white man for miles around, the nearest mining camp was close to a hundred miles north, but even though the odds of the tinkling bell being on a horse were slim and none, Jack would remain convinced to the end of his days that he and his mates and Captain Dan had indeed repeatedly heard the horse bell sounding as the animal moved about the swamp.

Jack vividly remembered the day the *Spray* returned to Cape Melville with Captain Dan bringing the news that war had been declared. It was one of those splendid, glowing tropical days, no wind, everything was still as a tranquil low tide lapped softly on the sand. Avoiding the rocks the lugger gently floated into the bay and dropped anchor. A vast contrast to that other beach a few months and half the world away when the transport ship *Lutzow* would drop anchor in Anzac Cove where men were 'bathing and dying'.

The first words the skipper greeted them with were 'war has been declared ... war between Britain and Germany!'

Jack recalled how astonished they had been when they heard the news. At first they didn't have any idea what he was talking about. Years later, he said:

Struth, that upset all our ideas of prospecting and everything. We didn't know how to take this. Of course I was mad then; I was going away to this war—the cheek of any country challenging my country, Australia, but I reckoned Australia would be silly not to join in this outside war, as I called it, and if Australia was going to be in it, I was going to be in it. So there and then I made up my mind. And they said, 'Oh, the whole damn thing will be over in a week or so, there'll be no war. The two most civilised countries in the world, they can't be that silly'.

Perhaps it was naivety such as this that led so many Australians to enlist.

War or no war it was business as usual for Moynahan. He was heading north to Port Stewart to deliver the mining camp's supplies and Jack, fired with impatience, declared that he was going south, on foot, to Cooktown. Moynahan tried to persuade him to wait where he was, but he might just as well have been telling a dog not to scratch its fleas. 'I packed my little swag, took half a damper and started off down the coast to get to the bloody war.'

In his first attempt get to Cooktown Jack had to wade across a number of estuarine creeks which fed through the swamps to the sea. These creeks were alive with saltwater crocodiles which came out of the swamps for a meal of fish and swam back at low tide. It was desperately slow for a man who wanted to get to war. Jack was 'highly indignant' at being delayed as he made camp that first night.

When Jack woke up the next morning he saw the camp was probably in the most dangerous place he could have chosen. He had slept on a long, sandy, narrow beach about nine feet high, nothing more than a ridge between the swamp and the sea. The swamp was noisy with wildfowl and alive with food and no doubt seething with young crocodiles. 'Millions of bloody crocodiles, and right where I camped the crocodiles could walk over that strip of sand and down to the sea for fish.' None of which did much to improve his temper, or his sense of security, when he made camp the second night.

All along the north Queensland coast grows the wild plum tree. Known as the Wongi tree, it was revered by Aborigines, travellers, Asians and European white prospectors. There is a legend which says that whoever eats the Wongi plum will always come back—Jack lived to prove this to be right. The Wongi tree bears a rich purple plum, which is very tempting, but very sour unless boiled. The tree grows about twenty feet in height with dense, green, bushy branches. When night fell Jack selected the thickest Wongi tree he could find and climbed up into its branches—he couldn't get the crocodiles out of his mind: 'I was getting scared. Crocodiles are bloody awful things, you don't know how swift they can be, they're not sluggish, they can go like bats out of hell over a short distance. Anyway, I couldn't resist it, it was back to my ancestors for me, I climbed up the bushiest tree I could see that was handy and camped there the night.'

All his efforts to get through to Cooktown on foot were thwarted the next day when he reached a river which had been scoured out by floods—it was very deep and alive with crocodiles and sharks. Jack recalled standing on the bank and roaring in frustration. He turned back to wait at the camp for Moynahan. Happily the lugger made the return run much earlier than anticipated and took all the men back to Cooktown.

From the minute Jack had decided he was going to the war it seems as if every obstacle were raised to stop him. First, he had

70

avoided becoming crocodile or shark food in order to present himself as target for Turkish bullets, and then there wasn't a recruiting office in Cooktown. The nearest place to enlist was Townsville, two hundred and fifty miles down the coast. This meant he had to take a ship, but of course he didn't have a single shilling, much less the fare.

Jack waited about the Cooktown wharf until the day the SS *Musgrave* was loading cargo for the trip to Cairns; he wasn't noticed when he slipped up the gangway and made for the bows. Then he remembered a coffin-shaped box that he had seen on the stern deck when he was leaning on the rail looking down at the people on the wharf, that first day he had arrived in Cooktown two years before.

Jack waited until the deck was clear, quickly opened the box, slipped in and pulled the lid into place after him. Inside the box were only a few signal flags which made it a little more comfortable for him, certainly more comfortable than trying to sleep in the Wongi tree. The boat was not leaving until the afternoon, and it was a hot summer day in Cooktown. All through that long, hot day he lay there, flat on his back in the box, sweating and cramping with his head hitting one end, the toes of his boots jammed hard against the other. Two small holes provided him with the only ventilation. Occasionally he took the chance of being found by raising the lid with his fingers to get a little more air. At nightfall, the boat was under way.

His troubles were not over. Jack said later that one of the first mistakes he made connected with the war was thinking the boat was bound for Brisbane. However its only port of call was Cairns and then back to Cooktown. If he hadn't heard two steersmen talking, he would have been carried back to Cooktown.

It was still night when the boat tied up at Cairns. The passengers and crew were in a great hurry to get ashore to take advantage of what was left of the night. The cargo was unloaded at a furious pace and very quickly the boat was deserted. Jack opened the box. There was total silence. The boat was in darkness except for the starboard and port lights. Slowly he sat up; he was bone stiff and aching to stand up for a good long stretch to get his body working again, but there, right before his eyes was the biggest, broadest policeman in the entire Peninsula. Big Pat, who was an 'elephant of a man', came to a halt approximately twelve feet from the bottom of the gangway. Jack sneaked around (which he did very well) keeping in the shadows right to the gangway opening, jumping down and past Big Pat before the policeman realised what was happening. Cyclone Jack was off and racing with Big Pat after him. This seems to be one of the few times when Jack lived up to his nickname.

Jack had come back to Cairns but this time it was different— he didn't have a swag or a stake in his pocket; he was homeless. Cairns was not the happy little town that it had been when he had first blown in. People thought that Australia was going to be invaded or burnt out and those engaged in industry or primary production feared that there would be no world trade. Everything had shut down and there was no employment.

Men had come in from the back country towns and were roaming the streets of Cairns. The outbreak of war had disrupted transport, the homeless wandered the streets and haunted the wharf, waiting for a ship to take them south to enlist. Jack described the period in those first few weeks preceding the mobil- isation of the country's resources to cope with wartime require- ments as a 'terrible depression'. Of course his only point of refer- ence was Cairns, so he assumed that similar conditions existed throughout Australia.

The first exhilarating response to war had subsided, and in its place was a mood of puzzled desperation. Every man in the homeless band had anticipated being instantly absorbed into the glorious army machine the second he arrived in Cairns. Instead, forced by hunger, they found themselves joining the Salvation Army food lines. Each had the notion that overnight they would be in uniform; however they still were wearing the clothes that they stood up in, the clothes they had been wearing when they left the cattle stations, mines and railway gangs and bush jobs. These con- fused, ragged, but enthusiastic volunteers were not cheered on by the multitude but, instead, moved on by the police. The great adventure had turned sour even before it had begun.

Jack joined the group and for some unexplained reason assumed its leadership. He took his place in the daily food lines and searched for shelter each night. It annoyed and depressed him that men who had come to serve their country should be treated like charity cases and criminals. Yet, neither he nor the others thought of giving up and going back to the bush.

Day after day, followed by one miserable night after another, they waited for transport. The Salvation Army gave them one good meal a day but nightfall found them shivering and forsaken. One bitterly cold, wet night Jack led the band to the railway shed, the only place he could think of where they could sleep undercover, provided they were quiet and didn't disturb the railway personnel. A long line of empty railway trucks offered the best hope for a good night's sleep. One by one the tired men slipped into a truck stacked high with bags and went straight to sleep only to be woken by flames. The bags that had seemed such a Godsend were filled with quicklime and the moisture in the air had set them alight. 'We woke up in fire and bloody hell. Didn't we jump out of that truck by God!'

That was enough for Jack. He didn't wait any longer for the authorities to open a recruiting office or to arrange transport but stowed away once again on the first available boat for Townsville. This time he was not successful in remaining undetected: the boat had scarcely left the wharf when he was discovered hiding in a lifeboat. But the reception was not what he expected: 'The crew lifted up the damn tarpaulin and saw me, and said, "All right mate," and they fed me with bonzer tucker under that tarpaulin, and they put in a billycan of tea.'

By the time Jack arrived in Townsville, Australia's target of twenty thousand recruits had almost been attained. The number of men volunteering from all levels of the community was so overwhelming, and the assessment of the numbers required so underestimated, that the army was able to be extremely selective. Only the strongest, tallest and most superbly healthy young men were being accepted. When John Masefield immortalised this body of men as the 'finest ... ever brought together in modern times' he was not indulging in romantic sentiment, but recording cold, hard fact.

When Jack presented himself at the Townsville recruitment centre confusion was the operative word for the day. The two recruitment officers, both ex-estate agents, worried over conflicting orders. At first they had been ordered to recruit every man they could get; then word had been received that no more men were required. The officers came to a compromise; they agreed not to disappoint all the eager volunteers and signed up another seven men.

Jack could not believe that after all the trials of getting to the point of enlisting, he now had to compete with two hundred men for selection. He didn't think he had a hope of being accepted. 'What chance did I have, with all the fine-looking, upstanding young chaps riding in from the back country—and me—skinny, sinewy, they called me.'

Apart from the fact that he thought himself to be scrawny, he was acutely aware that he looked like a wild man: 'I had a great scraggy, dingy red beard, we all grew beards up in the Cape York Peninsula to keep away the mosquitoes in the wet season.'

It was his awful appearance that caught the eye of the recruiting officers. Stunned curiosity forced them to ask him where he had come from. Jack told them he had been mining and that he had tried to come overland to get there early but the 'bloomin' sharks' had scared the hell out of him so that he had had to wait for the lugger and the rest of his party. When Jack had finished his tale and answered all their questions, he was a dead-set certainty for the front row.

Chapter Nine
WAR

... the queer psychology of lawful killing ... you saw a Turk's head,
you saw his moustache and his eye glaring along his rifle sight; you
fired too, with your breath in your belly, then rushed forward,
screaming, to bayonet him, to club him, to fall on him and tear his
throat out ... and he met you with a replica of the berserk, frightened demon that was yourself.

I.L. Idriess *Daily Telegraph Pictorial* 12 November 1929

THOUGH much has been said and written about the First World
War by historians and countless others, we find, even now,
that the horror experienced at the front, and the sorrow at home
throughout the duration of the war, have not cast a shadow over
that 'crystallising point in the evolution of a national pride and consciousness'.

Jack kept a daily record of this 'crystallising point' in his
diaries, which he later used to write *The Desert Column* first published in 1932. The Author's Note to the book begins, '*The Desert
Column* is more than my diary. It is myself.'

The book which is said to be 'Jack' is remarkably controlled.
It presents an almost dispassionate record of events, battles and
manoeuvres and day-to-day life in the trenches. Jack's account is
unembellished—only rarely does he make a personal comment and
those that he does make pale into insignificance when compared
with the nerve-shattering tableaux of death, dying and mutilation
on almost every page.

Throughout the book runs the courage, determination and
cheerfulness of the Anzacs, named by the Turks 'the mad bushmen'. It is a graphically written document which is as visual as any
product of the cinematographer's art. He doesn't only recall the
horrors of war: 'The dearest memory, the memory that will linger
until I die, is the memory of my mates, these thousands of men
who laugh so harshly at their own hardships and sufferings, but
whose smile is so tenderly sympathetic to others in pain.'

Jack also remembered those other men, the Turks, as being

ruthless, but first class fighters and good men: 'they obeyed, as far as we were concerned, what we called the rules of war and, stone the flamin' crows, they could fight.'

'The rules of war' included temporary truces to bury the dead of both sides; the confiscation of Major Birdwood's sawn-off shotgun by his superiors after the Turks had complained that its use was a violation of international law; the observation of the humanities by the enemy, who were known to throw water and food from the safety of their trenches to wounded Anzacs who could not be brought back to their own lines while still under the fire of the same Turkish 'Good Samaritans'.

Jack never commented on the bewildering, contradictory aspects of what appeared to be random carnage at Gallipoli. It seems to have been to him simply a case of 'ours not to reason why'. It was not until the desert campaigns that, war weary, he began to commit to his diary comments of censure and questions. Even then he was not moved strongly to condemn and as an old man in his eighties he was to remain mildly surprised that the propaganda machine of both the Australian and British armies had misrepresented not only the enemy, but the quality and strength of his arms and munitions:

> All our skite about our modern weapons was tommy rot. The Turks had better arms than we, my oath they did. Their rifles could out-shoot us. In bloody action in Palestine, we'd be hiding behind the bloody hilltops with the Turkish bullets whizzing by, and our bullets couldn't make the distance.

Although Jack was right in the thick of the fighting from 19 May 1915, two weeks after the landing at Gallipoli, he was destined to live through the war theatres of Gallipoli, Sinai and Palestine and was often in the front line with the 5th Light Horse Regiment.

By 29 May, eleven days after landing, he had grown accustomed to being under fire. During those periods when he was pinned down in the dugouts by heavy shelling ('high explosive has its own terror'), he continued to write his diary, sometimes lying on his back and complaining how awkward it was, and cursing because he and his mates were unable to fire a shot in return.

Jack was sapping (reconnoitring) in Shrapnel Gully, right up to Quinn's Post the night a Turkish mine blew up that desperately held hill, an instance which history records as sparking a bloody battle and to which Jack referred to as being 'only one of those local affairs. It is all dammed local.'

Jack spent the night with bayonet at the ready waiting for 'God only knew what' while the Turks hurled hundreds of bombs at the shattered trench which was Quinn's Post. Jack was close enough to hear the Turkish shouts of 'Allah!' over the sound of the bombardment as they charged. That night Captain Quinn and fifty Australians were killed; however the toll taken of Turkish soldiers, according to Jack, was fifteen hundred: 'Our supports and the survivors united and went over the top with bomb and bayonet and mad Australian strength and cut the Turks to pieces in the very frenzy of their victory.'

Jack never seems to have felt either anger or hatred for the enemy. His strongest comment was directed at Australian officers invoked after he had witnessed the shelling and shooting of a group of Australian infantry being drilled right in sight of the Turkish artillery observation post: 'We have just witnessed a shameful, horrible thing ... Such tragic idiocy, drilling soldiers on a battlefield that is night and day under fire. It was a case of sheer murder. The officers involved should be shot like mad dogs.' Strong words for Jack.

Of the officers he served under he was prepared to say that there were those whom he respected and with typical even-handedness he said that others were pigs but that he supposed they couldn't help it; although there were a number he hated, there were those whom he liked.

Along with every other Australian soldier, Jack found it extremely difficult to find anything to recommend the British officers. In his opinion they demanded strict observation of army protocol to disguise their own ineptitude and bolster their egos; they were only too willing to use the Anzacs to protect their own troops. An order by a British officer to get back into a filthy uniform crawling with lice—after he and his mates Stan, Morry and Bert had bought khaki shirts with their own money (the six shillings a day which King George V thought was too much pay for any soldier) to wear on twenty-four hours leave—did nothing to improve his opinion of them.

Jack was not fearful for his own safety. Years later at an Anzac gathering of the 5th Light Horse Regiment in Brisbane, Major Jack Cain recalled how a fearless Jack Idriess volunteered to blow up single-handedly 'Beachy Bill', a lethal gun emplacement trained on Anzac Cove. The Turks were using the gun with great efficiency and causing many fatalities and casualties among the Anzacs. Jack was commended for volunteering though he was refused permission to undertake the dangerous mission by Colonel

Harris who felt that the position was too well guarded. Many letters from Frank Byron of the 5th Light Horse who wrote regularly to Jack made mention of the incident which was often discussed at Anzac Day gatherings in Brisbane:

The Major often spoke of it to me and wondered if it could have been successful but he said, 'What a risk Jack would have had to take—Jack Idriess would have to be a gamer man than I to go,' and Major Cain was recognised by his men as a 'pretty good soldier'. And he rose to the rank of major and was awarded the Military Cross!

On 30 May Jack was wounded for the first time. The wound to the right knee, though superficial, turned septic. He was sent by hospital ship, the SS *Franconia*, to the Egyptian Government Hospital at Alexandria which proved fortuitous because the wound, like most other wounds, had only been dressed and not treated. Had he not been shipped to Alexandria he would have inevitably lost his leg.

While Jack made light of his leg wound and the fever caused by infection, both were bad enough to keep him in hospital for approximately eleven weeks before he was fit enough to return to action. During his long convalescence he filled in the time designing plans for what he called 'war inventions'. These he sent to 'the Brigadier and Admiral Robertson'. Just what the inventions were he did not record but he did note that 'naturally I got no reply'.

The first week in September found Jack back at Gallipoli and in action at Lone Pine. The route through the trenches to Lone Pine ended in a tunnel, the floor of which was 'uneven with puddle holes of putrid water'. The tunnel smelt like 'a cavern dug in a graveyard where the people are not in their coffins'. This is not surprising for that was virtually what it was.

We are in Lone Pine now and the stench is just awful; dead men, Turks and Australians, are lying buried and half buried in the trench bottom, in the sides of the trench and built up into the parapet. They have made the sandbags all greasy. The flies hum in a bee-like cloud. I understand now why men can only live in this portion of the trenches for forty-eight hours at a stretch.

Under these conditions it is hard to imagine how anyone could maintain their sanity, much less keep a sense of humour. The first Turkish sap (a covered siege-trench) was just fifteen feet in front of the Australians. The Turks couldn't hold it and the Australians couldn't take it. Any movement during daylight hours meant death, so the Turks contented themselves with sneaking in at night and throwing bombs across into the Australian trench.

Jack continued to snipe and write in the diary which he said was his one link with sanity, his safety valve. Apart from the dead and dying, bombs and bullets, nature was also contributing to the horrible conditions. Flies swarmed in such numbers that it was impossible for the men to get food into their mouths, lice filled their uniforms and bred under the incubator conditions formed by the seams, the men were covered in filth and rashes from the continuous lice bites, maggots fell into the trenches, 'not the squashy yellow ones' but 'big brown hairy ones'.

While Jack commented wryly that it was comical to watch the replacements trying to stick it out and ignore the maggots and crawlies, Lone Pine seems to have eroded his stoic veneer, for the diary entries show an understandable crack or two:

> Of all the bastards of places this is the greatest bastard in the world. And a man's boot in the firing-possy has been dripping grease on my over-coat and the coat will stink forever. We are supposed to be 'sleeping', preparatory to our next watch. Sleeping! Hell and tommy! Maggots are crawling down the trench; it stinks like an unburied graveyard; it is dark; the air is stagnant; some of the new hands are violently sick from watching us trying to eat. We are so crowded that I can hardly write in the diary even. My mates look like shadow men crouching expectantly in hell. Bombs are crashing outside, and—the night has come! The roof of this dashed possy is intermixed with dead men who were chucked up on the parapet to give the living a chance from the bullets while the trench was being dug. What ho, for the Glories of War!

Before the end of a week at Lone Pine Jack had fulfilled his mates' predictions that he would be 'outed' just as all the wounded men had who had returned with him had been. Once again he was wounded by a bomb, only this time it was a much closer call. Jack had just enough time to throw his overcoat over it before it exploded, mortally wounding the man in front, and damaging Jack's right arm. It was this wound which would cause him to write *Forty Fathoms Deep* with his left hand in 1934, nineteen years later.

That evening Jack had been searching for any sign of life among the heaps of crumpled khaki bodies by the last rays of the setting sun:

79

Some are rotting without either shape or form. The boots last the longest. Within a few yards of my periscope lay a tale telling how furiously both sides died. The Australian's bayonet is sticking, rusty and black, six inches through the Turk's back. One hand is gripping the Turk's throat, while even now you can see the Turk's teeth fastened through what was the boy's wrist. The Turk's bayonet is jammed through the boy's stomach and one hand is clenched, claw like, across the Australian's face. I wonder will they fight if there is an afterworld.

Jack was more fortunate than either the Australian or the Turk. After the bomb blast he was taken to the dressing station on the main beach, where he waited out the night to be taken off the next day by the hospital ship *Salta*. It was not a good night to remember:

> I nearly cried sometimes—I was not hurt at all—but those hundreds of poor maimed chaps lying there on the sand were trying to help one another with a joke, a whispered word—a smile—a look.

This second wound received at Lone Pine gave him a brief respite—being wounded was the only respite that any living man got at Gallipoli. Jack does not mention the severity of his wound; however, it seems to have kept him at the Egyptian Government Hospital in Alexandria for at least six weeks. During this time he once again turned to inventing and once again he didn't record the nature of his invention except to say that a Captain Dwyer had surprised him by showing enough interest in whatever it was to want to show it to a submarine officer.

At the hospital Jack had found himself in a bed beside Gus Gaunt, one of the men from Queensland's 5th Light Horse, who had also been on the *Salta* with him. Gus was one of the many who would continue to stay in contact with Jack for the rest of their lives after they had returned. An interview with Gus Gaunt published in the *Sunday Sun and Guardian* in November 1933 is an astute observation of Jack the separatist who had the ability to distance himself from the men and the devastation around him by using his diary as his confidant and as an escape hatch to maintain his sanity:

> Nearly four years abroad with Idriess gave one the opportunity of studying the man at close quarters. To even his closest associates Idriess was an enigma, and to get a word out of him was almost as great a problem as to fathom his thoughts. Of a reserved and

unassuming nature 'Jack' Idriess never argued the point, as was so common amongst even the smallest coterie of 'Diggers' when together; he was a silent listener to all their arguments, and to their whys and wherefores of how the war could be won.

A flicker of amusement might pass across his mostly sphinx-like face when some inebriated 'digger' in lurid language denounced the actions of GHQ over some stunt that appeared stupid and valueless. If asked to express his views on the actions of the 'Heads' he remained silent; he was later on to express his thoughts in words, via *The Desert Column*.

Jack Idriess gained neither promotion nor any decorations—he was just one of those thousands of diggers who abhorred limelight ... he took his duty as a matter of course and carried on, without looking for reward or wishing for fame.

Chapter Ten

THE DESERT COLUMN

BY 4 December 1915 Jack had been declared Class B by the medical board. Still unfit to return to Gallipoli he was placed on guard duty in Alexandria at the Ras-el-Tin convalescent home in Alexandria adjoining the sultan's palace and harem. Knowing that there was a secret world behind the stone wall of the palace was deliciously tantalising. Somehow he managed to get in a little guard duty between writing in his diary and blowing kisses to three of the sultan's ladies. The women who peered down at him from the barred windows indulged the infidel in his long-distance flirtation by returning his attentions with smiles, waves and signs of the Coptic Cross.

Alexandria was a hotbed of rumours and menacing unrest. The word was out that the Greeks were intending to join forces with the Arabs for the purpose of celebrating Christmas by assassinating all Christians and foreigners. Jack, and the other Australians, New Zealanders and the few English soldiers who were also convalescing, determined to meet any attack with fierce resistance. The attack did not materialise.

All able-bodied men were still on Gallipoli and the news was bad. Jack itched to get back into action with the 5th but, failing that, he tried to enlist with the recovered wounded in the Composite Regiment being formed to quieten the Senoussi Arabs who had started a holy war in the Tripoli desert.

3 January 1916 was a day of mixed emotions for Jack. He was delighted to be detailed to rejoin his regiment in Cairo, reluctant to leave behind the security of the convalescent home, and stunned to hear of the evacuation of Gallipoli—so stunned that he could write nothing else in his diary except 'We could not believe the news of the Evacuation'.

Three days later he was back with the regiment at Ma'adi. The reunion was not the happy event that Jack had anticipated. The diary entry for 6 January reads like an obituary for the regiment and a salute to the fallen:

It was real lonely, wandering down the old familiar lines, looking for familiar faces, and saddening to find only an odd one here and there. I think the boys of my regiment were the nicest lads in the world. We landed on the Peninsula nearly five hundred strong. Our casualties were eleven hundred and fortyfive. As fast as the reinforcements dribbled across, they were knocked. Only two original officers survived right through the Peninsula without being casualtied away. In my troop, there are only four old hands left, and two of them are first reinforcements who came over with us.

Missing familiar faces brought the war into sharp focus. Suddenly he wished that 'this damned war was over'.

Five weeks passed before Jack was to make another diary entry. When he did, he noted, 'I haven't much felt like writing up the old diary.' During those five weeks he had endured a deep depression. The depressed usually stop talking and become withdrawn. As Jack wasn't a talker, he stopped writing. For a man who already lived inside his head, this would have been like shutting off his safety valve. As he was naturally withdrawn, few would have guessed that Jack Idriess of the 'sphinx-like face' needed help.

The days at Ma'adi were filled with constant drill, training and manoeuvres. Doubtless the strict routine and physical effort which left little time for brooding was responsible for extricating Jack from depression.

A large army of Turks was reported to be massing in the Sinai and moving on the Suez Canal for a second attack—the first attack early in 1915 under Djemal Pasha had been repulsed by British troops. Numbers of British troops had gone to France and Europe after the evacuation of Gallipoli, leaving the Australian Light Horse, the New Zealand Mounted Rifles, the British Yeomanry and some artillery to keep the canal secure. These men and their horses had to shape up like case-hardened steel and become capable of travelling great distances without water. To this end they were trained in the desert, tempered by hours of intense heat and cold and sandblasted by the never-resting desert wind.

By 5 March Jack and the 5th were at Serapeum on the Suez Canal. The Turks were rumoured to be only a day's march away. The reinforcements were animated with excitement. Most of them, Jack observed, had never heard a bullet. He added that the 'old hands just smoke away and take things as a matter of course'.

Somewhere between 4 and 12 April Jack arrived at Salhia where General, later Sir, Harry Chauvel, Commander of the Australian Desert Mounted Corps had set up headquarters, as

Napoleon had done not many more than one hundred years before. From this time on he was committed to the desert.

At night, wrapped in a greatcoat, Jack stood Listening Post, staring out into the desert, not daring to move and knowing somewhere there, out in the darkness, were both Turks and Bedouins moving ever closer. It was quite obvious to the Australians that the Bedouins were treacherous spies and killers but the British allowed them to fraternise with their troops and camel drivers. It was Jack's opinion that the British didn't want to win the war.

By the end of April, Jack seems to have regained his equilibrium and was taking an interest in all that was happening. Once again he was writing between his four-hour watches. At the main outpost on hill 383, Ion L. Idriess, Trooper 358, assessed the positions of the outposts, the regiment, the brigade, and the infantry and theorised on the strategies that would be employed to defend the canal. He came to the conclusion that the authority and power of England, and thousands of lives, might well depend on 'this sunbrowned outpost gazing away out across the desert'. The regiment was comprised of sections of four men:

> The section lives together, eats together, sleeps together, fights together and when a shell lands, dies together ... Our life is concentrated in a section ... We growl together, we swear together, we take one another's blasted horses to water, we conspire against the damned troopsergeant together, we growl against the war and we damn the officers up hill and down dale together; we do everything together—in fact, this whole blasted war is being fought in sections. The fate of all the East at least, depends entirely upon the section.

Jack, Morry, Stanley and Bert Card were a 'section'; the four served together throughout almost the total desert campaigns except when they were briefly separated for two or three weeks in April of 1917. The breakup of the section which had fought together for so long profoundly angered Jack to the point that he was moved to damn to hell whoever was responsible—a curse that he had never even levelled at the enemy!

These four, together with Gus Gaunt 'who fights and growls in another section', survived to return home at the end of the war. Bert Card went to work at a department store in the Valley, Brisbane. Stan became the manager of a plantation in New Guinea and Morry took to the land and established a pineapple and banana farm. Gus ultimately became the supervisor of the Brisbane Sewerage Department. The five, though dispersed, were to keep in

contact with each other until their deaths. Gus, the most regular letter writer of the group, kept track of the others after the war.

They fought together at Romani on 4 August 1916. Jack wrote in his diary:

> The troops have been fighting day and night ... in fierce charges—attack and counter attack—galloping their horses to within point blank range of the Turks—scrambling on their horses when the Turks came raging around them, only to gallop back to turn around and fight again. Men and horses are desperately in need of sleep.

At El Katia, Morry tried desperately to swap places with someone who would hold the horses so he could go into the firing line with Jack, Stan and Bert—but no one wanted to be a horse handler. Here the Turk was fighting in a snarling fury over every inch of ground. It was here that Jack, blind with fear, lunged forward into a long, bare patch of sand with the squadron following him. The Turks held their fire until the squadron was well in the open. It remained a mystery to Jack that any man lived through that murderous crossfire which he claimed was worse than any at Lone Pine. He refused to feel guilty about his mistake because he simply hadn't been able to avoid it.

That same day Bert discovered a well from which the entire squadron managed to obtain a long, cold drink. The thirst-crazed men formed a defence around the well and held off the Turks while each man drank his fill. The oasis was reputed to have a well which was known as the Holy Family Well and Jack was sure that this had to be it; the precious liquid was nothing short of a miracle for men who had been fighting for days on end with only a quart of water each.

The four rode and fought together through the battle of Bir-el-Abd, along the El Arish track. The Turks were six thousand strong, well fed and rested and relieved by reinforcements continually arriving from El Arish. The Anzac Mounted Division was only half that strength and had no reinforcement support:

> Outnumbered, and outclassed by the Turkish batteries, the Anzac Mounted lay on their bellies firing through it all with a deadly cool steadiness: that unflinching steadiness has saved us again and again...Riflebolts clicked distinctly, jerking out the empty shell, ramming home the new—as definitely and remorselessly as fate.

Lying in the open under heavy shell fire Jack reached the

stage where he didn't give a damn—if he were to be killed, he would be killed, and that was the end of it.

The 5th were convinced that they had beaten the Turks at Romani and were waiting for the order for the final bayonet charge; instead they were ordered to retire. Jack believed that they could have finished the Turks off but of course he didn't know that the Turks had them surrounded.

They retreated, fought, retreated and fought; Morry took Bert's place in the front line beside Jack so that Bert, 'a poddy little fellow' who was completely exhausted, could take a break while he held the horses. Jack, Stan and Morry continued to fight and carry back the wounded—it was unspoken law that the Light Horse carried their wounded with them.

Jack remembered that awful retreat of tired horses and tired men, some asleep in their saddles, their heads dropped to their chests, moving through the night in the shadows of the padding Camel Corps which had brought them food: bread, jam, condensed milk and bullybeef. Horses fell, exhausted, the wounded moaned, the agony of their wounds magnified by the swaying and bumping of the cacolets mounted on either side of the camels.

When at last they sagged into Oghratina the horses had to be fed and watered, for the success of the war and the lives of the Light Horsemen depended on their horses.

It seemed to him that he had only just closed his eyes before they were back in the saddle again and riding to push the now retreating Turks. Keeping the Turk on the run and never letting him rest meant the Mounted never rested either. The exhausted men of the Anzac Mounted Division did not know that the tide of battle had changed—this was the beginning of the British advance.

Jack, Stan, Morry and Bert seem to typify the resilience of the Desert Mounted Division. There were the good days when they were glad to be alive and enjoyed each other's company, either scouting on their own, running down the stray Bedouin goat for meat, or, when their own horses were sick or wounded, stealing horses from other regiments, particularly those belonging to English officers.

At Bir-el-Abd, Jack joined the horseless. Staying at the front had become an obsession; under no circumstances did he want to be detailed as a member of the troop taking the horses back to Dueidar. After several attempts to steal a horse from the New Zealanders, he managed to 'pinch' a horse from a man who had, in turn, stolen it from some other luckless soldier at El Katia, earning himself the nickname of 'Bedouin Jack'.

At Hod-el-Amara, in good spirits, he brought his diary up to date, noting with a derisive 'what tommy rot!' the rumour that the Government was sending a journalist to write the history of the war. It was Jack's opinion that no mere observer could ever record the experiences and emotions of the fighting men.

While other men talked to each other Jack 'talked' to his diary. He was not concerned with technicalities but rather the humanities, or more precisely, the lack of them. He was a man who had come from a land where caring for his fellow man was almost a sacred duty, a land where a man was your mate and even if he was a bastard, should he need help, you gave it. Even in the thick of battle he had witnessed Turks individually extending incongruous compassion when they allowed the wounded to be carried to safety, shooting at the rescuers only when they had returned to the fight. In light of all of this he found it totally incomprehensible that the British could let thirteen thousand fresh infantry men remain in their redoubts while the battle surged right up to them, and watch while the thin line of mounted men was driven back again and again without ordering them to help. Neither could he understand how British officers could have marched the 42nd Division, East Lancashire lads, untrained in desert warfare, out from Bir-el-Nuss to help with the Katia battle. Hundreds had died, or gone mad digging for water in the hot sand with their bare hands, or had dropped, exhausted in the desert, long before nightfall—without ever firing a shot. Once again he registered both mystification and disgust for the intelligence of the British officers and thanked God for the Australian and New Zealand officers. While he was not naive enough to expect any form of mateship from the field officers in battle, he did expect support. Then, after he had mulled over the complex situation, he decided, again with typical fair-mindedness although not entirely convinced, 'perhaps field officers see it differently'.

By March of 1917, after almost two years of war, Jack's gung-ho attitude had faded. No longer was he prepared to see both sides or make excuses for those he did not understand. He was angry that British officers, who had never seen desert duty, were being placed over officers who had proved themselves in the field. The sight of dead and wounded men became harder to accept as part and parcel of a bloody war. It was as if he had placed his emotions on 'hold' for the past two years.

The sickening sound of bullets thudding into the faithful horses and the sight of the lustrous brown eyes widening in shock, or dimming, as the animal died were becoming too much for Jack.

The horses followed their masters like dogs over rugged terrain where it was impossible for men to ride; they carried them, galloping, into the most terrible battles. They charged through shelling and shooting, dying men and dying horses, without faltering and with the smell of blood and death filling their nostrils. More than the screams of any man, a horse screaming in pain filled Jack with a terror that turned him to water and the sight of their distress racked him with an unendurable anguish which at times blotted out all reason.

Then came the battles for Gaza and a chance meeting with Garnet Aitchison, the schoolteacher from Nigger Creek:

In the evening on the plain before Gaza I was smoking and cleaning my rifle when a chap strolled along enquiring for Jack Idriess. I looked up and saw in the starlight the grin on the face of Garnet Aitchison. We had a great yarn about old Nigger Creek. Aitchison was in the ambulance corps. A big attack was coming off in a couple of days' time and he expressed the pious hope that if I was 'knocked' his ambulance might pick me up before the Turks or Bedouins did. He also visited me the following night away across the plain.

The first battle of Gaza confused and sickened him. 'Men are dying this morning—writhing on the green grass of the Holy Land! God knows why.' He accepted General Dobell's order to retreat when the battle was won as being reasonable if they stood to lose large numbers of the mounted regiment; however, the order to polish up bits and stirrup irons after the battle sent Jack and his mates into a fury. These were men who had seen two years of duty and they knew what targets the glint of sun on metal provided for the Turkish snipers. Even so, they were prepared to back their own ability to outsnipe the Turks but for that they needed to be down on the plain fighting, not sitting on the hills surrounding Gaza cleaning their gear while other men were being killed. Naturally Jack wondered, yet again, if Britain really wanted to win the war. What he and his comrades didn't realise was that the mounted regiments were too valuable to lose.

When it came to sniping Jack was a match for Johnny Turk; his youth spent in Broken Hill hunting for food had provided excellent basic training but it was at Gallipoli and in the desert that he perfected the art of camouflage.

This knowledge and experience in sniping and commando tactics he was to give to the young soldiers of the Second World

War when he wrote the Guerrilla Series, published in 1942 and 1943. The first four titles of this set of handbooks, *Shoot to Kill*, *Sniping*, *Trapping the Jap* and *Guerrilla Tactics*, were published in 1942, while *Lurking Death* and *The Scout* were published in 1943. Reports have it that copies of *Sniping* are still used for reference by army trainees at the Singleton Army Camp in New South Wales. In recent years *Sniping* was stolen by an American publisher who, after recognising its value to the gun-crazed Americans, blatantly infringed copyright in 1978, the year before Jack's death in 1979.

Overcome by a great despair Jack feared that the Gaza campaign was about to become Gallipoli all over again, a thought that was also being voiced in Whitehall. The infantry were well entrenched on both sides, so well dug in were they that very little damage was inflicted on either. Observing the situation Jack sarcastically commented that, given a constant supply of food, arms, and their families, the antagonists facing each other down the plain could well live to a ripe old age in comparative safety. A miasma of despair shrouded the regiment when the *Egyptian Gazette* ran the headlines: 'Defeat Of Twenty Thousand Turks Near Gaza'; knowing that the report was a lie made the men question the truth of the reports of victories in France. Without access to accurate information, and fighting a war with no visible end, Jack felt isolated from the rest of the world and lost in a land which, compared with the jungles of the Cape York Peninsula, was hell's back yard. Suddenly he began to envy the wounded going past.

Throughout the fighting Jack had nurtured the idea of inventing a quick-firing rifle. It was his plan to turn the rifles, by the addition of a simple mechanism, into a machine-gun. After he had proposed the idea to the major who in turn referred it the colonel, he was given leave to go to Cairo to put it before the military authorities.

The train to Cairo was packed with soldiers who were on leave or on special duty. Gone was the old lightheartedness of the early days of the campaign which would have had them singing the night through. Scarcely a word was spoken throughout the long night. Each man squatted on the hard floor of the truck locked in his own thoughts, probably, like Jack, victims of their memories.

In Cairo Jack presented his invention and was amazed to find the British were not only interested but helpful; furthermore that they intended to send the plans to the Invention Board in London. By 24 June, however, he was back in Palestine and temporarily attached to New Zealand Brigade Headquarters while he developed his gun with the aid of Armourer Sergeant Major King, a New Zealander. A month later, after the rifle had been assembled out of bits and pieces of scrap by King, whom Jack said was a wizard with all things mechanical, they tried it out, and found that the rifle fired and ejected shells and reloaded with such speed that they could not see the bolt work.

29 July: 'The rifle has turned out trumps. King and I are to take the model into Cairo to be tested before the Inventions Board.'

The rifle was not tested in Cairo until 21 August. After the successful test it was decided that it would be sent to an experimental gun factory in England and both Jack and King were to take it there. At the last minute orders came for both men to return to Palestine. King was bitterly disappointed that the trip to England had been cancelled. Jack declared that he didn't give a damn—the luxury of sleeping in a bed, good food and no lice had been enough reward. This was not an assumed attitude; at no time in his life did Jack ever crave for material possessions or rewards.

Jack did not keep any record or plans of the rifle but a letter of Gus Gaunt's states that an ordinary rifle, with the addition of Jack's mechanism, weighing approximately one pound, could fire six hundred rounds a minute. What eventually happened to the gun is not known. Probably the Hotchkiss gun influenced the War Office against the Idriess invention.

By the end of August the entire Anzac Division had been classified as B Class and sent, on General Allenby's orders, to Marakeb beach for a month's rest. Allenby considered the men to be suffering from battle fatigue (the understatement of the decade). Jack thought that this was a miracle which could only happen in 'this land of miracles'.

At Marakeb the men swam and slept and drank all the fresh water they wanted. The reason given for retiring the Anzac Division to the beach at Marakeb was that they were 'overworked'. They were—but it appears that their condition did not stop the Anzac Division from being used as guinea pigs to test the effectiveness of gas and gas masks.

The Anzac forces were no strangers to gas warfare, having used it, albeit ineffectively, during the disastrous second battle of Gaza. Because at Gaza the gas had dissipated harmlessly in the desert air, one must assume that some intense work had been undertaken in the meantime to produce 'huge clouds of gas and fumes' which stayed suspended long enough for the men to 'waddle silently into another awe-inspiring cloud' a few short weeks later. Could it be possible that the compassionate reason given for resting the Anzac Division at Marakeb was cynical and sinister?

The sinister aspect behind the beach vacation and its disastrous potential does not seem to have occurred to Jack for he found gas training 'interesting'. He thought that the men were such a frightening sight and such 'weirdlooking monstrosities' that the Turks would run in terror at the sight of them emerging from a cloud of gas—it never entered his head that he and his comrades might enter that vile vapour and not live to terrify anybody.

In June 1917 General Allenby replaced Sir Archibald Murray as Commander-in-Chief. With him had come new troops and a change of title which had saddened the Anzacs—'The Desert Column' was now the 'Desert Mounted Corps'. The desert was swarming with mounted men, infantry and gun batteries. Observation balloons flew overhead and the navy had joined the show. Everyone knew that the dense concentration could mean only one thing—a hell of a big push was coming.

A census taken at the end of August 1917 revealed that just over a hundred of the original members of the 5th Light Horse Regiment were left. These men had all been wounded, some twice. The balance of the regiment, some four hundred men, was made up of reinforcements, half of whom had also been wounded.

By 22 October the men of the Desert Mounted Corps knew they were facing the thick of battle again. As ever the one vital necessity was water for the tens of thousands of men and their beloved horses. German engineers had blown the wells of Asluj and Esani which lay about thirteen miles south of Beersheba. The Desert Mounted Corps' task was to ride ahead of the infantry and develop water for the following hordes. This they accomplished by 25 October, and by 1 November had established a reservoir of water and were standing by at Asluj waiting for the troops to mass at the water before they rode on Beersheba, in what has been hailed by some as the greatest charge and battle in cavalry history. In *The Desert Column* Jack outlined the battle plans:

> Chauvel is in command of the Beersheba operations. The plan roughly is: the Anzacs must smash Beersheba; immediately word of success comes through, the 21st Infantry Corps assisted by the Navy is to vigorously attack over the sand-dunes between Gaza and the sea, Chetwode is to rush his divisions against the strongholds of Tel Sheria and Hareira, the Yeomanry Mounted Division is to attack with the 20th Infantry Corps, the 7th Mounted Brigade is to attack the southern trenches. Immediately the Anzac and Australian Mounted Divisions break through Beersheba, Chauvel is to smash his way right through to behind Gaza.

As far as Jack was concerned the Desert Mounted Corps had a thirsty job to do and there would be 'merry hell to pay'; he wondered if his luck would hold. At the same time he had an overpowering sense of the vast scale of the plan which was designed to smash the Turk's right flank. It was almost too much to comprehend. Just like every other man riding, Jack accepted no thought other than that they would take Beersheba on that first day—to fail would have meant the whole front would have been lost and the army would be committed to a more disastrous Third Battle of Gaza. Failure did not come into their calculations.

Those who wish to read the graphic details of the battle for Beersheba, from the morning's first magnificent charge to the eventual taking of Beersheba at sunset on 2 November 1917, must read *The Desert Column*. Never before or since has anyone told it better than Jack:

> At a mile their thousand hooves were stuttering thunder, coming at a rate that frightened a man—knee to knee and horse to horse—the dying sun glinting on bayonet points ... The last half mile was a berserk gallop with the squadrons in magnificent line, a heart throbbing sight as they plunged up the slope, the horses leaping the redoubt trenches...

By mid-December, after the fall of Beersheba, the Desert Mounted Corps had driven the enemy back one hundred and twenty miles. Outside Jaffa Jack went down with a malaria known as Jaffa fever. This strain of malignant malaria and the strain contracted from Cape York stayed with him, and recurred throughout his life. Jack seems to have spent a number of days lost in the delirium of malaria fever, spasmodically recovering sufficiently to fight before lapsing back into delirium. He recorded that they were lashed by icy rain and that the weather was cold—indeed it was, for snow fell on Bethlehem. He wrote that he was too sick to notice or care what was happening but he knew that they were dug in under ceaseless shell fire and he thought that the Turks were being reinforced again and again from the Balkan and Russian fronts. The world was an inferno of machine-gun and rifle and artillery fire made worse by hand grenades. 'If hell is any worse then I don't want to go there.'

Somehow the doctors managed to pull him through the fever. Then one morning, feeling much better, Jack went on sick parade to have his septic sores dressed when a shell exploded. He should have been blown to pieces; instead he was hit by a dozen or so shell splinters. 'Port Said Hospital, 2 January 1918—I am to be returned to Australia as unfit for further service. Thank heaven!'

Many years later in the early days of the Second World War Jack and Sir Donald Cameron were exchanging memories at a 5th Light Horse Regiment reunion in Brisbane. Sir Donald Cameron had served as a member of the 5th Australian Light Horse regiment throughout the First World War, and had been its Commanding Officer from 17 October 1917 until the regiment was disbanded in August 1919.

The two discussed the amazing and little-known situation where, in the closing encounter of the desert campaign, Turks and Australians joined forces to fight as allies against the Arab Bedouins.

Attached to the draft of an article which he no doubt planned to polish for publication at a later date is a pencilled note: 'Would have been a wonderful last chapter to end *The Desert Column*. But was too badly wounded before this final episode. I.L.I. 1971.' The draft carried the title, 'The Southern Cross and the Crescent: The Last Episode of the Palestine Campaign', and reads:

Ran into Sir Donald Cameron, genial commander of the Queensland Scotties. He was our OC, before he grew a handle to his name, while I was only a roughneck trooper in the 5th Light Horse. The tough old sheepman-soldier hasn't changed, except that he's grown another wrinkle or two.

'What do you think of this new war Idriess?' he grinned.

'Blest if I know, Colonel. We'll win in the long run, but it's going to be tough.'

'Maybe. I think I'll join up.'

'If you do it may end in another Ziza for you.'

The grin faded from the rugged face, we saw again the sun scorched hills of Palestine, he slipped back to the last fight of that war. Ziza! Four thousand five hundred Turks with artillery cornered by the 5th Light Horse Regiment, thinned by casualties into only 400 strong. The fight, the cheekiest in the whole World War, and then—clouds of human vultures on camel and pony and foot hurrying to the slaughter—Bedouins, torturers of the wounded but—our Allies! This Turkish remnant of an army hampered by wounded and dying men. These desert jackals swarming in their black robed thousands meant that the throats of the Turks would be cut to a man. The Turkish Commander was frantic to surrender to the Australians but daren't, the Light Horsemen were too few in number to protect his men.

'Hold your arms,' advised Cameron. 'Protect yourself when necessary, and I'll guarantee to hold the Bedouins off.'

Grimly the Australians seized a position which commanded both friend and foe, though necessarily effective as far as their rifles could reach. Then began as strange a fight as history has ever seen in all those battle scarred hills of Palestine. The glowering Bedouins withdrawing from Australian rifles to attack where those rifles could give the Turk no protection. The Turks crouching low, sweating blood and salt while struggling to carry their sick and wounded close to the Light Horsemen's protection, then snatching up rifle and machine-gun to fight back frantically wherever the Bedouin attacked. Every now and then the crawling Arabs captured a Turk, hauled him from his rifle pit as a boy would haul a rabbit from a burrow. On such occasions the Turk would squeal like a dying pig even before the Bedouins drove the knife into him.

Cameron threatened the Bedouin chiefs that if they dared attack the Turks in force then the Australians would attack them.

It was perfect discipline. Intense heat, foemen's rifles poking from every rock, the trapped Turks massed in gun pit and trench that echoed their heart beats as they awaited that last long, terrible cry. The Australians, fingers itching on rifles and machine-guns, covered the detested Bedouins for critical hours, longing for the order to fire. One shot, and hell would have broken loose in an all-in fight that would have blazed into a massacre one way or the other. Towards sundown the strain was at breaking point, the 2nd Light Horse Brigade, still miles away, were galloping to the rescue but thousands of fresh Bedouin were arriving, clamouring to overwhelm Australian and Turk alike. Both Australian and Turk well knew that under cover of darkness the Bedouins would come swarming like clouds of bats from the night. At sundown came a distant shout, heads were turned, wild laughter broke from the Australians. The 7th Regiment was coming fast, shadow horsemen in the dark.

It meant the boil-over one way or the other. Cameron won, defeated the Bedouins' momentary hesitation by swiftly marching into Ziza. The 5th Light Horse scrambled down into the Turkish trenches and then began the strangest incident in all the startling annals of warfare. Australian and Turk, foeman and foeman, crouched shoulder to shoulder against the Bedouin—our Allies! But the 7th regiment hovering out in the darkness and the knowledge that other regiments must be hurrying up, took the guts out of the Bedouin. They snarled around Ziza all night, creeping up to the gun pits, firing erratic shots, creeping back to creep forward again, awaiting the long drawn, wild scream to plunge forward in one overwhelming rush. But their chiefs were as undecided as they. At dawn they faded away before the oncoming 2nd Brigade.

That dramatic episode ended the war between British and Turk. Before long, Australian and Turk may again be fighting, but fighting as they fought in the very last action of their war, fighting shoulder to shoulder.

'Twill be the justice of fate should Cameron command a Division of Australians and Turks.

Chapter Eleven
THE WALKING WOUNDED

IN the early months of 1918 Jack was brought home badly wounded to Sydney. The doctors at the 14th Australian General Hospital, Cairo, had unsuccessfully tried to remove all splinters of the shell which had knocked him out of the fight but he was still carrying several pieces embedded in his body. No one would attempt to remove a large piece lodged against his spinal column—to have done so would have proved fatal. This souvenir of his last day at the front he would carry with him to the grave. Apart from this potentially lethal foreign body there was a large fragment in his right thigh and numerous other pieces of shrapnel, especially in his left leg.

Initially Jack was relieved to be classified as unfit for further service but he hadn't counted upon being discharged in Sydney on two crutches with the pronouncement that he would never walk again with or without them. Ion L. Idriess, late Trooper 358 of the 5th Light Horse AIF, had run out of luck—or so the army doctors thought, but they didn't know Jack.

In 1912 a group of business men, captained by one Snowy Baker, had bought the Sydney Stadium. Reginald 'Snowy' Baker was an exceptional athlete who excelled at every sport he chose to participate in. A silver medal winner for middleweight boxing in the 1908 Olympic Games, he was also a swimmer, diver and a horseman extraordinaire. Snowy was more than brawn, he was also skilled in promotion and publicity. Apart from sponsoring a magazine, *Famous Fights of the Stadium*, he also published the widely circulated *Snowy Baker's Magazine* which promoted physical culture and patriotism and ran advertisements for his physical culture correspondence courses.

Jack responded to one of Snowy's physical culture advertisements and became a living endorsement of Snowy's expertise and methods, disproving the doctors' verdict by hanging his crutches over the doorway of the stadium's gymnasium—and leaving them there. Jack also learned the art of self-defence with boxing lessons from Snowy's brother Harold. After his stint with

Snowy, there was nothing to keep Jack in Sydney. Kate Windeyer, the step-grandmother who had taken care of him after Julia's death, had died, and his sisters and father were all living in Grafton, so he took the opportunity to join one of Snowy Baker's travelling boxing exhibtions touring country towns, which included Grafton. The following newspaper report of 23 August 1918 in the *Grafton Argus* is not a shining example of reporting accuracy for Jack never rose above the rank of private, nor did he see action in France:

> Last Night's Rally…Huge and Enthusiastic gathering…Clabby then boxed three rounds with Sgt Idriess, who was but recently returned from France. Sgt Idriess made a good showing with the champion who found it difficult to use his famous loop-the-loop hit, and states that Idriess is the best boxer that has faced him during the present march.

Jimmy Clabby of the 'famous loop-the-loop hit' held the World Champion Lightweight title. Clabby, an American boxer, was one of many boxers Baker imported to Australia.

Without wishing to detract from Jack's possible ability in the boxing ring, one has to wonder if Jack's 'good showing with the champion' was staged to promote Baker's boxing courses. Jack, however, was not interested in life as a boxer; as far as he was concerned the trip north with the boxing team was a means by which to get back to the Peninsula.

The one-night stand at Grafton provided him with the opportunity to visit his family and leave two metal trunks, a big round haversack and an army kit bag at the home of his married sister, Ildyce Morrison, affectionately known to family as Dycie. This baggage and his diaries from the front stayed behind the door of the Morrison spare bedroom on the verandah for many years.

The personal relationships within the Idriess clan had not improved. Walter Owen Idriess had re-married some years earlier. Although the new Mrs Idriess, one Amy Scott, had been a close friend of both Walter and Julia when the Idriess family lived at Lismore, according to Ion Morrison, Jack's nephew, the elder girls refused to acknowledge or accept her as their step-mother. Although Walter and Amy lived in the same town as the vivacious Idriess girls, they were steadfastly ostracised by both Esmé, and Ildyce, the latter refusing even to speak to Amy. By 1924 some semblance of civility was restored to the situation by Jack who arranged a meeting between Walter and Ildyce's son, Ion Morrison. Recalling the meeting Ion remembered Jack thought it deplorable that the grandfather and grandchild, young Ion, had never met. However the meeting did nothing to soften the family's attitude to Amy.

Always with Cooktown as his goal Jack kept travelling north. In Brisbane in March 1919 he witnessed the trade unionist march which created a riot in which nineteen people were wounded when they twice raided the headquarters of the Russian Association. The sight of two lines of police constables armed with fixed bayonets standing fast shoulder to shoulder to meet the violent mob at the Russian quarter in South Brisbane sickened him and he became more disgusted when he learned that there were returned service-men in the crowd of rampaging hooligans.

The discord between the family members must have seemed trivial and annoying to a man who had just come back from a major fracas between nations, but the discord in the city disturbed him more; little wonder that he wanted to go bush and stay there.

He didn't get away from Brisbane until sometime in 1920, staying long enough to give his blood in transfusion to another returned solider at the Mater Misericordiae Public Hospital. The small newspaper cutting carrying the heading 'To Save A Life—Willing Sacrifice—Soldier's Noble Action' from an unnamed paper dated simply '1920' claims, in a highly graphic report, that Trooper Ion Idriess, late 5th Light Horse Regiment, gave his blood in the first blood transfusion carried out in Brisbane.

When Jack finally did get back to Cooktown he resumed his friendship with Dick Welch. The two pooled their resources to buy horses, tools and supplies for an extended prospecting trip but there was no possibility that life could ever be the same for either of them. Dick had spent his war years in France and had returned home after suffering extensive wounds in the legendary mud and blood at the Somme, which eventually led him to find solace in alcohol and, finally, death. It is hard to reconcile the sunny-natured Dick, the boy of pre–1914, with Dick the morose alcoholic who bit-terly regretted he had not died at the Somme with a gun in his hand. It was the news of Dick's death in the late 1950s that prompt-ed Jack to write My Mate Dick, published in 1962.

The first four years back in the Peninsula after the war appear to have been spent with Dick traversing the Peninsula from the Cooktown base in search of gold or any other payable metal and sandalwood, with an occasional trip on a lugger fishing for trochus shell or bêche-de-mer.

Together the pair, 'the walking wounded', walked or rode north, to Somerset at the Finger Point on the tip of Cape York

Peninsula and to the old goldfields of Ebagoola and the Coen. They found only a few nuggets that the Chinese had missed and evidence of much they had taken away on mules to the coast, from where it had been picked up by lugger and illegally shipped out of the country. They knapped (chipped the rocks to test for ore) in the gullies along the Rocky, Batavia, Claudie, Alice and Nisbet Rivers and covered Gordon's Iron Range and Portland Road which many of the old prospectors believed was John Dickie's lost goldfield. They dropped on to the track Christy Palmerston had explored over half a century before, and crossed the dividing ranges of the Byerstown and Windsor, there to find sandalwood which they took back to Cairns via Mounts Carbine and Molloy, and on to Mareeba. Then they made tracks right across the Peninsula to the eastern edge of the Gulf of Carpentaria through the sea-level Mitchell country where missionaries were zealously attempting to impose their beliefs, against all opposition, on local Aborigines.

The country was wild and the Aborigines were dangerous but somehow Jack and Dick managed to pass unharmed from one tribal land to another. Gifts of Nigger Twist tobacco, sugar and flour to the more aggressive Aborigines helped to ease a number of potentially explosive situations, while at night it was the precaution of setting up camp, rigging the mosquito nets and making a show of crawling under them and later stealing out to sleep elsewhere that saved them from being speared as they slept.

It was during this period that Jack went 'walkabout' with a northern tribe, while Dick went back to Cooktown for supplies. During this time, because of the trust that the Aborigines placed in Dick, Jack had the privilege of witnessing ceremonies which few white men have ever seen. Detailed accounts of these rituals and other facets of Aboriginal life which Jack saw and recorded during his lifetime were eventually to appear in *Our Living Stone Age* published in 1963, and in *Stone Age Mystery* published in 1964.

Jack continued to keep his notes and to send his paragraphs to the *Bulletin*'s 'Aboriginalities' page. But it was not until 1924 that, aged 35, he began to extend himself to longer articles. The first appears to have been an article entitled 'Heroines All', subtitled 'Women of the Far North—Great Heart and Dreams'. He was still writing under the *nom de plume* 'Gouger'.

The eleven years spent on the Cape York Peninsula were also punctuated by visits to Grafton and Sydney; an extensive trip to New Guinea; work on Thursday Island and Brisbane wharves; one long trip up the Queensland coast in a small, unreliable cutter with one of Jardine's grandsons; and a memorable stint marooned on Number One of the Howick Island group which resulted in the writing of his first book, *Madman's Island* (first published in 1927, revised and re-published in 1938).

Early in 1922 Jack and Dick had returned to Cooktown to sell what little gold they had and to buy supplies for another trip. As usual, they found themselves holding up the bar of the West Coast Hotel—the West Coast had still retained its place as Jack's favourite watering hole since the first day he had arrived in Cooktown twelve years and a war before.

Drinking at the West Coast that day was another prospector, Charlie, also badly wounded during the war. The three reminisced and swapped prospecting yarns over a beer when a Malay, whom Jack described as being 'a wild and woolly bloke', threw down on the bar what he thought to be stones and asked them to identify them. The stones were a mixture of tin and wolfram, a bad combination to separate but still valuable.

The Malay had been shipwrecked and marooned on Number One Howick, an island he called Hammock Island, and was later picked up and brought back to Cooktown. Jack and Charlie decided immediately to go to the island on the off-chance they might find a good patch of wolfram; Dick preferred to stay on the mainland with his horses. So began the chain of coincidences that ultimately led to *Madman's Island*.

It was Captain Dan Moynahan who took Jack and Charlie on his schooner to the island, the same Captain Dan who had put Jack ashore at Cape Melville, and who had brought the news of the declaration of war and taken Jack back to Cooktown in 1914.

There was one reef of wolfram, and another small reef of wolfram and tin on the island. Charlie and Jack crushed one and a half tons, packed it into canvas bags and waited for the schooner to return to take them back to Cooktown. Dan, however, never did get back and they were marooned there for seven months before a Japanese fishing lugger manoeuvred close enough for Jack to board—Charlie refused to leave.

Both men could have died there had they not been able to spear fish after their supplies ran out and it would have been possible for Jack to have been shot and killed by Charlie in the months waiting for Dan to return, for Charlie had a problem.

Charlie had sustained an injury during the war which had necessitated the removal of what he claimed to be nine feet of his intestine, give or take a foot or two. The 'miracle' operation had been carried out at Guy's Hospital in London, before he was sent home with an ingenious spiral silver tube implanted in his stomach.

The doctors had also given him a funnel to insert into the tube and prescriptions for huge bottles of chemicals which he had to mix with a pint of water to pour into the tube to clean out the gases, which if left to accumulate would cause his death inside forty-eight hours—the time span was fortunately under-estimated. He also had instructions to write just two words, 'Still living', and post them to Guy's Hospital every two months.

All would have been well if Charlie had packed his funnel and chemicals when the pair shipped out for the island but Charlie and Jack had overdone it the night before they left for the island and Charlie forgot his life-saving equipment.

After a few days on the island Charlie began to swell up, a 'horrible sight' according to Jack. The first intimation that Jack had of Charlie's predicament was when he said, 'Stone the bloody crows, Jack, I've gone and forgotten my belly juice.'

In reply to Jack's startled 'What?', Charlie showed him the hole at the end of a vivid red scar running down the right side of his body and explained. Jack recalled that at the time all he could think was, 'Struth, here is a man who is going to swell up and bust and I'm here with him, marooned on a lonely island and God knows when anyone will ever pass this way, so I said nothing. There was nothing to say except "Stone the bloody crows!"'

Partridge's *Dictionary of Slang* credits Jack with popularising in print the saying 'stone the crows' and that the expression was used widely to denote not disbelief but surprise at learning something new. In this instance I think Jack was using it in both contexts.

Apart from being a man of uncertain humour, Charlie was also an inventive one, who had no intention of dying until death actually kicked him in ribs and forced him to roll over. As the months crawled by Jack came to regard his tenacity with mixed emotions.

Charlie fashioned a substitute funnel from wire and the canvas bags which they had brought to fill with wolfram and tin. For two hours each day he would lie in the water just off the beach and pour salt water down the funnel; the salt water worked to a degree but only if Charlie never failed to doctor himself each day. Slowly the lack of adequate medication began to take its toll and Charlie started to become even more morose and evil tempered, until finally he lapsed into periods of madness, and began to shoot at Jack, forcing him to stay away from the only water on the island.

The following months Jack spent in a state of fear and tension on the other side of the island, his every sense, waking or sleeping, tuned to outwit Charlie who, in his madness, was extremely cunning. Somewhere during this period Jack found the log book of the shipwrecked Malay and used it keep a daily diary which formed the basis for *Madman's Island*.

After Jack was rescued and taken back to Cooktown Charlie refused to leave the island for some time. When he eventually did come back to the mainland Charlie went gold prospecting at the top of the Peninsula, where he died of malaria.

In the closing paragraph of *Madman's Island* Jack claims to have been feeling 'wonderfully fit and ready to start life all over again', after his harrowing experience on Howick Island. And 'I walked eagerly through town in search of my old mate Dick'. While a fitting end for the book, akin to the hero riding off into the sunset, this was far from the truth, for he was in ill health and his nerves were stretched to breaking point. He took himself south over the border into New South Wales, to recuperate at his sister Dycie's home in Grafton.

Jack settled down at Grafton for a short time. He had his own entry to the room on the verandah where he kept mostly to himself, preferring not to be a part of the family. On rare occasions he would share a meal with them but mostly he ate at the Grafton Returned Soldier's and Sailor's Imperial League. The family had no idea therefore that while he was recuperating he was using the log book entries to write his first book.

Over the preceding years Jack's *Bulletin* paragraphs, written while he was in the Peninsula, had attracted the attention of Alec H. Chisholm, then editor of the *Daily Telegraph*, editor of the *Argus*, Melbourne and later editor of Angus and Robertson's *Australian Encyclopaedia*. Apart from his literary work, Chisholm was a dedicated ornithologist who, in the pursuit of this life-long passion, had written to Jack asking for descriptions of rare Peninsula birds, which Jack supplied. The correspondence between the two men was sufficient for each to regard the other as a friend. It was to Chisholm that Jack sent the manuscript.

Chisholm in turn submitted the work to George Robertson of Angus and Robertson, booksellers and publishers, accompanied by a letter dated 12 April 1923 in which he wrote that it had been 'written under the most extraordinary circumstances by a bushman friend of mine in Queensland'. Although the letter never mentioned Jack's name nor the title of the book there is very little doubt that his 'bushman friend' was Jack.

Robertson returned the manuscript, unread, because the Firm was turning its endeavours to the selling of British and

American books rather than continuing to fight the unequal battle of the rising costs of printing and binding which had escalated with the forty-four hour week.

However it was not long before A&R were printing and publishing Australian works again after finding a 'young master printer' who had kept out of the hands of the Master Printing Association, the equivalent of today's Printers and Kindred Industries Union. Even so, it would be another three years before Robertson would find the manuscript for *Madman's Island* back in his hands.

The story of how *Madman's Island* came to be published, as told by Jack, is a beguiling mixture of fact taken out of context and publicity hype, with one or two slight variations—an art at which gentle Jack the storyteller excelled. The more expansive version has it that the publication in 1927 of the first edition was pure coincidence and reads as follows...

Jack, while holidaying in Sydney on the proceeds of the inevitable shammy (a small bag made from fine oiled leather) of gold, just happened to visit Chisholm to expand upon the sighting of some rare bird. During the conversation Jack told Chisholm, then the news editor of the *Daily Telegraph*, about his experience on Howick, at which point, Chisholm suggested that Jack should write a book about the episode; to which Jack replied that he had done so, while he was sitting on the peak of the island and that as luck would have it, he happened, by chance, to have the manuscript with him. On hearing this, as Jack reports, Chisholm

> ...grabbed his hat in one hand and my arm in other, I didn't have the faintest idea what was going on ... and marched me straight across the road to Angus and Robertson, right up the stairs, still holding on to my arm, right up to this long giant of man with a great big black Ned Kelly beard and a very austere, severe, distrustful-looking countenance. Chisholm ran me up beside him and said, 'Here you are George, I've got your dream, what you wanted, at last. The great Australian novel.'

The author's note to the revised publication released in 1938 carries a similar story, only this time he is told to return with the diary—he doesn't have it under his arm and it isn't in manuscript form. In this version Robertson has a smiling face and kindly eyes and is not at all 'severe' or 'austere'.

The first publication in 1927 written with what Jack consistently referred to as a 'love interest' was a total failure, selling only three hundred copies. The romantic story line was said to have been Robertson's brain child and the reason for the book's failure—Robertson never denied this. In the original log book Jack's entries are written in pencil and there is a rather amateurish attempt to add a romantic storyline at the end which he probably wrote at the time to amuse himself. It would seem that Robertson might have simply indicated that Jack should make more of the book's existing romantic aspect, not add it.

While Jack would have had the world believe that Lady Luck had been conspiring that day to get *Madman's Island* into print, she had in fact, been working on it for three years, with a little assistance from Chisholm, and a nudge from Jack.

In 1925 Jack continued to write regularly for the *Bulletin* which was always 'good for a bob'. And he tried his hand at more long articles which found a market in publications such as the *Australian Woman's Mirror* and the Brisbane *Daily Mail*. For the women's magazines he wrote about the women of the Peninsula in stories such as 'The Honour Dance' and 'Sheer Grit' subtitled 'How a Woman Wooed Fortune in the Northern Wilds'. For the *Australian Woman's Mirror* he used the *nom de plume* 'Little Jack'. The *Daily Mail* published such lusty tales as 'Three Times Dead and Still Alive' and 'The Alligator' to which he signed his own name, Ion L. Idriess, maintaining 'Gouger' for the *Bulletin* and also occasionally using 'Stannifer'. In 1927 he added the *nom de plume* 'Up North,' also in the *Bulletin*.

In June of 1925 he wrote a reader's appraisal of a book entitled *The Money Web* for A&R. The attached letter was addressed to Mr Shenstone who had become Robertson's right-hand man in the late 1890s. Jack's address is given as 378 Park Road, Paddington. Just how long he stayed in Sydney, or why, is not known. How he came to be involved in the criticism of this book is a total mystery but it does prove that he was no stranger to A&R prior to his meeting with Robertson.

Before the year was out he was back at Grafton. Life at the Morrison home would have been a pleasant experience for they obviously were people who were able to resist interfering in his life. But Jack was unable to resist the gold bug; it really didn't matter where he was, if there was a possibility that gold might be found, he just had to go and do a little prospecting. While he was staying with the Morrisons he managed to infect Ildyce's husband, George, with mild gold fever.

Jack and George Morrison were very firm friends. George's family had come from Scotland bringing all their goods and chattels with them and settled on Goodwood Island on the lower Clarence River. There they established a private sugar mill, the last private sugar mill to hold out against the giant Colonial Sugar Refining company. The elder Morrisons had employed many Kanakas from the Cook Islands, who didn't want to go home when the government of the day decreed they were to return.

George could best be described as a 'gentleman farmer'. He had travelled widely studying farming in the United States and Canada before he met and married Ildyce when he was forty-five years old. George is also said to have founded the National Party together with Lloyd George.

George Morrison, a gentleman of the old school, was a Grafton estate and stock and station agent when Jack and he went in search of the yellow stuff in the Clarence Gorge below Glen Innes. It was Jack's belief that one of the biggest gold strikes in Australia would be made there but George and Jack were not to prove his theory.

By July, 1926 Jack had tired of Grafton. He had moved to Brisbane and was looking forward to travelling north with one of the grandsons of the Jardines of Somerset. The purpose of the trip was to carry out a prospecting and geological survey expedition for the Queensland Mines Department, after which he planned to go on to Thursday Island. This he did, leaving Brisbane in 1926—his Torres Strait days had begun.

Chapter Twelve
TORRES STRAIT DAYS

IN July 1926 Jack wrote to George Robertson asking him to pass on his address as Brisbane GPO should A. S. Le Soeuf of Taronga Park Zoo contact A&R before mid-August; after August, Le Soeuf was to be advised to address his mail c/o the Thursday Island GPO.

Le Soeuf, who had recommended the Taronga Zoo site and supervised its design and building, had been the zoo's director since 1903. A reader of the 'Aboriginalities' page, Le Soeuf, like Chisholm, had called upon Jack's knowledge of the Peninsula's birds and animals. While Chisholm wanted only descriptions of birds, Le Soeuf's needs were more ambitious. He wanted both specimens and descriptions from Jack of the 'strange animals seen in out-of-the-way places'.

Le Soeuf had written to Jack from England that he would make inquiries at A&R as to Jack's whereabouts when he returned. This was probably the first of the countless occasions that A&R were to act as a point of contact for the wandering Jack Idriess.

In the same letter Jack told Robertson about his proposed prospecting trip with Jardine—grandson of the first Government Resident and Police Magistrate, Captain John Jardine of the 44th Regiment of Foot and the first Adminstrator of the historic Somerset House settlement at the tip of Cape York Peninsula. Jack wrote that they planned to explore two tracts of land, which were likely to prove to be gold bearing, for the Queensland Department of Mines which was financing the trip. Jack was engaged as the mining expert, while Jardine was the navigator and both were experienced bushmen. In one of the areas to be surveyed the explorer de Goleuse and his party were said to have perished at the hands of the Aborigines; 'chewed up,' wrote Jack. It was said one man had survived to bring back a gold specimen, which a bank manager apparently declared as rich as any that he had seen at Ballarat.

Jack wrote to Robertson that he had his reservations about the other tract which Jardine said was 'utterly dead land':

Jardine declares there is neither animal nor bird in that country, only a dead silence. I cannot reconcile this with my own extensive knowledge of the Peninsula. However it promises to be an interesting trip, and I would go to the North Pole if I thought there was a chance of opening up a goldfield there.

Jack, who preferred to keep his feet on terra firma, objected to the use of a boat as a means of transport. 'I firmly believe in horses. A man is then travelling over country all the time.'

When Jack left Brisbane he was well equipped to write. In place of the school exercise books he usually made his notes in, he took with him a large, hard-covered book. Unlike most of his diaries the majority of entries in this black-covered book are dated and all are written in ink.

Beginning on 22 August 1926 when the twenty-seven foot cutter, the *Somerset*, chugged down the Brisbane River, Jack regularly kept the diary, missing only a day or two here and there until the end of the trip. The last dated entry is 24 November 1926. There are several entries after that date—the day he and Jardine went ashore approximately fifty miles from Cape York to walk inland to where Jardine expected to find de Goleuse's goldfield. On that date he wrote that the 'Skipper', Bootles Jardine, was anxious to get back to Brisbane for Christmas, and 'Hoo-blooming-hurray! This most wretched of trips is finished at last'.

From the time the *Somerset* left the Brisbane River the entire trip was a miserable, and often death-defying, experience. Jack's diary is a litany in which the sea, the *Somerset* and the *Somerset*'s engine assume human characteristics. Throughout the trip the traitorous engine was supremely capable of resisting all of Jardine's exhortations to behave in a temperate fashion, neither dialogue, or mollification, or vilification, seems to have been able to persuade it to relinquish its disobedient and dishonest behaviour. To Jack, all three—sea, wind and engine—seized every opportunity to combine and tyrannise, particularly when total destruction was a possibility. Jack formed the opinion that there is very little poetry in 'sad sea waves' and that 'the sea is merciless and is only fit to be hated'.

Jardine's good humour seems to have deserted him along with the engine's reliability soon after leaving the Brisbane River, while the third member of the party, a man named Pen, deserted at Townsville on 15 September. By 23 September, after enjoying a few days ashore, both Jack and Jardine had exhausted their funds—Jack had one ha'penny, and Jardine seven pence ha'penny. They put to sea again, with Jack Mitchell aboard to replace Pen. Mitchell was 'a man of many parts', according to Jack, but by 4 October he was completely disenchanted with the sea and the engines' capricious ways, and left the *Somerset* at Cairns.

By 10 October Jack had returned to Cooktown. 'We steamed into the little bay of quiet waters, and so I came back once more to the old town.' Cooktown greeted him as an old friend while it also turned out enthusiastically to meet the international flyers, Williams and MacIntyre, when they landed their sea-plane on the blue waters of the bay, an event which was captured by Jardine on 'cinematographic' film.

Jack's delight in being back in Cooktown was short-lived and his morose mood was not improved by visiting an old flame. For some reason the visit proved to be a bitter disappointment: he noted in his diary the following day, 'last night was the saddest night of my life'.

The further north the pair travelled the more Jardine's humour deteriorated, and being in Cooktown did nothing to improve it. From being spasmodically unpleasant he had become downright 'piggish'. Jack, who was indulging in a little deep sighing of his own over what appears to have been unrequited love, concluded that Jardine's churlishness was the result of mooning over the wife who was waiting for him in Brisbane.

From Cooktown they sailed to Lloyds Bay, approximately two hundred miles beyond Cooktown. Here Hughie Gilbert's Sandalwood King headquarters had once stood. Gilbert had established a crude settlement for 'his people', a handful of white men and the hundreds of willing Aboriginal workers who cut sandalwood. An entrepreneur, Gilbert owned hundreds of packhorses and a small fleet of luggers with which he shipped tons of sandalwood, worth thousands of pounds, to Thursday Island. His packhorse teams brought a never-ending stream of the precious timber into Gilbert's settlement. So large was the settlement that, after the luggers had unloaded the wood to be shipped to the Orient from Thursday Island, they were reloaded with stores for the return trip south to Lloyds Bay.

Gilbert had also maintained dozens of outlying camps, and the pack teams which brought the sandalwood to Lloyds Bay would return laden with food, tobacco and the much prized tomahawks for the Aborigines who cut the wood for him. Not only did Gilbert treat the Aborigines well, he also demanded that his white employees did likewise.

The settlement had witnessed many wild scenes which few writers could have imagined. When the Sandalwood King died, nature silently closed her lush green hand over the great empty land and the settlement disappeared without trace.

The trip had revived many memories for Jack. Lloyds Bay was no exception, for he and Dick Welch had worked briefly for the Sandalwood King. When the Somerset had passed what were again the heavily wooded foreshores of Orchid Point, he experienced a sense of loss and a certain emptiness that came with knowing that, with the passing of Hughie Gilbert, a roisterous era which had lasted for many years had ended.

He wished once again, as he had done in Cooktown, they would find a goldfield on this trip which would open up the Peninsula and bring it back to life. He had his doubts, however, that this would happen, for Jardine seemed to him to be sailing into the unpeopled north without any true destination. In fact he became convinced that they had more chance of finding gold on the *Somerset*'s deck than in the country Jardine had indicated as gold bearing.

However Jardine did have one destination in mind which had nothing to do with gold seeking—he was going home for a brief visit to Somerset which stood twelve miles from Cape York. On 14 November they entered Albany Pass and anchored in tiny Somerset Bay. Under relentless siege by white ants, Somerset House looked down from the hillside and across the waters of the Pass. This was not Jack's first visit to Somerset—there were not many places on the Peninsula that he and Dick had not visited at one time or another.

The historical romanticism of the place appealed deeply to Jack. On his previous visit to Somerset House he had been given several volumes of Captain John Jardine's journals. These carefully kept records documented the establishment of the white settlement at Somerset and the 'white invasion of the Strait'. It was reading these journals which eventually led him to research the history and the customs of the Murray Island people and to write *Drums of Mer*, first published in 1933.

After landing at Somerset Jack and Jardine rested for two days. Jack wrote, 'It is heaven sleeping and eating on solid ground once more.' The quiet beauty of the Somerset nights briefly restored his inner peace:

I just had a moonlight walk under the great rows of palms. Shadow fronds disputed the splashes of moonlight on the path. Pinpoints of stars twinkled serenely above. A cool wind kissed my face and rustled the blowing leaves. It was far away from the world, the feeling among these many palms. A man could easily have let himself go and believed himself in another world.

At the close of the second day the wind had dropped and the pass was calm, which meant that they would have to leave again to search for de Goleuse's land of gold. Jack faced the thought of boarding the *Somerset* with a soul full of revolt. 'How I hate the idea of the whole business. It will be all rush by sea and land, on starvation tucker, with, I believe, not the slightest hope of success.'

Jack's scepticism about the possibility of finding gold in the area proved to be correct. Jardine had no idea where de Goleuse was supposed to have made his gold find.

At the end of the trip which had lasted four months they had survived howling gales and high seas, been dangerously close to starvation and travelled through some of the most savagely lonely country that Jack had ever seen. They had crossed miles of country between the sea and the head of the Jardine River, country which at that very time was being put to the torch by unseen Aborigines, and they had narrowly escaped being trapped by the raging fire. Jardine was right however when he described the area as lifeless; it was utterly barren. Although they assumed that the fire had been lit by wandering Aborigines, there was no evidence to support the theory—not one track of man, reptile, bird or beast.

Jack finished the trip exhausted and totally disenchanted with Jardine: 'How awfully thankful I am that the trip is over. It has been the silliest wild-goose chase I have ever even heard about. The skipper's idea of [the] de Goleuse find is equal to a schoolboy's, his vaunted plan of the find is non-existent.'

It would appear that de Goleuse and party never existed, or were known only to the Jardines, which is of course a possibility. The 'silliest wild-goose chase' ended with Jack and Jardine returning to Somerset. The last paragraph in Jack's diary closes with 'in a few days we are walking to Cape York. I might try a bit of country there simply because I don't know what else to do. The Skipper goes to Brisbane and good riddance to him.'

After walking the twelve miles from the old Somerset settlement to Cape York Jack must have revised his plan to 'try a bit of country' and made the return trip with Jardine, for he spent Christmas 1926 with the Morrisons at Grafton.

A press interview with Jack about the adventurous trip north appeared in the *Grafton Daily Examiner* in 1926 after he returned. It carried the headlines: 'Thrills at Sea...A Story of Treasure Trove.'

110

In that interview Jack described the terrors of the storms, hurricanes, a fire on board the *Somerset*, being blown out to sea, and barely escaping being smashed to pieces on the jagged coastal shoreline. He begins with a description of Somerset House:

> The solemn, big house frowns down from a hill overlooking the shore, an old-time cannon frowns at you. You climb the winding path up the little hill, and two cannon sneer at you from the verandah steps. The weeping coconut tree, where men were flogged, still stands. England endeavoured to establish a large port here, but the glory of Somerset departed when the settlement was abandoned.
>
> But the BISN Co.'s boats when passing always salute the old house, and there are always free berths for two of the F. L. Jardine family to any part of the world—an honour in recognition of the prompt and noble aid of Jardine at the time of the terrible *Quetta* wreck.
>
> It was Jardine's brigantine, the *Lancashire Lass*, that discovered by accident on February 18, 1891, when Aboriginal boys were diving for beeche-de mer [sic] at the northern end of the Great Barrier Reef, the only genuine treasure that was ever recovered from Australian waters. During diving operations one of the boys brought up a heavy lump of corroded silver dollars cemented together by the action of sea water. The dollars were of the Don Carlos period, and there was only one gold piece, a Ferdinand of 1819.
>
> The dim outline of an old wreck was discovered, and grim old guns were found lying among the ribs of the wreck. One gun was salvaged, and is now staring out across Albany Pass from Somerset House Beach. But the spot of the old wreck has never been re-located, for during the night a storm sprang up, the anchor chain snapped, and the *Lancashire Lass* was forced hastily to put to sea.

By Tuesday 11 January 1927 Jack had crossed to Thursday Island and found casual employment as a waterside worker on the Thursday Island wharves.

The population of Thursday Island (its native name is Wai-ben) was polychromatic—a mixture of Torres Strait Islanders, Malays, Chinese, Sinhalese, Filipino, Japanese and Europeans. Slim two-masted luggers, their prows protected from the jaws of the reef by a band of copper, rocked at anchor off-shore. The cultured pearl industry had not yet come to Thursday Island—neither had pearl buttons been replaced by plastic. The luggers and their diving crews were mostly engaged in diving for the conical trochus shell (from which were cut the pearl-shell shirt buttons which sported a red flash) or fishing for bèche-de-mer.

Jack took up residence at Jack McNulty's Federal Hotel and at night would knock out a tune on the piano, the same piano which a group of ill-bred, Second World War Australian soldiers stationed on the island were to push off the hotel's balcony in order to obtain its wires to go trolling for kingfish.

McNulty also had a collection of Spanish coins and the register in which the survivors of Her Majesty's Royal Mail steamer, the *Quetta*, had signed their names in 1890. When the *Quetta* struck a pinnacle of uncharted, submerged rock the night was calm. The sea claimed the steamer and 130 lives in three minutes. Anyone with a little imagination and a sense of drama would have been interested in the turbulent past of the Strait's islands and its many shipwrecks but Jack had more than an interest. The scraps of memorabilia were beginning to form the framework of a work which could reach saga proportions. Each new piece of information led him to another and, with the zeal of a dedicated detective, he followed every lead. This curiosity led him to the Thursday Island Court House where he was allowed access to 'four cobwebby volumes of valuable official records, which had been unearthed from an old lumber-room in the Court House'.

From the time that Jack had read Jardine's journals he had vaguely considered the idea that he might someday write a work of fiction based on historical fact. At that time the ill-fated first publication of *Madman's Island* with its 'love interest' had not yet been released so he had every reason to hope that it might be a success and to consider the possibility of writing a second book. If *Madman's Island* had been published and recognised as a failure before he went to Thursday Island he might not have had the confidence to research and gather the material for *Drums of Mer*.

While Howick Island had been a proving ground in more ways than one, Thursday Island and particularly Murray Island (Mer or Maer to its people), approximately one hundred and fifty miles north-east of Thursday Island, were islands of pure joy for Jack.

After the endurance trip from Brisbane to Somerset which had ended in a desperate flight from the flames of an advancing bush fire, life on Thursday Island was not hard to take. The people were a happy-go-lucky lot with plenty of time. Their philosophy of 'think about it tomorrow' was one which Jack found easy to adopt. Here, as in Brisbane, he received his Unemployment Insurance

Contributions Book, which indicates that he worked, on average, one or two days each week from January through to August 1927. There are no entries for the months of September and October but during November, December and January 1928 once again, he was employed for approximately two days each week. He was later to lay claim to having worked at loading and unloading every ship that passed through Thursday Island during the periods he was there, a fact that he was very proud of and quite a change for the man who had previously made a fetish out of declaring himself to be lazy.

Between his stints on the docks he took any work on offer, pearl diving on *The Dancing Nancy* or working with the construction gang building the unmanned lighthouse on Restoration Rock. He almost lost his life re-laying an undersea cable between Peak Point and Thursday Island.

Jack had been working on the loading of a ship bound for China when he was offered a few weeks' steady work re-laying the thirty miles of cable. Jack and his mate Ginger stood for days in the bow of the boat to keep the cable on the reel as it was wound up from the sea 'covered with barnacles, chewed up by shell worms that crunched on the wheel, a mass of queer rubbery things'.

The oarsman had to keep the boat steady and straight in the boiling cross seas but there were times when he was unequal to the task and the boat would momentarily be out of control. On that near fatal occasion the nose of the boat flew high in the air and the 'bloody cable slipped sideways'. Jack and Ginger took to the water, otherwise they could have been cut in half by the cable. Jack found himself being pulled down to the sea bed. Somehow, with a super-human effort, he managed to wrench himself sideways before the full weight of the cable could fall on him and crush his chest.

Jack's imagination had been fired when he had seen McNulty's collection of Spanish coins, and reading the names in the 1890 register and Court House Records fuelled the flame. The Jardine journals had provided the first threads of what might have proved to be only 'the white man's point of view' of the conquest of the Strait. But here on Thursday Island there was much more. He began to find snatches of tales about massacres, cruel native customs, mysticism, and the fate suffered by shipwrecked whites at the hands of the islanders. The most intriguing stories were those of the 'Lamars', the white survivors of shipwrecks whom the natives sometimes adopted as their own children, believing that a loved one's spirit had returned from the Land of Shades and was inhabiting a pale and different body. For the first time Jack was researching to write of history and experiences that were not his own.

Jack's most valuable contact on the island was the Reverend W.H. MacFarlane, Mission Priest of Torres Strait and Administrator of the Diocese of Carpentaria. MacFarlane, together with his wife and children, had for many years been resident on Thursday Island. The Reverend, himself a writer, was also a 'living mine of Torres Strait ethnological lore' and was well known as the 'Wandering Missionary', a title he had earned because he regularly visited every little island in the strait on the cutter *Herald*. MacFarlane brought God to natives who had been the most feared and proud warlords in the region. He did it not with fear of hell fire, or by force, but by gentle suggestion.

The two men became firm friends, and Jack spent many hours with MacFarlane when he was at home on Thursday Island and regularly accompanied him on his cruises aboard the *Herald*. During these trips MacFarlane brought Jack together with island historians. These old men trusted MacFarlane with the secrets of their people and in turn they came to trust Jack who wrote, 'Cruising with MacFarlane, landing in out-of-the-way islands, and hearing the story from the lips of the last Zogo-le, was fascinating work.'

Many years later Mrs MacFarlane remembered Jack as being strong featured, of sturdy build and five foot seven or eight inches tall. She recalled that he usually dressed in dark trousers, open-necked shirt, or the island people's popular button-fronted cotton coat. These coats were known as 'ten to ones' meaning 'ten to one, he got no shirt on'.

Jack most enjoyed Mrs MacFarlane's cucumber sandwiches and he always commented, 'by Jove you know how to feed the brute'. She was never privy to the conversations between MacFarlane and Jack when they discussed the native practices and customs; such talk was for 'men only'.

Life for Jack on Thursday Island continued to be pleasant. His spasmodic workload allowed him plenty of time to write and research and he continued to write for the *Bulletin*. An article entitled 'Men Who Made the *Bulletin*' in the Easter edition, March 1928, finished with mention of 'the most indispensable of them all, the men and women who do most to give the *Bulletin* its special character—the character by which it is known all over the world; the great army of contributors, led by such men as Ion L. Idriess who knows the wild North as other men know Collins Street.' Ion L. Idriess had arrived.

Ion L. Idriess however was not especially interested in what was happening back in 'civilisation'. All he needed were the cheques that his work provided. Jack was captivated by the islands of the Torres Strait, especially Mer and had no real desire to return to the mainland.

Mer, now known as Murray Island, unlike all other islands off the Barrier Reef, is volcanic. It surpasses all other islands of continental origin, which are but pieces of the mainland isolated by sea. Its robust jungle growth is the result of crumbling volcanic lava which bestows on Mer a rich, red soil.

In 1930, three years after Jack had wandered on to this tropical paradise, Dr Younge, leader of Great Barrier Reef Expedition of 1928–29 wrote of Mer: 'The beauty and luxuriant vegetation of Mer cannot be portrayed in words. Only Samoa can be compared to it, and the climate of Murray Island is infinitely superior to the oppressive steamy heat of Samoa.'

While Younge was awed by the obvious, Jack was steeped in the lusty brutality of a civilisation which had for centuries fed on the rituals of death which were paralleled by the vigorous jungle growth which fed on decay while reaching for the sun.

Dr Younge's work *A Year On The Great Barrier Reef* was published in 1930 but Jack's *Drums of Mer* was not to be published until 1933. The resounding failure of *Madman's Island* mid-1928 would undermine Jack's self-confidence and deter him, for some time, from attempting to have a work of fiction published, even if that work was based on fact. Fearful of another failure he was later to put aside the unfinished manuscript of *Drums of Mer* to concentrate solely on long newspaper and magazine articles.

Chapter Thirteen
THE TURNING POINT

GOLD prospecting in New Guinea had been banned until 1922. The lifting of that ban and the issue of the first miner's right in New Guinea in 1923 led to the discovery of gold in large quantities for the first time in 1926.

The news of large gold strikes in New Guinea set the Australian government on edge. Fearful that the New Guinea goldfields would become another Ballarat if the influx of prospectors was not controlled a law was introduced requiring each aspiring millionaire to lodge a five hundred and fifty pound bond before landing. In theory if a man did not find gold he could be returned to the mainland without incurring government expense.

Jack first heard of this momentous event during a brief visit ashore at Townsville while sailing north with Jardine. The idea of going to New Guinea had been at the back of his mind since finding that the Mer headhunters had regularly sailed to New Guinea to trade with the natives on the Fly River. The thought of combining a little gold prospecting on a rich field with research across the Torres Strait appealed to him but he needed five hundred and fifty pounds before he could land.

Madman's Island had been released in 1927 while Jack was living at Thursday Island. On its release Jack sent Shenstone of A&R a batch of handwritten personal messages, which he asked Shenstone to cut out and paste inside copies of the book and forward them to the people on a list of names and addresses which he had included. These became the first of the Idriess autographed books.

Over the following forty years Jack was to autograph many thousands of his books. It is still possible to find Idriess works in secondhand bookshops which bear the familiar 'Cheerio' and signed 'I.L. Idriess' or 'Jack Idriess'. The demand for Jack's signature grew with the demand for his books. Jack took the compliment seriously, and he requested that the customer let him know what occasion was being celebrated so that he might inscribe a suitable message. Books were also sent back to A&R by booksellers all around the country for Jack's autograph. As an old man he still paid a weekly visit to A&R's bookshop to autograph books that customers had left for that purpose.

By mid-1928 it was obvious that *Madman's Island* was doomed and there was no hope of enough sales to provide him with the fare and bond money to land in New Guinea. As soon as Jack was able to find a berth on a craft sailing to New Guinea he took a position as a crew-hand on a cutter. It was 'a leaking old tub' engaged in the questionable business of recruiting island divers for pearling and as gold carriers for the New Guinea gold-fields. This was the only way for him to get to what seemed to be the Promised Land. Once there he planned to jump ship, take off through the back door into the jungle, prospect for gold and leave as a rich man by the front door.

Bringing gold out of the New Guinea jungles was not an easy task. Despite the brave efforts of the patrolling authorities the New Guinea cannibals were killing and eating almost every native carrier who attempted to bring out the rich ore from the New Guinea gold-fields. The carnage—or more accurately, the shocking banquets—reached epidemic proportions and carriers were at a premium. By the time Jack was on the high seas the prices being paid for carrier 'recruits', which had started at two pounds per head, had rocketed to twenty pounds. 'Recruiting' turned out to be a polite term for 'black-birding', an occupation which didn't sit well with Jack.

All Jack wrote about his attempt to land illegally near Eddie Creek, New Guinea, was that the cutter had hidden near the mouth of a river waiting for an opportunity to land but it was too close to a Dutch penal settlement to do so. His plan was thwarted when the old cutter was chased out to sea by a patrol boat.

Jack must have landed somewhere, however, for there are various references that indicate he spent the greater part of 1928 travelling along the Fly River. Dr Ion Morrison, Jack's nephew, recalls that Jack came back to Grafton in the closing months of 1928 bringing with him a large collection of spears and other weapons from New Guinea as a present for the young Ion Morrison and as gifts for a museum. Many of the spears which formed a large display on Ion's bedroom wall were tipped with poison and required careful handling.

It was impossible for Jack to stay in any one place for long. From Grafton he went briefly to Brisbane, staying only long enough to buy three blocks of land at Ann Street. The buying of anything so important was quite out of character for Jack and obviously he didn't take the purchase seriously for the land was eventually sold for rate monies which he neglected to pay. It would seem that Jack took as much notice of councils as he did of the taxation department. By 1929 he was back at the Morrison home.

1929 brought down the curtain on the boom years in the Australian economy. In tandem with the country's economical downturn Jack's health began to falter. In the first half of 1929 he was diagnosed as having cancer, which prompted him to write a long emotional article on the subject for the 13 July issue of *Smith's Weekly*. While he intimated the disease was terminal, he didn't disclose the site of the cancer. It was assumed by Dr Ion Morrison that it may have been one which Jack was later to have removed from the back of his neck in 1950.

Believing that his days were numbered he turned to his past, reading the war diaries which had lain for eleven years locked in the haversack behind the door in his room on the Morrison verandah. Still the recluse Jack resumed his old habit of dining at the Returned Soldiers and Sailors Imperial League, taking very few meals with his sister's family. Occasionally Jack visited his other sister, Esmé, his father Walter and step-mother Amy, and his youngest sister, Katie, who also were still living in Grafton, but for the most he kept to himself, writing the work which would ultimately become *The Desert Column*.

The author's note in *The Desert Column* states that it was a proud sister who sent the diaries to the publishers with the instruction that they must be published. This was not the case, judging by the forthright tone of Ildyce's letters which Jack kept over the years and a statement which he made about an unnamed member of the opposite sex who told him, 'You haven't got the heart, or what you vulgar men call the guts, you haven't got the guts to stick to writing.' It seems most likely that it was Ildyce's verbal assault that shocked him out of his introversion and provoked him to attempt another book after the failure of *Madman's Island*. It would also account for Ildyce's possessive attitude towards both Jack and his success.

Whoever the 'member of the opposite sex' was, her pep talk had the desired effect on Jack. Ion Morrison recalls how he used to rush home from school each day to read what Jack had written. Jack's daily output depended on how much he had to read each day—some days he might produce twelve pages, or as few as one or two. The work, written in pencil across the horizontal width of the page with two to three line spaces between the lines for editing, was not really a task of writing but rather one of editing which eventually reduced the diaries by some twenty thousand words.

Late in 1929 Jack had finished the book and had crossed the Queensland border again, returning to his old Cooktown stamping ground to do a little prospecting in the Laura River district. It was here that he claimed to have made his decision to leave the bush for the city life.

There are two versions of how Jack 'came out of the bush', both of course from Jack, and both are probably a mixture of the facts. As Jack told it, he simply turned his horses loose and told the storekeeper at the Laura that he thought he'd be back, and then he went to Brisbane to live it up a little on the contents of a small shammy of gold. The other version is much the same. He let his horses go, told the storekeeper that he might be back but that he had to 'choose whether to die like a dingo beside some hollow log and die happy' or to put in the rest of his life in the city.

Why would Jack, a man who had tried city life many times, a man who loved the outback and the jungle, suddenly decide to give the city another go at a time when other men were deserting the cities in their hundreds in the hope of living off the country to survive the Great Depression? I believe that the answer lies in his reference to dying like a dingo and his choice of residence in Sydney: the house at 5 West Street, Paddington, was immediately behind Sydney's St Vincent's Hospital. Figuratively speaking there are few things that will bring a true-blue bushman out of his saddle: starvation, a woman, or death. In Jack's case it wasn't a woman, and he had a better chance of starving in the city than if he stayed where he was. I believe he came to Sydney to get medical attention for cancer.

♦

THE American stock market crash at year's end had very little to do with turning Australia's bohemians into bums, or the rich to poor and the poor to destitute. Neither could the failure to float two public loans in London in January and April be held entirely responsible for the Depression—the rot in Australia had set in long before. Ten years of government borrowing to the tune of some thirty million pounds each year had produced an economic structure that relied on benign world economic conditions. The World Depression which had begun in 1929 forced the price for wool and wheat to fall dramatically, the wells of overseas capital had suddenly dried up and export prices had taken a sharp decline. It was the failure to obtain annual loans and the drop in export prices that placed the country in a position of severe budgetary crisis and reduced the national income by ten per cent. By the end of 1929 the new Labor government under the leadership of Scullin, a party which had not held office since 1917, a government which was comprised of inexperienced men, was facing the inherited problems of nationwide depression.

The Depression was tightening its stranglehold on the country when Jack took up residence in the room under the stairs of the house in Paddington in February 1930. The full shock of the steep fall of government revenues and problems in meeting overseas repayments was being absorbed by the workers. Escalating unemployment was clearly evident in the city. It seemed five and ten pound notes had mysteriously disappeared overnight. For Jack there was little chance of finding work to pay the weekly rent of five shillings.

Jack, who had been a member of the Waterside Workers Federation during his stay at Thursday Island, went straight to the shipping docks thinking that he would readily find employment loading or unloading ships. His Thursday Island experience however did not impress the Sydney Waterside Workers Federation and he was refused work. Right to the end of his days Jack recalled this rejection with some bitterness. However, the Transport Workers' Bill which had been brought in by the Bruce-Page government in 1928 requiring men to hold a licence before they could obtain work on the wharfs, and which was designed effectively to stop employment of strikers, had most likely blocked Jack being employed as a Sydney wharfie, for there is no evidence that he ever held this obligatory licence.

1930 saw the unemployment figures climbing rapidly towards the thirty per cent mark. Men from all strata of society fought for any job, no matter how physically exhausting the job might be. Jack Lang, the leader of the NSW Labor Party, made his power play by capitalising on the fears and resentment of the working classes, claiming that the Depression was a conspiracy mounted by the employers to destroy the workers' living standard, a standard that the Labor movement had fought for long and hard. A large man, blunt and domineering and aligned with the most aggressive elements of Labor, he loudly denounced the policies of economy, retrenchment and deflation.

In August 1930 Sir Otto Neimeyer of the Bank of England came to Australia as a guest of Prime Minister Scullin to attend the Premiers' Conference and to look into the financial problem and give advice. After casting a jaundiced eye over the situation, he came to the conclusion that the Australian living standard was in excess of its means and that belt tightening was the best medicine for the day. Clearly this was not the advice the premiers had hoped for but it allowed the ruthless Lang to preach the policy that Neimeyer was the emissary of the Old Lady of Threadneedle Street and that the real motivation behind his visit was to force the Australian government to cut wages and place the Australian worker back in the hands of the British capitalists and financiers.

For those people with hungry children wearing threadbare clothing, for those people who had sold their furniture to pay the rent and faced being evicted from their homes, for the 'sussos' who were forced to accept the stigma of joining the dole queues for food coupons, for those begging on the street, for those living under sheets of scrap iron in 'Happy Valley' at La Perouse, for the thousands of men who took to the track in the hope of finding work in country towns and who were often hunted from town to town by the police, for all those people, Neimeyer's remedy reeked of the unyielding and heartless credo of the British aristocracy which they thought they had escaped from long ago.

Alone in Sydney, unemployed and virtually unemployable, Jack's only alternative to the dole queue was his writing. The idea of an unknown writer attempting to compete with trained journalists seemed to Jack to be an impossible thought. He recalled thinking, 'God's truth ... what's going to happen here? Well I've got to try.'

Calling upon his diaries he began to write. For the rest of his life Jack was to claim that he hated writing, which seems to be an inexplicable contradiction from such a prolific wordsmith. It was not the writing that he resented, but the need to write which kept him anchored in one place when he ached to be away wandering. The Depression, however, forced him to develop the discipline needed, and before long scarcely an issue of a newspaper or magazine appeared without an article, paragraph or letter to the editor bearing Jack's name. While the well-educated were reading *The Fortunes of Richard Mahony* the masses, both well and barely educated, were reading Ion L. Idriess.

Jack was bemused to find that his past was not a wilderness but a treasure house to which he alone held the key and that his memories were stronger currency than the currency of the country. To his surprise he found that he could sell anything he wrote. He fulfilled Tom Peel's prophecy: people in the cities did want to read about the out-of-way places he had lived in, they wanted to know about the strange animals and the eccentric characters he had seen and met. All the years he had spent wandering the outback and the jungles and the Coral Sea islands had not been to no avail. It almost seems that his life up to that point had been lived for the purpose of delivering the opiate of escapism to thousands of people suffering under the Depression.

His readers who were clustered in the drab grey suburbs of the cities and in towns along the coastal belts were Australians who had lost touch with the identity that they had of themselves as bushmen (the vision of themselves as bronzed coastal Aussies was not quite in place).

A whole generation of men who had reached adulthood in the cities tried to return to the bush, where they were often unwelcome, to take up a life they were no longer fitted for. Shocked and dispirited the wilting cornstalks were totally disoriented.

Jack became their man—a cult figure who restored to them their image of themselves as the embodiment of the Australian bushman. He endorsed their myths, entertained them with his storytelling of wild people and wild places, bringing relief from ugly reality. Even more, his readers identified with him—he was a bushman, a man's man, a mate. He had rolled his swag and humped the bluey all over Australia, he knew what making do was all about and he knew what it was like to be hungry. To cap it all, he was a Returned Soldier, one of the legendary 'blooded' Anzacs.

If ever there was a right time and place for any man, the Depression of 1930 in Sydney was the right time and place for Ion L. Idriess.

Chapter Fourteen

LASSETER'S GOLD

Without a job the threat of starvation provided the best incentive for Jack to produce lively articles calculated to seize the imagination of both editors and readers. He discovered the Mitchell Library and began to research material from which he created pieces of historical interest, writing on topics such as the arrival of electricity in the Clarence ('Let There Be Light'), the opening up of Australia's dead heart through transport, communications, radio and the flying doctor service ('The Camelman'), the romance of Norfolk Island and the voyage of the Bounty ('The Deathless Past').

Stories of a white man, James Murrell, who had lived with the Queensland Aborigines for seventeen years after being shipwrecked, led him to research the fate of the barque *Peruvian* and that of the surviving seven passengers. They had come ashore on the Queensland coast after being wrecked in the Coral Sea while sailing from Sydney to Peru in 1846.

Researching for this story, 'The Tragedy of the *Peruvian*', rekindled his enthusiasm for the Torres Strait work and he began to delve further into the records of shipwrecks in the Coral Sea, and in particular those which had occurred around Murray Island. One reference led to another and eventually he found his way to 'Father Chester of Sydney, who granted him access to the records and diaries of his father, Lieutenant Henry M. Chester, who had established the seat of Government at Thursday Island, and who later hoisted the flag on New Guinea.'

Jack's mind overflowed with stories. He was often involved in writing more than one book at a time, sometimes working on two or three simultaneously, while producing one or two articles at the same time. Just as an expert juggler would throw in another ball amongst an already impressive number circling overhead, Jack would nonchalantly throw another project into the mix. The Lasseter story was one of these.

Jack had come to Sydney in February of 1930. The following month, Harry Bell Lasseter made his appeal to John Bailey, president of the Australian Workers Union, for funds to search for the gold reef he claimed he had found while prospecting for rubies near Alice Springs in 1897. Lasseter presented himself to a group of union officials and mining experts who interrogated him to assess his credibility. He managed to convince a significant number of officials that it was an opportunity too good to miss. If the reef did exist, its discovery would have improved the economic pain of the 1930s Depression just as the discovery of Kalgoorlie's gold had eased the 1893 Depression.

After a visit to Canberra to investigate Lasseter's background, Bailey returned to Sydney. The Central Australian Gold Exploration Company was quickly floated and inside twenty-four hours, five hundred pounds had been subscribed to mount an expedition dedicated to finding Lasseter's reef.

Jack avidly followed the press for any item relating to Lasseter and the expedition, and filed the cuttings away. Whether he kept them because he planned to use the information later or because of his fascination for gold and gold prospecting is not known. It may simply have been because Lasseter appeared to have a chance of opening up a new goldfield, something Jack would dearly have liked. For now, the best that Jack could do was to keep writing. The continued publication of his articles paid his rent and food and allowed him to turn his attention once again to *The Desert Column*. He had one large hurdle to clear before he could get it published by A&R—Robertson himself.

The year before, 1929, Jack had visited A&R after receiving a letter notifying him of the fate of *Madman's Island*. He was told that the book was a failure and had been remaindered (the best way for any publisher to dispose of unsold books) and that he should not nurture any idea of becoming an author. In the face of such discouragement Jack deemed it inappropriate to mention *The Desert Column*. To be told that *Madman's Island* had failed was bad enough, but to see row upon row of the book on sale at sixpence a copy in Anthony Horden's book department was definitely demoralising.

Jack took himself back to Grafton. However, it was not long before he pulled himself out of his despondency and hit upon the idea of approaching both Brigadier-General L. C. Wilson and Lieutenant-Colonel Donald Cameron to read the manuscript of *The Desert Column* for accuracy.

Wilson had commanded the 5th Light Regiment for over two years from July 1915 to October 1917, and Cameron had taken over Wilson's command, serving from October 1917 until the disbanding of the unit in 1919. Jack's strategy was brilliant both in his selection of the two commanders to comment on the work and his timing—November, just prior to the Armistice Day commemorations. The two men confirmed the book's accuracy and commended it to the general public, each writing a paragraph stating their approval of the work for inclusion in the book.

Going one step further, they compared *The Desert Column* to Erich Maria Remarque's *All Quiet On The Western Front*. The English translation of *All Quiet On The Western Front* which had just been published in London was being hailed as the most revealing and devastating account of the war at that time. Wilson and Cameron declared *The Desert Column* to be the greater work. Their response was better than Jack had hoped for. Seizing the opportunity he reported their comments to his press contacts, neglecting to mention that *The Desert Column* was only in manuscript form. The item was syndicated through the major press and by the sin of omission it was assumed that the book had been published and that Wilson and Cameron had been approached by the press for comment. As a result Jack was also approached by the press and subsequently found himself widely quoted.

The publicity brought the existence of the diaries to the attention of the director of the Canberra War Memorial who wrote asking Jack to present the diaries to the Memorial. Cameron, then a member of parliament, reinforced the request. Jack complied with this request sometime between November 1929 and February 1930. He later added further notes and some assorted pages which were placed in the strong box which housed the diaries—where they can still be found today.

At this time Jack backed his play by sending the manuscript to General Harry Chauvel GCMG, KCB, the late Commander of the Desert Mounted Corps. No doubt he quoted Wilson and Cameron to Chauvel and at the same time he asked him to write the foreword to the book.

On 9 July 1930 Chauvel returned the manuscript.

I am sending back by same post your history. I am most awfully sorry I have kept it so long but the fact is I got very interested in it and read it right through instead of skimming through it and I have only a very occasional evening at home which I can devote to reading. I will be very glad to write a 'foreword' but only if the remarks about the treatment of our wounded after Romani and Magdhaba are expunged. This was a bad show but it was all thrashed out at that time and those responsible dealt with. It is no good raking it all up again—raising bitter feelings and distress again amongst the relations of those that died. I don't quite like the way it actually ends either.

You want to avoid any expression that has the slightest tinge of blasphemy or may be thought to have. Otherwise the book is excellent and very graphic.

Armed with the Chauvel foreword together with Wilson's and Cameron's written verifications of accuracy and recommendation, Jack played his ace in the hole and scrawled Robertson a pencilled note designed to appear as if he was soliciting Robertson's assistance:

I have just completed a war book to which General Harry Chauvel has written a fine introduction. Could you recommend me a firm of London publishers, likely to accept such a book? Would not trouble you only I'm blessed if I know who to send the book to and no one in Sydney can advise me.

At approximately the same time the Lasseter expedition was somewhere west of Alice Springs moving towards Ilbilla. Blakeley, the only experienced bushman with the party and its leader, was beginning to speculate on Lasseter's veracity, while at the same time Lasseter was not impressed by Blakeley's leadership—in short the prospect of finding gold had become somewhat tarnished by suspicion.

Meanwhile, in Sydney, Robertson was not unaware of Jack's flourishing popularity. Neither would he have missed Jack's articles dealing with various incidents from the Palestine campaigns. Pieces such as the 'Night March on Gaza' plus snippets and quotes from Jack, Wilson and Cameron in reference to *The Desert Column* would have drawn the work to Robertson's attention. Robertson walked right into the crafty bushman's trap by asking to read the manuscript. This time however, Robertson did not rely on his own judgement—he had the manuscript professionally read.

The reader's report on *The Desert Column* was not at all negative. Dated 10 October it read:

This is the fifth war manuscript I have read within twelve months. The other four, for reasons given, I did not recommend. But the intrinsic qualities of *The Desert Column* compel me to recommend it, even if present conditions forbid early publication ... Sergeant [*sic*] Idriess would have made an admirable war correspondent. Nothing of interest within his purview appears to have escaped him. Scores of interesting anecdotes and vignettes enliven a narrative that has very few dull pages ... *All Quiet on the Western Front*, I understand, is responsible for *The Desert Column*. But the spirit of the books are as different as the men who wrote them. The filth and the suffering horrors of war are of course in both. But Idriess hasn't dwelt on them, ad nauseam. He never lost his optimism nor his sense of humour nor his interest in little things. One cannot imagine a trifle like this in *All Quiet*: 'Just now we heard a riotous hullabaloo, and jumping from our dugouts saw a hare racing across a sandy hillock. All hands cheered the hare, they yelled and laughed.'

One closes *All Quiet* sickened–if one has the stomach to read to the end. One finishes *The Desert Column* with regret.

Like General Chauvel I 'recommend this book'. ... The style, notwithstanding some grammatical errors, is, on the whole, good. If Serg. Idriess were as good a stylist as he is a soldier *The Desert Column* would be a masterpiece. Recommended.

The Depression was intensifying. Despite the reader's recommendation Robertson decided to delay publication of *The Desert Column* until the Firm's finances were less strained. He was also concerned that the public might find war a subject too depressing to contemplate and would not buy the book—the Scot did not want a second Idriess failure on his hands, any more than Idriess did.

A few days before the reader wrote his report on *The Desert Column* the Lasseter expedition out in the desert near the West Australian border had almost ground to a halt. Diplomatic relations had ceased to exist between Lasseter and Fred Blakeley, the party's leader. Errol Coote, a journalist and pilot who had also been appointed as the expedition's deputy leader had crashed the expedition's Gipsy Moth *The Golden Quest* at Yai Yai a few weeks before. When Coote returned to the party with the *Golden Quest II* in the last weeks of August, he and Lasseter finally made a reconnaissance flight south-west towards the Petermann and Blood Ranges. Once back on the ground, Lasseter, according to Coote, not only told Coote that he had recognised the landmarks, he also drew him a map in the sand. For some odd reason Blakeley was not told of these events. Both Lasseter and Coote allowed Blakeley to continue the search to the south-west for another week. One hundred miles later, short of water in country that the expedition's Thornycroft truck could not cross, Blakeley decided that it was time to abandon the search and turned back to Ilbilba.

At Ilbilba Lasseter made it clear that he would not give up the search, and Blakeley made it obvious that he believed Lasseter to be a cunning confidence man. At this time a young German, Paul Johns, with his team of five camels blundered into the expedition's camp. Lasseter agreed to continue the search with Johns. Blakeley put Johns on the payroll for a period of two months, eagerly unloaded two tons of stores for the two men and returned with the rest of the party to Alice Springs.

On 14 September Lasseter and Johns set out from Ilbilba with three ill-fated camels and headed for the Petermann Ranges. They were not, however, to get very far before they were forced to return to Ilbilba when two camels were poisoned and another ran its foot through a stake.

While the Lasseter drama was drawing to a close, Jack was finding life in the city an 'imprisonment'. On the surface it appeared that he had coped with the transition from bush to city but the image of himself as a professional writer who would live supported by the pen eluded him—as it continued to do for the rest of his life.

Although he was creating a new life for himself he still yearned for the freedom of the bush. All that he had known seemed to be irreclaimable, even his training at the Broken Hill School of Mines seemed to have been squandered. He forced himself to write, knowing that if he didn't, he wouldn't eat. Although he was always totally familiar with his subjects, the knowledge didn't change his attitude. He was frustrated and irritable. Fretting for open spaces and endless skies he substituted Sydney's Hyde Park for the bush.

The Lasseter story had started a gold fever epidemic. Trapped in the little room under the stairs Jack envied the men who were taking to the bush to try their hands at gold prospecting, but at the same time he pitied them. The majority of men were going bush blinded by the hope that if gold had been found before, it would be found again and that it would be found by them. Few, if any, would have known what type of country might produce minerals, much less gold. Jack knew that unless a man understood 'rocks' or learned to look for the different granites, types of quartz and a dozen different rock formations where various types of metals could be found, he had no more hope of finding gold in the bush than he did in Hyde Park.

Any one of Jack's admirers would be familiar with the publicity story which tells how a hungry Jack Idriess, strolling through Sydney's Hyde Park in 1930 with not even two-pence in his pocket to buy a meat pie, was suddenly struck with the brilliant idea of writing a book on gold prospecting. This story of the background events that led to the writing of *Prospecting for Gold*, repeated many times over the years, is a simplification of the facts.

When Robertson had placed *The Desert Column* aside to wait for a propitious publishing date which embodied both financial consideration and public acceptance, he had inadvertently given Jack a marketing lesson. Jack knew that there was a market for a simply written handbook on prospecting for uninitiated gold seekers—all he had to do was write it and have it published. First, however, he wanted to show Robertson tangible evidence that a demand existed for the book which would justify its immediate publication.

On 31 January 1930 a Letter to the Editor was published in the *Sydney Morning Herald*. Quite a lengthy letter, it outlined a plan Jack felt should be advanced to the mining authorities of the day proposing the establishment of a Gold Search Association. The letter detailed a workable proposal listing all the elements needed for such an association to assist unemployed men who had an interest in searching for gold to pursue their goal efficiently. The formation of such an association and the publication of a detailed booklet on gold and where to find it would, Jack suggested, serve two purposes: it would put food into the mouths of hungry Australian families, and the gold reserves obtained would speed the country's recovery from the Depression. The letter was signed I. L. Idriess. It was intended to serve as a lever to convince Robertson to publish such a book without delay. The patriotic intentions expressed in the letter, however, I believe were sincere. Throughout all his life Jack's faith in his fellow Australians, his country and its potential, never vacillated. He was also impatient when the country's progress, especially in northern Australia, was not as expansive as he felt it should have been.

A few days after the publication of the first letter, a second Letter to the Editor from Jack appeared in the *Sydney Morning Herald*. This time he wrote that he was sorry that he would be unable to reply to the 236 letters that he had received in response to his first letter and hoped that all those who had written to him would understand. He also wrote that he could not cope with the swarms of visitors or the telephone calls that he had received.

It would appear that the number of letters that Jack claimed to have received was not as overwhelming as suggested. Jack kept every piece of paper and letter that ever came into his hands. I have been through all his papers which date from 1913 to 1978 and not found one of these letters, which in view of his bowerbird fetish is strange to say the least. It was the second letter which proved to be the touch of genius needed to convince the publishers that a prospecting handbook would be a best-seller.

Prospecting for Gold was written in long hand—as were all his books—in three weeks. It was typeset, printed and selling inside five weeks, from start to finish. Released in February 1931 it achieved a sale of two thousand copies inside the first ten minutes and was hailed by professional mining men and mining authorities alike.

Mr F. S. Mance, Under Secretary for Mines at the time, summed up the publication: 'Mr Idriess has certainly succeeded in his objective which is to provide information which will be of service to the man who is setting out on his first prospecting venture, as well as the more experienced prospector who is desirous of adding to his sum of knowledge.'

A letter dated 15 August 1931 from Francis Lundie of the Australian Workers Union quoted Mr Hockey, General Engineer and Manager for BHP, as saying, 'The book was one of the most useful printed on the subject,' and that 'he always took along a dozen or so of them and left them with prospectors with the aim of assisting them.'

Then the following year on 25 May 1932 when the book was in its third edition inside twelve months, Mr W.G. Woolnough from the Department of Home Affairs wrote to Jack: 'You will have the great satisfaction of knowing that you have put many worthy unemployed in the way of making "Tucker" and a few in "easy street".'

There are letters from men who thanked him profusely for the simple way he had written a book which had enabled them to find enough gold to keep their families fed. Some are quite poignant in their gratitude and tell of the number of years that the writers had been unemployed and what a blessing his book had been to them. The most amusing letter is from a prospector who used a number of explosive expletives to describe 'This **** Dago Idriess' who 'knows how to get gold out of the **** ground'.

By the time *Prospecting For Gold* had been published Jack had begun to deal with Walter Cousins. Cousins who had joined A&R as a boy was well on the way to becoming the Firm's publishing director. Jack and Cousins were to form a lasting friendship and a fine working relationship that would endure until Cousins' death.

◆

THE Depression had not eased. Destitute people in the inner city who had come to the end of their meagre resources struggled against eviction. The homeless, cast on the streets together with their remaining pitiful belongings, were a common sight. The number of people openly begging in the streets had increased and small plaques declaring 'No Hawkers or Canvassers' appeared on the grey paling fences in both the working-class and nob-hill districts.

Evictions on the land were as common as evictions in the city. Many farmers were unable to meet their commitments and as a result storekeepers and rural suppliers were sliding into insolvency. Whilst it was true that many families left the land, it was also true that many people left the cities to live with their country relatives in the hope of supporting themselves on what they could produce from the land. At least in the country they had access to boiled wheat and treacle, the original 'cocky's joy', to supplement their diet.

For a little light relief the disillusioned and the hopeless gathered in School of Arts and church halls to give each other moral support and to find some comfort in community singing or take pleasure in the weekly dance.

Pinned together amongst Jack's collection of personal memorabilia were three pamphlets. The first, dated 4 June 1931, advertised a 'Grand Gala Night' at the Paddington Town Hall; the second, undated, invited all to enjoy 'Old Time Dancing' at the Australia Hall, admission one shilling, while the third offering 'Community Singing and Concert' was dated 31 May 1931. They were placed in that order, perhaps because Jack is said to have met Eta Gibson at a dance at Paddington Town Hall, although in later years Eta said that she met Jack in 1932.

Eta was a vivacious lady who loved to dance. Many times she told her children the story of how she had first met Jack who, she said, found no favour with her at first. Dressed in his bushman's long all-weather coat and wearing his broad-brimmed hat he looked to her like the original bush roughneck. Not Eta's type at all. Just how Jack managed to prevail on her to change her opinion she didn't say but the persistent and determined Jack Idriess obviously managed to win her affection. One has only to look at the photographs of Julia, Jack's mother, and Eta, to see that Jack would have been instantly attracted. There is a striking similarity between the two women—both had enormous eyes of the same shape, and each had the same direct gaze which gave them an expression of haunting intensity. The sight of this woman dressed in a whispering, lustrous, taffeta dance gown and wearing lace gloves, her hair curled and waved, would have sent his mind spinning back in time to Broken Hill and Julia dressed for the ball. All the years of avoiding emotional commitment came to an end when he met Eta.

Jack had not come to terms with Julia's death. I have no doubt that Jack subconsciously perceived Eta as the mother figure and projected on her both his love and his guilt for being the instrument of Julia's death. Of course he would have expected Eta to be the paragon of all the virtues, as was the Julia of his romantic memory. Ultimately Eta was not to measure up to Jack's impossible expectations.

Eta Gibson (née Morris) is somewhat of an enigma. Born in Horseforth near Leeds in England, she claimed that her father was a Welsh Romany gipsy. Perhaps this was fact but Eta was said to have had a lively imagination. Eta and Jack shared a trait—both told several versions about their lives and backgrounds, each tailoring their stories to suit the occasion and the listener. No doubt there was an element of truth in them all.

Eta was to tell her good friend and neighbour, Val Pepper, an equally vivacious lady who lived next door to the Idriess family at Kensington in Sydney in the 1940s, that she had been pregnant and unmarried when she left England early in 1929. Under the shadow of this disgrace she had migrated to Australia. Eta met a horse trainer, Jesse Gibson, on board ship en route to Australia and he had married her to legitimise the unborn child. The version that she told her daughters varied a little in that the occupation of Jesse Gibson was given as a doctor of medicine and that Eta's mother's dying wish had been for Eta to marry 'Doctor Gibson'. In fact Jesse Gibson was a gardener.

The child, a son, Maurice Beresford Gibson, was born in Sydney in 1929 and unhappily was killed in a motor accident at Tennant Creek in 1949. Eta's flair for the dramatics came to the fore when she told her daughters that the boy of twenty had bled to death when his jugular vein was cut after he was thrown to the stony roadway. The death certificate, however, gives the cause of death as 'fractured base of the skull'. The father's occupation is given as 'gardener'.

Eta claimed to have been a nurse at Guy's Hospital in London before coming to Australia. This too is doubtful, because she never seemed to want to obtain her nursing registration papers from England, papers which would have allowed her to nurse in Australia, a desire she expressed many times to Dr Ion Morrison, Jack's nephew. Eta also said that she had been a domestic at Carnarvon Castle on the border of Northern Wales.

It is most likely that Eta, domestic or nurse, did conceive of a child to a doctor. It is also most likely that her mother did want her to marry the doctor but the doctor did not share the same desire. Given the circumstances the truth probably is that, unable to marry the doctor, she decided to remove herself and her perceived disgrace not only from her family but from England by coming to Australia. While travelling from England she married Gibson, who was ever after referred to as 'Doctor Gibson'.

In 1952 Wendy Idriess visited England and made contact with one of Eta's sisters. The sister was not only surprised to find that she had a niece but puzzled as to why her sister had not kept in contact with the family, which suggests that Eta's mother had kept secret the reason behind her daughter's departure, telling the family only that Eta had married a 'Doctor Gibson' and that she lived in Australia.

It is said that Jack never knew that Eta was married to Gibson, neither did he know about the child, Maurice, for some long time after meeting Eta. There is also the story of how Gibson, drunk and crazed with jealousy, after confronting Jack with both accusation and revelation, fought with him, throwing him down the stairs of the old Hyde Park Hotel in Sydney. I suspect that this is also a romanticised version, for the story came from Eta. If the news was indeed broken to Jack by Gibson under such dramatic circumstances, one has to wonder how she kept the existence of the child hidden from Jack. Why did he not suspect that something peculiar was afoot? Did he never take her home after the dances? If he did, how did she avoid asking him into the house? The answer will never be forthcoming so I can only conjecture that Eta, who told Ion Morrison that she had nursed private patients, told Jack that she was unable to invite him inside because it was not her home, or because she was going on duty.

Years later Eta said that she met Jack in 1932 which becomes even more confusing because her daughter Judy was born in 1932. Did she successfully manage to hide the existence of two children from him or did she hide both a child and a pregnancy?

Eta and Jack shared one of those love-hate relationships which are the bread and butter of fiction writers and the cause of crimes of passion. At a very basic level the discrepancies between them start with a large age difference for Eta was assumed to have been fifteen years younger than Jack. This is assumed because she would never divulge her birth date except to say that she was born 10 December. She was a city girl who hated the bush and would not compromise. Eta loved a gay time, people, parties and dancing, while Jack was a quiet man used to his own company and happy with it, and his contentment was found in the solitude of the bush. Jack was attracted to her possibly for all the wrong reasons and expected her to live up to his idealised vision of his mother. Not only could Eta not measure up to Julia, she was also married and had one, perhaps two, children.

I do not believe that it was the existence of the child (or children) or Gibson which created Jack's greatest trauma but the knowledge that he had sacrificed his freedom and betrayed the memory of Julia. His confusion went even deeper as the years went on for, while he liked and admired women, he also despised them, using derogatory terms which do not bear recounting. It is possible that when he finally committed himself to Eta and her offspring he did so in an unconscious attempt to atone for Julia's death. As the reason for his sacrifice was no longer clear to him he turned against all women, torturing Eta as he tortured himself.

◆

THAT other enigma, Lasseter, was still very much in the news. In May an article entitled 'Dead Gold Seeker Claimed As Husband By Two Women' queried whether Lasseter was a bigamist and once again threw the whole question of the existence of the lost reef open to debate. The estimated value of the reef (if Lasseter's claim that the specimens he had taken from the quartz reef thirty years earlier had really assayed at three ounces to the ton) was sixty million pounds. To regain sixty million pounds in gold, after the shipping of twenty million pounds of Australia's gold reserves to England, would have gone a long way to easing the country's financial stress.

Lasseter's body was reported to have been found by Bob Buck in March 1931. Apart from the Depression, gold and Lasseter were the main topics of the day. Encouraged by the success of *Prospecting for Gold* and the popularity of Jack's press articles, Cousins urged Jack to write a book on the Lasseter saga—Jack didn't need to be pushed.

George Ferguson, then scarcely in his twenties and the man who would eventually become a publishing director of Angus and Robertson, drove Jack, mid-1931, to the Lasseter home at Kogarah in NSW to buy from Mrs Lasseter the diary which was said to have been found with Lasseter's body. Ferguson recalled that there was a great air of excitement about the project and that the buying of the diary by Angus and Robertson was a 'hush-hush' affair.

Controversy has since arisen over *Lasseter's Last Ride*. It has been implied that Jack, not Angus and Robertson, bought the diary, and that Jack alone published the book, that Jack was responsible for sales of the thirty editions by 1947 and the fact that it is still in print today. The implication is that Jack was besotted with the contents of the diary and that it was his only source of reference. None of this is true. Jack began to piece the work together in June of 1931. He interviewed all the members of the expedition and was given access to the records and correspondence of the Central Australian Exploration Company. These records were made available to him by the company's secretary, Mr E. H. Bailey, and he had lengthy interviews with Fred Blakeley, the leader of the Central Australian Exploration Company, the brother of Arthur Blakeley who was then Minister of the Northern Territory. Of course, he used the diary as well.

Jack, who interviewed those who had been on the expedition, was in a better position to record the facts as told to him than those who have come later. These people can only make educated guesses based on reports and the diary. There have been stories of how Lasseter was seen after he was supposed to have died, and there have been stories that the man was a bigamist. Perhaps he was, for amongst Jack's papers is a letter from a Mrs Florence Lasseter to Mr I. L. Idriess, c/o Angus and Robertson NSW, in neat and legible handwriting, signed Florence Lasseter:

> In the Melbourne *Herald* I have just read an account of a book you have written about my late husband Lewis Herbert Lasseter. I do not know if you were aware of my existence or not, as I believe there is a woman in Sydney posing as Mrs Lasseter.
>
> Had I known you were writing this book, I might have been able to give you many interesting details of his life. Personally I was unaware that anyone could write a book about a real person without first consulting his family. I would be glad if you would send me a copy of the book as I would very much like to see if your information has been correct.

She concluded with 'the *real* Mrs L. H. Lasseter'. It is interesting to note that Mrs Florence Lasseter referred to her husband as 'Lewis Herbert' Lasseter which contrasts with Lasseter's public name of Harry Lasseter and Harry Bell Lasseter. That they are one and the same person is demonstrated by the signature L. H. B. Lasseter on a receipt, 8 July 1930, for fifty pounds from Fred Blakeley who led the ill-fated Lasseter expedition. This is also confirmed in a letter from an elderly gentleman, one J. E. Picton who lived close to, and was a friend of, Lasseter's father and knew Lewis Herbert Lasseter both as a small child and as an adult.

This letter details Lasseter's entire life: his childhood in Ballarat and Geelong up until the time he boarded a schooner and sailed to the South Seas and thence to America. It tells of his return to Australia in 1911, his employment by the Department of Public Works in Sydney, his work as a road maintenance man at Tabulam on the Clarence River where he later took up a selection, apparently married, became a market gardener and built an unusual house 'on poles'. Lasseter lived there for some years until war broke out, at which time he joined the navy and served on a minesweeper. He returned after the war to South Kensington where Picton was living. He told Picton that he was divorced and had married again. Lasseter lived in the Kensington area up until a few months before his departure for Central Australia with the expedition to find the 'lost' reef. Up until that time Lasseter was looking for work and had visited Picton carrying his carpenter's satchel. Picton directed him to the Daceyville School, where a new wing was being built. This letter cites dates, place names and events in Lasseter's life which could very easily be verified.

Picton's letter confirms that there was indeed a Mrs Florence Lasseter and a second Mrs Irene Lasseter. It shows that Lasseter, and his second wife and child, did not return to Australia from America until 1911. It also details Lasseter's life in Sydney right up until the time he left with the expedition to Central Australia. All of which shows that it was not possible for Lasseter to have been prospecting in Central Australia at any time during the thirty years prior to 1931.

Therefore, on the face of it, there never was a gold reef to lose or find!

However, in spite of this, Lasseter had enough knowledge of gold prospecting to convince most of the syndicate, if not all, to believe in his claim. Lasseter's knowledge was also, possibly, added to by his father, for Lasseter senior had served in Her Majesty's Navy on a man-of-war and had deserted to follow the lure of gold on the Ballarat goldfields. It is also possible that the gold sample Lasseter is supposed to have brought from his 'lost reef' came from either Ballarat or the Lady Jersey mine.

I have a heavily marked copy of *Lasseter's Last Ride* which was given to me by Jack's daughter, Wendy. This copy belonged to Malcom S. Stanley, member of the group who assessed Lasseter's claim. Stanley had meticulously written notes throughout the book and pasted in newspaper clippings of the day and others through to 1936. Confirmation of the bigamist story occurs here on several occasions and Stanley further implies that Blakeley, the leader of the expedition, knew about this. Stranger still are several mentions of Lasseter having been seen and spoken to by two men who knew him when all were sailing on a ship bound for the United States and further, that Lasseter was alive and living in Salt Lake City in the USA. Confirmation of these face-to-face meetings took place after Lasseter's reported death. Which brings us back to Picton's letter and the statement that Lasseter had left the country many years earlier for the United States and confirms the American connection.

Whether Lasseter was a bigamist or not would matter little, for bigamy seems to have been the order of the day—the aviator Bert Hinkler was, amongst others of the time, also a bigamist. It could however have some bearing on the reason why Lasseter hurriedly left Ilbilba after agreeing that he would wait there for Johns to return with fresh camels and supplies from Alice Springs.

It has also been implied that something untoward happened between Lasseter and Johns and that whatever it was is 'shrouded in mystery'. I have read most of the press reports relating to the event and find nothing to suggest a mystery about their parting. Johns' account of the parting is certainly straightforward:

> Crossing the Warburton Range, we zigzagged a great deal, endeavouring to make contact with Lasseter's country. At this time our supplies were running low, the camels in poor condition, and, to aggravate matters, two died of eating poison bush and another ran a stake through its foot and had to be turned loose. It was now necessary to return to our base camp at Ilbilba, and we made a direct line for it, avoiding Lake Amadeus, and accomplishing the trip in seven days, during which time the camels had no water. I then decided to ride to Alice Springs to pick up fresh camels, Lasseter remaining at Ilbilba until my return.

I find nothing mysterious implied here by Johns, in fact it seems to be a very logical plan. Stanley claims that Lasseter wanted Johns to leave him and go on to Alice Springs for two reasons: 'he got rid of Johns having learnt to manage the camels'. With regard to two letters which Lasseter gave Johns to carry to Alice Springs, Stanley makes an interesting claim:

> The letter or rather the two letters, 1) to the committee in Sydney, 2) instructions to the Commissioner of police at Alice Springs to hold Johns for attempted murder. This letter, delivered by Johns personally, imparted to the Commissioner Lasseter's imperative

instruction—the Commissioner took no notice of it—he was waiting for Lasseter to come in.

If Stanley is correct in his claim that Lasseter had sent Johns back with a sealed letter to the police requesting Johns' detention, it would answer the question as to why Lasseter didn't wait for Johns to return, but quickly left Ilbilba for the Petermann Ranges. There was no point in waiting for someone who could not return.

There are one or two other unanswered questions. Why didn't the exploration company request the airforce to continue the search for Lasseter after they had found the *Golden Quest II*? Most interesting of all, why has the question never been asked how a man afflicted with sandy blight, trachoma, a man who wrote in the diary later obtained from Mrs Lasseter that he was unable to see because of the resulting blindness of the progressing disease and that he could not take an accurate shot at natives who were threatening to spear him, nor see well enough to find food for himself—how could this man continue to write in his diary without any visible change to his handwriting? The handwriting is firm, flowing and perfectly legible. The lines, written on unlined paper, run straight across the page and on the line immediately preceding the statement 'beaten by sandy blight' can be seen the word 'for' crossed out by a straight, firm line and replaced by the word 'against' written above it. Some days later when the condition no doubt would have been worsening, he states, 'Keep spit on my fingers & rub ... eyes to keep them open ... they smart & burn, it's awful'. The writing however is still firm and if it were not for the charred condition of the paper, perfectly legible—and still the lines are straight. All of which shows, I believe, that he could see clearly and that he was not as affected by either the trachoma or by failing health as he repeatedly claimed throughout the diary.

Stanley further makes the astonishing claim that the second expedition mounted after Lasseter's death found the reef or at least found a reef:

> On Blakeley's return—the crowd in Sydney laid all the blame on him, his report was unfavourable, the committee did not want that so they collected more cash & one man gave 500 [pounds] towards fitting another expedition, they found the reef—in ironstone caps containing no gold, the crowd lost all its subscribed capital, I knew many of them, fortunately I mistrusted Lasseter, I kept out and stayed out.

Maybe a reef exists—maybe it doesn't. Perhaps Lasseter died in the desert. Bob James, alias Bob Buck, found a body and buried it, a body which he claimed to be Lasseter's, but was it? There was never a coroner's report called for or carried out. Perhaps James found Lasseter alive and took him to civilisation (as was rumoured) where Lasseter buried himself in the previously established obscurity of an assumed identity in the United States. There are many unanswered questions and no matter how many people address the mystery, no one approaches it without bias.

I would like the answer to two questions. Firstly, why didn't the airforce plane continue its search for Lasseter after finding the personnel of the downed *Golden Quest II*? Surely the continuance of the search in the hope of saving a man from death was a decision to be made by the federal authorities and not the expedition company? Secondly, why didn't the government put a stop to the many subsequent gold expeditions which followed in the path of the original group?

Could it be that Lasseter was indeed a bigamist and that members of the Scullin government did a trade with him—his safe conduct out of the country and a massive cover-up in return for the location of the reef and its gold? It is odd that James, alias Buck, found the body and then led another company expedition a few months later, maybe the same expedition which Stanley claims found the barren reef, and by chance found the legendary diary. All this after the reported sightings of a very much alive Lasseter.

If the federal government was not interested, the mining ministers for the states of Western Australia and South Australia certainly were. So great was their interest that there were publicised plans to place all unemployed miners in the field in search of gold, and there was an additional scheme which called for the cooperation of all other state mining ministers to do the same. Was this interest purely because a chap named Lasseter had died in search of a reef which he said was rich? Or could it be that the whole scenario was set up as a diversion offering hope to the suffering masses after John Bailey, president of the Australian Workers Union in 1930, took Lasseter's story to Canberra?

Lasseter had written to Arthur Blakeley MP about the reef in 1929. It would have been easy for Blakeley to have ignored the letters, regarding the claim as being possible but not probable. Given the disastrous changes which were happening daily on the economic front in 1929 the letters would have had little chance of serious consideration. According to all reports the AWU acted purely on their assessment of Lasseter's verbal credibility. I find this hard to believe. Arthur Blakeley MP would have at least run some check on Lasseter's background. I believe it probable that he found a record of Lasseter's marriages and from that point the scam developed, which would explain the friction between Fred Blakeley, the MP's brother, and Lasseter, and further explain Stanley's claim that Fred Blakeley knew about the bigamy charge. The hiccough was Johns who happened to blunder onto the scene. Fred Blakeley left Lasseter and Johns, no doubt agitated and anxious to get back for further orders.

Fortunately Lasseter and Johns had trouble with the camels, or did they? Maybe Lasseter was forced to take Johns into his confidence and they agreed on the story that he would return for Lasseter after he went to Alice Springs for help. Johns, however, hadn't counted on Lasseter giving him the letter which would hold him in Alice Springs. With Johns safely detained Lasseter was free to carry out the plan as originally conceived, scuttle into the great unknown, mark the reef and wait for Bob James alias Buck to find him and take him out. James returns but reports only that he found the body. Subsequently Lasseter is seen, which is not part of the plan, so James makes another trip for the exploration company and conveniently finds the diary, the evidence that is needed to convince everyone that Lasseter is dead.

The entire nation had its morale lifted! Lasseter's reef was still glittering in the heavens, beckoning the unemployed, a mass the government didn't know what to do with. The government could have put miners into the field to search, not just for Lasseter's reef, but for any goldfield in Western Australia or South Australia, and the miners would have gone—gladly. This would have solved a large unemployment problem with the bonus of perhaps finding a gold reef big enough to boost the gold reserves.

Who did what and why to this day has remained a secret. If Jack had indeed been an opportunist, as has been claimed, he would have used the added information which he had to promote the book, or to publish yet another, for he had enough material to do so. Jack essentially was a researcher who liked to ferret out the facts; if he had doubts about Lasseter he shut them out, perhaps blinded by the myth of the man and his gold reef, just as those who wanted to believe then, and still believe now, in a glittering Eldorado in a lonely desert without benefit of hard evidence.

Almost as soon as *Lasseter's Last Ride* had rolled off the presses in July 1931 Jack was busy searching for another title which would have popular appeal. Walter Cousins and he by this time had established a fine working relationship. The two would meet for morning tea in Cousins's office to discuss possible publishing projects. It was at one of these meetings that they hit upon the idea to approach the Australian Inland Mission for permission to write the story of the work of the Mission and in particular the achievements of John Flynn.

Jack's third book, ultimately the one to outsell all his other works, *Flynn of the Inland* was the result.

Chapter Fifteen
LIFE IN THE FAST LANE

A SERIES of letters, written by Jack to Walter Cousins between June and August 1931, just prior to the publication of *Lasseter's Last Ride* in September, show that Jack the prospector, now professional author, had developed a keen sense of promotion and publicity. These letters to Cousins, often accompanied by newspaper cuttings, would be the first of the many on this topic to be received by Cousins and others at A&R in the coming years.

Jack was determined not to let *Prospecting for Gold* slide into obscurity. Any report related to gold which appeared in the press he cut out and deliberated upon the possibility of turning the event to his best advantage. After due consideration he forwarded these, together with his suggestions, to Cousins.

A newspaper clipping attached to one of the letters read, 'The Western Australian Minister for Mines In Melbourne To Arrange Exhibition of Golden Eagle Nugget'. This prompted Jack to point out to Cousins that he should contact the Melbourne booksellers with the suggestion that they mount window displays featuring *Prospecting For Gold* together with rocks painted with gilt to resemble gold nuggets. Such a display he felt sure would stimulate sales of the book.

A South African review of *Prospecting for Gold* from a Johannesburg newspaper which read, 'We wish a South African would do the same for South African diamond mining as Idriess has done for Australian gold mining' brought forth a more ambitious plan. In his letter to Cousins Jack suggests that 'the S.M.H. write a par on the statement and also say that the Department of Mines N.S.W. helps the mining industry here more than the South African one does.' Jack's sphere of promotion was not confined to publicity. He was an instinctive marketer and among the first to attempt to sell books through non-traditional sales outlets and to suggest the use of direct mail. Always in search of additional market places he went out in the field and acted as an unpaid book representative. 'I was talking to the organiser of the Centralian Gold & Aerial Transport this afternoon. They propose to open a store in

Alice Springs. They will stock both *Prospecting* and *Lasseter's*. I asked him to give us a list of their shareholders to circularise.'

By the end of September *Prospecting* was selling steadily as was *Lasseter's* and Jack was free to proceed with the manuscript on the work of the Australian Inland Mission and John Flynn. Cousins, in agreement with the proposed new project, left Jack to approach the Australian Inland Mission for permission to write its history.

John Flynn was the first man to inaugurate an aerial medical service for a civilian population, and for this alone he is widely known in and beyond Australia. He was the guest of honour at the First International Aviation Congress held in Paris in May 1929. All nations were interested in the inauguration of this Flying Mission in the wilds of Northern Australia, and John Flynn as the founder was invited to visit England, Italy, France, Germany, Switzerland and America. Although the Australian Inland Mission was backed by the General Assembly of the Presbyterian Church of Australia, now embraced by the Uniting Church of Australia, the Mission was non-denominational.

The 'wireless' played a very important part in the then new medical aerial service. The AIM had a contract with Qantas to supply a plane and pilot any time. Cloncurry, the first base of the flying doctor operations, represented only one circle in the dream of John Flynn. He envisaged six circles of service to gird the whole of Australia's remote districts with facilities for flying doctors and hospitals.

On 21 October 1931 Jack wrote to the Reverend Milliken of the AIM requesting permission to write a book on the work of the Inland Mission. 'I suggest the work of Padre Flynn and the others who have helped him, their work, struggles, trials, dreams and the results attained and the results hoped to be attained.' Always with an eye to net the most sales he pointed out to Milliken that 'a fine time to launch the book would be at the Bridge opening when it is expected that there will be an additional 20,000 people in Sydney. As this is only a few months hence, the time is limited.'

The following day he also wrote to the Mission's Publicity Committee requesting permission to write the work and further offering the Mission the opportunity to sell the book when written. It was a respectable business deal in which A&R offered the book to the Mission for four shillings a copy, to sell at six shillings a copy, 'a profit of 2/- per book'.

Cousins was not about to let A&R's rising star, Ion L. Idriess, slip from his grasp. Jack had become extremely popular in a very short time, his public profile was growing daily and he was capable of turning out a prodigious amount of work. It was obvious that if Idriess and Cousins could keep coming up with topics of high general appeal it would be possible to keep the presses rolling. The proposed book had everything. The subject, John Flynn, was a highly visible religious humanitarian, the author had a devoted following and the work had the bonuses of a ready-made sales outlet and a captive audience in the faithful.

The AIM Publicity Committee was suitably impressed, for on 24 November 1931 the Reverend J. C. Milliken wrote to John Flynn saying 'the Publicity Committee has decided to get Ion L. Eidress [sic] to write a book on the AIM' and further that the Committee had decided to name the book *Flynn of the Inland* ...we have placed you among the immortals'. Milliken constantly misspelt 'Idriess'—even after the book was published—as either 'Eidress' or 'Eidiress'.

Jack met the opening of the Sydney Harbour Bridge deadline. The manuscript was completed and read by the AIM by 15 January 1932 and the publication was in the bookshops by March—the bridge being opened on the 19th of that month. The release of *Flynn of the Inland* of course was a minor event in the face of the historic action of Captain de Groot of the New Guard. Captain de Groot, dressed in the uniform of the British Royal Hussars, made his daring dash on a broken-down racehorse to cut the blue ribbon with his sword ahead of Premier Jack Lang. Idriess found the incident very amusing; he had no time for politicians and expressed the opinion that they were all 'bastards' and that the country would be better served if it were run by public servants.

The additional twenty thousand people in Sydney must have contributed to the sales of *Flynn*; the first edition of two thousand copies was sold out inside the first few weeks and it was back on the presses for a second edition of two thousand five hundred before the end of the month. By June 1945, twenty-four editions later, 56,924 copies had been sold. Accurate records have not been kept since but the book is still in print and sells well today.

Among the numerous review cuttings of his books which Jack kept was a copy of the *Sydney Morning Herald* review of *Flynn of the Inland*. It was this article which earned Jack the title of 'The Boswell of the Bush' a phrase which stuck with him until his death. The *SMH* reviewer waxed lyrical:

With apparently artless art the thread is drawn out gathering as it goes the simple primary colours of a pattern very close to nature. In conversational style the completed study is built up, and history is revealed while scarce we know it. The method, in part, at least, is that of Boswell. And throughout, as is fitting, the high aim in view and the means by which it is accomplished transcend the telling, transcend even the man.

Attached to the review clipping was a handwritten, unsigned internal A&R note:

This will tickle you! When Idriess came in this morning the first thing he said was 'Who is this bloke Boswell? I don't know whether to take it as a compliment or not.' We gave him *Everbody's Life of Johnson*. I explained that it was abridged: he said 'What's abridged?' ... and he wasn't joking. Isn't it marvellous how he can write?

Whether Jack was a stylist or whether the academics thought he could write was of no concern to A&R—his books were selling by the thousands. The following month, April 1932, encouraged by Jack's popularity and the success of his previous books, and his glowing acceptance by the reviewers, A&R overcame their concern that the public would find *The Desert Column* too depressing to read in such dark times and published the book.

The Desert Column is by far his greatest work. However whilst it went into three editions in 1932 and is still in print, it had only sold 24,174 copies by 1944, a respectable number but a little under half the numbers sold of *Flynn of the Inland* and *Lasseter's Last Ride*. Perhaps the original assessment that the topic was too depressing was correct.

As soon as he had finished the Australian Inland Mission history, he concentrated on his days in the jungles behind Cooktown. Using his diary notes, he wrote *Men of the Jungle*, perhaps started in tandem with *Flynn*, or in record time between January and March 1932.

Many years later in 1976, aged eighty-seven and still writing, he would tell Kylie Tennant in an interview: 'I have trouble getting started. Then I go hell-for-leather to get the damn thing finished.' While he might have had some technical difficulties getting the opening chapter up and running, paucity of subjects was never a problem.

In March 1932 he wrote to Sampson, the Cooktown chemist of 'great fever mixtures' fame, asking him to approach Charlie Patching, 'the Father of Cooktown' to write the foreword to *Men of the Jungle*.

Sampson's letter in reply carried two pieces of bad news. Patching, he wrote, was no longer physically capable of carrying out Jack's request. He asked Jack to write the foreword and to send it to him to give to Patching to read and sign. The second disturbing piece of news was that Dick Welch, Jack's friend and travelling companion, was back in Cooktown and that his health, due to injuries received in the battle of the Somme in France, had badly deteriorated and that he was drinking heavily.

The news disturbed and depressed Jack. Although his Cooktown days were twenty-one years and a war behind him he had not stopped to consider that Charlie might be coming to the end of his life. But it was the news of Dick Welch which distressed him most. Patching had lived a good, long life but the vision of the once sunny-natured Dick, now a morose alcoholic, angered him and brought the memories of war flooding back.

Jack's life was a whirl of activity. He still continued to turn out lengthy articles for magazines and newspapers such as the *World's News*, the *Sunday Sun & Guardian*, *Daily Telegraph* and others, while at the same time writing and researching his books. He was beginning to receive requests from various groups to undertake addresses. A retiring man, he preferred the written word to public speaking engagements. Therefore he refused a request from 'The Sane Democracy League of Australia' to speak on grounds that he was having trouble retaining his own sanity while maintaining a busy schedule.

Somehow he managed to fit in a social life which not only involved Eta but a lady who sent him many letters addressing him as 'Mr Man'. These letters which usually contained the phrase 'honour bright and shining' also referred to his weakness for 'little sweet cakes'. The trickle of fan mail had grown and now he had the added chore of answering all letters. One of these letters, simply dated 1932, from Mary, alias Miss 'Clara Bow', offering him her services as 'charwoman', was addressed to him c/o The Grampion Flats, Eaton Avenue, Kings Cross. Jack had left behind the room in Paddington.

The only reference to New Guinea found in Jack's notes relates to his abortive attempt to land at Eddie Creek for the purpose of prospecting. In the 1930s however Jack was also a member of a group which formed the New Guinea Club. At eleven o'clock each Thursday morning at Thorne's Café, Castlereagh Street, the pale-skinned Sydney patrons were treated to sights of northern suntans and the parchment-coloured skins of malaria sufferers. Sipping tea on Thursday mornings at Thorne's could be found ex-

New Guinea planters, people visiting from New Guinea on shopping sprees or meeting sons and daughters who were receiving their formal schooling on the mainland, together with the odd academic and district officers and their families on vacation in the south. In short, whoever was in town. Jack somehow fitted the Thursday morning social into his busy schedule.

Short reminder notes asking him to call at Thorne's Cafe and messages left for him by New Guinea people establish, in part, that he did spend some time in New Guinea apart from the brief skirmish at Eddie Creek. It is impossible however to pin-point the year or years that he visited there. Therefore, as his New Guinea contacts were numerous and his acceptance by the reigning New Guinea clique at Thorne's came in the early 1930s, he presumably visited there in 1928 during his Torres Strait days.

Jack also kept numerous letters from a lady, Ali Innes. Ali, who also took tea at Thorne's when visiting Sydney, was the wife of the publican of the hotel at Salamana, New Guinea. The letters from her indicate that Jack used the hotel as a base during a protracted stay pre–1930. Although not overt the letters show that Jack and Ali shared a mutual fondness for each other. They contain a restrained theme of affection and overtones of the sweet misery of a love which, controlled by Ali's married status, could never be fully expressed. Ali continued to write letters and poetry to Jack for many years. Obviously the two kept in constant contact, for although the letters were never dated apart from naming the day on which they were written, she always had each of his new addresses. Unhappily Ali Innes died a few brief months before I began my research; it seems she was the very last person, had she lived, who could have supplied times and dates and perhaps given some personal details on the movements of Jack Idriess in New Guinea.

The manuscript of *Men of the Jungle* was completed in March 1932, so Jack immediately started work on the fascinating New Guinea epic—the historical *Gold Dust and Ashes*, utilising his New Guinea contacts. He had also written to Mr Wells of Wells and Co., Chartered Accountants of Adelaide (accountants for Guinea Airways) some months before, possibly while he was still working on *Flynn* and certainly while writing *Men of the Jungle*.

Gold Dust and Ashes is the incredible story of the opening up of the New Guinea goldfields. Set against a background of cannibalism, black-birding, death-defying feats of heroism and extensive alluvial goldfields, the book documents the efforts of Cecil John Levian, a man of wondrous vision and persistence who fought against almost insurmountable odds to bring air services to New Guinea. Guinea Airways was founded principally for airlifting the first dredge, necessary to win the alluvial gold from the Bulloolo, and carrying the glittering stuff out of the steaming jungle. Apart from overcoming transportation problems encountered in difficult terrain in a country where there was no road system, the establishment of a New Guinea air service was of paramount importance to overcome the loss of native carriers to the cannibal inhabitants.

The writing of *Gold Dust and Ashes* met with full approval and encouragement from Cousins. Jack had hit on yet another winner and there was no end to his ideas, nor his urge to have the material for another book almost compiled before finishing his current work. With this in mind, while working on *Gold Dust and Ashes* Jack wrote to all state police commissioners requesting both permission and the names of police personnel to contact in order to gather together the material to write 'the mounted police book', a work which would ultimately be titled *Man Tracks*.

By August 1932 *Gold Dust and Ashes* had passed the manuscript stage and Wells, the Guinea Airways accountant, wrote to Cousins requesting A&R to print 'a De-luxe edition of 50 copies'. These he offered to pay for as he wished to 'place some in influential quarters home and abroad'.

Men of the Jungle was released in September and by December six thousand copies had been sold. The book was reviewed in glowing terms—it seems that Jack was everyone's golden boy. The only reviewer to fight against the popular opinion was employed by the *Labor Daily*, who tried desperately to find an adverse criticism. The closing paragraph stated, 'A fault in this book is the use of the term "from whence", whence as used means "from what place" … so the word "from" is not necessary.'

In January 1933 however H. M. Green, the literary historian, of the Fisher Library at the University of Sydney and a reader for A&R, wrote to Jack with a view to giving him a lesson or two on the finer points of writing. He too found 'from whence' to be a mark of illiteracy. As Green was not moved to write to Jack until after the book was in its third edition I assume that his criticism was not prompted by Cousins but that he acted from his own initiative. Whatever his motivation was he didn't remotely disturb the Idriess ego. Jack did not deign to answer the letter until May:

Dear Mr. Green,
I've gone over your corrections in *Men of the Jungle*, but I'm afraid I'm too dense in the head to absorb them. If I could, no

doubt it would teach me a lot but I don't think the reading public would note the difference. Times move so rapidly and the public are in such a hurry that I doubt whether they would bother in the least about the finer points of writing—whatever that may mean.

If a man writes a successful book he writes it, if he doesn't, he doesn't and that's the end of it.

Thanks very much for all the trouble you have taken. My regrets are that I am such a bad pupil.

Wishing you the best of luck,

Yours sincerely,

Ion L. Idriess.

As was the custom with all his mail, Jack had answered Green's letter in longhand and passed it on to Cousins to be typed and forwarded. Cousins however must have felt that Jack had been a little too patronising for the typed copy was left in the Cousins/Idriess files, marked 'Not to be sent'.

Many years later when over forty of Jack's works had been published and he was still attracting a large audience while continuing to draw complaints from literary circles, because he wrote the way he talked, the widely respected H. M. Green was to give him then what might be the only praise ever to come from the establishment: 'The most popular of descriptive writers. He knows the wildest places in Australia. It is largely owing to him that these places have become to us more than mere spaces on a map. He loves excitement, adventure and outlaws.'

The Desert Column was in its fifth edition by September 1932 when Jack received a letter from the Board of Trustees, Imperial War Machine, South Kensington, London, thanking him for a copy of the work: 'I am directed by His Royal Highness, The Prince of Wales, President of the Board of Trustees, to thank you for the gift mentioned overleaf which you have presented to the War Museum. I am to assure you that your generosity is greatly appreciated.'

The letter however did not please Jack as much as did the receipt of a letter from John Masefield, the Poet Laureate, from Boar's Hill in Oxford which read, 'It is a pleasure to us to read of the wonderful Australians. Your book is a vivid thing, and records a great unit's share in a great campaign most thrillingly and telling-ly.' I wonder if H. M. Green might have found 'thrillingly' and 'tellingly', though correct, a little jarring.

Both letters delighted Cousins who thought that they could be used in promoting the books. He was particularly glad to have the Masefield letter although he felt that both he and Jack would have been better served had Masefield commented favourably on Jack's style. The literary pundits, who were honing their razors in preparation to slash the upstart from the bush down to size, made him uneasy. Cousins didn't share Jack's philosophy. He wanted it all—a best-selling author who was also applauded by his peers.

November found Jack staying at Katoomba with Eta and an unnamed girlfriend. While Eta and her friend were enjoying the change of air and books that Cousins had sent them, Jack was hard at work revising *Gold Dust and Ashes* and writing Cousins his usual letters full of promotional ideas. Somewhere along the line he had hit upon the idea of selling a set of ten Idriess books. With that in mind he wrote to Cousins suggesting that *Madman's Island* be reprinted and sold for two shillings and sixpence, reminding him that the Firm had mooted a possible reprint of the book in October of 1931, a year before. 'The Chief [George Robertson] and Mr Shenstone told me that they didn't lose by the first publication of *Madman's Island*. The Firm had suggested 'cutting out the romance that had been tacked on at the end'. Jack was all for that.

At that time, including *Madman's Island*, six Idriess books had been published. The seventh, *Gold Dust and Ashes*, was almost a *fait accompli*. Jack was hoping that *Drums of Mer*, the manuscript of which was now complete, would soon be the eighth and that the new project, 'the mounted police book', when written, would bring the count to nine titles. He needed another title for the grand total to reach ten, then the set would be a possibility.

Throughout November the letters continued to fly back and forth between Cousins in the city and Jack at Katoomba. Cousins kept Jack up-to-date with the news, and posted on the sales of his work. On 9 November Cousins sent Jack a note which said, 'The 5th edition of *Flynn* sold out today. We are now selling the 6th, and Bert tells me that 100 have already gone out of the 3000. Hope we have to reprint for Christmas.'

Later, Cousins again wrote to Jack:

Told Bert you threatened him with your gland treatment if he did not get a move on and the result has borne fruit. 520 of *Flynn* & 450 of *Lasseter* have been sold from the editions in today. *Lasseter* is in its tenth—congratulations.

By 16 November Cousins was totally convinced that the Idriess set should be published. Delighted with the response to *Lasseter's Last Ride* he wrote to Jack, 'What a great foundation we are laying for the set idea. We will be issuing 40,000 catalogues this year—double the number of last year, so hope for bigger sales.' Obviously A&R were then at the forefront of aggressive publishing marketing tactics. 40,000 catalogues in today's market place would be excessive and an absolutely astounding number to print and circulate in 1932, one of the toughest of the Depression years.

◆

JACK was riding the crest and not prepared to be disturbed by anyone, certainly not a critic. In one of his shorter notes to Cousins he sent a message to Robertson's secretary, Rebecca Wiley, in reference to a critic. 'Tell Miss Wiley that wop-eyed N.Z. cow doesn't know a book when he sees one. He is the sort of critic who brushes his hair with a curry comb.' Critics were all horses to Jack.

During Jack's absence from Sydney 'the Chief', George Robertson, had begun to take a greater interest in the phenomenally popular author who was turning out best-sellers on almost a three monthly basis and it was becoming increasingly evident to him that Jack was capable of continuing to do so.

Every publisher aims at having a number of best-sellers in progress for the Christmas market but with Jack in the A&R stable it was Christmas every three months. Already, although *Gold Dust and Ashes* was still being revised, Jack had begun to drop the odd article in the press featuring New Guinea, designed to whet the public's appetite for the book when it was released. Feature articles such as 'Shark Eye Park Who Found Guinea Gold' and 'Lone Prospector Among Cannibals Passes Through Sydney' which appeared in the *Daily Telegraph* during October had already created an interest, and Robertson had no doubt that Jack would continue to keep the interest building with more in the same vein. With this in mind Robertson decided that *Drums of Mer* should be published when the sales of *Gold Dust and Ashes* were beginning to fall, thereby achieving the best market potential for both books.

The roistering *Gold Dust and Ashes* did not need any assistance to stay among the best-sellers, in fact Robertson would have had a long wait had he waited for declining sales. *Gold Dust and Ashes* stayed up there with the best of them with five editions, a total of eight thousand copies being printed and sold between April and September of 1933, when *Drums of Mer* was released. *Gold Dust and Ashes* by 1945 and nineteen editions later, was still holding its own, selling 40,924 copies.

On 22 December 1932 Robertson wrote to the Reverend MacFarlane the 'Wandering Missionary' in reference to *Drums of*

Mer, quoting the response that he had from T. E. G. Tucker, Emeritus Professor of Classical Philology, University of Melbourne, 'the best editor we ever had'. He looked over the manuscript and reported as follows:

> Idriess is something of a genius. Apart from his evident knowledge of the natives and their customs he has a graphic power greater than that of any writer I have read for years. His accounts of a battle of canoes, a wreck of a flotilla, and other events are the finest things of that kind that anyone out here has produced. I have gone over the whole thing twice because of my desire to see an unusual writer win more than local success.

In stating that 'Idriess is something of a genius', T. E. G. Tucker had given Robertson a greater recommendation for *Drums of Mer* than he had expected. The publication of book number eight was about to become a reality.

Chapter Sixteen
THE DEMANDS GROW

WITH the revision of *Gold Dust and Ashes* behind him Jack turned to editing *Drums of Mer*. Although Professor Tucker had found the manuscript an exceptional piece of work, another unsigned reader's report advised against its publication 'until the economic clouds roll by and then only a condensed version with the C'Zarke's fantastic journey cut out altogether because of inaccurate astronomical data'. This was a polite way of saying that the reader thought that Jack was off with the pixies.

The 'inaccurate astronomical data' contained in the original manuscript of *Drums of Mer* referred to by the reader was the account of how C'Zarke, the Zogo, the great Au-Zogo-zogo-le and Au-Maid-maid-le, head of the Bomai-Malu, by using his extraordinary powers transported his mind into the world of outer-space where he claimed to have seen and spoken with Abob and Kos, the Flying Men, who had come from the sky to teach the islanders how to make stone fish traps or to have built the traps themselves, off the shores of Murray Island, Mer.

A footnote which appears in the first edition of *Drums of Mer* makes oblique reference to the deleted material:

> As the writer of this story, I would like to explain what the remnants of the Zogo-le assured me the great priest saw in these 'mind' travels of his. Such, however, might only prove of interest to students of the occult. To other readers, such an attempted description might read as a fantasy.

When he was an old man in his eighties Jack called the story 'sheer bloody fact'and insisted on the existence of the Spirit Men:

> The fish traps were built by the Spirit Men, huge rocks bonded with some cement we don't know—they'd enclose half an acre of sea— the great waves sweep in a thousand miles or more to beat against them, but they never knock down those walls. Abob and Kos were two clever men. You could walk along the wall and spear fish of any

size you wanted. There were pools that dug into the rocks at depths and sizes according to the fish coming in.

On the back of some old typed material of Jack's I found the following notes written in his own hand:

> That strange little race...that untold centuries before we flew to the moon had their strictly believed legends of such as Abob and Kos, and the score of others, Supermen who flew down from the skies to teach them things, so that they could continue to exist and fight their way through nature and enemies by land and sea and air, and continue to live and learn their culture of continuous life.
>
> Supermen from the skies, who taught them of mesmerism, and many other weird things, Supermen flying down from the skies to teach them also how to build the great stone fish traps of Mer and Eroob, traps that have withstood the fury of the open sea of centuries of cyclones.
>
> Even to this date of the fantastic 'Whiteman's Civilisation', our best engineers have not succeeded in doing this. Nor, incidentally, would our 'Wisemen' believe this when at long last I brought this information down here.
>
> But—'we are fading away'.
>
> So what odds!!!
>
> Ion Idriess 1971.

The Reverend MacFarlane endorsed the belief in the Spirit Men. Jack met MacFarlane, the Wandering Missionary, on Sabu Island off the New Guinea coast, resuming their friendship which had begun on Thursday Island. There MacFarlane introduced Jack to many native island historians and in many cases he interpreted for Jack. Had it not been for the timely documentation of their customs and the grim head-hunting practices as told to Jack and MacFarlane by the last living Zogo-le (one of the governing priests) the secret rites and rituals of the Murray Islanders would have been lost forever. *Drums of Mer* would come to be regarded for many years by the Murray Islanders as the bible of Mer.

Robertson, however, was unprepared to have MacFarlane influence his thinking. Even if the clergy endorsed the existence of extra-terrestrial beings he had no intention of letting Jack jeopardise either his own or A&R's credibility by publishing the material. Consequently he ordered the deletion of all references to 'flying men' with supernatural powers. This decision would irritate Jack for the rest of his life.

Drums of Mer, first published in September 1933, was in its fourth edition by December of the same year and had sold eight thousand copies. By June 1945 twenty-four thousand copies had been sold.

During the same period, September to December 1933, *Flynn of the Inland*, *Men of the Jungle*, *The Desert Column*, *Gold Dust and Ashes* and *Lasseter's Last Ride* were also reprinted, and approximately eighteen thousand copies of Idriess books were sold during these four months. Each title was back on the press inside the first three months of 1934. These printings were in addition to the editions of the same works totalling approximately twelve thousand copies printed and sold in the first eight months of 1933. No figures are available for *Prospecting for Gold* but it would be safe to estimate sales of approximately two thousand copies. Using these A&R figures it is possible to estimate that some thirty-four thousand Idriess books were sold in 1933, and that twenty-seven per cent of the Australian population of eight million had bought and read at least one of Jack's books when the Depression was at its height.

♦

THE letters he had sent in 1932 to the police commissioners brought an even greater response than he had anticipated. Permission had been granted and in many cases the names and addresses of police officers had been supplied. This new work was now uppermost in his mind.

His aim was to produce an epic of factual record, and to portray these men while they were engaged in carrying out their hazardous duties under harsh, lonely conditions. In his letters to the officers he had outlined his desire to make the Australian Mounted Police as famous as their Canadian counterparts.

Tales of heroism and daring poured in from all over the country, and in a few cases he received whole diaries which had been meticulously kept by patrol officers. After reading the letters it was clear to Jack that compiling the work would be a difficult and protracted task. The material which came in was good, but to get the accurate details he needed to give the book colour and life he found it was necessary to write yet more letters asking specific questions. While Jack waited for the answers, he began the research for another book. With Cousins's blessing he planned to write a seventy-five-thousand-word biography of the Salvation Army's Commissioner MacKenzie.

Although Jack was intent on keeping up his output he was

not so engrossed that he didn't take a lively interest in current events. On 26 January 1933 he wrote to F. E. Baume, editor of the *Sunday Sun* in support of the paper's view that Australian films should find public and government support. Of course, by endorsing the need for films with Australian content he no doubt had his own books in mind as possible film material. The letter shows also an acceptance of women engaged in the workforce, even though such participation in commerce was not readily accepted by most men of his day.

Throughout January he had his head down working on *Drums of Mer* and under a constant workload, much of it self-imposed.

On 5 February he wrote to Farmer Whyte, a media man in Canberra: 'I got one of the nicest compliments when I returned yesterday; it was a request from the Blind Institute people to transcribe *Flynn of the Inland* into Braille. I liked that better than if it had been from some big overseas publishing firm asking to print whole editions of my books'. *Flynn*, like many of his books, is still being transcribed into Braille and also being recorded for talking books for the blind.

On 15 March Jack wrote to the widow of C. J. Levien:

I am glad that you like *Gold Dust and Ashes*. The 2nd edition is nearly sold out and I am sure the book will be the means of the name of C. J. Levien being remembered as the Cecil Rhodes of the Mandated Territory. The window show here has sold *Gold Dust and Ashes* at the rate of 200 per week for the shop [A&R] alone, also the sales of *Lasseter's Last Ride*, *Flynn of the Inland*, *The Desert Column*, *Men of the Jungle*, *Prospecting for Gold* have jumped surprisingly.

While Jack had been staying in Katoomba he had written one of his many letters to Cousins and suggested that the window displays featuring *Gold Dust and Ashes* should also contain his other books. Obviously in this instance Cousins had acted; the effectiveness of the exercise was able to be measured in increased sales of all Idriess titles. By mid-March *Gold Dust and Ashes* was in its third edition.

Earlier in the year a friend of Cousins, Mrs Robertson of Central Queensland, had written suggesting that Jack should collaborate with Daisy Bates to bring to publication her book of West Australian native customs. Cousins had given the letter to Jack and asked him to reply. Cousins was not particularly interested in the project; he felt that there were more 'important books waiting to be written' and that while such a book would no doubt be of value in the future, there was very little chance of it being financially rewarding at that time.

Jack answered Mrs Robertson, his letter echoing much of Cousins' sentiments. He named the Australian market potential as being 'eight million and only a few of these who buy books'. He was concerned that he would be out-of-pocket if he wrote the book and felt that he would be better advised to write another book of his own first. Then he closed with, 'Meanwhile, here is thanking you quite a lot for your suggestion, which appeals to me very much indeed. It is the type of book I would like to write, and I dislike writing books.' This from a man who had written four best-sellers in a year!

The end of March found Jack doing a lecture tour of primary schools in the Orange district of western NSW. At a public function he was welcomed to the district by the Mayor of Orange. The local paper quoted the mayor who hailed him as 'famous author'. The paper also reported on a gold mining venture that Jack and three of his friends were engaged in on the Macquarie River. Somehow between all his activities Jack had managed to find time to become involved with three old New Guinea mates in prospecting for gold—his first and only love. Their plans did not succeed, for the Department of Mines returned the money that they had paid for the leases, stating that they could not be granted due to some old law.

During his stay in Orange Jack received a letter from Cousins. Attached to the letter was a newspaper clipping from the Melbourne *Age*. Under the heading of 'Australian Novels– the Best Fifty' the author of the article, one A.C.W., ranked *Madman's Island* as No. 34 and wrote that 'Ion Idriess comes in places near the rank of masterpiece'.

This unexpected acclaim of the book which everyone had discounted as not being worth the paper it was written on prompted Cousins to write, 'We will have to re-publish *Madman's Island* the sooner the better. Anyway as soon as you get back I think we should consider bringing it out in a revised ed. We will get a new jacket for it and I will have it ready to show you on your return.'

Jack was in great demand. The find of a fossil marsupial lion's tooth at Molong in NSW sent him to the district to collect more of the fossils and to bring them back to Sydney for the *Sunday Sun* which in turn placed them before the curator of the Sydney Museum.

His writing began to cover news items such as a piece on the Greater Public Schools Regatta or Head-of-The-River boat race held in those days on Mortlake Bay, Parramatta River.

A letter to Jack from Cousins reported that 'the last year's sales of books in Australia has put the sales of Australian books far ahead of those from overseas', which was excellent news for Australian book publishers, especially as they had been continually fighting booksellers who consistently pushed books from 'home'.

The old magazine, the *World's News*, had changed hands in 1932. Now controlled by George Warnacke it was running under the banner of the *Australian Women's Weekly*. Warnacke approached Jack asking him to write for the new magazine. Jack thanked him for the request but refused because he was 'snowed under with work'.

Although he was exceptionally busy he took the time to write a note to Farmer Whyte in Canberra to tell him that Warnecke was soliciting writers to contribute to the new magazine. 'George Warnecke has started a new women's paper which appears to have a big chance of success'. How right he was.

His workload was made heavier by many writers who asked him to verify their facts when they wrote material on areas with which they were not familiar. Farmer Whyte occasionally called on Jack for this service. In reference to one of Whyte's articles, 'Peaceful Papua', he wrote that the piece was almost correct with the exception of Whyte's reference to head-hunting: 'However head-hunting is still going on in the mountainous interior towards the Dutch Border, where the Kukukulus still take a head or two. The last time I was at Boigu word came one morning from the mainland of a raid on the Werida people, and eleven heads were taken.' If Jack had stated when 'the last time I was at Boigu' had been, it would have been possible to get a firm date of at least one of his visits to New Guinea.

It is difficult to assess the depth of his relationship with Eta in 1933. There is a brief note dated 10 May to Constable Morey of the Mounted Police based in Darwin which says, 'I arrived at the Quay at five past eleven. It transpires that the Girl Friend, complaining she never saw enough of me, had put the clock back an hour. Hence, all through the woman's fault as usual, I failed to farewell you and Mr Caird.' I assume that the 'Girl Friend' was Eta.

On 11 May 1933 Jack overcame his shyness and took his first speaking engagement to address the Amateur Fisherman's Association and, flushed with his success, wrote to the Reverend Frank Walker accepting his invitation to address a Methodist meeting. And on 16 May he wrote to a Miss Bedford saying, 'I appreciate the honour of being elected a member of the P.E.N. Club.'

As far as Jack was concerned there were no authors other than Australian authors and he did his utmost to encourage the writing of more Australian books. With this in mind he wrote to Frank Reid of Bowen, North Queensland, and urged him to sit down and write of his experiences with the Camel Corps. 'The adventures of the Cameleers would make a unique book if treated with dash and personal feeling, not too much blood and guts and obscene stuff.' Reid ultimately wrote the book which was entitled *The Cameleers*. In the same letter Jack told Reid about *Drums of Mer*: 'My next book comes out in September ... a blood-thirsty story of the Torres Strait Islands. It is the natives' own story of themselves, their fights etc. Plenty of action and blood and thunder in it, but according to native historians, all pure fact.'

Ten days later he wrote to MacFarlane on Thursday Island begging him to get a photograph of Gelam and the crater of Mer: 'All island romances of fiction have a crater and buried treasure. But if I had a photo of our crater then I could prove that it really existed.'

On the same day he wrote to MacFarlane he answered a letter from Brian Fitzpatrick of *Sun* Newspapers. Fitzpatrick had written to Jack asking him to write an article for the *Sun* dealing with the 'coloured question'. He gave Jack the title 'The Black, Brown and Brindle of the North'. Jack went to some lengths to explain why he could not and would not write the proposed article:

I wish I could comply. But you see, many of these people are my friends. The question is involved to an extent quite unrealised by the people down South. I have worked with and travelled with the ordinary half-caste, whether black, brown, white or yellow, as similarly I have met the well-educated coloured people and moreover been a guest in their homes. The trouble is that I know these people intimately, particularly the coloured folk of Cape York Peninsula, Thursday Island, the islands of the Torres Strait, and quite a number of the coloured people who count of the South Pacific. Quite numbers are proud of their family blood but are very unhappy at the thought of colour.

You see, there are innumerable degrees in 'colour'. Quite a number of owners of large plantations, of pearling vessels, traders and business men too, have coloured blood in their veins, but such would never be guessed at by people down here. And they are trying to live it down. To give you an idea of what I mean. Not very long ago, a highly polished guest at the Metropole was really a coloured friend of mine, son of a highly respected man up North. The lad had come down here for his wedding. He married a Sydney girl who alas did not dream of the tragedy which might possibly be. Well, that lad is a gentleman to the finger tips; when he or his brothers are down here they are guests at some of the nicest Sydney homes. I have been a guest and have been treated with the nicest of hospitality at this lad's island home.

I know personally many such, and as I can only write of life as I have seen it I could not write a serious article without putting at least some of my convictions in it. And this would ill repay friendships.

Jack probably knew a large cross-section of 'coloured' people in the north better than anyone else in Sydney and he had a deep respect for their powers of clairvoyance and mental telepathy. Since the time he had spent on the Peninsula travelling with of its native tribes and the extensive time compiling the *Drums of Mer* material on Murray Island he had become fascinated by psychic phenomena. Many times he had seen the Aborigines respond to warnings from their brothers, warnings which came unbidden, and many times saved them from death at the hands of enemy tribes. There were instances of his own psychic experiences; together with the recounted experiences of others they convinced him that such phenomena were not imagination.

One of Jack's experiences had taken place on the night of 16 December 1916 while he stood sentry duty outside Maghdaba on the perimeter of the Plains of Palestine. While thinking of Phoenicians, Babylonians, kings of Persia, Roman legions, the Saracens and Crusaders and Arab hordes, he saw phantom soldiers 'gather in curious groups around the dying Anzacs. And I could see quite plainly the spirits of the Anzacs arising and staring at the weird soldiers gazing so silently back.'

The scene became very real for him:

I forgot my duty—clean forgot everything except a shadowy sense of desert and real live phantoms all around me. There was this calm steady sort of chap standing beside me explaining, not in rough speech, but putting pictures in my mind and before my eyes lucidly and clearly; showing me the huge armies who are really watching our tiny army all along the old Darb el Sultani right from Egypt to Palestine.

As further proof of psychic phenomena there was the vision shared by hundreds of men a few nights later in the same area. On 25 December 1916 troops riding back from the Maghdaba engagement were suddenly enshrouded in blinding clouds of dust. The column of exhausted men, their nerves strained to breaking point, had not slept in four nights and they had ridden ninety miles. All were snatching sleep in the saddle when hundreds saw the 'queerest visions—weird-looking soldiers were riding beside them, many were mounted on strange animals. Hordes walked right amongst the horses making not the slightest sound. The column rode through towns with lights gleaming from the shuttered windows of quaint buildings. The country was all waving green fields and trees and flower gardens. Numbers of men are speaking of what they saw in a most interesting, queer way. There were tall stone temples with marble pillars and swinging oil lamps—our fellows could smell the incense—and white mosques with stately minarets.'

The men didn't mind speaking openly of their collective vision because at that same time General Sir Harry Chauvel and one of his officers had galloped off into the darkness, both men thinking that they had seen a fox.

Jack delved into the occult over a long period of time. In 1931 after Lasseter's disappearance he and several of his friends had held the occasional séance in the hope of locating Lasseter. There is an undated letter from a gentleman in residence at Raraku in Mosman which contains a map drawn by a Mrs Scott while in a trance, showing the location of the reef. The writer notes that he 'weighed a rabbit's ectoplasm' at the exact time of the drawing. There is no statement of whether the drawing of the reef was dependent on the weight of the rabbit's ectoplasm or if each was an unconnected act. Obviously neither resulted in the finding of the lost reef.

Jack was still studying the occult in 1933. A letter to Frank Reid, himself a witness to the strange scene after the battle for Maghdaba, would imply that both were in search of a reliable medium. Reid had written to him requesting confirmation of the veracity of Eleanor Morrell, a psychic medium whom he was considering visiting on a trek down from North Queensland. Jack answered his letter on 1 June: 'Eleanor Morrell has a good name down here. However I saw her some time ago and was not at all impressed. I am quite convinced of survival after two years of study of various phenomena. But it is extraordinarily hard to come in contact with a medium who can produce anything that counts. There are numerous circles down here and the comparatively few good mediums are all constantly engaged, they rarely leave the one circle.'

Jack wished for the ability to engage in a little clairvoyance himself. The replies from the police constables in the outback were coming in but many still missed the little details that Jack needed. Once again he wrote to all the constables, only this time his questions were more specific.

Chapter Seventeen
TOP GEAR

1933 was Jack's year. People wanted to see him and hear him and newspaper editors urged him to write more articles. In between all these engagements his Letters to the Editor appeared regularly in most Sydney newspapers and to add to the frenetic pace he took to the air waves on radio 2KY.

The *Bulletin* was still Jack's favourite magazine. When the editor, S.H. Prior, died, Jack attended his funeral. The passing of this man, whom Jack felt he had come to know through the letters which accompanied the many cheques he had received over the years, closed an era in Jack's life.

The loss set him thinking of the many odd places he had been when he had received a *Bulletin* cheque and prompted him to write a tribute to Prior and send it to F.E. Baume of the *Sunday Sun*. 8 June 1933 he wrote:

> Enclosed is an appreciation of S. H. Prior. I have often seen his name on a cheque, and wondered what kind of a man he was. It was the *Bulletin* cheque, one of those funny ones with the cartoon of the quaint old gentleman who never has any money, so he pays his way with an IOU. I have cashed those cheques in the most unlikely places, in bark shanties in the Never-Never, at far out stations right away towards the rim, at lonely opal fields, at isolated gold camps in the farthest North, once even to the Japanese skipper of a pearling lugger on the shores of the Arafura sea. And the cash part has never been questioned, in such confidence is the 'Bushman's Bible' held in the far outback.
>
> I have known a storekeeper, in delight at cashing such a cheque, frame it and nail it above the counter to be pored over and discussed by the nomad travellers from far and wide.
>
> At receiving S.H. Prior's first letter, I felt a warm glow to the meaning of the lines. I had scribbled an article from a lonely but fertile valley tucked away among the mountains in Cape York Peninsula. He wrote an awfully nice letter with just the right sort of encouragement and through it all a wish that Australians should be

taught to know all about her furthest away places so that we should know where to send pioneers that they might pave the way for future Australian homes.

Throughout years of wandering, I received an occasional letter, each breathing a quiet spirit of comradeship and an unbreakable faith that ours was a wonderful land, and that the very best that any man can do is help her in any way in his power, no matter how big, no matter how small.

On 15 June he wrote to Mrs I. Grey of radio 2KY who had asked for copies of his radio scripts. She had queried the existence of the eccentric characters of *Men of the Jungle* and mentioned that she had a friend in northern NSW. Jack answered that the 'manuscripts of the radio talks might not be available as the typists souvenir them as curiosities', and, in reference to *Men of the Jungle*:

It merely is an everyday account of our life up there for some years. Even the names of all the persons mentioned are their true names, as are the districts. Since the book has come out, I've got letters from some of the people mentioned recalling the 'old days'. The 'Old Hatter' is a general favourite among readers ... his real name is George Stewart, a well-known resident of Mt Molloy up to a couple of years ago when he died.

Then he closed the letter with 'If ever I'm going Nor'West in NSW I'll call on your friend—hope she's a "she" with the curves in the right places!'.

I do not know if the reference to Mrs Grey's friend was the type of flippant remark that Jack thought was expected of him or if he thought that it added a certain dash to his persona or whether, in his own way, he was flagging the fact that he was living alone and available. Possibly it was a little of each, although unnecessary, for according to his nephew, Dr Ion Morrison, Jack's only problem with women lay in defending himself from their attentions.

On the same day he received a letter posted from 'Native Camp Ooldea' written by Daisy Bates in which she outlined her work and life with the natives of Western Australia and thanked Jack for a copy of *Flynn of the Inland*, *Men of the Jungle* and *The Desert Column*. In her letter she wrote that the West Australian Government had returned her manuscript of native customs as having 'no commercial value'. Obviously both Cousins and the West Australian Government shared a common lack of vision together with an eye for profit. If either had published the work it would have been an acquisition which, although perhaps not commercially profitable at the time, would have been of great value to posterity and a publication which in years to come would have brought much acclaim.

Jack's opinion of the treatment of the Aborigines by whites was generally highly valued and he had come to be regarded as an authority on the subject. A cutting of an editorial which appeared 19 June reported on the British Commonwealth League Conference and examined the treatment of Aborigines by white Australians. A witness at the Conference, Miss Ruby Rich, 'a lady whom Sydney had long known for her publicist energy, especially in the cult of racial hygiene', had read a document from a western missionary's wife which claimed that the Aborigines were 'enslaved, debauched, and mauled by the white people'. The press was at once scandalised by these comments but relieved by a statement from its favourite author: 'Ion Idriess, a witness to be trusted came forward with a wholly different picture and a quite reassuring story concerning the life of blacks in contact with white men which refuted the information from Miss Rich.'

At that time Jack no doubt presented the facts as he saw them. However, in the following year, which he was to spend in Western Australia, and during his reading of detailed reports written by Constable Morey while stationed at the mission settlement on Groote Eylandt in that same year, Jack formed a different opinion, not of the average white settlers, but of the missionaries in charge of the education and welfare of the Aboriginal mixed blood girls on Groote Eylandt.

Despite all the public acclaim the promotion of his books was still uppermost in his mind. A&R had attempted to reach the German market by selling the translation and publishing rights of *Lasseter's Last Ride* and *Gold Dust and Ashes* to a German publishing house, but the Germans had declined due to 'the present worsening economic climate'. The home market was excellent but Jack decided to do a little judicious marketing of his own.

On 11 July he wrote to Snowy Baker at the Riviera Club in Santa Monica. Baker had long ago taken up residence in the United States and was well connected in movie circles:

> You will be puzzled to remember me perhaps after all these years, but I am one of the bone-heads you licked into amateur shape in your Sydney studio days. Since then, but only in the last couple of years, I have become a fairly well known author. So in memory of the old days and some punches I haven't forgotten I'm taking the

liberty of sending you copies of my books. Perhaps the right crosses, with which your brother in particular rattled my jaw, put some sense in my head and made me 'use it' as he so often insisted. Anyway I've learned to use my head better than my hands, and here are the books.

The astute Baker recognised the gift of the books for what it was. He wrote thanking Jack for the books but warned him not to trust 'movie people or movie rights'.

The gathering of the material for the mounted police book was not going well. The answers to his letters were coming in but somehow the men continued to miss the point. Once again he sent out more letters.

There are many people who have dismissed Jack's work as being equivalent to the efforts of the average reporter. The mounted police book, *Man Tracks*, disproves this criticism. Only someone who had experienced living on the track in desolate, lonely country, someone who had been taught to observe the tracks and signs of man, animal and reptile in the bush, someone who had lived with Aborigines, someone who had instinctively noted the changes in terrain as he travelled through the outback, could have asked the detailed questions of the police in the field as Jack did. Only Jack would have had the temerity to have kept asking for details about the same incidents, the same areas, of the same men for over a year, in order to compile and write *Man Tracks*.

He used every ploy he could think of to make the policemen respond with the material he needed. He flattered, entreated and appealed to their national pride: 'The Australian Mounted Policeman is unknown and it is only fair that he should take his place in the historical annals of the development of this country.' And, 'The book will almost certainly, in time, be "on the pictures" and I want every story in it to eclipse the stories of the Canadian Mounted.'

Getting the information was still like drawing teeth from a jaw locked in death. When all else failed he sent the typed stories to each contributor asking them to add to, or to change and correct. In these drafts he left spaces in the copy for the contributor to write in the missing information. Still the work dragged on.

Because of the attendant problems related to acquiring the multiplicity of details he wanted, and despite all his efforts, *Man Tracks* was not published until 1935.

Jack's fan mail came from many people. Most wrote care of A&R and some praised only the publisher for the publication of

Jack's books. All letters were passed on to Jack. One from the Dean of the Faculty of Medicine, University of Melbourne, written to A&R, was as follows: 'I have read with immense satisfaction *Men of the Jungle*. This is the real thing that I have been waiting for. I congratulate you on the service you are doing to Australia in publishing a book like that. It is a splendid antidote against the hothouse degeneracy of some recent English effusions, I value the book highly.' No word of acknowledgement for the author.

Jack kept all his fan mail. Among these letters were many which asked him for assistance to find the most likely place to look for gold. Many told harrowing details of the length of time the writers had been out of work, some for three years or more, and each hoped that Jack might be able to point to some undiscovered goldfield which would alleviate their financial distress.

Some writers became regular correspondents and regarded Jack as a friend. One of these was a Helen Walker who always addressed him as 'My Friend'. Judging from the tone of her letters she seems to have been a young girl. Not only did she ask Jack questions about the books and the people that he wrote about, she also wrote of her life in a North Queensland tent town and about her family. Helen's letters continued to come to Jack for a number of years and Jack answered them all in detail; never once were his letters to her short notes, and he always inquired after her family.

There is one letter which he received on 26 July from Norm, an Anzac mate living in Brisbane, which gives the only indication in that otherwise fulfilling year that all was not right with Jack and that he was 'unhappy and in difficulties'. Norm extended his sympathy and his 'hopes for his peace of mind'. Just what Norm was referring to is difficult to say. Maybe the news of Dick's death had disturbed Jack, but as he did not keep a draft of his letter to Norm, as was his usual habit, I can only conjecture that the subject matter was personal and perhaps involved Eta and her children, Maurice and Judy, or knowledge that Eta was pregnant.

While Jack was researching *Man Tracks* he formed a firm friendship with Mr C. Treadgold of the Office of the Police Commissioner, Police Department of Western Australia. Treadgold became heavily involved in the compilation of the material for the book. Taking a deep interest in it he sent Jack much detailed information about native tracking practices and a large number of photographs. It was also Treadgold who carried out the final proofing. Clearing the work for its accuracy Treadgold had the last word on what was to be published.

One of Jack's problems lay in obtaining enough stories of

'white desperados' or a 'few good cattle duffing yarns'. On 17 July he wrote to Treadgold:

> This week I am starting on the Mounted book, with the object of having it ready for publication in March next. I have not got sufficient of quite the type of copy I want. Considerably more than enough has come in to write a full book of strong native interest. But the reading public, I feel certain, would greet more heartily a book in which there was a 50% 'white interest'.
>
> There is material among the Mounted men for a really epic book. I would very much like to feature, among other things, some first class stories where fine endurance and tracking feats have been performed. Readers would be keenly interested in this phase of police work. I can get the endurance easily enough, but for the tracking I would have to use my own knowledge and imagination to a fairly large extent. Several excellent stories of this description have come in, but the writers do not seem to grasp what I want. They will write of tracking natives for hundreds of miles but will give no details at all of how they did it. They answer that it is all in a day's work but don't seem to realise that the man in Pitt Street would be intensely interested to see them do that work.

Treadgold responded with a wealth of detail and three new stories. Jack was delighted with two of the stories.

Although he still felt uncomfortable in front of an audience Jack changed his mind and accepted an invitation, which he had previously refused, to address the Agricultural Bureau at Hawkesbury College on 28 July 1933. The topic selected by the Bureau centred on his experiences with the Aborigines. The address was duly reported in the press and Jack was quoted as saying 'I have never known a single shooting or poisoning of an Aboriginal by a white.' Which was true in Jack's case.

Jack's life was getting out of hand. The 2KY radio programme was responsible for additional fan mail. Letters poured in from listeners, and he answered them all along with his regular fan mail. Somehow he managed to find time to dash off a note to his sister Ildyce's husband, George Morrison, in Grafton, 7 August: 'I have been doing a lot of spouting lately and all very well. Never thought a few years ago that I'd be standing up on a platform telling city people things.'

By August 1933, the Depression was showing positive signs of easing. 'Things are fairly cheerful down here', he wrote to Frank Pryke on Pryke's return to New Guinea from Bathurst, 'what with big wool sales and gold at eight pound per ounce, not to mention quite an appreciable livening up of the building trade, most people have the tail up. The share market has been sky high since you've been away, share buyers and sellers must have turned over many thousands these last three weeks especially. Splendid reports are coming in from W.A., an old time official of the Mines Dept. just returned from the west told me that the activity on the fields over there reminds him of the boom days.'

Despite his highly specific letters to the mounted policemen he was still unable to get the responses he needed. He decided that the only way to get the material he wanted was to go on an extended trip and visit all the police stations that he could in the outback. So once again he wrote to Treadgold:

> Bar any unforeseen circumstances, I will visit Perth approximately towards the end of September or early October. This Mounted book is looming up in importance and it looks as if I'll have to do the job in a very thorough manner...from Adelaide and Port Augusta I wish to come straight to Perth. I am looking forward to meeting you and will take the opportunity, if I may, of getting as much first hand material as I can...I have an idea in my mind of from the West going around Australia and of visiting, if possible, as many of the most isolated Police Posts as I can. I would like to go through the Kimberleys and from there across the Territory. From thence down into the Centre (or into the Centre from the west then back into the Kimberleys). From the Territory across the Gulf country into Queensland.

The two men continued to correspond regularly for many years after the publication of *Man Tracks*. Treadgold, after such protracted exposure to Jack's passion for detail, formed the habit of cutting articles and reports of unusual crimes in Western Australia and the Northern Territory from the Western Australian newspapers and forwarding them to Jack. While they formally addressed each other as 'Mr Treadgold' and 'Mr Idriess' over many years of corresponding, 'Mr Idriess' built up a formidable file of information on crime in Western Australia which related to the outback, police and black tracker exploits, heart-rending tales of either dead or alive, lost and found whites, and the stray story of restless Aborigines breaking out of the lock-ups and a few native wars. No doubt it was Jack's intention to use this treasure trove of fact in future books.

Jack's popularity continued to boom along with the improving economy. In the midst of everything C. J. A. Moses, the Talk Editor of the ABC, decided not to be outdone by 2KY and asked Jack to handle a general outback programme speaking on various items of interest. This was too much.

On 29 August he wrote to Moses:

I suggest that Joe Bourke, Patrol Officer New Guinea who was in command of the punitive expedition that razed the notorious Kaisenik Village and who was in the thick of the excitement during the cannibal outbreaks, would be an interesting speaker for the ABC. He also opened up the Bonang Track to the Eddie Creek gold-fields at the time of the dysentery epidemic; one of the early men into the field, won gold in a very large way. He has led several expeditions into unknown country. Before the goldfields at Keranga Creek, he was a plantation manager. Always a first-class raconteur.

Although Jack had no intention of doing any more radio work and no intention of taking on any more writing than he could handle he didn't let the requests lie. Wherever possible he turned the editors towards other writers or in the case of a Mrs Drayton of New Guinea, who had sent him some interesting material in the hope that he would use it, he personally visited Baume of the *Sunday Sun* and suggested that Mrs Drayton be asked to write an article as 'she could use the money'.

Throughout the period of collecting the *Man Tracks* material Jack was being bombarded by newspaper and magazine editors with requests for him to write articles. Twice he refused the Melbourne *Herald*, saying that he had too much work. The editor, A. Watkin Wynne, was persistent and came back with a third request. Jack refused again because he was planning to take the extended trip to Western Australia. However, when Jack was pass-ing through Melbourne on his way to Perth and points north, Wynne managed to contract Jack to write a series of ten articles about outback Western Australia for the Melbourne *Herald*.

Jack was expected to be an authority on all things relative to the outback. On 6 September he received a telegram from the *Courier Mail*, Brisbane: 'Mr Idriess, c/o Angus and Robertson. Will you do article Japanese luggers responsibility native trouble Arnhem Land if so telegraph one thousand words tonight. Sligo *Courier Mail*.'

Jack had one or two theories of his own about the Japanese and had long thought that these people were not only casting acquisitive eyes towards Australia but that their fishing boats were also being used for more than 'fishing' in the accepted sense.

Jack had been correct when he had written to Treadgold that his books were being increasingly used in schools as educational material. In September and October 1933 excerpts from *Gold Dust and Ashes* were reproduced in school magazines issued to primary school pupils. Excerpts from Jack's books would continue to be serialized in school magazines for many years. Ultimately a book known as *Gems from Idriess* would become required reading for school children.

Before leaving on his West Australian trip Jack attempted to pull 'The Fighting MacKenzie' manuscript into draft form.

Known to the soldiers at Gallipoli, the Peninsula and through the French theatres of war as 'Mac', MacKenzie had been the first Salvation Army Chaplain to be appointed to the AIF. Prior to that he had served with the Salvation Army for many years in China.

When Jack had started to research 'The Fighting Mac' the plan had been to publish it as a companion volume to *The Desert Column*. It was to have been a book which, in theory, would have had all the pathos of a man torn between his moral and religious convictions, fighting shoulder to shoulder with the men of the 4th Battalion, to which he was attached.

The name 'Fighting Mac', given to MacKenzie by Sydney returned soldiers, had led Cousins and Jack to think that MacKenzie had carried arms. Although it was true that Mac had wanted to accompany the men of the 4th in the Lone Pine assault, 6 August 1915, he had given up the idea when he was refused permission to accompany them if he didn't carry a rifle with fixed bayonet. Jack found that Chaplain MacKenzie could hardly be hailed as a dashing figure.

However MacKenzie's contribution to the morale of the men had gone beyond praying for their souls and the safety of their bodies or accompanying them into battle. His colonel, Onslow Thompson, had put him in charge of the distribution of gifts sent to the troops by the Comforts Fund. MacKenzie turned the distribution of these gifts into a pleasant weekly interlude by instituting a weekly 'sing-song'. His community singing gatherings, which entertained and eased the tension for many, came to be regarded as the greatest gift he handed out each week.

MacKenzie had one other claim to fame; he was responsible for the Lonely Soldier letters. It distressed Mac to see disappointed diggers who did not receive letters from home at Mail Call. Determined that all the men would receive a letter he wrote to his friends at home asking them to write and requested that they ask their friends also to write to A Lonely Soldier, c/o Captain MacKenzie, 4th Battalion. In due course Mac was receiving sacks of mail from home. He carried these letters in his pockets to give to those who didn't receive correspondence at Mail Call.

Jack managed to come up with an outline for the book but the substance was lacking. Both Jack and Cousins agreed that although MacKenzie was a warm and caring individual, the instigation of 'Lonely Soldier' letters, gift distribution and sing-songs were just not enough to build a best-seller on. This was an instinctive marketing decision built on the understanding that the reading public would have preferred the recounting of human conflict, bloody scenes and terror, to the story of a man doing a quiet job behind the lines.

Before the decision was taken to drop the project Jack had completed a large part of the manuscript. Although it had been given the thumbs down he kept it, planning to attempt to salvage it at a later date.

With the end of 'The Fighting Mac' project he turned his efforts towards promoting himself in Western Australia. Several articles appeared in October in the *West Australian* in Perth. One, 'A Land Forgotten', referred to the old Jardine Plantation on the Cape York Peninsula as being the only coconut plantation on the mainland of Australia and referred to what Jack believed to be the growing Japanese interest in Australia.

By 1 November he had left Sydney, staying at the Royal Artillery Hotel on Elizabeth Street in Melbourne on his way to the western states.

The train trip from Sydney had taken twenty-four hours and Jack's mood was not good on his arrival in Melbourne. Alec Chisholm, then editor of the *Argus*, together with Charles Barrett and a group of press photographers, was waiting to meet him at the station. Chisholm and company had met both preceding trains; after two unsuccessful attempts to shower the visiting celebrity with fuss and fanfare their sense of occasion and mood of hearty greeting had dissipated. Alec Chisholm had lost all his bonhomie, resorting to swearing roundly, while Charles Barrett, being of religious bent, struggled to retain his Christian charity.

Barrett, who was known to both Jack and Walter Cousins, was frantically involved in organising an exhibition of Aboriginal artefacts and Australian 'bush' books for the coming 1934 Melbourne Centenary celebration. All profit from the exhibition was to be donated to the Australian Inland Mission.

On 8 November 1933, still in Melbourne, Jack wrote to Cousins that he been a 'guest at lunch with Theodore Fink "Melbourne's millionaire", Sir Keith Murdoch and a half dozen lesser bods'.

Sir Keith Murdoch's *Herald* pressured Jack to write articles for publication while he was travelling in the West, as did Chisholm for the *Argus*. Barrett, wishing to foster his sponsor's continuing goodwill, urged him to accept the *Herald* offer 'for his own good'. Jack however consistently declined, as he had done in the past, due to his heavy workload.

He was not seduced by all the attention being lavished on him, neither was he unaware of their reasons for doing so. Barrett needed him to gather Aboriginal artefacts from northern Australia for his exhibition and Jack knew Barrett was also using him to ensure that Angus and Robertson would support the exhibition with large numbers of books for display and sale. He knew that articles about western and northern Australian Aborigines, in which there was a keen interest due to the recent Caledon Bay massacres, would increase the *Herald* circulation, which in turn, would create greater public interest in Barrett's exhibition.

He was not excessively concerned about Barrett's transparent manipulations, nor was he of a mind to be coerced by lunches and chauffeur-driven cars. In fact he was most relaxed until a meeting with the arrogant son of an English publisher, a Mr Lane, changed his mind. The young man's derogatory remarks about Australian publishing and Australian authors were like 'a red rag to a bull'. Jack wrote to Cousins:

> Mr Lane expressed the opinion that my phenomenal vogue will not last. He thought that poorer and poorer books would be produced until the public would not buy them. I said that a new era had more than dawned for Australian literature, that it would never look back, that better writers than me would arise and their sales would help my books yet again and cement the demand for Australian books. I gather that overseas bookmen look with great disfavour on this increase in the popularity of Australian books, and that they are only just beginning to be alarmed that the 'vogue' might last.

It was his desire to obtain greater publicity and support for the struggling Australian publishing industry that had moved Jack to sign a contract with the *Herald*'s Watkin Wynne to write the series of ten articles. He had notified Cousins of his contract with the *Herald* and warned him not to breathe a word to anyone about the fee of ten guineas per article and payment of fifty per cent of the syndication profit.

Before Jack left Melbourne the *Herald* took the opportunity to promote the writer now under contract by publishing one of his articles on 7 November about how and where Jack and his mates had enjoyed the running of the Melbourne Cup while prospecting on the Cape York Peninsula. And a follow-up, published on 8 November, 'Pageant of Colour ... Author has first visit', reported on the running of the Cup and Jack's impressions of the gala day.

Cousins was suitably impressed by Jack's contract with the *Herald* and reported on 10 November that Christmas sales were 'working up well'. Then, on 15 November Cousins cautioned him against becoming involved in a proposal to commit *Lasseter's Last Ride* to film: 'every picture made in Australia to date has been spoilt because of stinted funds.'

Encouraging signs that Australia was pulling out of depression continued. Wool sales were predicted to reach a record for the season, mining all over Australia was very active and the building trade was picking up; however, retail sales were still sluggish. As far as Jack could see the booksellers were not pulling out all stops to boost the economy. The window displays, or rather, the lack of Australian books displayed in Melbourne bookshop windows, upset him. He wished again and again that A&R's 'Mr Liddle was in Melbourne to brighten up the bookshop windows'.

Close to the end of November Jack moved on to Adelaide. He was disgusted to find that Adelaide bookshops were featuring English novels: 'I am convinced that there are scores of thousands of Australians who have not heard of Australian books.'

Disenchanted by the lack of awareness shown by the bookselling fraternity in Adelaide he moved on to Port Augusta. His ego smarting, he wrote to Cousins in stunned disbelief. 'They've never heard of Idriess! Ticket collector, publican, PO Clerk or otherwise have all failed to recognise the name of Idriess!' Cousins reminded Jack he had warned him not to expect too much adulation from the town on the edge of the Nullarbor.

Crossing the Nullarbor by train to Perth gave him a view of Australia which he had never seen before: treeless, endless and arid. 'This is the State of big distances with a vengeance, a hard country too.' But the unforgiving landscape beckoned him. 'I can smell romance everywhere here.'

Arriving in Kalgoorlie he almost forgot Australian publishing and the fact that he had become a writer. He found a large town bustling with crowds in the street, a mile of shops. All the talk was gold, gold, gold. Some stores had models of mining machinery at work in the windows, while others had dryblowers, windlasses, cowhide buckets and all manner of mining tools for sale on the footpaths outside. Jack briefly caught gold fever but managed to overcome the infection with indignation when he found not one copy of *Prospecting for Gold* in any of the shop windows. To compound the shock, there was not one Australian book to be found in any of the 'so called bookshops, only two bob English novels!'.

In typical Idriess crusading mode he made straight for the newspaper offices to 'put the newspaper men right as to A&R and Australian publishing and soundly bagged overseas publishers'.

Arriving in Perth on 17 November he went directly to the West Australian Police Secretary's office. Treadgold was holding the material for the proposed 'police book' which had been gathered at Jack's request from all over the state. He was taken aback by the amount of the material handed to him by Treadgold: 'two great piles of paper which I could hardly carry for the weight.'

A car was placed at his disposal. Apart from setting to work reading the police material he made his usual bookshop inspections. In Perth, as in Adelaide and Port Augusta, he found that there was little awareness of Australian publishing. Once again he took himself to the newspaper offices and 'disabused quite a lot of minds. I hope that they publish it all, not like the Melbourne press who ignored my statements about Australian publishing being equal to anything overseas. To each reviewer I explain a lot about Australian books in the hope that in the future they will get a better reception.'

During his stay in Perth he was asked to visit all the bookshops and spend an hour or two autographing books. Coldly he refused for he thought this to be a cheap and shoddy way to gain advantage over other authors who were not able do the same. Apart from the moral objection he couldn't see enough stock on hand to autograph!

While the Perth population might not have been especially aware of Australian publishing or Jack's other books, they were aware of *The Desert Column*. Jack observed that almost every man in Perth wore a returned soldier's badge and that the 'returned spirit is very strong here'. Everywhere Jack went he was quizzed and congratulated on *The Desert Column*.

The excessive amount of information the police had provided him with almost convinced him that he should stay a while longer in Perth and rush the writing of the 'police book' for publication in March 1934 as originally planned. However, Treadgold had made the necessary arrangements for him to travel north to join a mounted police patrol going through the Kimberley so he had no choice but to leave the work until he returned.

Before he left Perth, the writer Ernestine Hill called on him to offer whatever help she could to make his trip north easier. Jack failed to see how this would be possible. One Emily Meares, also concerned with his well-being, provided him with five introductions to station owners in the north. Jack didn't avail himself of the courtesy, all five notes written on blue linen paper, enclosed in their blue linen envelopes, remained sealed until I opened them myself some fifty-four years later.

It was Treadgold however who provided, as far as Jack was concerned, the most practical piece of equipment for a man proposing to travel through dangerous territory where the Aborigines, in many areas, could not be classed as friendly—he was given a Colt .44. Treadgold insisted Jack take it and not hesitate to use it if it became necessary.

The element of danger didn't concern Jack, this was what he had come for!

Chapter Eighteen
PERTH TO BROOME

WHEN Ernestine Hill visited him yet again in Perth Jack took her for 'tea and cakes', but the lady did not tell him anything of interest. He wrote to Cousins that Ernestine's visit 'ended up in my advising her on her book to be; she is a nice little sort though and as she has wandered quite a lot and has a good style of pen she ought to turn out a decent book. The little writing that I have seen of hers I like better than any other writer I know except for Davison's *Man Shy*. I've wondered why she did not keep our acquaintance in Sydney after Baume's introduction.'

Jack also reported to Cousins that he had received a visit from representatives of the naval department. He was asked if he would 'keep his eyes open up North—especially on the coast' and to report any information at all that he felt might be of interest to the navy. As Jack was determined to do as little travelling by sea as possible he refused their offer of charts on which to pin-point any activities which he found to be suspicious.

Reports in the local press that an English company was equipping an aeroplane in Perth with a view to using it for aerial gold searching tickled his funny bone. 'The idea of finding gold from the air seems ridiculous to me, it is hard enough to find it with pick and shovel on the land'.

Most of Jack's letters written to Cousins from Western Australia and the Northern Territory during 1934 closed with a cheeky message to Rebecca Wiley, whom Jack always called 'Bess'. It appears that Rebecca Wiley had joined the Firm as a teenager. Working part-time, she had been responsible for addressing book mailing wrappers and keeping customers up to date with advance information on forthcoming publications. Her responsibilities embraced the operation of the Firm's switchboard and the book-shop's cash desk.

Jack was just ten years old when Rebecca, aged nineteen, gained full-time employment with A&R. Rebecca's employment ceased with A&R for a period of five years during which time her mother and a sister died. When she ultimately resumed her employment in 1909 she assumed control of the Mailing Department; Jack was experiencing his first season gouging for opals at Lightning Ridge. Later, when Jack was associated with A&R, he took some delight in writing notes such as 'Remember me to Bess and tell her to keep her knees together' and 'By Jove it is hot here, it would even thaw out our Bess' obviously amused him, if not Rebecca. Clearly not all Jack's thoughts were centred on the lofty pursuits of literature and the promoting of Australian publishing.

Jack had wined and dined at Parliament House in such august company as that of Sir James and Lady Owen, Sir John Kirwan, A. A. Coverley, member for the Kimberley, F. J. Wise, member for Gascoyne; he had been irritated by a patronising 'colonel's lady' who asked him at a civic reception given by Sir James and Lady Owen, 'Are you famous? You're a poet and I haven't read any of your books'. This was enough for him to decide not to stay in Perth for the coming Christmas festivities. He upped his ports, packed his colt .44 and set out for Meekatharra en route to Derby on 6 December 1933.

♦

MEEKATHARRA, four hundred miles from Perth, is harsh land. The town simmered in a vast expanse of low, grey scrub. The surrounding red apologies for hills were clad with ironstone. A blistering hot sun fused the landscape into a surrealist tableau of white heat. Meekatharra was a wild, colourful town. What appeared to be dust storms in the distance heralded the coming of big cattle mobs which moved into town almost every day. The squatters were hard-bitten types, the wrinkles around their eyes etched into weatherbeaten skin by the cruel West Australian sun.

Day and night the pubs poured balm for parched throats. Wild drinking bouts could last for twenty-four hours and fist fights were not unusual. 'A few days ago there was a bonza,' Jack wrote to Cousins. 'A Dago stabbed a man in the back, a free fight followed in which the Police joined, the big sergeant laying them out right and left. He back-handed a fellow who attempted to stab him in the back and when the chap ran for his gun the sergeant simply took it off him. How men can fight in this heat has got me beat.'

Jack was an interested and bemused spectator. He had witnessed and been in a number of fights in the past, but few of such savage intensity. The lack of respect for the law exhibited by the locals made him feel as if he had regressed a century into a western frontier town.

Soon after arriving in town Jack was visited by a number of station owners. Surprised, he greeted men who had travelled almost four hundred miles to invite him to visit their holdings. One or two of these visitors had come from properties which were situated on the fringe of the white-inhabited country which lay far to the east, holdings surrounded by land peopled by Aborigines who had little or no contact with white Australians. Jack was greatly impressed by the effort the men had made by coming to Meekatharra to extend to him their invitations of hospitality.

'There are a dozen books here in Meekatharra, a man could spend years here easily, without dreaming of going further north,' he wrote to Cousins.

Hot Meekatharra was no stranger to authors. Green's Pub had hosted a few notables. Curle, Priestly, Prichard and Hatfield had stayed there, and some 'Yank' scientists seeking some remarkable beetles. Jack broke the tradition by dossing down not at Green's Pub but at the 'Big Pub'.

The publican's wife at Green's was aggrieved: she would have liked to have had Jack's name on the register. But what else could be expected of writers? Novelists and journalists passing through joyfully presented both legs to the locals to be pulled. Avidly they absorbed every tall story. Then, not content with obviously extreme subject matter, the wordsmiths embroidered it, writing reports and books which, as far as the people of Meekatharra and surrounding districts were concerned, were a far cry from the truth.

Katharine Susannah Prichard was judged to be responsible for the distortions which appeared in print. A young policeman told Jack that the attitude of the locals towards her after the publication of her novel, *Coonardoo*, was one of derision and anger. They believed that her sensitive treatment of a melancholy relationship between a white station owner and an Aboriginal woman fictionalised the life of the man whose hospitality Katharine Susannah Prichard had accepted while staying at his property, Turee, prior to writing *Coonardoo*. In their eyes Prichard had inferred in her book that her host was a 'gin-man' and 'more'. It is hard to decide which was regarded as her ultimate sin—the suggestion of cohabitation between black and white, the abuse of her host's hospitality or that a white woman had written about such an embarrassing subject.

The locals also told Jack about their most infamous character, 'Brumby Leike'. In Perth the police had assured him this desperado

179

would tell him with shameless gusto tales of how he 'beat 'em', ''em' being the police. To hear his stories however, Jack would have had to prove himself to 'Brumby' to be innocent of all association with the police. Jack was assured that if he failed to convince 'Brumby' the police were also poison to him, then the wild man would simply shoot him. Jack found no difficulty in passing up that opportunity.

Before Jack left the district he trekked the one hundred miles or so to the gold town Wiluna, a relic of the old roaring days. Trucking was fast outstripping the camel as a method of transport but here, in the closing days of 1933, camel carts were still hauling gold-bearing rock from the mines to the crushing plants in town.

Unable to avail himself of all the invitations to visit the outlying stations he had received during his brief stay at Meekatharra he reluctantly took the seat that the police had booked for him in the mail truck which left town once every two weeks.

Jack left every town walking backwards, tormented by the nagging fear that behind him lurked a priceless story he had missed, a place he should have explored, or a 'character' he should have met. At the same time, he was excited by the possibility that an even greater tale was about to unfold, one which he would miss if he didn't move on.

At every stopover it was the same story: 'There is a man you must meet! He is only fifty miles away but,'—pause—'that is, if he's there now. But if he's not, he's sure to be back in a month or so.' Several reasons forced him further north at a pace he would not have chosen. One of these, his unresolved personal involvement with Eta, lent a degree of urgency to his movements.

It is only possible to conjecture on what passed between Eta and Jack prior to his departure. I assume that when she told him she was three months pregnant with her third child, his arrangements with Treadgold to accompany the mounted police patrol were too advanced to be cancelled.

The question uppermost in his mind would have been the identity of the child's father—Jesse Gibson or himself? Under the circumstances he would not have approached the trip in pleasant anticipation and, once committed to it, he placed himself in the tortuous position of wanting to be in two places at the one time. 'I wish I was not tied up with that unfortunate affair in Sydney,' he wrote to Cousins in reference to Eta.

Another reason was the fabled 'wet' which was brewing in the Capricornian skies. In reality it was the weather and Treadgold's travel arrangements with the police that kept him on the move, not the desire to return to Sydney and settle his problems.

Reluctantly he took the mail truck to Marble Bar as arranged and made a brief call on Constable Morrow at Peak Hill. His stopover was just long enough for him to form the opinion that the constable was a decent chap and Peak Hill an 'awful place'.

He would have liked to have had the time to stay longer at Marble Bar but Derby was still a long way off. The heat was unbearable and sapped his every inclination to write. He decided that the only way to write books about this land of intense heat and vast distances was to 'loaf through it'.

Loafing, however, was not on Jack's agenda. While he might have claimed to be a lazy man, nothing in his life confirms this point of view. His output during the journey never wavered. Despite heat, constant rain and incessant travelling, he wrote, almost daily, long letters to Cousins and met the contract with the Melbourne *Herald* to supply the ten articles. He also researched and wrote *Forty Fathoms Deep* in draft form, while at the same time gathering material for seven other titles.

While Jack was at Marble Bar he chatted with the Australian Inland Mission Sisters. The women told him that the Bar was a beautiful garden in winter. He found it hard to believe, for the landscape appeared to be one of utter desolation.

From Marble Bar Jack took the train to Port Hedland. His first impression was that Port Hedland, like Marble Bar, was a raw, uninviting place but perhaps marginally more interesting. As he moved north Jack was staggered by the accuracy of his descriptions of Lasseter's and Flynn's country, not only each district but right down to such small details as rocks, animals, grasses and birds.

'I am rather scared in a way when I see it all rolling out before me,' he wrote to Cousins. 'The men out here and those from the Rawlinson and the Petermann Ranges swear by the books and do not question anything in them in the least. It is rather sincere flattery but I only now fully realise what awful mistakes I could have made. This state is entirely different to the eastern states.'

During his short stay at Port Hedland Jack found that the RSL librarian had been buying imported books rather than Australian publications. Like most people the librarian believed that the imported books, priced between four and eight shillings each, were cheaper than Australian books. By the time Jack left for Broome three of his books were on order from Alberts, Perth's biggest bookseller, and Cousins had been advised to post a catalogue to the librarian in Port Hedland.

The push was on to get to Broome but he was forced to cool his heels for a week in Port Hedland while the skipper of the little steamer that made the run to Broome waited for the weather to settle at sea.

While waiting aboard the ship he accepted an invitation from one of the 'boys' who had been delegated to ask him to join their group and have a drink with them. The 'boys' were all interesting men:prospectors, cattle and sheep men, motor transport men, windmill men and airmen. They had heard of Jack and most had read *Lasseter's Last Ride* and *The Desert Column*. This interesting assortment declared themselves to be 'honoured' by his company, but it was Jack who felt honoured and a little embarrassed when they declared him to be the man who 'really writes the real facts of life in these places'.

Steamer and air services out of Broome were about to cease for the duration of the wet season. Jack knew that if he missed these transport facilities his only other travel option was to take the ninety-mile 'Madman's Track' from Port Hedland to Broome. The police and locals assured him that this was a feat for only the game or the foolhardy.

Try as he might he was not able to get either police or civilians to take him over 'Madman's Track'. The waterless track, a horror stretch fit to be traversed only in good weather—either on foot, with mules, or on horseback—had them all bluffed. So he resolved to wait for the steamer. Jack arrived in Broome by sea from Port Hedland on 23 December 1933.

Jack regretted that he had not been able to travel the track which ran around Eighty Mile Beach; it was the only strip of country between Broome and Perth he had not seen. To make matters worse word had come, prior to his departure from Port Hedland, that people at a station out on the edge of the track were expecting him to visit. Jack had been sorely tempted to throw caution to the winds and take the chance of reaching the tiny 'one horse' settlement of De Grey, but he knew the possibility of getting through to Broome from there was very slight. The fact that he was now carrying twenty-seven letters of introduction to station owners along the way had made the trip seem all the more inviting.

Western Australia was hard, dry country but the fifteen hundred miles he had traversed between Perth and Broome had shown him nothing to compare with any one hundred miles of the wild Cape York Peninsula. It was the tamest 'wild' country he had ever been in and it was easy for him to understand how 'motor cranks' and women 'scribblers' had been able to make their way around 'wild' Australia following the same route. Jack was convinced that Peninsula men would laugh in scorn at any 'terrors' the nor'-west had to offer. However, having seen much that the elements could turn on without notice, he covered himself when later describing the country by saying, 'of course I could come a thud'.

On Christmas Eve he wrote to Cousins: 'I am staggered, for from Perth to here no matter in what isolated spot, some book or other of mine is known. Mostly *Lasseter*, *Flynn* and among the returned men *The Column*. *Lasseter* is the red hot favourite. I heard the strangest types of men talk of that book as I used to talk of *Robinson Crusoe* when I was a kid.'

Most of the people at the stations, from the owners to the hands, the men at lonely mining camps, and the personnel at telegraph stations, were great readers. All cared for books and handled them with great reverence.

Jack was a little bemused, perhaps even put out, to find that very few books were bought; people relied on each other to pass them along. At that time the north of Western Australia operated like a giant lending library. At each outback station, every mining camp and every telegraph station, reading material—of any kind— was parcelled up when read and given to the mailman to pass to another reader at his next stop. At the same time, the senders received a parcel of reading material which the mailman had picked up at his last call. This system operated for thousands of square miles.

Jack, the promoter, was quick to see that there was an opportunity for sales of hundreds of books a year if only the people of the outback were given a publication which advised them what books were available, and where to buy them.

He advised Cousins to get a directory of addresses of stations from the Perth Lands Department, and addresses for the inland telegraph stations from the Perth Telegraph Department. He admitted that the mining camps were a little harder as the population was transient, but there was always a nucleus of people who formed a permanent community. He offered no suggestion though on how to approach this market segment.

Cousins wrote telling him that war books had not sold well over the Christmas period but it was expected that sales would pick up as the year moved on towards Anzac Day. Jack had an answer for this also. He observed that there was a keen market throughout RSL organisations around the country. These were just waiting to be tapped he said, and suggested that suitable mailings to RSL clubs would no doubt bring rewards. He registered surprise that there was a strong feeling of warmth towards returned men and their experiences.

Jack had been disappointed by the material given to him by the police. He was in search of accounts in which the white man was the villain. Stories about treachery and murder by Aborigines abounded, but his aim was to write a book which did not present an unbalanced picture. It wasn't until he reached Broome that he got his first three good stories since leaving Perth.

Jack was itching to get into the Kimberley but the area had been declared impassable; even the police looked blank when travel during the wet was mentioned. There was no point in going to Derby because it was more than half deserted, as were most of the stations right through to Wyndham, the people having gone south to Perth to stay 'over the wet'.

Jack was certainly not interested in taking a rest for three months. He wanted to get on with the work he had come to do. At the same time he was concerned about what was happening back home.

'It is the Eta business that is worrying me,' he wrote to Cousins. 'I would not hesitate to stay under ordinary circumstances but I feel a bit troubled. If I stay it will mean another three months here probably. I have left her ample money until March. After that I'll get you to keep one hundred pounds out of my royalties and pay this to her at the rate of not more than three pound per week.'

As usual Jack was torn between moving on and staying to glean all the available material. If the police patrol he was to accompany did not leave for unknown country Jack determined he would leave Broome for Derby and take off with pack-horses into the Kimberley on his own. While he was reaching this decision, the wet moved in, and the lay-up season began in Broome.

The pearling fleet, its captains and crews, including the divers, were in port taking a well-earned three-month break. Jack found himself in the right place at the right time for he was able to collect material which otherwise would have stayed at sea for nine months.

He stopped fighting the urge to start another book. While putting together *Forty Fathoms Deep*, this 'Pearl' book, as he called it, developed into two. 'I couldn't resist the other, though I fought against it. It is incomparably easier to write than the Broome book. A straight hero right through, MacKenzie, second in command of James Clark (Pearl King) when they sailed for the Azores and opened up that Dutch possession,' he wrote to Cousins. The MacKenzie manuscript written at that time and intended as the second book after *Forty Fathoms Deep*, remains unpublished. By mid-February both books were three-quarters written, and he had settled into a comfortable routine in Broome. Getting into the Kimberley took second place.

Broome, lightly touched by the depression, lazed languidly on the left shoulder of Australia and casually carried on its great pearling industry. The inhabitants took as little notice of the rest of the continent as the southern states took of them. The climate was very hot. The most stimulation anyone was prepared to incorporate in any one day was the sight of the brilliant red and purple bougainvillea vines. Occasionally someone would take umbrage about being misrepresented by a southern newspaper, but, by the time the next mail was due to leave, the energy to write a Letter to the Editor in protest would have evaporated.

'This is a land where there ain't no schedule. The people simply don't know what it means to plan to get started on time, it isn't the custom. They won't travel in the wet at all and are adverse to helping any "mad" man to do so,' wrote Jack.

Broome bewitched him. Its people were polyglot. Malay divers, aristocratic Japanese, Chinese, Greeks, Indians and Europeans rubbed shoulders with European Australians and Aborigines. There were the wanderers, the white flotsam and jetsam, and there were the wives and children of the pearlers.

In the town the delightful streets were lined with shady trees. Every house with its windows latticed against the remorseless sun and flanked by dense gardens, lush with tropical plants thriving in the rich red soil, seemed a sanctuary of cool mystery. There were also questionable lanes, where it was advisable to 'watch your back'. Here the houses almost butted against each other, the shade was not cool and inviting but full of menace.

At night the air was thick with the scent of frangipani. Coconut palms cast deep, jagged, abstract-shaped shadows. Above, molten silver stars blazed in a blanket of electric blue. The night brought out jealous lovers and pearl thieves with the possibility of tribal fights between the imperturbable Chinese Tongs. To the casual observer all seemed idyllic, but beneath the beauty of tropical nights the air seemed to crackle with excitement.

A collection of exotic ships rode at anchor in the port. Chinese junks and all manner of strange craft from around the world rubbed planks with the Broome pearling fleet. The thirty-eight foot tide regularly slipped back to the deep ocean, leaving all ships high and dry lying drunkenly on their sides.

An incurable romantic, Jack revelled in the cosmopolitan

atmosphere of the town. Broome with its harbour, silver town, pearl town and oyster town, was to Jack, as it has been for many others, the most fascinating place in all Australia. He loved all the different coloured races and the whites; none was subdued, they were all 'damn cheeky' and self-assured, there was work about and they were making good money. For Jack, his stay in Broome took on the aura of a Robert Louis Stevenson South Sea romance.

He wired Cousins: 'Copy excellent for book this district alone am seriously considering remain to collect it.' Cousins, received the wire with delight. The idea of having a ten-volume Idriess collection to offer for sale on an instalment plan was starting to become a real possibility.

Chapter Nineteen
INTRIGUE AND PIRATES

BROOME was Jack's Aladdin's Cave of exotic tales. He gave up fretting about moving on to Derby and through to the Kimberley and became part of the colourful mosaic.

The knowledge of pearling which Jack had gained working dockside on Thursday Island in 1928 stood him in good stead. Accepting him without question, the pearlers asked him to sail with them when the fleet put back to sea. Quietly he set about cultivating Nishioka, the 'big gun' Japanese, who, charmed by Jack's equally enigmatic presence, willingly acted as interpreter between Jack and the Japanese pearlers. Even Elles, the poker-faced Singalee pearl cleaner, supposedly worth over 150,000 pounds, kept him supplied with stories.

The pearlers took a liking to Jack although they despised writers. Here, as in Meekatharra, other writers had soured the locals by writing malicious and false stories about Broome and its people. Jack won their confidence because he was not concerned with the town's sordid gossip or half-truths which previous writers had eagerly sought. Rejoicing in the fact that his fellow artisans had missed some of Australia's best material, he moved easily around the waterfront and immersed himself in the life of the town and its inhabitants.

Every day more divers came ashore bringing tales that even Jules Verne could not have imagined. Jack reported back to Cousins that the stories, authentic to the last detail, had never been put on paper before. 'I am getting so much it's becoming difficult to write and keep up the pace.'

While Jack was busy recording the tales of Broome he found time to write the foreword for *The Yellow Joss*, a collection of short stories which he had somehow managed to put together during the hectic output of 1933.

Jack never trusted anyone but himself to make the right choice of photographs to illustrate any of his works. Over the years he would meticulously study every detail of all the prints of each scene, many of which he photographed himself, until he was

satisfied that the print he selected was the most accurate represen-
tation. *The Yellow Joss* was to be the exception.

The wet was closing in fast and Jack had no choice other
than to stay in Broome. In desperation, because he was unable to
select the illustrations for *The Yellow Joss* himself, he wrote three
pages of detailed information to Cousins as to where he might get
the best photographs for the book and closed with 'I have been
thinking so fast of so many things here that I forget the names of
the wretched stories but please see that the natives are not dressed
up as mission natives for those mentioned are ones from around
Cape Melville, Normanby, Escape River, Kendall River (still canni-
balistic as they were in my time).'

The rain began in earnest. Much to everyone's satisfaction it
proved to be a record wet. Jack was impressed. It was obvious that
he had no chance of leaving Broome for Derby, or for any other
place, so he wrote again to Cousins asking him to take care of the
financial arrangements for Eta:

> Now, as to those royalties you wired about. Would you place them
> to my account in the Commonwealth Bank, with the exception of
> one hundred pounds. I hate having to ask you to arrange this for
> me, but would you pay Eta three pound per week from that hun-
> dred, at twelve pound per month this means she would only have
> to visit the shop [A&R] once a month. This arrangement would take
> that wretched business off my mind. I don't know if she has ever
> visited the shop, but if so and you know her address would you let
> me know. If she comes in after you receive this would you tell her
> the arrangement, and that I am held up by the wet season. I don't
> care to write to her address when I don't know whether she is there
> or not.

Cousins wrote to Jack in early January. The letter contained
no mention of Eta. Cousins continued to nurture their plan for the
set of ten books. Reinforcing the project he counselled Jack not to
worry about West Australian readers borrowing copies of his
books, as opposed to buying them. Cousins was working on the
theory that it was all for the good because these people, when the
Depression eased, would buy the set of Idriess books when it was
published.

When Jack had written to him about the need for a brochure
or a catalogue he had immediately put into production a four-page,
quarto-sized brochure featuring *Drums of Mer* on the front cover.
This he promised would be circulated heavily in the West. Cousins

gently reminded Jack of the hard times the country had weathered:

> Things should be better now. The wool position should improve business generally. It's a great surprise packet for Australia. No one dreamed of getting such prices. Previously booksellers must have nearly gone broke, because very few orders were reaching us for anything. Our best customer is about two years behind with his payments.

Cousins was also having second thoughts about the Daisy Bates project. The decision taken in 1933 that Jack should not collaborate on her 'History of the Western Australian Tribes' worried him. He could see no reason why the work, written at the request of the West Australian government but returned to her by the Labor Premier as 'offering no commercial return', should not become her biography.

As biographies seemed to be Jack's forte, Cousins suggested that on his way back to Sydney, Jack should take the opportunity of visiting Mrs Bates at her home at the Native Camp, Ooldea in South Australia where she lived with Aborigines, many of whom were still wild and reported by Mrs Bates to be cannibals.

Cousins wrote to Jack, 'If you do get a chance to call on her do so, but above all do not miss Kidman. His life story would make a great volume. He is a national figure and a book about him would live for years. He must be an old man now, and it might pay you to see what can be done before it is too late.'

In the same letter Cousins made reference to a young man who had a map of Lasseter's country. The man had claimed to Cousins that the map had been given to him by an old prospector and that he was intrigued to find a number of things mentioned by Lasseter marked on it. He further mentioned that the man was mounting a four-man expedition once again to search for the lost reef.

Jack was too absorbed with what was happening in Broome to give Daisy, Kidman or Lasseter any deep thought. He was doing what he wanted for the time being and he was content with the production of the sales brochure.

The police had wired Jack to come to Halls Creek and he felt sure that the subject of the communication was Nemarluk, one of the most feared and respected Aboriginal renegades in the north. A courageous leader of his tribe, Nemarluk had vowed to rid his land of all whites.

Jack was delighted with the invitation as the police promised

189

to assist him to undertake trips into the unpeopled badlands north of Derby.

Jack rushed a letter to Cousins. 'No scribbler, overseas or otherwise, has been there before. If Nemarluk only comes out and spikes a few I'll be right in it.' It never occurred to Jack that he might be one of the few 'spiked', for Nemarluk was not known to ask questions before spearing his victims.

In Broome the stories were coming at such a pace that Jack's wrist, still carrying the splinters from a jam-tin bomb in Gallipoli, seized up. He was forced to use his left hand to write *Forty Fathoms Deep*. Writing with his left hand was slow and frustrating but he was proud of his dexterity.

Depression settled on his shoulder once again. Eta had written to him telling that she was 'in all the trouble in the world'. Baby Judy had fallen out of her cot, she mentioned doctor's bills and an assortment of other troubles. She wanted money. Jack had left her ample ready cash to see her through until March; nonetheless he directed Cousins to give her what she wanted out of the hundred pounds mentioned in his last letter. 'When she goes through that she will have to dashed well wait. Blow women.' Despite this, Eta was ever pressing on his mind. His letters to Cousins always contained several mentions of her.

Jack pushed himself to get all the Broome material in another month. He continually corrected and enlarged the stories so as to have the book in an advanced state when he finally sat down to finish it. He decided that if he was held up by the wet or anything else he could finish it right there; in fact he hoped to have it all clear to be posted to Sydney by the end of February.

Jack's depression over Eta was short-lived. A few weeks later his old buoyancy had returned. He was still getting great copy from some pearlers but others amongst them had changed their attitude towards him. A few pearl dealers were afraid that he was a customs spy on the lookout for illicit pearl profits which they had not declared in their income tax returns. His most prized informant, the 'big gun' Japanese, Nishioko, now regarded him as a naval secret service officer who had been sent to Broome to spy on the Japanese pearlers and accordingly withdrew his cooperation. Jack lamented the loss of Nishioko's help as being 'unfortunate because my mine of information has closed like an oyster'. He turned to Elles, the Singalee, and later wrote that he was 'probably the most wonderful pearl cleaner the world has ever known. His sensitive fingertips could feel the "life" in a pearl.'

Though Jack was sorry he wasn't able to get more wonderful

tales from the Malays, he was content with the knowledge that he already had enough material for two books.

While Jack pretended to be bemused as to the reasons behind the suspicions of both the Japanese and the pearlers he enjoyed the game immensely. He wrote to Cousins that the Japanese gentleman's guess about the purpose of his visit to Broome was much closer than that of the pearlers, which managed to intrigue Cousins.

Neither Jack or the Broome pearlers guessed that Nishioka might have had good reason for withdrawing his help. In view of the war that was to come, it is likely that the Japanese pearlers were engaged in spying under the cover of pearl poaching. It would also seem that Australian Military Intelligence in Broome was unaware of the possibility of spying being undertaken in northern waters at that time; and that Australian Naval Intelligence in Perth had not communicated their suspicions to Broome Military Intelligence officers.

Later that year in October, Captain Goldie, the Military Intelligence Officer at Broome, captain of the ketch *Ninilya*, would report observing Japanese ships poaching the pearl grounds at Rueapebe Islands and that they had been sighted within two miles of Bossut Lighthouse. Reports of the sightings in the southern press stated that these Japanese ships were 'sampans'. Captain Goldie, humorously critical of the fanciful reporting, wrote to Jack saying that the Japanese vessels 'were of European design, seventy feet overall in length, with a beam of some thirty feet and weighing from thirty-five to forty tons and without marks or sails, and propelled by diesel or semi-diesel fired engines'. The ships were built, engineered, equipped and supplied with a year's stores in Japan. Goldie assessed that each would have cost the Japanese the equivalent, then, of fifteen thousand Australian pounds and that Australian made ships of the same design would cost around seven thousand pounds each. Japan, although financially handicapped, was then on the move and no one had the wit to question the over-sophistication of ships seemingly being used for pearling.

Jack and the captain were good friends. Jack lived for a time aboard another of Captain Goldie's ships, the *Heralk*. Later Goldie was to write that he was 'positively ill' when some *Bulletin* reviewer tried to show his superiority by criticising Jack's technical diving details contained in *Forty Fathoms Deep*.

Jack, absorbing all the stories available, did odd things like sleeping in a graveyard (where Con the 'hoodoo' man told him 'they' really talk) and spending a night on the bishop's verandah seeking the bishop's ghost—the bishop did not favour him with his presence.

During this time the movie pirates were raking the literary seas for easy prey. *Gold Dust and Ashes* had caught the attention of a film group. Quite unashamedly they hoisted up the Jolly Roger and announced that they intended to go to New Guinea to film *Gold Dust and Ashes*.

Jack had been told about the proposed film by Waterhouse of Price Waterhouse (involved at that time as investors and accountants for Guinea Airways) before he had left for Western Australia but he had not been too concerned. Jack's contract with A&R tied down the movie rights and it didn't seem possible that anyone would invite legal action from either A&R or himself by using the work without buying the film rights.

It wasn't until Jack was in Broome in February 1934 that Cousins wrote to let him know that the pirating was indeed afoot. Jack was outraged. He recalled a conversation that he had with Waterhouse who, when he realised what he was saying, had pulled up short when telling Jack about the proposed film. Waterhouse was unconcerned about Jack's legal rights as author; his position was that any film at all would have been an advertisement for Guinea Airways and the gold mining company Placer Development. Jack told Cousins that Henry Price had also warned him about the 'picture men'. Price had been specific about one man, an ex-employee of Fox Films known as the 'Captain', who during dinner one night at the Sydney Press Club had openly stated his intention to use *Gold Dust and Ashes*.

It seems that a company had produced a successful travelogue. This had been presented to Fox Films as a film concept for *Gold Dust and Ashes* and Fox had been interested. Jack advised Cousins that, from what he been told, the result had been what he would have called a 'patchwork'.

He wrote to Cousins: 'I presume the photographers have taken scenery and interspersed here and there parts of the story. Apparently some of the characterisation of *Gold Dust and Ashes* has been introduced as intended.'

Jack was most upset that by doing it this way the future of the book would be spoiled and he urged Cousins to take a strong hand to stop any further unlawful use of the work.'I believe Fox Films will only deal with us if they are forced to: I suppose they are considering how far they can legally work on the book without paying for it.'

By 1 March the problem of the film pirating came to a head.

The 'Captain' turned out to be Major Guinness, of Guinea Expedition, Film Producers, and an editor or ex-editor of Fox Movietone News. Guinness had contacted Cousins with a verbal offer of one hundred pounds for all the rights, which Cousins took the liberty of telling him that Jack would not listen to. When Guinness then made the counter-offer of five per cent of gross takings, the offer was treated with the suspicion it deserved.

'How will you know what the gross takings are?' Cousins wrote to Jack. '*Gold Dust and Ashes* is too good to throw away on speculation of this kind. I told Guinness that in this case I could not decide for you, but would forward his letter and scenario. Please return the latter.'

In the same letter he told Jack that Wells, the administrator of Guinea Airways, was in Sydney and that he would like to see a film of this kind. However Cousins had told Wells that Jack had better ideas; nonetheless he enclosed a letter from Wells asking Jack to consider the proposition. Cousins ended by saying, 'If this is the party that set out to do *Gold Dust and Ashes* without mentioning a word to you I would have nothing to do with them.'

Jack read the scenario and the letter from Wells, to which he responded:

> That alleged offer to film and the scenario on *Gold Dust* [made] me pretty mad. It is from the band of shysters who set out from Sydney to pirate the book. They actually boasted about it, when drunk...I am surprised at Wells. I had imagined he felt me crude in numerous ways but thought that he gave me credit of knowing the difference between a penny and a ten pound note. He and Waterhouse want Guinea Airways and Placer Development boosted in any way at all. Well, I have served their purpose and boosted their concerns in a way they would never have got otherwise, but they have served my purpose too. I have given them excellent value for what they have given me, but that ends the mutual arrangement. It is a common failing for a man to think he has brains but the other goat has none at all.

Reluctantly Jack posted the scenario back as Cousins had suggested. He feared that Guinness and Co. would go ahead with the film in a less barefaced form and that he might need a copy of the script to be able to prove piracy.

This was to be the first of many such encounters with film production companies. Over the years ahead Jack was to find that many such organisations believed they had a right to steal some of his works simply because those works dealt with historical fact.

It was not only the piracy of *Gold Dust and Ashes* that worried him that February. His personal life was still a source of deep concern. Eta wrote to tell him that she had heard Kingsford Smith was going out after Lasseter's lost reef. This was good news; anything which promoted sales was always good news to Jack. This time however, Eta had written Jack a long letter which was most unusual, for her correspondence to him was usually limited to telegrams requesting money. In the letter she asked him for four pounds per week instead of the three pounds she had previously received.

Jack wrote to Cousins. Calculating that this would mean sixteen pounds per month he asked Cousins to give it to her until 'that hundred pound is gone. After that, if I have not returned, she can do as she jolly well likes, somehow I think I have been more than fair.'

Jack had already left Broome when Cousins sent him a telegram: 'Received today letter for you from Kidman's secretary at Adelaide asking if you are prepared write life Kidman and what terms.'

Chapter Twenty
Derby Days

Jack, as always, was in a state of wanting to be in several places at once. Reluctantly he left Broome, with a wealth of material still untapped. Eagerly he moved on to Derby, anticipating stories which would be characteristic of the area. At the same time he wished that he was at home to settle his affairs, both personal and business.

The citizens of Broome gave Jack a send-off when he boarded the *Centaur* for Derby on 5 March 1934. They introduced him to tourists, planters and tin men returning to Malaya and to sheep and cattle men who were returning to the Kimberley after vacationing in Broome, or further south in Perth.

The presence of the 'great personage' caused quite a flutter, especially when the chief steward and the purser, both of whom had read *Gold Dust and Ashes* and *Flynn of the Inland*, spread the word around the ship that the author was aboard.

Derby, named after the Colonial Secretary of the 1800s, was situated on the coastal plain, where it merged with the saltpans and blundered into the sea. From the seaward approach the town was low lying and three parts encircled by marsh, saltpans, mangroves and bush. The bush to the south was uninhabited. To the north by sea lay Darwin approximately nine hundred miles away, Wyndham being the only port between.

The surrounding land at that time was peopled only by Aboriginal tribes. Derby was separated from Broome, Wyndham and Darwin by hundreds of miles of barely inhabited country, while to the east lay hundreds of miles of almost uninhabited, rugged country. Here the great King Leopold Ranges waited as they had done for countless ages. Behind the Leopolds lay 'The Land That God Forgot'.

Instinct drew Jack on to the King Leopolds. The range, with its weathered plateaux and amphitheatres of ancient rocks, deeply scourged and dissected by wild currents, forms a rugged natural barrier, as does the embattled Cader Idris escarpment of Jack's Welsh forefathers.

Jack arrived in Derby irritable and anxious to get into the ranges and beyond. Soon after he arrived he wandered out along the jetty, the town's largest structure. The long, long jetty, like a scrawny arm protruding from a quicksand bog, straddled endless mud and sand. Soaked to the skin, Jack looked out through the incessant rain towards King Sound where the thirty-five foot tide had retreated, exposing the mangroves, cliffs, headlands, bays and islands. From where he stood there was nothing to indicate that the treacherous waters at the mouth of the big inlet were a navigator's nightmare. The sound was a jigsaw puzzle of land and sea.

Wet and dispirited he mused on the good luck of having passed safely through the forty miles of the deadly, swirling waters of the sound. He was in no mood to recognise the navigating skills of the *Centaur*'s crew. Jack thought Derby was 'a terrible hole of a place' but he was never to forget King Sound:

> The great Sound fascinated me; its maze of waters, its changing moods, its elusive peace and raging passions sweeping its forty-mile course inland to Derby. Pausing for hours of slumberous breath only to gather strength to rage back to sea again, it seemed to be a thing of life. Peaceful, turbulent, never to be trusted, changing daily—not only with the weather but with every wind, every turn of the tide, every cross rip. Quiet, then murmurous with coming movement—then hissing, swirling, rumbling with action.

Jack lodged himself at the Port Hotel. The wet continued to run its course, days of steady soaking rain falling from a sky that could not be seen were broken by periods of good weather which usually lasted about two weeks.

Jack spent the wet days staring from the hotel balcony at the long jetty pushing its way through the forest of mangroves out into the sound. At high tide the water stood within one hundred yards of the hotel and the small town was locked in the watery embrace of perfectly level marshes to the right and left. Nearby the Fitzroy River emptied endless torrents of muddy brown water from far inland into the sound.

On 7 March he sent a telegram to Cousins: 'Prospects for copy exceptionally bright.' Scarcely had Jack arrived in Derby than his spirits lifted. As always the promise of abundant copy set him off like a terrier after a rabbit, and he received a letter from Cousins a day after his arrival which contained information that a four-page circular of his books was to be widely distributed throughout Western Australia inside a few days. Cousins didn't say how the distribution was to be carried out but Jack was satisfied that the push was on.

In Derby he found his first patrol police station and there he received a first-hand authentic account of a case from the man on the job. He would use it in *Man Tracks*.

The material in Derby, as he had anticipated, was unique. Here were the true outback pioneers, horse thieves, 'gin-men' and wild Aborigines, and the first humorous stories of the trip. The population of Derby numbered about one hundred and fifty, white and black. The 'aristocrats' among the non-whites had Chinese blood, and he observed that the girls were 'strikingly pretty, good dancers and extremely clever'.

On dry days he would take a walk around the town with some of the men, check at the post office for any news from Cousins and stop along the way to talk with the townspeople. The trip to the post office was generally fruitless. During the wet no steamers called at Derby; only the government ship *Koolinda* would, perhaps, call once or twice. There was an airmail service but this was only possible if the plane could land without being bogged in the mud that surrounded the town. Apart from this service Derby had no contact with the rest of the continent for the duration of the wet.

After the post office stop, making as much noise as the cockatoos screeching in the bottle-shaped baobab trees, Jack and his companions would go on to Billy Adcock's store, then to the general meeting place, Jack Knopp's store. Mostly the party would finish up at the single-storied Scott's Club Hotel to swap a yarn or two with the boys who were there waiting out the wet. It could take them two or three hours to cover the three hundred yards from the Port Hotel to Scott's Hotel. This was a land of 'lots of time'.

At night, if it was fine, all the town would gather to watch the teams of men and girls playing basketball by the light of carbide lamps.

On wet nights, listening to the sound of rain and the 'windborne, moaning rumble of water from the sound', Jack would nurse his impatience to be off. The pitch black nights alive with howling winds and sheeting rain depressed him and caused him to brood, and listening to Womba Billy did nothing to improve his mood.

Womba was a white Australian who had been taken as a baby after his mother had died and had been reared by an Aboriginal woman. Adopted by her tribe Womba was fully initiated into the tribe by the time he was fourteen. He spoke thirty-eight native dialects fluently and possessed the 'three languages', the language of the tribe, a sign language, and the sacred language.

Womba's nights however were full of bad dreams and often while tossing in his drunken state he would fall out of bed. After hitting the floor he would pick himself up and shamble to Jack's room to talk, for Jack was a good listener. He would talk most of the night away, mostly in pidgin English for it came to him more easily than English. Sometimes when he became excited he would lapse into pure Aboriginal.

Womba's story was full of pathos. By the time he had reached fourteen half of his adoptive tribe had vanished, victims of white man's diseases such as pneumonia and consumption. His people had fled camp after camp, abandoning each as places cursed. Then the whites had claimed him and tried to 'civilise' him.

Jack spent many nights listening to Womba's story. He heard how Womba had laughed when a 'fellow' tribesman had speared a white stockman ('served him right Jack—served the cow right') and how he had been a crew member aboard a black-birding ship until he realised what was being done to 'his people', and how he had then released some thirty Aborigines by using a ruse before making good his own escape into the bush.

But he experienced the greatest tragedy of his life when he lost his daughter Lucy. The child had been taken from the care of Womba and his wife under the law which then gave the Protector of Aborigines the care of half-caste children. This inhuman law ruled that an Aboriginal camp was no place to rear a half-caste child, preferring instead that children be torn away from their natural parents and placed in mission homes and centres where they were not only desperately unhappy but often exploited.

Womba could not forget the sight of his wife, Mungatty, running from the camp to meet him, her face streaming with blood where she had cut it with a broken bottle in her grief after the child had been taken. Womba told Jack that Mungatty, was 'in sorrow' and that the memory was continually with him.

Womba was not the only sleepless person at the Port Hotel. Derby was full of outback characters waiting for the wet to pass and all of them, it seemed to Jack, had made the Port Hotel their headquarters.

There was 'Bunch 'em up' Gardiner, a tall, thin man with a white moustache and always spotlessly clean, drunk or sober. 'Bunch 'em up' couldn't manage to say much without using the phrase 'bunch 'em up' which had labelled him. His past was a secret. No one knew much about Gardiner except that he had been educated and schooled to go into the clergy. In his cups he told Jack in a nervous whisper that he had fought in the Boer War and had ridden with Breaker Morant and Lieutenant Handcock. Gardiner said that he was to have been shot by order of a British court martial with Morant and Handcock but had been saved from the firing squad by some 'big influence', the identity of which or whom he never divulged. 'Bunch 'em up' was the scourge of the night for he never seemed to need sleep.

Then there was 'Blue Bob the Bastard from Borroloola': tall and wizened he was always challenging someone to 'yard' him. For the most part he was ignored but his challenge had been accepted during the last wet at Fitzroy Crossing where 'yard' him they did—on the end of a chain padlocked to a log by a lonely creek.

For three months of the year Derby, like Wyndham and Broome, was host to an assortment of men who came to stock up on provisions for the far-away homesteads, provisions that would have to last throughout the coming nine months' 'dry'. The bouts of buying were interspersed with wild bouts of drinking and any other entertainment that helped to pass the monotony.

The most popular evening entertainment at the Port Hotel was the bullfight. The 'bulls' were usually two drunks (Jack was agreeably surprised to find that bulls of the horned, four-footed variety were not actually brought into the pub). The two human antagonists would get down on their hands and knees, roar about, upset the pot plants and then scratch and paw at the dirt from the pots and spread it all over the place, 'sniff each other's arses', lower their heads and with a roar charge each other full on. It was Jack's hope that they might crack their skulls. The sham fight would usually progress past the point of fun until one of the 'bulls' sustained an injury; then the fighting would escalate into an event of deadly intent. The noise disturbed Jack and distracted him from his writing; he was less than amused.

At last came the chance that he had wanted before he had left Sydney—a patrol was being organised to bring in several native murderers, including Toolwanor, alias 'Nipper'. This was not to be the average patrol. Its purpose was to apprehend the murderers whose killings had frightened their tribesmen into seeking white man's justice—but their camps had to be found first. As a result of Inspector Treadgold's guiding hand the local police sergeant had made arrangements for Jack to ride with the patrol. The plan was to go north and then east off Walcott Inlet, past Port George and into the inland, where the country was supposed to be the most inaccessible in Australia.

Fired with the knowledge that he would be the first writer to venture into this inhospitable territory, Jack waited impatiently for the order to come from the police inspector in Broome for the patrol to proceed. Cousins kept writing to Jack, keeping him up-to-date with events in Sydney and advising him of what was happening on the sales front. As the result of Jack's constant prodding Cousins came up with the ultimate mailing list—the Kimberley electoral role.

Cousins, dedicated to the idea of a set of Idriess books on hire-purchase, had wanted to wait until a set of ten was available, but he finally decided to ride with the eight Idriess titles already in publication.

The Yellow Joss was about to be released and instalments of the *Man Tracks* manuscript were being lodged regularly in the A&R strong room. Cousins knew that he could offer the eight titles, and with confidence promote and announce the forthcoming two titles in an enclosed letter. In the mailing package he enclosed a form with the four-page illustrated brochure, the form to be filled in and returned by the receiver if they wished to receive an A&R catalogue annually. The offer in the brochure was for any or all titles at two shillings and sixpence down, with payments of six shillings a month. Cousins and Jack hoped that most recipients would order all eight titles.

The saga of the pirating of *Gold Dust and Ashes* continued. Cousins wrote: 'Re Major Guinness. This man had been awfully polite up to date. But when I phoned him re *Gold Dust* film he was very, very abrupt. I'm afraid we have spoked his little scheme. Serve him right.'

Jack wrote back to tell Cousins that he had met a man who was selling a medical book entitled *Vitalogy* priced at four guineas. Both Jack and the bookseller himself were nonplussed at the success of the idea, especially since the man, a New Zealander, had been told by a bank manager in Kalgoorlie that it was utterly impossible to expect to do business. Money was very tight and the country was still in the last throes of Depression, but the man had gone ahead and had lived by selling his books for two years in the Kalgoorlie district alone. Jack thought that it augured well for the A&R project. If this man could sell thirty copies in Broome and seventeen in Derby, which Jack had described as 'a little hole', run a decent car, and travel the country extracting money from men who were 'hard heads who never buy a thing in their lives, men who are still wondering how he talked them into parting with their precious four guineas', then this was the man to sell the Idriess set.

The rains had started again in Derby and all the rivers were running bankers. Jack had nearly used up all his copy and was greatly irritated by the constant rain and the fact that the patrol could not start.

Jack, however, was not sure that everything was at a standstill because of the big wet: he felt that a pending commission into native affairs was contributing to the delayed departure of the patrol. The police were reluctant to move in any direction. Alert and sensitive to the prevailing mood of restless boredom in Derby they were also hesitant to turn their backs on the populace, knowing that anything could happen at any time—and it did.

Demon alcohol ruled in Derby. The general attitude to the rest of Australia was 'ter hell with 'em', an attitude which was used as an excuse by any irresponsible person, Australian or visitor alike, to do anything they had half a mind to.

It was a visiting alleged journalist from the *London Morning Post* and his 'hobo cobber' who realised the fears of the police. These two were involved in an all-out drunken brawl after which, egos more battered than bodies, they had staggered off to the native camp and pulled an old blind Aborigine out of his bed, beat him savagely about the head with sticks and almost killed him in a fit of pique. Jack was sorry that they were only sentenced to six months' gaol; if the sentencing had been left to him they would have been deported.

Jack clung to the hope that each day's mail would bring the order to start the patrol. Common sense dictated that he should accompany a patrol that was going out either from Derby, Fitzroy Crossing or Halls Creek but he was so resolved to get into the country in the north that he determined to push into the wilds alone if the patrol did not eventuate.

Obsessed by the desire to be the first writer to go into what was described as some of the most inaccessible and dangerous country in Australia, and driven by an unshakeable conviction that all his writing had now to be done from his own experience, he decided that if the order didn't come he would make straight for the Fitzroy Crossing when the rain had finished and the tracks were passably dry. 'I can't return without getting into the wild country, otherwise I'll have no more weight to put into my future books than any other tourist who makes out he's an explorer.'

His trip through Lasseter and Flynn country had been a great object lesson; it proved to him how necessary it was to actually experience the country that he was writing about if he wasn't to make a fool of himself or, worse still, be classified like the

201

self-styled adventurer Terry, who was known as 'The Main Roads' Explorer'. At Derby, Terry was called the 'Three Ts' or 'The Terrible Terry'. He wrote to Cousins, 'I don't want the cows to ever have the chance of alluding to me like that, as they surely will if I don't get off the beaten track...If it were not for this Eta business I would simply buy a team and roam about and write three or four books from here; there is ample material.'

Noted Australian author, Mary Durack, and her father stopped at Derby en route to Wyndham while Jack was in this 'do not pass go' situation. He described Durack as a 'splendid old pioneer type' and Mary 'as a very nice quiet little girl'. When he learned that Mary had just finished a manuscript and had sent it to Endeavour Press in London he was outraged, and in his own words 'roused on her and the old man severely'.

Jack wrote to Cousins, 'I cannot imagine why anyone would not support their own people. The more books that are published in Australia, the more printers, binders, editors, typists, packers, salesmen and booksellers and people in the bookshops are needed and employed, right down to the reviewers and newspaper people and the newsboys in the streets.'

Some fifty years later Dame Mary remembered meeting Jack, whom she described as a quiet man who showed his work written in pencil in school exercise books to both her father and herself. She did not recall him 'rousing' on either of them.

It was Sir John Mitchell who had advised Mary to send her work to England. Jack thought that Sir John had done this after seeing the advertisements which Endeavour had placed in Australian papers.

Jack believed that the bulk of the Australian public took advertising on face value and were even gullible. He was disconcerted to find that if a company represented itself as being well established and large, the people believed it to be so. Consequently he thought that Angus and Robertson, with integrity, should indulge in a little 'blowing of the horn' now and then. He was convinced that Mary would have sold thousands more of her books and got twice the royalty if she had sent it to the 'Old Firm'. He wrote to Cousins that Mary was preparing a manuscript for the following year and said that he had extracted a promise from her that she would send it along to A&R. No doubt he felt content that he had applied the nail that would save the shoe.

While in Derby he had managed to see a little of the fringe of the desert here and there without the assistance of the police. The tracks still remained impassable and, even though a few shearers had chanced them, prudence dictated that he should wait at least another two weeks when he was assured the wet would be finished. He hated the idea of waiting around Derby for another eight to ten days but there seemed no possible hope of doing otherwise.

Then the Kimberley, recharged, at last began to move. The boat tied up again and disgorged over a hundred shearers, a number of meat workers and drovers. The town was suddenly overflowing with noisy, drinking, brawling men. The atmosphere was charged with expectancy and impatience.

At last the word that Jack had waited for came, and on 28 March he wired Cousins: 'Leaving here on northern patrol in about a week.'

The wet however had not backed off. On 30 March it was blowing a gale and the rain thundered down again. On 1 April, in high spirits, Jack wrote to Cousins.

> On Wednesday we leave on this patrol. The crowd here are an easygoing bush lot and have been very decent to me. This morning when I let them know I was going on this northern patrol, there was much surprise and congratulations. It appears that certain writers, tourist-explorers, journalists etc. have been in the habit of writing about their country 'without leaving the wharf'! Hence the idea of this scribbler seeing the country, and a wilder part than any of them have seen, appeals. By the way it might be judicious if you, as chance occurs, let certain Sydney people know of this fact too. Our 'ero is not keeping to the beaten tracks.

On 2 April Jack wrote to Cousins that word had come through that fourteen natives and one white had died within a few hours at Fitzroy Crossing of some mysterious sickness. There was no doctor at the Crossing, only a policeman with medical knowledge. The 1934 influenza epidemic had begun. If Jack hadn't been delayed going out on the patrol he would have arrived at Fitzroy Crossing when the epidemic was at its height.

Laurie O'Neill, the young policeman leading the patrol, was credited as the quickest traveller in the country. The patrol was being mounted with sixteen horses and mules and two black trackers, one of whom, Larry, was considered the smartest in all the Kimberley. He had been with the police all his life. When he was a small child his parents had been running with Pigeon's Gang, and when the police closed in, young Larry had been shot in the leg. In order to save herself his mother had slung him away into the bush and left him. The police had found him and brought him up.

The other tracker, Davey, was a self-styled ladies' man. Just when everything was ready Davey got himself put behind bars for mixing with the town's Aboriginal girls. This would not have been such a heinous crime under normal circumstances but he had been caught with a group of male lepers who had come for women at the town's leper camp. Rather than hold up the patrol O'Neill put the boy in gaol until the last minute when he could be put on his mule as the patrol rode out of town.

Jack was unconcerned about leprosy, he just wanted to get on with the patrol and away from 'Bunch 'em up' Gardiner—'the noisy blasted swine hasn't slept in the last one hundred hours, I wish he'd break his blasted neck!'

The route which the patrol planned to take lay through wild territory and no one anticipated that they would eventually travel over one thousand miles. As it had been the heaviest wet for many years travelling was expected to be heavy and difficult for the first two weeks. In view of these factors it was impossible to accurately assess the date of their return.

'If you don't get a wire from me sharp on two months it will mean that we'll be a fortnight or so overdue,' he wrote to Cousins. 'I think Eta is all right, that and the time this trip is taking are the only worries on my mind.'

Cousins received a telegram dated 3 April 1934: 'Leaving with patrol tomorrow morning.'

Chapter Twenty-one
MANHUNT PATROL

THE purpose of the patrol was multi-faceted; it was to check on the welfare of the scattered settlers over the range, to arrest half a dozen Aboriginal murderers whose killings had frightened their own tribesmen into seeking white police protection, to check the station Aborigines along the route for venereal disease and leprosy and to bring any sufferers back to Derby for treatment.

A most impressive task for any party, it becomes more impressive when one considers that all this had to be undertaken by one constable in charge of two trackers. It is even more surprising that a civilian should have been given permission to accompany police on business which had all the hallmarks of being both difficult and dangerous.

On 4 April 1934 the patrol filed out of the Derby Police station yard. 'Slippery the mule doing his snorting best to buck his pack off—Mandy tying herself in a knot. Larry and Davey, the trackers, rode ahead followed by the twenty-odd packhorses and mules, then Constable O'Neill and myself. Before us, under a bright sky stretched the Nor'-west Kimberley.'

Young Constable Laurie O'Neill was 'a fine type of the Western Australian Mounted Police. Tall and strong with the long swinging walk of the bushman, a boyish face and a smile that hid a determination that was alertly quick to swing into action.' Not yet thirty, O'Neill already had twenty thousand miles of patrolling to his credit.

The trackers were alike only in the colour of their skin, their tracking skills, and their love of their taxing work which gave them authority in the eyes of their fellow Aborigines.

Old Larry had grown grizzled in the service of the Western Australian Mounted Police. After the police had picked him up and reared him when he had been shot in the leg as a child, he had become a valued tracker. Except for periodical walkabouts he had stayed with them ever since.

Davey, the smart young Aborigine who fancied himself as a ladies' man, always washed his clothes the day before arriving at any homestead where he knew there would be young Aboriginal women working. Laurie felt sure that he would finish up wearing a shovel-bladed spear thrown by some jealous husband. Davey, only three years before, had been a *munjon* (wild bush Aborigine).

The Kimberley offered a visual feast of changing terrain, birds, animals and plant life. The wet had rejuvenated the land and in its wake everything flourished in the moist, warm earth.

The patrol moved through country that was awash with the reflected light from lagoons, and coloured pastel by the blue and pink water-lilies suspended on the shining surfaces. The air was alive with the sound of noisy wild ducks. Disturbed by this unexpected intrusion they took to the wing, sending shafts of coloured light spearing in all directions as they broke the sheets of translucent water.

The patrol soon left behind the scenic splendours of Six Mile Lagoon with its brolgas, wildfowl and colourful yellow water-lilies and crossed a lightly timbered plain covered with seven feet high patches of tall wheat grass.

The first night they made camp twenty miles out from Derby and moved on the next morning to cross the Lennard River, which was at that time a fury of swirling flood. Not quite three months later they would cross that same river, its ire spent, and by then nothing more than a series of water holes. A few miles beyond the river a low line of hills pushed crests and spires, sway-back tops and purple-grey walls above the plain. Once across this range the group headed to a line of green trees that clustered along the banks of the Barker River.

It was evening when they came up on Scotty Saddler's station hands building a log fire to last the night. Scotty and his cattle were not far behind. The cold night was warmed with hours of reminiscences told by Scotty, a well-preserved man, who still had a trace of his Scottish accent.

The next morning O'Neill, the trackers and Jack gave Scotty a hand to drive his cattle over the Barker River. Then, after tracking down and loading up their mules which had wandered off in the excitement of the crossing, they left Scotty and rode for the Napier Range, 'a jagged line of broken turrets carving the sky line. The face of the Napier was ever changing, always presenting a new facet at every turn; dull red hills, bold bluffs of heavy purple, bastions of bluish-grey rock above lawns of wheat grass.'

That nightfall they camped 'in a world of strange shadows' at Fletcher's Camp. This was a lonely waterhole among weird hills; it had been the favourite camp site of a Constable Fletcher when he was out on patrol. Fletcher, who had been stabbed to death by a Malay in Broome, would never see the camp again.

The next morning they pushed on to Mount Hart Station, riding through the foothills of the King Leopolds. Here the baobab trees clung to the pink bluffs like 'fat grey spiders'.

To reach Mount Hart the party had to zig-zag up steep hills and down into valleys, digging for toeholds, only to climb again to see panoramic stretches of range after range. Slowly they made their way along the divide until before them lay the hollow ringed by the small hills which cradled Mount Hart homestead. The area was known as the Kumumbullabulla and was the home of Felix Edgar and his overseer, 'Bunch 'em up' Gardiner, the same noisy, insomniac 'Bunch 'em up' they had left behind in Derby, and who was to die in Felix's arms of fever at Yabagoody Well not long afterwards. Felix himself was also to die of fever at Derby, a little over two years later.

Felix Edgar's station at Mount Hart was a setting for a wild west romance—Australian style. The station was ringed by hills which provided hidden vantage points in which the Aborigines could hide and spy on the homestead. Outside, feathery leafed poinciana trees shaded the grave of Chalmers, Felix Edgar's former partner, once known as the uncrowned king of Derby. Not long before the arrival of the patrol he had shot himself.

Jack wrote to Cousins on 11 April from Mount Hart:

A chance of writing today, the mailman calls at this place now and again. We are one hundred and forty miles from Derby now. I've got corns on my arse as big as doorknobs. The first cow I mounted chucked me clean over his head, to the huge delight of the aborigines. I've ridden all the blasted mules and horses in creation since then, or rather feel like it...So far, every man 'over the range' has died violently.

It seemed to Jack that here in the outback, suicide, murder and death by misadventure were the only ways to quit life; no one seemed to die quietly in old age.

Felix had come ashore in 1881 from a four-masted brig, the *Hamar*, after she had been badly knocked around by a storm in the King Sound. The *Hamar*, high and dry, found ground where Derby now stands. Felix and his mate, Tony Cornish, had bought fourteen hundred sheep, a small mob of horses and cattle on behalf of the Kimberley Pastoral Company which had taken up land on the Fitzroy. They had pushed the horses and cattle overboard so that they could battle for themselves and landed the sheep. Most of the horses and the cattle survived but it took Tony and Felix a long time to round up the animals which, driven by thirst, had wandered far inland in search of water.

To Jack, Felix was the epitome of a pioneer, the type that he revered, not only because of the man's physical ability to survive the rigours of a comfortless and dangerous life, but because Felix had been there when exploring, pioneering and settling were the only way of life.

That night, savouring his cigarette, he lay listening to Felix. Still and silent in the darkness he was enthralled, like a small boy afraid of breaking the storyteller's narrative. He absorbed the old man's tales of how individuals and big companies had gradually crept up the Fitzroy and settled the West Kimberley. Here was true romance told by a man who had 'done things in the days when our beards were black'. This was what Jack had come so far to see and experience—the rough outback and its people.

The patrol camped overnight at Mount Hart and halted for a day's 'spell' to shoe their horses. Jack was pleased to rest his tender behind, ease his aches and pick the grass seeds out of his pants.

Felix had been relieved to see the patrol arrive. He knew that in the hills unseen dark eyes were watching every movement that was made around the station. The dogs that constantly prowled the homestead had been more restless than usual at night; their occasional growls and ceaseless movement told him that the bush Aborigines were slipping into the home perimeter to communicate with the station Aborigines. In recent weeks these wild Aborigines had systematically killed and eaten thirty-six milking cows. Felix was worried. He knew that his own boys would have told the watchers on the hills that he was about to leave the station on muster; he also knew that the second his back was turned they would come in and raid his storehouse. Much to Felix's relief the day the patrol had arrived the Aborigines had taken off for the hinterland, leaving behind the station blacks.

Jack's felt city hat, with a handkerchief attached to the brim at the back to keep the sun off his neck, fascinated the Aborigines. The stockmen kept giving him curious glances, while the station women subsided into gusts of giggles at the sight of him. Apart from being a strange sight, his presence with the patrol provided a source of gossip. The homestead Aborigines were puzzled as to who he was. As trackers were supposed to know everything, old Larry assured them that Jack was an 'inspector'. Of course the trackers themselves did not know what his position with the patrol was and they had no intention of admitting it.

Laurie O'Neill made the decision to accompany Felix out of the homestead to give the appearance that the patrol had come to work the muster with him. The plan was to ride with Felix and his plant for a few days mustering and, when near to Laurie's objective, the patrol would cut away without prior warning. This action would serve a two-fold purpose: it would gain Felix time to get the muster completed before the bush Aborigines stripped his store-house and it would throw Laurie's quarry, Toolwanor (alias 'Nipper') and others, off-guard. Laurie's reasoning and the loyalty of his trackers appeared to be confirmed when they reported to him that the smoke signal, a wisp of pale blue smoke that spiralled into the sky forming a stationary black column, carried only the information that the patrol was still at Mount Hart.

Jack was keenly interested. He was sceptical that O'Neill and his men would be able to take their man unawares, on his own turf, by pitting their white wits against what seemed to him to be formidable odds. He wrote to Cousins:

> We've been wonderfully lucky, it hasn't rained since we started, but we've had to swim two flooded rivers. As usual I gave the trackers a laugh. O'Neill made a boat out of a fly ribbed with packbags, put some of the packs aboard and pushed her out. The blasted current soon swept me off my feet and I clung to the boat, my legs getting tangled up with the trackers. I was more of a hindrance than a help but you can bet your sweet life I did not let go, just thought of Bess and hung on. Your hero didn't cross back again but stayed safely on the other side while O'Neill and the trackers brought the rest of the stuff across. A few years of city life soon takes the kick for that kind of work out of a man.

On 12 April, 'dawn broke softly, cool and beautiful. The sun came stealing up over the hills'. The brief moment of peace was not long lived. Calls from a bird or two were the first sounds but then all was pandemonium. The police line was ready to leave in a moment but Felix and his retinue were unprepared. Felix began to roar on discovery of broken surcingles and girths that had not been repaired, and he continued to roar to the accompaniment of yells from the boys and much commotion from the women who were getting the breakfast.

At last, breakfast over, the repairs were carried out, and the equipment which consisted of pack bags, strings of hobble chains, tarpaulins, a wide assortment of gear and food for twelve or more people for two months, was all assembled in the stock yard ready for packing.

Felix sat on his big bay horse, occasionally flicking his stock whip around the uncooperative mules. Like an army general, he sat bellowing commands to his troops until finally all was saddled, sorted, packed and lashed down to his satisfaction.

Jack took in all the details, his keen eyes missing nothing. He committed everything to memory and notes which he later used to write *Over The Range*, his eleventh book.

After padlocking everything that could be secured Felix gave the keys of the kitchen to the home Aborigines who were staying behind. Then he gave the order for the unruly group to move off.

Big Paddy rode up front with the trackers, the stock boys were spaced at intervals along the string of mules and horses, while bringing up the rear were the three Aboriginal girls dressed in trousers, hats and smiles. Among the group rode Boghole Willie, 'the most willing and the most stupid' and Brandy, son of Whisky, wearing an old felt hat and a stock whip looped around his shoulder.

Jack rode behind with Laurie, who stopped to caution the station Aborigines not to listen to the *munjons* if they should come in to raid Felix's storehouse.

Jack continued his observations: 'I rode behind on the old grey, keenly interested in that most interesting of all hunts, a man hunt. It hardly seemed possible that wild men in their own country, with all its natural resources allied against the opponent, could be captured by one solitary white man and two trackers. My job was simply to mind my own business.'

The patrol left Felix's station on 'a glorious day. Vision so clear that shadows of the trees away on the hills were perfectly distinct. As we rode through kurrajong and coolabah, box and gum, musical with birds and over miles of waving grassland it was good to be alive.'

The party travelled over some of the 130,000 acres that Felix had bought from Sir Sidney Kidman when the latter had abandoned Glenroy Station.

After leaving Mount Hart they rode on with Felix and his mustering party to the first wall of the Leopolds and entered Gardiner's Gap. So well hidden was the opening that the trackers in the lead were instantly swallowed up, vanishing from sight before Jack and Laurie, who were the last of the party, had entered the mouth of the gap. Once inside and surrounded by the towering walls they followed a small wandering creek that stopped here and there to form tree-lined rock pools. Then, without warning, the party rode out on to a grassy valley that stretched away to where the Precipice Range runs parallel with the Leopolds. 'To the north towered Mount Chalmers.'

Jack, the romantic, was thrilled to ride through the gap which had only recently been made known to 'Bunch 'em up' Gardiner by the Aborigines and as a consequence bore his name. For many years men had ridden right by it, as they had ridden by many such other passes while seeking to make the Leopolds accessible from the coast. Jack imagined what it must feel like to go where no white man has ever been before.

As a frustrated explorer Jack envied and appreciated the achievements of those explorers who had gone before him. He disliked pretension and misrepresentation and refused to allow himself to be referred to as an 'explorer'. He was determined that the reputation of being a 'Main Roads' Explorer' would never be his.

After leaving Gardiner's Gap and the grassy valley behind, the group rode towards the Isdell River. With superb attention to detail which surpasses the ordinary traveller, Jack recorded how he saw the Leopold Ranges:

> The ranges run approximately from east to west, ending in a hopeless tangle at the rugged coast. To the man riding north they appear, as a rule, before him like parallel walls, their summits usually rimmed by sheer cliff faces. The majority are flat topped. Straight 'through' a range may only have a width of three, five or ten miles, then will appear a grassy valley, often stony, from three to ten miles wide and twenty or more long.
>
> Across this valley looms another range, another wall-like barrier. By narrow passes through these ranges the traveller passes into valley after valley. Some ranges however, are a series of steep rounded hills. These are crossed by riding up a negotiable spur, then over a divide and down into the lower country. The ranges seldom rise more than two thousand, five hundred feet, with isolated peaks up to three thousand feet. The entire country has a grandeur peculiar to itself.

Jack rode in the brilliant light of the Kimberley. Places named after men who had not long died or were still alive strengthened his sense of 'new' country, yet, somehow, all was old. Three years later, when he wrote *Over The Range*, the story of the Kimberley patrol, it was subtitled, 'Sunshine and Shadows in the Kimberleys' emphasising the impression made on him by the brilliant light and rich purple shadows.

They met Bill Connell, another man who had chosen to live away from his own kind. Jack, who was not unused to his own company, marvelled at the character and the personality of these men who were able to live in isolation for months and years. Bill was the epitome of the stalwart types who were thinly scattered 'over the range'. Bill lived back in the hills, two days' ride from the wells, his only companions two very old Aborigines and two big dogs. Without transport, he lived on the Aboriginal food he hunted with his trusty old Aboriginal friends.

Stopping there for the night they brought Bill Connell up-to-date with all the outside news, while he gave them the news contained in the Aboriginal 'smokes', and the death of one Murphy in the West Kimberley, which Laurie knew nothing about. Bill had known all about the coming patrol long before it had arrived and the fact that a stranger, wearing something 'odd' on his head, was travelling with it.

Once again, lying silent in the night, as he was to do for many nights to come, Jack soaked up the colourful stories of good and bad whites and blacks, strange animals and the unusual story of the crying voice, a piteous wail that rose at night from a lagoon and made the hair on the back of the necks of all who heard it stand on end.

The ill-assorted, riotous cavalcade moved off the next morning leaving Bill behind to muse upon his solitude for another year.

On reaching the Isdell River which marked the boundary between Felix's property and that of Maxted and Smith, the patrol abruptly left Felix as arranged. The manhunt was now on in earnest.

♦

The banks of Isdell River were lined with tall Cadjaput, Leichhardt Pine and Screw Palms. Gladly the group travelled in the sun-dappled shade of the tall trees as it followed the river towards Grace's Knob:

> Later that day we rode over a low divide and down on to a black-soil plane well grassed with bundle-bundle, Mitchell, Flinders and ribbon grasses, with occasional patches of spindle grass amongst which stood up the sweetly edible mimosa bush.

Mid-afternoon they came upon an Aboriginal camp by the river. Laurie sent his trackers on ahead to observe. They reported back that they had seen no sign of Toolwanor. It was here that Jack was to observe for the first time some of the tactics that Laurie would employ to flush out his man. They halted outside the camp, biding their time until sunset. If Toolwanor was hiding out, he would be waiting until dark before coming into camp. That would be the time to move if they hoped to catch him.

Laurie sent Larry and Davey across the river to wait. They had orders to ride into the camp from the opposite side when he and Jack came within full view of the Aborigines. If Toolwanor had slipped into the camp the sight of the two white men would flush their man into the arms of the oncoming trackers.

At the appointed hour Laurie and Jack crossed the plain at a gallop with the line of following packhorses and mules stretched out behind them. Simultaneously, the trackers moved in from across the river. However they were not rewarded by even the sight of a fleeing shadow. The women and children stared at the group as they entered the camp. Tribesmen, heavily scarred and with deeply wrinkled faces, approached Laurie and the two trackers.

Taken by surprise by Davey's rapid questioning, the tribesmen admitted that Toolwanor had been camped with them, but that he had left to hunt flying foxes. They claimed they had heard nothing more of Toolwanor. However, they let slip that a native named Oomagan had killed another tribesman. Laurie abandoned the search for the time being and moved the patrol on to pay a visit to Maxted and Smith, two young cattlemen who had taken up the pick of the country Kidman had abandoned around the Isdell River.

The homestead was a short distance up river from the Aboriginal camp. They had not gone far when old Peter Bextrum strolled into view from behind a huge baobab tree. Peter, who worked with Maxted and Smith, told Laurie that the two men were away mustering. Peter Bextrum was one of the many staunch friends the Aborigines had throughout the Kimberley. They trusted him. He understood the Aboriginal mentality, he counselled them, he doctored them and did his best to battle the dreaded venereal disease which was so quickly wiping out large numbers of the race. He was very concerned about what appeared to be a sudden virulent outbreak of leprosy, the 'Big Sick'. Throughout the afternoon Peter questioned Laurie at length about the disease in the hope that the constable's knowledge would assist him to recognise and treat the insidious killer in its early stages.

Night fell suddenly. As the hurricane lamp was being lit in the Maxted and Smith homestead wild chanting broke out in the Aboriginal camp a short way down the river. Laurie had just packed a little food into an easily carried bag when Larry appeared at the door. Laurie picked up his hat, and with a smile and an almost imperceptible nod strode from the room.

'He's gone after Toolwanor,' Peter quietly answered Jack's unasked question.

'Tonight?' Jack asked incredulously.

'Yes, he knows that immediately after dark a runner will leave to warn Toolwanor. That's Davey's country out there, he knows where Flying Fox camp is … they'll have a hard time, but they'll bring him back tomorrow.'

Shortly after midday Laurie and the two trackers came back to the homestead—with Toolwanor, just as Peter had predicted. Jack would have liked to have been in on the capture, but he had to settle for a detailed description of the night's events.

As Peter had stated the going had been rough. Laurie, Davey and Larry had clambered down rocky ravines and pushed through the thorny scrub along a rock-filled gorge; then they had climbed over a rough hillside and down another gorge. They knew that they had reached their destination when, in the small hours of the morning, the musty, fetid, smell of the flying fox colony filled their nostrils. The dull red coals of a fire glowing under a clump of giant paper-barks by a sandy creek bed had confirmed that Toolwanor was close by. The trio had then taken cover and settled back and waited for the runner they knew would come.

The runner had come like a shadow. Without so much as a whisper another two shadows took him.

The vast silence of the bush ticked on until near dawn when Laurie and his two trackers rushed the camp. They surprised a few Aborigines who were sleeping there but Toolwanor had vanished. It took Davey only a few brief seconds to pick up Toolwanor's tracks and to set out—with Laurie and Larry hard on his heels—to run his man down.

Davey had accurately guessed that Toolwanor would go to ground in a hideout in a gorge they had both used in the past. Swiftly circling wide of Toolwanor's path, Davey had out-distanced him. He had scarcely taken cover among the boulders before Toolwanor appeared. Like a flash of black lightning the tracker had him down and had snapped the handcuff shut on one wrist. Toolwanor had not come quietly. A wild fight had followed before Davey managed to snap the cuff over his other wrist.

After a minor confrontation with Toolwanor's woman and much pleading by Toolwanor with Davey, who had been his past accomplice in minor crimes, to let him go for 'old times' sake', Laurie and Larry caught up with them. The woman, Chalba, followed her man and the patrol back to Maxted and Smith's place.

Jack was told that Toolwanor's 'white feller name' was Nipper and that he was accused of having killed a fellow Aborigine, one Burrin. Toolwanor admitted to the killing with some pride, adding, as he pointed to Chalba, that Burrin had tried to steal his wife. He declared, with no malice at all, that a certain Ungandongery (white feller name Charcoal) had assisted him in the exacting of his vengeance.

After Nipper had been captured and Charcoal's name had been mentioned, the Aborigines camped downstream from Maxted and Smith's were only too ready to give details of the murder. Indeed there was a surfeit of informants. Larry listened to all of them, only finally to wrinkle his face with a knowing grin. He stated, 'These feller all about lies ... know too much!'

The next morning the patrol left Peter and the homestead by the Isdell. With Nipper on the chain, and his woman following, the enlarged party forded the river and pushed on. They were in search of Charcoal. In the late afternoon they clambered up a steep rocky rise to gain access to the tablelands of the Phillips ranges. Once there they made camp for the night.

'Next morning's awakening was glorious,' wrote Jack. 'The brightness of the spreading colours of the rising sun slowly dimmed the morning star. Bird voices broke out everywhere.' After breakfast the group moved on through a narrow valley, Larry and Davey bending over their horses to point out the tracks of men they knew. Toolwanor eagerly pointed out the tracks of strangers. Laughingly he also pointed out the refuse left by burnt-out campfires and detailed the names of those who had gathered there. Jack listened and watched the black men in fascination. Although he had many times seen the Aborigines practise their formidable tracking ability during his days on the Cape York Peninsula, he never failed to be amazed at what they could see—and what he couldn't.

They had crossed a tableland 'that eventually seemed to break over the rim of the world'. It was here that they came upon two hunting dogs followed by an Aboriginal huntsman and his woman:

The man upright and fearless was daubed with ochre bars of red and white, his forehead band brilliant with tufts of parrot feathers.

He carried a woomera and two excellently made shovel-nosed spears; a stone knife was shoved through his human hair belt.

By judicious questioning Davey had obtained directions to the nearest white man's camp, and the information that Charcoal was hunting his way across country to the 'white man' property of Dave Rust. Davey got his information and the informant gained a pocket knife. The painted warrior found it hard to believe that such a chance meeting would have made him the proud owner of such a wondrous knife.

Fred Russ also had a holding in the near vicinity—near vicinity being only a relative term in respect of such vast distances. Because O'Neill could not be sure that Charcoal was not at Russ's place 'chucking his weight about' he decided on a detour to check out the Russ property. Charcoal was not there but an Aboriginal woman badly afflicted with VD was and so was a male leper. These two, together with Jack Campbell, joined the trek to Dave Rust's homestead. The original party of four had now grown to nine.

Finally the party reached Rust's pine-walled thatched hut. Jack Campbell, the half-caste who worked for Dave, approached the hut with apprehension to unlock it. It had been some time since the place had been inhabited, or been under the watchful eye of Jack Campbell. All shared the common fear that the bush Aborigines would have broken in and cleaned out the next three months' supplies. Had this happened Dave Rust would have had to start all over again. He been forced to do so in the past, and if necessary would have done so again. Jack admired the continuing endurance of men like Dave who, in the face of hardship, disaster and theft, kept coming back for more of the same with never a thought of quitting.

Dave's place had not been broken into. The hut held all the usual settler's equipment which Jack was now familiar with. Its walls were lined with pictures of men dressed in kilts and tossing cabers, lassies and sword dancers, Scottish terriers and castles. It was easy for Jack to visualise the hut's owner at the end of a day picturing himself back home in Scotland.

Dave's hut stood near a chain of reedy waterholes, beside which was a newly fenced patch of bright green peanut plants. Over all hung an air of utter wildness. 'The courage of a man to plant peanuts in such a place' impressed Jack. This was Gnoungundooda—a pioneer's home in the most primitive sense.

It was here that Laurie caught up with Ungandongery, known as 'Charcoal', and Oomagun, who does not appear to have acquired the white man name which was then so prized by the Aborigines.

Late that afternoon Laurie held an impromptu inquiry under the trees by the waterholes. The Aborigines squatted in the dirt in front of him. Davey, the police tracker was a 'local' who knew every district within a large radius and proved to be a very competent interpreter.

The appearance of the patrol had convinced Toby, an ex-tracker, that it was time to terminate his current walkabout with the tribe. His pidgin was good, and as he had been travelling with the tribe for some time he was well informed on current tribal happenings. In his eagerness to gain the favour of the patrol he acted as Counsel for the Defence.

Jack was keenly interested in the scene which was played out before him. He recorded not only the events but committed to paper some of the best descriptions of the Northern Territory bush Aborigines ever to be written.

The 'trial' over, the prisoners were placed on a neck chain. The infamous chain, the subject of much criticism by those who believed its use to be inhumane, was in fact far more humane than the handcuffs that replaced its use for a time in other areas. Ultimately, the regulation requiring the use of handcuffs was rescinded in favour of the proven, kinder method of chaining prisoners. The following description of the treatment of Laurie's prisoners illustrates the more benign aspect of chaining:

The prisoners were put on a chain. Not a very impressive chain; Nipper had carried it a hundred miles and not noticed it; one day he had carried a kangaroo as well. The chain is strong but light. A loop of it is placed loosely around each man's neck and the loop padlocked. There is ample room between each man to allow them to walk, drink, or do anything in comfort—except run away. They could even do that, and swiftly, but they would become entangled around a tree, or else fall and bring the others on top of him. Thus linked around the neck, equal distances apart along the chain, their arms are perfectly free. This is absolutely necessary when marching through the bush. Hands must be free to brush away branches, grass and vines, and allow them to carry on the march. When climbing a hill, clambering down into steep gullies, or winding along boulder strewn gorges or down slippery banks or across deep streams, their limbs are thus free. They must have their hands free, too, to attend to themselves in a dozen different ways.

By the time the patrol was ready to leave Dave Rust's holding the number of people in the group, including the original three police personnel and Jack, had grown to fifteen. Eventually Laurie was to lead almost forty people back to Derby. This large number was made up of his prisoners, their women and two children, witnesses for the Crown, and the sick.

Chapter Twenty-two
THE LOST TRIBE

LAURIE admitted to Jack that most patrols were lonely, nerve-racking affairs, especially if he had what he considered 'a bad bunch to bring in'. Inclement weather reduced visibility and brought sudden raging torrents, which slowed their progress and increased the danger threefold.

The strain escalated with the approach of night—camp had to be made before dark. Establishing the camp was not a simple undertaking. All stones, large or small, had to be removed from the radius of the chained prisoners, and all tufts of grass had to be uprooted to ensure that no stones were hidden in the roots. The prisoners' matted hair also had to be searched for any stones that may have been concealed there during the day. This ritual was meticulously carried out every evening prior to the lighting of individual fires for each prisoner. Despite all their precautions Laurie, Jack and the trackers endured the endless nights with their nerves taut. With ears straining they listened for a faint tapping which would indicate a stone was being used to break the links in the chain which had been surreptitiously heated in a fire.

The mood of the Aborigines changed dramatically when they were travelling through taboo or enemy territory. The women clung together in fear, apprehensively casting sidelong, wild-eyed glances at every bush and clump of grass, while the men were silent and watchful. The sudden cessation of sound always drew a reaction from Jack and Laurie—it could have indicated anything from an ambush attack to an impending escape attempt.

The search for Burrin's remains, Toolwanor's victim, took them through several areas where both Aborigines and white men expected death to come, without warning, in the form of a shovel-nosed spear. This sense of dreadful anticipation was increased after they had recovered Burrin's bones.

To show a white man where a body had been buried was one thing, but to have him put the bones into a canvas bag and carry them away with them was an act that invited the spirit of the dead man to follow his bones wherever they went. Gloom and superstition took a stranglehold after Davey returned empty-handed from several hunting trips. The group firmly believed that the spirit of Burrin had walked before him and frightened the kangaroos away. Larry insisted that he had even seen the spirit's tracks and no amount of logic could convince him that this wasn't possible. Davey supported Larry.

They continued towards Walcott Inlet. At night the Aborigines kept low fires. The women spoke only in subdued, serious tones; gone was the laughter, the chants and the songs. It was around these campfires that Jack learned more about the spiritual beliefs of the Aborigines than most men would have learned in many years of living with them. Under the spell of superstition, and fearful of the lurking malignant spirits, Larry and Davey clearly expressed their convictions without resorting to camouflage or the childish stories usually reserved for inquisitive whites.

The paralysing fear persisted and threatened to completely freeze the party in the middle of no man's land. They needed food. As the absence of kangaroos for the pot seemed to be the one factor that confirmed the vengeful spirit's presence, Laurie ordered Davey to take a rifle and keep walking until he did get a 'roo. Meanwhile he pushed the rest of the party towards the sound of a waterfall which Davey told him was named Bulwallingarra, adding that no white man had ever been there before.

Jack found this hard to believe. Both he and Laurie pored over Laurie's official map and found that none of the accepted explorers' routes had crossed this particular area. Hann had missed it in 1898, as had Brockman in 1901, while Bradshaw's route and Allen's were nowhere near, nor any track taken by Dr F.M. House. Crossland's expedition of 1905 did not touch the area, neither did Price-Conigrave's 1912 expedition. Easton's Kimberley Exploration Expedition of 1921 had crossed the Charnley farther towards the coast. Laurie was nonplussed. 'I've done twenty thousand miles of patrolling in the Kimberleys,' he said, 'but this little corner is new to me. I know every man over the range, but I haven't heard one describe this particular spot.'

Jack recorded that they followed a river along flats that were well grassed while continuing towards the sound of the waterfall. He was sure that if a cattleman had come across the river, he would have followed it in search of good grazing land. He also knew that if a prospector had passed this way, he too would have followed the river to test it as a sluicing prospect.

Just a little over one page in *Over The Range* is devoted to what would have to be the first published record of their discovery—

the first sighting by white men of an age-old corner of Western Australia:

Blocked by a mass of trees and boulders we stepped from rock to rock up a low hill-side, and presently saw a long stretch of slippery rock gleaming under the sun, ribbons of water racing down it. A bee-eater in a shimmer of gold, green and bronze sped by, his two long tail-quills holding our interest as he sped above the rock that, like a slippery road one hundred yards wide, was a rapid and not a waterfall. It ran between black, pink, and grey walls ten feet high. At the head of this rapid was a large circular pool ringed with black rock as if cut by the chisels of pigmy giants. A sprinkle of sand was marked by tracks of freshwater crocodiles, the only sand along the whole quarter-mile length of glistening rock. Above this pool gleamed a further long slope over which water raced, then another walled pool, emerald clear, with fishes swimming in it. Above it was still another slope across the top of which ran a broad causeway of steel-hard rock. Ten feet below the fury of countless wet seasons had torn away the softer rock. Beyond a further pool the long slope of smoothed rock rose rapidly to its summit silhouetted by a fringe of green pandanus palm. This was the lip of a low tableland. And here gleamed the top pool where, from around an island of rocks and palms, two green streams swept out on to the bare rock to join in a swift race down into the Charnley.

Turning around and looking down this we saw that the series of falls ran approximately from north-east to south-west. Down that quarter-mile slope the vertical fall was probably not much more than one hundred feet, its centre sparkling under a thin ribbon of water. But what a magnificent sight it must be in a heavy wet season with a raging fury of water tearing down there. We could see flood-marks twenty feet high. Such a volume would be overwhelming, roaring down that quarter-mile slope with its hundred-foot fall. This once great torrent was now withered and old. It had been a mighty stream in ages past when these hills were mountains. The dwarf trees on the summit, the prickly scrub, the weathered sandstones, the old-time plants like the tufts of coarse spinifex grasses and pandanus palms, were the grey hairs in this very, very old land.

Davey had kept walking (with Burrin's spirit by his side), hunting the kangaroos for another two days. Each night when he returned without meat the Aborigines shrugged and turned back to the fires and 'civilised tucker'. Then at last the curse was lifted:

Davey came back to camp with a 'roo—they had crossed the boundary of Burrin's country.

Davey said this was his country and where he had undergone his initiation. He was delighted to be on his own territory but not so the other Aborigines. Their fear was obvious: not only were they in another tribe's territory, they were also nearing sacred country and tribally they were forbidden to tread on the ground. They were 'stepping like cautious cats ready to dodge and run at a movement'.

While the others grew more serious and more subdued Davey became more animated and told them stories that they would never have heard from him had the circumstances been different. 'Before the "big sick" came this had been the great meeting place where at certain times of the year the men of the Walcott Inlet marched to meet the men of the Isdell, of the Gibb and the Hann and the Upper Charnely. The Ngarinyin and tribes equally as far away marched here to fight and initiate their young men.'

The entire group—prisoners, the sick, witnesses and women, followed by the pack horses—had climbed, in single file, a precipitous spur that appeared to lead to a 'dead-end amongst scrub-covered bastions above' to reach the 'Charoo'. The path however had widened out into a scrub-covered plateau.

'It was an old looking plateau; old rocks, old trees, coarse tufty grass that might have been among the first species of grass to grow in the world.' Jack observed that a rider below would have passed by never suspecting its existence. It was easy to understand how it had remained undiscovered.

Davey explained complex rites, and even told them of 'the eating of the heart, kidneys, and liver of a slain enemy by the warriors of his tribe, but not the organs of their own men'. Whilst they drew the line at eating their own men, he told them that they occasionally took a young plump lubra into the bush, killed her, and after cooking her, ate the entire body. He assured them, however, that this was only done on special occasions.

Jack was not surprised or shocked. Cannibalism had been in common practice in the past on Cape York Peninsula. The Aborigines there had made no secret that, given a choice, they preferred to eat the hapless Chinese who came to the Palmer River in search of gold. The Chinese, named 'long pig' by the Cape York Aboriginal because they were 'sweet', were a delicacy prized above the white prospectors, whom they said were 'tough and salty'. Historical records show, however, that when it came down to it the Peninsula Aborigines were neither selective nor finicky.

Davey's explicit descriptions did nothing to encourage his fellow travellers to feel at home. Laurie moved the miserable group forward. Going ever deeper into the forbidden territory they passed huge stone heaps which were obviously markers of symbolism and tradition.

Jack noted that in some places stones had been placed in patterns over several acres, but grass and low-growing shrubs were beginning to creep over these larger ritual grounds, evidence that they were no longer in use and that the people were dying out. He felt then, in 1934, that it would not be long before the undergrowth would obliterate all trace of this Aboriginal tribe's age-old beliefs and practices.

Suddenly, on this lost plateau bordered on all sides by deep valleys, they came upon the men of Charoo—Aborigines who had never seen a white man before:

> We took the men of Charoo by complete surprise. They stared, seemingly incapable of movement. Here and there a half-poised spear trembled in a nerveless hand; one old warrior frantically chewed his beard, his eyes like those of an animal paralysed with fear. All crouched in whatever attitude they were in when we appeared among them. The women covered their faces with claw-like hands; children buried their heads under the mothers. The warriors were glaring at our horses, more than at us. When we dismounted I would not have been surprised had they dropped, for one legend of those people is that in the faraway ages half-man, half-animal beings had come to their ancestors and told them the laws.

On that first day they encountered only twenty-five of these 'pre-historic' people and another twenty-five the following day.

> Throughout the whole patrol they were the only people we met entirely in the stone age, though we met some hundreds who were just beginning to discard their stone weapons for rough hewn tools of iron. But these people carried nothing but stone axes, stone phallic knives, stone spear-heads, secret stones, magic stones, medicine stones; human hair belts around the waists of men; the wildness of Eve in the eyes of the women. They were carrying their 'spirit' bones too. The old witch doctor wore an eagle's claw through his nose and a necklace of human knuckle-bones. At first glance they looked just like animal men and women and cubs—and smelt like it too. They lived materially right down to nature, while living, too,

day and night in a spirit world. Laurie battled hard to gain their confidence. Their fears gradually became tinged with a frightened curiosity. But we would not have held them a moment had it not been for the reassuring presence of Davey.

Davey eventually gained the partial confidence of the people and fear gave way to interest. After a while he was able to take Jack and Laurie to a place further down the plateau to a waterfall where the laws were made.

Both men had stood silent for some time. Jack, as he observed, felt the urge to 'leap out and over' while Laurie was moved to say, 'It all gives one rather a queer feeling.'

No doubt both were a little over-awed and understandably so. They had travelled far under less than ideal circumstances in the company of murderers, they had stumbled upon a lost tribe and broken ground which was imbued with centuries of primitive superstition. At this time Laurie O'Neill and Jack Idriess were indeed 'men who had done things'.

While they stood there, lost to the world, the Old Men of Charoo enacted out a strange pantomime which Davey interpreted. Through this they explained that here the laws of the stone-age men had been made. They told of a time when man was a lonesome thing terrified by convulsions of nature, chased by gigantic animals and monstrous birds and serpents. Among other things they told of the days of the under-gods, half-man, half-spirit, that were sent from the World of Stars to teach laws to man upon the earth.

These were a people who had never been seen before and most likely have never been seen since. They never left their hidden plateau, and the tribes that visited them were forbidden to mention the place because of its sacred associations. Sadly, despite their isolated location, and even though they had never been in contact with the white man, the people of Charoo were doomed— leprosy had reached them.

Chapter Twenty-three
RETURN TO DERBY

ONE of the newspaper clippings waiting for Jack with his mail when he returned to Derby from the Kimberly patrol was written by the Sydney journalist, Colin Simpson. It made Jack cringe. The three paragraphs had appeared in the *Sunday Sun* on 15 April 1934, just a few days after Jack had left Derby with the patrol. It carried the heading 'Expedition Seeks Wild Tribes' and was sub-headed 'Ion Idriess Explores the Kimberleys'.

On 12 June Jack wrote a five-page letter to Cousins which closed with:

> Have just glanced at that par of Colin Simpson's. He refers to me as 'exploring'. I don't like this at all, he can write anything roman- tic he likes but leave out 'exploring'. That is a job for the 'main roads' explorers'. Exploring in Australia was finished long ago. In my talks at various times I have had to contradict the Press when they referred to me thus. It makes a man a fool to those who know.

Jack apologised for 'answering in short' because he had fifty-four letters to reply to and two articles to write for the Melbourne *Herald*. Already several residents of Derby were talking about dashing off articles about the patrol for the southern press. Jack was concerned that if these articles, by-lined 'Our Special Correspondent', appeared in other papers before his articles reached the *Herald* the editor may think he had not honoured his contract. Due to the sensitive subject matter he planned to send his articles first to Treadgold in Perth. This would create a further delay but he had no wish to embarrass Treadgold or the police who had shown him more than average consideration.

While Jack was roaming about the Leopolds and the Kimberley, a 'lady novelist' from New York had visited Angus and Robertson in the hope of finding an Australian publisher for her work. Cousins reported that he was unimpressed by her writing but he found her travelling companion, the Associate Editor of the American *Good Housekeeping* journal, a valuable contact. Both ladies assured Cousins that Jack's *Men of the Jungle* was 'just marvellous'. The Associate Editor thought that *Men of the Jungle* had a good chance of being accepted for serialisation by the magazine and assessed that the rights would bring about six thousand US dollars.

Later, after his return to Derby, Jack wrote to Cousins in reference to the *Good Housekeeping* journal, that while 'two million is a big public, it would be difficult for a bloke to skite about being published in a magazine called *Good Housekeeping* ... The title puzzles me, it sounds like a woman's paper for making recipes.'

Cousins did not acknowledge the comment. Evidently he found the publication of the works of one his authors to a public of two million adequate compensation for any possible aspersions that might be cast on the author's manhood. Accordingly he forwarded not only *Men of the Jungle* to the magazine but also *Gold Dust and Ashes* and *Lasseter's Last Ride*. The editorial staff of *Good Housekeeping*, however, declined the opportunity to publish Idriess, thereby saving 'a bloke' the embarrassment of having to admit to being published in a magazine with such a 'sissy' title.

Before leaving Derby Jack had sent films and manuscript back to Cousins. Cousins acknowledged receipt of 'MS in a Capstan Cigarette Box and two spools of films together with negatives from Constable O'Neill'.

People wrote to Jack for information about all number of things and Cousins sent the letters on to him. They covered topics such as 'What steps an ordinary outback farmer should take who wishes to sell sandalwood and information regarding the NSW market'. A note from Cousins was attached: 'Scribble something out.'

At that time Jack was beginning to be irritated by the mounting number of letters from people who expected him to answer their questions on any and all topics. He had not yet learned to conserve his time and protect himself from the enormous drain on his energy which his public exacted from him. In later years, when the world was beating a path to his door and he was suffering from frequent recurring bouts of malaria, the constant enquiries and visits from fans and cranks sorely tried his patience.

◆

DURING the previous two months Jack had traversed the country as far as Port George on the coast and the Prince Regent inland. Riding with the patrol he had crossed the country from the East Kimberley right through to the West Coast. He returned claiming, with a certain amount of pride, that 'I know enough about patrols now and the nor'-west Kimberley to last me a lifetime'. Briefly he outlined the results of the patrol to Cousins:

> There is a book in this patrol, we covered twelve hundred miles (mileage not made out yet) got two lots of murderers and witnesses, witnesses for another murder, twelve lepers, etc. not to mention three skeletons. About the least known country in Australia I should say. Interesting country and just enough people in it to give it the human interest touch. There were only a dozen or so whites all told.

Jack's letter to Cousins reports that they had brought back twelve lepers. (A newspaper report in the *West Australian* dated 22 June 1934 by a 'Special Correspondent' states that the number was ten.) Jack noted that throughout the entire trip they had seen many others similarly afflicted with the disease but the size of their small party had effectively stopped them from bringing them in.

The diseased natives were also often unable to be persuaded to leave their tribal land for the magic of 'the white man's medicine'. Fearing Laurie, Jack, the trackers and their monstrous horses and mules which most had never seen, the Aborigines had slipped away to hide deep in the bush when the patrol approached.

On his arrival in Derby Laurie had placed the lepers in the Derby Leprosarium for treatment; six decamped in the night. Once outside the Leprosarium's iron fence they had turned north and travelled through marsh lands in an attempt to return to their tribal lands.

Constable Laurie O'Neill, giving evidence before the Aborigines Commission on 21 June, told the pathetic story of how the trackers, after following the escapees for twenty-five miles, had captured five of the six at the end of the first day. The search for Jungolongoh, the sixth man, known on the patrol as the 'Big Leper', had to be halted when nightfall had made it impossible for them to follow his tracks.

When daylight broke it was easy for the trackers to pick up his trail. The soles of his leprous feet had dropped off on the way into Derby; now with every footfall the blood from the badly swollen and broken skin left the story of his last agonising journey imprinted on the earth.

The tracks showed that Jungolongoh's companions had quickly outstripped him. At first, fearing pursuit, he had hobbled on, expecting to be overtaken by the trackers, but the knowledge that he was in hostile territory would have turned his fear to terror, anticipating an assassin's spear sighing through the night air to cleave open his back. When the night, peopled with spirits and devils, closed in on him, superstition completed his torment. It was clear to the trackers that alone and lost the man had wandered in circles. They saw that here and there he had made sudden lunges into the bush only to turn and rush back. In other places, in a frenzy of pain and fear, he had torn down bushes in an attempt to gain a branch to defend himself should he come face to face with the killer he was sure was on his trail.

His tracks had stopped at the edge of a mangrove creek. Jungolongoh never crossed the water. Perhaps, as he slid down the creek's sheer wall the notorious King Sound tide was rushing to the sea and sucked him along with it. The trackers believed however that he had fallen prey to the king of lizards—the crocodile.

Laurie's evidence, given before the Aborigine Commission, was a stark statement of facts. The Commission, however, was not told of the care that Constable Laurie O'Neill had given the 'Big Leper' when bringing him in for treatment. Laurie O'Neill, a humane and caring individual, had been deeply distressed by the suffering of the man. When Jungolongoh's feet had first begun to swell badly Laurie had cut up his boots and given them to him to wear. After that the party was able to travel only for a further two miles before the soles of the leper's feet began to break away. Laurie had then cut up a shirt and bound the man's feet in an attempt to give him a measure of comfort. However, by midday the same day Jungolongoh was hobbling far behind. Once again Laurie called a halt. After examining the man's feet he found that the soles were peeling off in layers inside the bandages.

Jungolongoh's eyes had widened in fear when Laurie indicated he was to ride a mule to save him further pain. He was frightened of horses but he was more terrified that the patrol would leave him. In strained guttural he had communicated to the trackers that he would try to ride the mule, not because of his physical condition but because he feared the wild bush *mujons* would kill him if the patrol were to ride off and leave him there alone. When Jack asked the trackers if he would have been killed had they left him behind, they replied unanimously, 'Quick feller!'.

The wretched man had spent an agonising day clinging to the back of the mule which was led at arm's length by his equally frightened wife. At sundown Jungolongoh had slowly rolled off the mule. His limbs were swollen and pieces of skin showed through the remnants of the bandages around his feet.

The group was forced to continue on in this way until it reached Kimberley Downs, where Laurie hurried on ahead to hire the mailman's truck to bring in his prisoners. His true intent was to save the sick Aborigines the stress of the remaining sixty-mile walk into Derby. For the Aborigines, all of whom had never even seen, much less ridden, in a truck, the ride into Derby was a mind-boggling experience. Jungolongoh unfortunately was not to be saved despite Laurie's best efforts.

The purpose of Jack's trip to Western Australia had been to get authentic material for what he called 'the mounted' book. During the process of collecting this material he amassed a wealth of stories about the north-west and south-west camel patrols of Central Australia, the desert patrols of Western Australia and the epic rides of the Queensland 'Mounteds'. He took down enough material for three books which dealt only with the day-to-day work of the West Australian mounted police: *Man Tracks*, *Over The Range* and *Outlaws of the Leopolds*. Of the three, perhaps *Over The Range* gives the greatest insight into the work of the mounted police constable.

The *Sydney Morning Herald* review of *Man Tracks* could have been written of *Over The Range* and *Outlaws of the Leopolds*. '[Idriess] writes, not fiction, but contemporary history, something far more valuable and enduring and, under his hands no less exciting to read.'

◆

DESPITE the fact that Jack had been on the move for the past two months he was in a hurry to get out of Derby. He made plans to leave town by motor for Fitzroy Crossing. He was eager to get back home but at the same time he lamented having only a week to spend at the Crossing: 'I could be a year with the material to be got there but I'm in a hurry.' In a letter to Cousins he outlined the rest of his itinerary: 'Another week at Halls Creek, a few days at Turkey Creek and a week at Wyndham. Then Darwin, then possibly Tennant Creek for a couple of days, then Alice Springs, thence Adelaide.'

However by 15 June his plans to leave Derby had changed. Nipper and Charcoal had been formally charged with murder and the inquest remanded for eight days. The trial had been held over pending the arrival in Derby of the Commissioner of Native Affairs, Mr Mosely. Mosely was said to be near Fitzroy Crossing and not expected in Derby in under eight days.

On 26 June he wrote to Cousins:

I received a wire from Eta asking for twenty [pounds], I did not answer. She had a hundred to her credit when I left Sydney, since then the four per week. Surely that should keep her. Somehow whenever I send her my address she wants money, it does not feel quite fair to me. However, I would not like her to be in want. If she asks for any extra, but only if you [are] sure it is a matter of emergency, please pay her what you think fit, out of any royalties if any are due me. And if the four a week is cut out please carry on if there are royalties due to cover it. The whole dashed thing is a sorry business.

By deliberately failing to answer Eta's telegram, Jack appears to have behaved quite out of character. He was not an uncaring man, neither was he miserly. To the contrary, there are letters in his files which show him to be a generous and caring individual. These are letters written by a number of people who were neither relatives nor personal friends thanking him for loans which had helped them over some particularly black periods. Although Jack was resistant to Eta's continuing demands for money he relented and wired Cousins on 28 June: 'Leaving Saturday Morning expect quick trip to Wyndham Morris allowance ok.'

Mosely heard the first of the Aboriginal murder inquests. Jack was modestly pleased that Mosely had remembered hearing him address a Perth Legacy Club and reported to Cousins that 'Mosely is a decent sort' and they 'got on well'.

The verdict was that Burrin died of wounds inflicted by Charcoal and Nipper, and that they be held in custody until the evidence had been submitted to the authorities to decide what action should be taken.

The inquest over, Jack was free to leave Derby. The only means out of town, apart from horseback, was the mail truck which left only once every two weeks for Fitzroy Crossing. Anyone wanting to travel on to Halls Creek was obliged to wait a further two weeks before the mail truck left Fitzroy Crossing. There was no recognised transportation from Halls Creek to Wyndham.

Fortunately, Bell, a Methodist Inland Mission man who had driven Mosely to Derby, was soon to return to Wyndham, so Jack arranged to travel with him at that time. The Reverend Bell was known as a 'lively sort' and a wanderer. Their route lay across 'civilised' country which didn't offer much in the way of copy and Jack hoped for a flying trip.

On 29 June Jack was able to write to Cousins that the embargo on his material had finally been lifted following the inquest and that he had forwarded the Melbourne *Herald* the last of the ten articles, thereby fulfilling his contract with them, and that now he considered himself a free agent. Even though he felt the contract tying him to the *Herald* had restricted his scope, the publicity hound in him decided that the syndication of these articles through Melbourne, Adelaide, Perth and Brisbane had given him 'a public not as used to me as Sydney. Which I think is an advantage.'

The fact that he had taken the trip to get material for a book and had picked up not only newspaper copy but money and publicity as well pleased him. As a result he suggested that Cousins offer the *Sunday Sun* of Sydney a coverage of the fever epidemic which was raging along the Fitzroy. At the time the Fitzroy area was stricken with a mysterious epidemic which was being referred to as 'influenza'. One hundred and twenty Aborigines and twelve whites had died. All the stations in the area were totally disorganised and the entire district was in an uproar.

At the bottom of page two of the 29 June letter to Cousins, sandwiched between his expressed satisfaction over the *Herald* deal and his anticipation of easy access to Darwin police material for 'the mounted book', he again addressed the problem of Eta's allowance: 'Re Eta and that allowance. Please carry it on at sixteen per month, if there's any royalties due please take it from that. If not let me know at Wyndham and I'll send some money down.'

The second Aboriginal murder inquest was scheduled for the afternoon of 29 June 1934. Derby was alive with rumours which told that some party or parties had been trying to get at the Aborigines and 'twist them'. No one knew why, but it was all very mysterious and the speculation made great gossip. Jack wouldn't even hazard a guess. He was prepared to report, however, that the 'old R.M. [Resident Magistrate] here doesn't like me for writing what has proved a widely commented on leper article'.

The same letter also contained detailed instructions for the photographer on the developing and numbering of negatives and films which he had sent back to Angus and Robertson for processing and safe keeping. It recorded the fact that he had also sent an unnamed manuscript. His spirits were definitely lifting. He was about to be on the move again and was looking forward to seeing new country and picking up more material in Darwin. Besides, the *Drums* brochure was all that he had hoped for. The letter closed with: 'Please put aside for me one of these "Drums [of] Mer" circulars...Au revoir, and best of luck to the old Firm.'

Chapter Twenty-four
WYNDHAM

JACK had hit the track again. At last he was on his way back home. Telegrams to Cousins kept him informed of his movements: '2 July 1934 Fitzroy Crossing WA 13.40 pm Expect be at Halls Creek Wednesday'; '5 July 1934 Halls Creek WA 5.45 pm Probably few days here then Moola Bulla Turkey Creek Wyndham.'

There was a letter from Cousins waiting for Jack at Wyndham when he arrived there on 17 July. He was glad that Jack was on his way home because he wanted him back on the job again. He observed that 'we must get a book out every six months if possible—otherwise interest in the other books seems to wane'. Then, as a none-too-subtle incentive, he wrote, 'Your royalties for Jan/June are two hundred and ninety-five pounds, which is considerably less than the same period last year I am sorry to say.'

Cousins reported that the sales of *The Yellow Joss* were good, although like all volumes of short stories it was not selling as well as a book on a single topic. In the same paragraph he lamented that they had not, as yet, the proposed ten volumes to offer for sale, agreed with Jack that an offer of eight titles was premature and applied a little psychological pressure by telling him that the sales representatives were continually asking for the set of ten. He observed that the appeal would have to be for the single volumes until they were ready for the 'big push'. Then in resignation he added, 'Wish to heavens they were ready—but I suppose we will gain in the end by having better times to help us.'

By July the public had overcome its aversion to short stories. *The Yellow Joss* was recognised as being as interesting as his other books and was on the press for its second edition. It became ultimately the first collection of short stories to sell consistently for many years throughout Australia and is now recognised as a collector's item.

As well as the letter, there was a telegram from Cousins: 'If no longer tied *Herald* few articles *Sun* may be advisable publicity purposes shall I tip Simpson Morris perturbed no letters advise you write.'

The trip between Derby and Wyndham had been interesting enough but he observed that there was nothing along the way that could be 'best seller' material. The seven hundred miles of main road, if it could be called a main road, was travelled by those he somewhat disdainfully named 'present day explorers and walk around Australia cranks', a remark no doubt made with Michael Terry in mind.

He reported he was a little nonplussed when Bell, the Methodist padre, had asked him to write something for the mission's quarterly magazine. Bell had shown him some past copies which carried Lasseter's photograph and a speech which 'The Terrible Terry' had given at a boys' school. Michael Terry had used the forum to make a direct attack on Lasseter and *Lasseter's Last Ride*.

Lasseter and Terry would not go away. While Jack still persisted in pretending that 'Terry doesn't matter' he was irritated by the man's sustained debunking of both Lasseter and himself. He went to some lengths to tell Cousins of Terry's latest publicised fallacious discovery of a 'great hidden valley of splendid agricultural land' in Central Australia. Almost gleefully he wrote that after the publication of a 'learned article, accompanied by a map' written by Terry, and Terry's remarks of wonderment that two well-known explorers had passed north and south of the valley and missed it, an 'old hand' had caustically replied in a later publication that Terry's great discovery had been applied for to the Lands Department by Carr Boyd some fifty years earlier.

His correspondence at this time also addressed a perennial problem. All his life Jack could not, or more to the point would not, see eye-to-eye with the Taxation Department. He acknowledged that he had received letters from the department forwarded to him by Cousins and waved them away with no more concern than he would have shooed away a bush fly. 'I got the taxation people's letters. I will write them, I wonder they do not save themselves the trouble of bothering me when I have no earthly chance of attending to the matter until I return to Sydney.' Jack viewed death and taxes with an equally jaundiced eye, while personal possessions rated little better.

The sickness thought to be gastric influenza which had ravaged the far north-west was finally identified as a rare strain of malaria. This malaria was responsible for the deaths of fourteen whites and a known two hundred natives along the Fitzroy River. The number of whites dead among such a small white population was staggering. The true mortality rate among the natives could

233

only be guessed at because the terror-stricken river tribes had fled to the bush, taking the plague with them.

Work on the stations during this epidemic came to a standstill. The largest sheep and cattle stations, which normally carried a hundred native workers, were each left with approximately ten survivors. The other properties sustained proportionate losses.

The police had telegraphed for medical help from Wyndham and Derby, but the doctors who were flown in were unable to contain the epidemic, which eventually extended down below Halls Creek almost to Derby.

The road from Derby to Halls Creek took the Reverend Bell and Jack through the fever area. On the trip they picked up a fever-stricken seventeen-year-old Aboriginal girl. Realising that the girl was dying they rushed her to the Halls Creek Inland Mission Hospital, where the sisters found that she was also suffering from venereal disease 'and treated her as the plague. [They] packed her off on the mail truck on the four-hundred-mile trip to Derby. She died a few hours later.'

Over the years Jack had seen numerous cases of venereal disease and had come to the conclusion that it was a very common human ailment. In fact the sexually transmitted diseases distressed him more than leprosy. While he was prepared to admit that the nursing sisters could have been morally offended by the girl's condition, he found their attitude and their lack of care inexcusable. In his opinion, as a man who had suffered assorted fevers and recurring malaria, a fortnight's medication with quinine for the fever would have saved her.

In recounting this episode to Cousins he showed his characteristic lack of emotional display. In the last two sentences of the two lengthy paragraphs, however, he did register, briefly, both disbelief and censure: 'The kid was half delirious when we brought her in. It was a first-class object lesson to me on Christianity.' Then, with typical even-handedness, he extricated himself from further emotive involvement: 'However it would be unfair to blame a very worthwhile organisation for the few weak links in the chain.'

Once again Jack was itching to get on the road. Wyndham was a 'quaint looking place' of which half appeared to be a tiny Chinatown. There was very little action in the streets; the delightful Chinese children and the odd drunk did not make great copy. A mile from the town stood the meatworks. The blood which trickled from the meatworks drain and into the Cambridge Gulf left a 'brickish red scum' floating on the surface of the water while it waited for the tide to carry it away. Jack found the sight of it repulsive; however, it did provide the material for what might be one of his best short essays, 'The Blood Hole', which appeared in 1960 in *The Wild North*, his second book of short stories.

◆

SUDDENLY he was tired of the trip. Everything was becoming a trial—if he waited for the boat to Darwin he would be cooling his heels in Wyndham for another five weeks. He hoped to take a truck on the four hundred miles overland to Wave Hill, there to wait for the Katherine mailman and then follow through by train to Darwin.

He received a telegram from Vickers of the Inland Mission's Melbourne headquarters telling of the proposed launch of a public appeal for funds to establish a flying doctor base at Port Hedland and Wyndham, and asking Jack to publicise the project.

Jack found most people knew *Lasseter* better than *Flynn* and that the AIM was doing little to promote *Flynn*. Even though every copy sold through the Mission brought it two shillings, money they desperately needed to carry out their work, the Padres did not believe in 'that sort of thing'.

In Jack's opinion he had provided enough publicity for the Inland Mission when he had written *Flynn of the Inland*. In addition he was not well disposed towards Vickers. The man had used extensive material from *Flynn of the Inland* in a series of lectures and had never once acknowledged his source, or the author. Further, the reticence displayed by the mission's personnel towards pushing sales of the book was difficult for him to understand; this, coupled with the lack of care administered to the dying Aboriginal girl at Halls Creek, had soured his attitude towards the entire organisation. Cousins agreed and was of the opinion 'the more you do for some people the more they expect'. Jack did not oblige Vickers' request for more publicity.

He came to the conclusion *Lasseter* was destined for 'immortality' and didn't hold out much hope for *Flynn*. However, in the years to come the two books ran a neck-and-neck race for top sales, with *Flynn* narrowly winning.

Two English weekly magazines dated 1911, the only reading material he could find, did nothing to improve his temper, but a *Drums of Mer* review notice which had appeared in the *Belfast Telegraph*, identifying him as 'a priest of the Torres Straits', raised a grin.

Irritable with the delay of his travel plans Jack turned his mind to the Kidman book and contemplated the spread of the market he should appeal to when writing it. The book had been simmering on the back-burner from the beginning of the trip; slowly it was coming to the boil. For the first time since the project had been raised he wrote to Cousins indicating that he was giving the proposal serious thought: 'Perhaps this book *The Cattle King* could be made of sufficient interest to every cattle man, grazier, and man on the land in Australia. As well to city folk. Anyway will think some more on it.'

Once again his path crossed with Durack who was travelling to meet Moray, his station manager. Jack had an invitation to visit the Durack station but he had only one thought in his mind—get to Darwin and then home. He hoped that Moray would offer him a lift to Darwin and solve his problem of getting out of the 'Land of Lots of Time.'

Jack was still in Wyndham when he received the first of many proposals to film *Drums of Mer*. The approach was made through Cousins by Claude Flemming, the producer of *Collett's Inn*, a musical comedy which ran for what was then a record-breaking one hundred nights in Melbourne, and at the time was breaking records at Sydney's New Tivoli Theatre. Cousins was somewhat enthusiastic about the prospect and felt that Flemming was not going about it in a 'niggardly manner'. Apart from *Collett's Inn* Flemming had also produced colour travelogues. Cousins reported that 'Miss Wiley saw one on London and says it was marvellous'. Despite many well-intentioned efforts, for many and varied reasons *Drums of Mer* has yet to come to the screen.

If, as Uncle Remus says, 'Everybody has a laughing place', Wyndham was not Jack's. On the contrary it seemed to be his place to be irritated. It had been bad enough that he was unable to report the patrol but now, adding insult to injury, it came to his attention that the facts he had written about the leper problem in an article from Broome, which had been published by the *West Australian* but scorned by the *Bulletin* and refuted by the Western Australian Health Authorities, were now proven to be correct. The Aborigines Commission had brought the existence of leprosy in northern Western Australia out into the open and the West Australian press was covering it daily. The West Australian Health Authorities had done an about-face and were planning to put travelling doctors into the field and hospitals in the inland. Methods of organising a systematic combing of the country for undetected leprosy cases were also under discussion. But with all the furore Jack had not seen any acknowledgement of his involvement: 'I have not seen one article mentioning me starting the question. The Royal Commission takes the whole credit. Similar thing with the Granites, and my article in the *Telegraph* just before the boom started.'

Time slipped by. Moray came in by air from Halls Creek, and ended Jack's hopes for a lift. No one had gone overland so he resigned himself to waiting for another two weeks in the backwater for the boat to Darwin.

During this two-week period the National Travel Association purchased the monthly magazine *Walkabout*. The association planned to make *Walkabout* the geographic magazine of Australia and was anxious to have Jack write an article for their first edition. By telegram they offered him ten guineas for an article of twelve hundred words on the Kimberley plus one guinea for each photograph used. Holmes of the National Travel Association said in the telegram, 'Cousins of Angus and Robertson cooperating', and also 'Charles Barrett personal friend of mine'. Jack failed to see what bearing either men had on whether he would or would not write the article; however, somewhat petulantly he agreed, but only because he had the time.

Unfortunately for Cousins, Jack was still in Wyndham and still in a bad humour when a copy of *The Yellow Joss* finally caught up with him. He liked the book but was disgusted with its jacket. Immediately he sat down to write one of his long letters, the first two pages of which were given over to the cover design: 'It has no selling power, neither does it portray the story.' The only point in its favour that he was prepared to concede was that he liked the colour. Sourly he noted that for once there were hardly any spelling mistakes and that he had little cause to be 'furious with Mr Lindley, he only cut out one little piece of supernatural business'. Mr Lindley had edited *The Yellow Joss* and is described by Beatrice Davis, who was A&R's first full-time editor and would edit many of Jack's books, as being 'the stern schoolmaster type'.

Jack was in no mood to be pleased with anything, not even the possibility of the filming of *Drums of Mer*. In the same letter he addressed the Flemming proposal with 'I don't feel enthusiastic. It may turn out all right but Australian attempts at picture production leave me cold. *Drums of Mer* has possibilities too good to spoil by a small picture but if he [Flemming] is prepared to do it properly then I will be willing too.'

With one week to go before boarding the boat for Darwin he wrote, 'This has been a killer of a trip. I hope to do business with the [Darwin] police quickly and come straight on down through to Adelaide. I am sick of the trip, I'm afraid this Eta business has taken the spice of things out of me.'

Of course, even though he was claiming to have had enough of travelling, the thought of the Kidman book was growing. He had begun to write it mentally, and was planning to visit Kidman on his way through Adelaide.

At long last the boat arrived and he was able to wire Cousins: '20 August 1934: Leaving for Darwin by steamer Wednesday.'

Chapter Twenty-five
DARWIN

JACK arrived in Darwin on 23 August and his mood improved with the change of location. Unable to leave for another month, he joined the crew on the lugger *Lotus* for a buffalo camp, his depression lifting as they cruised east to Point Blaze and then west towards Port Keats where Nemarluk, the renegade Aboriginal killer, and his warriors had massacred the Japanese on their lugger, the *Ouida*.

While the morally self-righteous people in the south were tut-tutting over the reported mistreatment of the northern Aborigines, Jack knew that faults lay with both sides.

It was no secret that Aboriginal men sent their women and young girls out in canoes to the boats which lay at anchor along the northern coast-line for 'the purpose of prostitution'. The Aborigines, however, saw nothing wrong in trading their women for tobacco with the sailors—European or Asian. The visits also provided a golden opportunity for the girls to steal whatever they could lay their hands on. If the girls did not return the next day with tobacco and an assortment of goods they were beaten.

Jack was on the *Lotus* when two young girls boarded the lugger—they were children of just eight and twelve years of age. He pencilled out an article entitled 'Black Velvet', which told of two children who were old beyond their years, the elder of the two having committed infanticide when she had given birth because 'picanin too much trouble me'. The article was sent to Cousins with the suggestion that it be sent to Baume of the *Sun* in Sydney as 'it should be sensational enough for him'.

The crass title 'Black Velvet', an artless attempt to be sensational, belied the gentle sensitivity of the story. He paints a poignant portrait of two children and their natural curiosity as they move about below deck, touching, smelling and seeking out the mysteries of the boat, of their pure wonder at being allowed to sleep under coarse blankets, of their sleeping faces dreaming the dreams of children, allied with the harsh reality of the adult purpose of their mission. The next morning the girls were sent ashore taking with them 'gifts' of soap, tobacco and other odds and ends.

After leaving the waters of the Clarence Strait, the *Lotus* had sailed up a river which was nothing more than a narrow gutter edged with steep, slimy mud banks and densely hedged with trees and mangroves. Away beyond the river and trees were the rolling plains on which grazed large herds of buffaloes. As the boat edged its way up the narrow waterway to the buffalo hunters' camp Jack imagined himself to be in darkest Africa. Enclosed by the mud banks and stifled by the steaming heat, he spent hours leaning on the boat rail watching the crocodiles slide down their muddy runways into the dark viscous waters to swim just ahead of the vessel, occasionally submerging to surface astern.

The skipper of the *Lotus*, Captain Cochrane, was an expert seaman and airman who had earned the title of 'the Pirate' after he had pirated two Malayan poras on the high seas.

Four weeks later, however, Jack was back in Darwin. He was disgusted with 'the Pirate' who, despite his reputation as being the terror of the local seas and a daredevil in the air, lost his lustre when he threw in the job at the hunting camp shortly after joining the buffalo shooters. As far as Jack was concerned, he was no bushman.

Jack regretted that the trip into buffalo country had not lasted six weeks; he observed that if it had, he could have gathered enough material for another book. He later found, however, that the four weeks he had spent sailing with 'the Pirate', and the short time he had spent at the buffalo camp, had been adequate for him to gather enough notes to write *In Crocodile Land* which was published twelve years later in 1946.

In 1934 Darwin was still a bush town, full of life and, according to Jack, classless. The people treated him as one of their own. Darwin excited him. To his great joy he found that the Darwinians had acquired the 'excellent habit of buying Australian books'. He was, however, not a little dismayed to find on his return from the buffalo trip that there was not a single room to be had anywhere. He also noted that not one solitary man was unemployed, not even in the back country, and to make it more exciting journalists were arriving every day to cover the great 'Round the World' Centenary Air Race from London to Melbourne, the first planes of which were about to touch down in Darwin.

Darwin was alive with action. Gold fever was endemic and the town was full of alleged mining engineers. Jack had seen his share of these 'experts' and voiced his doubts about their credentials. All the talk was of Tennant Creek and Katherine and there was the odd rumble to be heard of a big gold find at the Granites.

The town was a melting pot of peoples and a trading centre for treasures won from both the land and the sea. Pearl shell was pouring in and buffalo shooters were making enough money to keep themselves satisfied, while crocodile shooters, those who had the nous to cure the skins correctly, were earning enough cash in a week to keep them for several months. Then there were those whom Jack named the 'gold talkers', those who told of fortunes to be wrested from the land, who always knew where it was, but who somehow never seemed to get it.

It seemed to Jack that Darwin was the Eldorado of the north and that there was a fortune waiting to be had by every man and his dog if they cared to bend their backs and take it from the land or the sea. There was plenty of money being spent but Jack shrewdly assessed that the real goldmine was the pub. So great was the ceaseless activity in the pub, and every room so over-crowded, that just keeping track of his belongings amongst the piles of swags, bags and trunks was almost an impossible feat, and it was even more difficult to get a bed.

On his return to Darwin after the buffalo shooting trip, Jack found he had to share a room. This didn't concern him; in his day he'd shared sleeping quarters in some very odd places with many strange companions. Jack was both surprised and pleased to find that the man he was sharing the room with was Tom Brady, an old acquaintance. Tom was an opal buyer to whom Jack had sold opal when they were both at Lightning Ridge before the war, some twenty or so years earlier. Brady had recently come in from a trip through the Musgrave Ranges in Central Australia, bringing with him an opal-cutting machine. He was busy all the time in a pokey little workshop which he had set up in a shed out the back of the pub. Jack surmised that Brady was on to a big find, but although both men had a high time talking over old times Brady never declared the source of his opal supply.

Darwin was still alive with stories of the Treachery Bay massacre by Nemarluk and his Red Band in April 1931.

Nemarluk, who had vowed to rid his land of white and yellow men, was feared by most. Jack admired the chief for his bush craft and his ability to keep his whole tribe constantly moving ahead of his white pursuers in the chase that had ensued after the massacre. It was claimed that these were a people capable of travelling fifty miles and more a day over the most wild terrain without stopping for food or rest until nightfall. Nemarluk had been captured twice and gaoled at Fanny Bay Gaol. The first time the authorities had managed to hold him for four months before he made good a daring escape. His freedom came to an end when he was relentlessly tracked and caught by the black tracker, Bul-Bul.

Bul-Bul was the 'Sherlock Holmes' of trackers. The very mention of the name Bul-Bul was enough to strike fear into the hearts of most criminals.

After Nemarluk and his Red Band had killed a number of Japanese, European and Aborigines, Bul-Bul, together with Mounted Police Constables Ted Morey, Jack Mahony and Tasman Fitzer, followed him into the wild country around the Fitzmaurice River.

Bul-Bul took no spears. He had to move and not be seen, he had to see and not be seen. Bul-Bul captured Nemarluk alive: there was no fight, Nemarluk simply woke one night in surprise to find himself handcuffed.

Nemarluk again escaped from Fanny Bay Gaol and Bul-Bul was once again on his trail. For twelve months Bul-Bul was never far behind. Nemarluk did not sleep in the same place twice; cunningly he devised a plan to keep circling back and travelling in the tracks of the police, a ploy which confused Bul-Bul. When the tracker became aware of the strategy being employed by his quarry the game was over, and once again Nemarluk was caught where he slept. This time the capture was not an easy one. Both were powerful men and each fought desperately as one tried to drown the other in the creek where Nemarluk had stopped to rest.

Mounted Police Constable Tasman Fitzer—for eighteen years the only police officer at Timber Creek, the most isolated police outpost in the north-west—was to write of Bul-Bul, after he had been killed in a motor accident, that he 'was tall, very wiry and of above average intelligence, he had all the guts in the world ... Bul-Bul was the greatest tracker the Territory has ever known'.

Some years later Jack met Nemarluk in Fanny Bay Goal. It was there that the two men struck up an acquaintance and Nemarluk was to make two beaded headbands for Jack, which survive today.

Jack not only knew Nemarluk, he also knew Bul-Bul and he had the respect of both men.

Jack was saddened to see Nemarluk imprisoned. While the world saw Nemarluk as a dangerous savage Jack saw him as a magnificent man. He was a striking individual with smiling eyes and perfect teeth which were startlingly white in his black laughing face. Full of friendly menace, Nemarluk struck fear into most observers, yet the set of his proud head above broad squared shoulders, along with his upright, athletic body, caused Jack to admire him.

Jack understood the depth of Nemarluk's hatred for the Japanese and the white intruders who had come, unasked, into his people's tribal lands of which he was chief. As such, it was not only Nemarluk's desire to protect his people and their lands from the invaders, it was also his obligation and duty. In a sense, Jack and thousands of other Australians had differed little from Nemarluk when they had fought and died in strange lands. There was, however, one essential difference between the two groups: the Anzacs were called heroes for fighting a war on foreign shores because they believed that their own country might be invaded, yet Nemarluk and his Red Band were branded as murderers for fighting in their own country to protect what were their territorial rights.

Nemarluk captured Jack's imagination and his sympathy. Jack was to devote eight chapters of *Man Tracks* to the deeds, daring, capture, escape and recapture of Nemarluk. In 1947 his final salute to Nemarluk appeared with the publication of *Nemarluk—King of the Wilds*. The book was written after he received a letter telling him of Nemarluk's death in Fanny Bay Gaol. The letter read, 'How sad it was to see that he [Nemarluk] had wasted away to nothing, he was so pleased to get your present of knives and pipes. It seems a rotten thing to keep a bush black here for more than five years.'

The author's note to *Nemarluk—King of the Wilds* strikes a forlorn chord; 'This is the story of Nemarluk, chief of the Cahnmah, King of the Wilds. One of the last of the Stone Age men, he deserved a better fate. I know the Wild Lands; I knew Nemarluk personally. I hope you will know him when you read this story of the last three years of his life. And that your sympathy will go out towards the Aboriginal, the last of God's Stone Age men.'

There was much happening at Darwin and the police, 'true mounted types', were extremely helpful; the offers of extended trips became so numerous that Jack resented having to turn them down and return home: 'If there was no Morris business to drag me back I'd dashed well double straight back here otherwise after I'd scribbled out a book or two.'

While he was in Darwin Mary Gilmore's book, *Old Days, Old Ways*, was causing a deal of controversy. He wrote to Cousins, commenting on the new book. 'Here the people live in the thick of the Abo question and such stuff makes their hair raise on end. It can do a lot of damage too at this time for the busybodies down south believe it. However for the sake of Mary and the publishers I hope the book proves a success.' He also took the opportunity to expound his theories on Australian publishing, still his favourite subject, proving once again that he had a sound, instinctive grasp of the marketing of Australian books:

> I am real pleased that Timms' novel is a success and hope it runs into numerous editions. Only by books being a success will there be a sustained run on Australian literature. The more books published that do not sell the quicker will the Public get again 'full up' of Aussie stuff. Whereas the more successes, the more will others sell. I wish Mary Gilmore all the luck in the world but privately I have been hauled over the coals over some of her statements here. It was awful, may be quite true according to Mary's sight, but the statements made were awful.

However Mary, publishing and Eta were pushed from his mind by the prospect of a trip to Tennant Creek, where two hundred and forty men had converged in the hope of finding gold. Several miners had asked him to go along with them to the Creek to try his luck. In view of the numbers already there, churning up the red dust, he reasoned that they would possibly arrive a little too late to share in a slice of the action. Even if he were too late, he could still make a stop at Tennant Creek on his way back home to pick up a little first-hand information.

The prospect of digging for gold, which he most likely would not find, had lost much of its appeal. Even if he did unearth any it would probably only be enough to stake him for yet another season to keep searching for the big lode which had always eluded him. The trip with the patrol had shown him that he was not up to fording swollen rivers or riding a horse for days on end, and apart from his somewhat failing physical abilities he seemed also to have lost the mental temperament needed to cope with the harsh bush life.

By then Jack Idriess, the quiet man who had built his reputation as a bushman, had not only grown used to the excitement of cities and towns, he needed the mental stimulus. By 1934 he only went bush in order to research his backgrounds for authenticity and to be sure that no one could accuse him of not having been to the places he wrote about.

Jack had become a newshound who thrived on intrigue and whose grand passion was collecting 'copy'. He had an instinctive skill for promoting his existing works and was honing that skill further by selecting topics for future books that would have an assured market.

So, despite the inner stirring of the old gold itch, he stayed in Darwin. Aged forty-five, with eight books to his credit, his outlook on life and earning a living had changed direction.

Chapter Twenty-six
THE CALEDON BAY MASSACRE

WHEN Jack first wrote to Treadgold in 1933 requesting permission to accompany a patrol, he noted that he had not been able to take up Mounted Police Constable Morey's previous offer to ride with the Territory Patrol to investigate the murder of six Japanese seamen at Caledon Bay, Arnhem Land.

The incident which had taken place in 1932 had become known as the Caledon Bay Massacre after King Wonggu (Wongo) of the Balamumu (Balamoomoo) tribe and his natives had killed the Japanese crews of the *Myrtle Olga* and the *Raff* while they were engaged in fishing for bêche-de-mer and harvesting trepang.

Balamumu, loosely translated in some native dialects, means murder. Various reports said this attack on the Japanese by King Wonggu and his men had been motivated by the Nemarluk killings in 1931. King Wonggu, a thoroughly untrustworthy and unendearing character, had, it was suggested, acted from much the same motivation as had Nemarluk. However, given the fact that the Japanese had foolishly locked up a number of the Balamumu women in their smoke-house and had, for some days prior to the attack, been shooting over the heads of the Balamumu whenever they approached, it seems more likely that the massacre was the inevitable result of provocation.

In the same letter of 14 August 1933 to Treadgold, Jack had noted that newspaper cables just received in the eastern states reported the spearing of a constable in Arnhem Land. When Jack later read the full report of the incident which took place on Woodah Island, he was relieved to find that the dead constable was not Morey, his Mounted Police Constable contact. The constable who had been killed was a man named McColl.

McColl, together with Mounted Constables Morey, Hall, Mahony and their trackers, had left the Roper River Police Post to track and arrest Wonggu and his band for the Caledon Bay murders. The group eventually covered a thousand miles over both land and sea in their search for the killer band, a search which ended in tragedy when Tuckiar, one of Wonggu's men, had speared McColl, cleaving his chest with a shovel-nosed spear.

When Jack had passed up Morey's offer to accompany the police party in 1933 he had done so with some regret. After the spearing of McColl he had viewed his decision with mixed emotions. The trip would have been exciting but, in view of McColl's death and the rest of the party's narrow escape from the same fate, it would perhaps have been a little too exciting!

Now, in the September of 1934, exactly two years after the Caledon Bay Massacre and nearly one year after the murder of Constable McColl, Jack was again faced with the prospect of passing up one opportunity in order to pick up another. That opportunity was to go gold prospecting at Tennant Creek but the thought of leaving a good story behind was too much for him. He stayed in Darwin to collect copy on the court proceedings relating to the murder of the Japanese seamen, and the subsequent events that led to the spearing of Constable McColl by Tuckiar.

In terms of the amount of material he collected, Jack's published works represent, to use that well-worn cliche, the tip of the iceberg. The size of his books was dictated by the prevailing economic circumstances. During the Depression years of the 1930s it was the cost of large publications that prohibited the full use of his material, while in the 1940s, the war and post-war years, the extent of the content was controlled by the lack of paper and availability of staff. In 1934 however, it was his integrity and respect for his information source which stopped him from fully reporting the aftermath of the Caledon Bay Massacre.

In Darwin that September of 1934, Jack worked very hard. He interviewed all the mounted police constables and took notes from their journals. It was not long before Jack was totally absorbed in the Caledon Bay Massacre story.

Jack had been out on the Kimberley patrol with Laurie O'Neill at the time Tiger and seven other Aborigines were brought to trial for the murder of Albert Koch and Stephen Arinski, two white prospectors who had been killed at the Fitzmaurice River in November 1932. The presiding judge, Judge Wells, had brought down the death sentence on the eight Aborigines on 30 May 1934. The Australian Board of Missions and humanitarians of all political persuasions had urged the government to spare their lives, but the government turned a deaf ear.

Judge Wells, acting on the verdict of the jury and employing the prevailing penalties for murder, which also provided an option for lenience, had explained to the Court before sentencing the eight Aborigines his reason for exercising the death sentence. Wells reasoned that if he did not resort to the extreme penalty the Aborigines would believe the white man placed a low value on life. Furthermore the judge observed that retributive justice was all a 'savage' could understand.

Wells was back at the bench to try the Caledon Bay murderers just prior to Jack's arrival in Darwin.

Under pressure from the Japanese Consul the Caledon Bay Massacre murderers had been brought to trial, found guilty and sentenced to twenty years hard labour on 1 August 1934. The authorities in Canberra were content. The sentences would placate the Japanese; justice had been seen to be done, without bringing forth an outcry against the harshness of the sentence from the churches or other citizens concerned for the welfare of the Aborigines.

The trial of Tuckiar for the murder of McColl, however, had all the overtones of a kangaroo court. No one really spoke or understood pidgin and the interpreters were inept. Constables Morey, Hall and Mahony, the only witnesses, were not in court. Through an interpreter it was alleged that Tuckiar claimed McColl had sexual relations with one of his (Tuckiar's) women—McColl had then attacked him. This attempt to blacken McColl's name was angrily quashed by McColl's fellow constables and by those men who were with him at the time, and Morey, Hall and Mahony were moved to write to the member for the Northern Territory, Mr Nelson, to defend McColl.

It did not make sense to anyone that Constables Morey, Hall, Mahony and the trackers, who should have been the Crown's key witnesses, were not present at the trial. The case had been pending for some months and to have brought the three constables and trackers to Darwin would have taken only three or four days at the most. During the Tuckiar trial Acting Crown Prosecutor Harris stated that Morey was 'somewhere' in Central Australia, and that the trackers were at Roper River; this was considered sufficient reason not to go to the trouble of finding them and bringing them to court.

Judge Wells concluded that there was only one inference to be drawn from their absence. As Jack noted, he said he believed that 'a deliberate attempt was afoot to defeat the ends of justice and that the true facts of the case would be withheld and that such practices would not be tolerated'. For this the judge was once again condemned by the Churches and Canberra. Obviously Wells was silenced, for Morey and his men were never brought to court to give their evidence.

For a brief period Canberra breathed easily. Then Judge Wells, only a matter of days after sentencing Wonggu's men to twenty years hard labour, exercised his judicial prerogative and directed the jury to bring in a verdict of guilty. Wells imposed the death penalty on Tuckiar for the spearing of Constable McColl.

The Government was acutely embarrassed by what could only be viewed by the Japanese as harsh retribution for the murder of an Australian but comparatively lenient treatment of Wonggu's men for the murder of the Japanese fishermen. Aside from any possible international condemnation, the electioneering government of Prime Minister Joseph Lyons could not afford to ignore the vociferous demands from church and humanist protest groups in the heavily populated southern states as had occurred in the Albert Koch and Stephen Arinski case. When these groups met in Sydney on 6 August they called for 'a more humane, scientific, and civilised policy towards the original inhabitants of Australia'.

Prime Minister Joseph Lyons, not content with making history as the first prime minister to make extensive use of radio for electioneering, was then chalking up another first by using an aeroplane for the same purpose. While campaigning around the country in the *Faith of Australia* piloted by Charles Ulm, Lyons found time to publicly condemn Wells for having sentenced Tuckiar to death.

Heeding the public outcry and, more importantly, aware of a possible loss of votes, an appeal against the sentence was hastily mounted in the High Court of Australia and Tuckiar was granted a reprieve.

The tension in Darwin mounted to fever pitch over the whole affair and there was talk of calling a public meeting to support Judge Wells against the Australian Board of Missions, the Mission Society in Melbourne, and the Council of Churches in Sydney, who were all agitating for the removal of Wells from the bench.

The rumour that Canberra also intended to release all Aboriginal prisoners under sentence of death or life imprisonment for murder set Darwin into a further uproar. There was no mention of releasing minor offenders, only murderers. This story prompted the comment that, 'if a man were an Aborigine he would be better advised to kill a man, than to rob him'.

Jack arrived in Darwin right in the middle of the uproar. The people of Darwin felt threatened and were angry at the church and political intervention and, isolated as they were, they were not prepared to tolerate the censure of people shielded in the safety of southern cities; city dwellers who could not comprehend that it was still possible to be speared or hacked to death in 1934.

Jack felt the public slap in the face received by the judge was most unjust, and believed that Wells deserved the highest praise for his 'fearlessness'. He supported the common opinion that pressure to withhold evidence in the McColl case had its origins in Canberra.

In September 1934 there was talk of a retrial of the reprieved Tuckiar in March of 1935. Mr Fitzgerald, Counsel for the Defence, had declared to Jack that 'new evidence, great new discoveries not before talked of' had been unearthed, and went on with what Jack called 'other tommy rot'. Jack decided he had to tread delicately and sort out the material to the best of his ability if he were to use any of it, for 'the police book must contain the truth'.

Jack continued to spend many hours sorting and sifting through the mass of evidence he had gathered from reports of the trial proceedings and the police material. He talked at length to all the men concerned with the Caledon Bay Massacre and the spearing of Constable McColl. He examined the private diaries of the men on that fatal patrol and gathered together evidence that was not given in court. He also talked with some of the Aborigines involved and the trackers.

Even though Jack was convinced he had all the facts from his police sources, he was worried that evidence he was unaware of might come to light and discredit the book if a retrial did eventuate. On the other hand, Jack the promoter did not miss the intriguing possibility that, if the book were to come out containing facts not revealed during the case, the retrial would be a 'blown bubble' and his public would be clamouring for his book. Finally, with remarkable restraint born of respect for Morey and his request not to disclose the source of his information, he made his decision to write only the facts as they were made public.

After the Caledon Bay Massacre and the subsequent spearing of McColl, the staff on Groote Eylandt and their charges were alleged to be in imminent danger of being slaughtered by the Balamumu Aboriginals. Constable Morey and his men had been detailed to protect them. While Jack was still in Sydney, just prior to his West Australian trip, he had received a letter dated September 1933 from Morey, presumably stationed on Groote:

> We had a very disastrous trip last time. McColl was speared to death—right through the heart. He was a splendid chap & we felt his loss keenly. Mahony nearly got his—spear went through his

hat—couldn't have been closer. We were all lucky to get out of it—
it was a case of the hunter being hunted and everything in favour
of black brother. Country couldn't have been bettered for an
ambush—thick jungles and dense scrub made things hard to see—
would have to put your foot on a coon before you would know that
he was there. We are only to act as a guard this time—received
instructions from Canberra that we were on no account to go hunting for the bunch that are wanted. We will be there until after the
'Wet' and then go out and round them up. It's going to be a tough
job—it's a hell of a country—just a maze of swamps, jungles and
saltarms and those old nigs are going to take some mustering.

The police however were never to bring in McColl's murderer. Incredibly, this task was allotted to and, more incredibly,
achieved by, the Groote Eylandt missionaries.

Unfortunately, Jack never used the material recorded by
Mounted Police Constable Morey relating to the missionaries' devi-
ous methods to coerce the native killers into giving themselves up
to them. Nor did Jack ever use the records and notes that Morey
kept during the six months he and Police Constables Hall, Mahony
and Graham were stationed on Groote. Fearing departmental
reprisals, Morey urged Jack to keep the material away from the
'news hounds' and if he did use any of it to 'keep mum (bloody
mum) about where you got it from'.

It had been the same with the Caledon Bay murders. Morey
had sent Jack copies of his minutely-detailed reports to
Superintendent Streeton in Darwin. These contained details about
the first Caledon Bay Patrol immediately following the murders of
the Japanese in 1932 and details of the second patrol, nearly one
year later, which ended with the death of McColl. The reports also
described the discovery, and temporary burial, of McColl's body
close to where it was found.

When *Man Tracks*, revealing only the bare facts of the
Caledon Bay Massacre, was published in March 1935 it did not contain such emotive material as it could have. This letter Jack received
from Constable Morey while stationed on Groote Eylandt is a good
example:

We are placed in a very galling and false position. We are here to
guard the Mission from a bunch of natives while missionaries go up
among the natives we are to guard the Mission from. The whole
position is farcical and Gilbertian. Frankly, we are seething with
resentment at being placed in such a false position. We are forced

251

to sit down and twiddle our thumbs while the missionaries are making overtures and making inquiries which is police work. Whilst still exultant over their murdering and pillaging along comes a boat loaded to the plimsoll with gifts, tobacco, lollies and supplication. The missionaries make friends with the killers and tell them that 'by-an-by he come back buildem house longa you fella'. They pose for a few pictures and (the Balamumu) are treated to a tune on the organ and gramophone. From the Missionary's viewpoint this is, undoubtedly, everything that it should be but from the point of law, order and justice it is fundamentally wrong and the weakness showed in allowing this procedure is deplorable. After the killers have been captured then is the time for the missionary to build his house and teach the natives the error of his ways but the missionary should never have been allowed to interfere with a service operation.

Jack, who had been compiling notes on this extraordinary affair, was confused. The police were confused. No official explanation had been given for the directive which had placed them on guard duty at the Groote Eylandt Mission.

The public observation made by the distraught Reverend A. J. Dyer, missionary on Groote, ignited things further:

...if a dictator would get the murderers, give them a public flogging, show them the power of the white garrison with a bayonet charge and big gun fire and the like, flog them and let them know that the next murderers would be publicly shot, this would be a lesson to them.

The newspapers had a field day. Headlines and stories about a 'black war in the North' set a cracker under the tail of the Attorney General, Judge Sir John Greg Latham, who, apart from holding the External Affairs portfolio, was also Lyon's Deputy Prime Minister.

On 24 November 1933 Latham rose to his feet in the House and, speaking as the Minister for External Affairs, addressed the question. He expressed concern that a recommendation by the member for the Northern Territory, Mr Nelson, to send a police party would do nothing to enhance Australia's overseas image concerning its treatment of Australia's indigenous people.

Nelson responded by urging protection for settlers in the North, and further that the Mission Party be backed up by a police patrol. Anything short of this would be, he felt, 'an incentive to engage in slaughter'. At this point Latham removed his External Affairs hat and placing his Attorney General's hat firmly on his head responded with the observation that 'it is not a political matter.'

Much to everyone's amazement the Mission Peace Expedition, headed by the Reverend Warren, who had returned to Groote from Tasmania in answer to the 'call', reported after its return to Darwin with the Balamumu killers that the Aborigines were terrified of the police. As there were no police in Arnhem Land, the question was raised as to who, or what, had made them 'terrified'. As the missionaries were the only people to have made contact with the Aborigines, the Darwinians placed the blame squarely on their shoulders.

To get to the truth, the Acting Chief Protector of Aborigines, Dr Kirkland, using six native interpreters, conducted an enquiry which lasted a week. The report that he submitted to the Administrator stated that the Mission party had told the alleged guilty Aborigines all they had to do in Darwin was to tell the government they were sorry and they would be sent back to the country. The missionaries promised the Aborigines no harm would come to them and that the missionaries would look after them. On the other hand, the Mission party threatened that if the Aborigines did not give themselves up the police would come and murder them in brutal ways.

Warren quite frankly sympathised with the Aborigines and openly condoned the murders. The constables were completely nonplussed by Warren's attitude towards the murderers of the Japanese, McColl and the two other white men, Trynor and Fagan. Arriving from a brief visit to Tasmania, Warren had been back on Groote Eylandt for barely three days when he began to ridicule the police, knowing that any friction between the missionaries and the police would lead to reports that the police were hindering the 'Peace Party'.

In reference to the threat of police brutality by the missionaries to the Aborigines Jack was to make one of his rare personal observations: 'The Mission party violated the privileges allowed them and abused every faith that was put in them.' The time he had spent in the company of the police in Darwin, plus the records and journals that he had access to, only served to endorse his opinion that the police in the Territory deserved to be fairly represented and not portrayed as brutal murderers.

While the Reverend Warren's duplicity may have surprised Jack, the police, who by that time had spent some time engaged in guard duty on Groote Eylandt, were beyond being surprised by Warren and his group. Warren had indeed previously outlined this very same course of action to Morey, to whom the disastrous implications of such a plan were patently obvious. Knowing the Caledon Bay Aborigines, especially the Balamumu, as he did, he was convinced that such a threat would not terrify them, but rather create a situation of kill or be killed. In view of the far-reaching damage that Warren's plan would do to effective police work in the area Morey wrote a letter of protest to Perkins, the Minister for the Interior, showing Warren to be an egotist, bordering on megalomania, who mangled the truth in subtle ways. He received no response.

The Reverend Warren had previously established the Roper River Mission only to subsequently move to Groote Eylandt because, in his own words, 'The half-castes were running away like the blacks do and we couldn't hold them, so we brought them over here so that they couldn't run away.' The Reverend Dyer, with equal frankness admitted the same thing.

While stationed on Groote, Morey continued to keep a record of the events surrounding the affair. He also kept notes on what can only be viewed as the callous and heartless practices employed, in the name of salvation, by the missionaries on Groote. These documents, which he asked Jack not to disclose, were indictments against Warren and the Groote Eylandt Mission personnel:

Girls have been put in the stocks, in fact this medieval practice appears to have been common practice until one girl, Esther, who could stand them no longer, burned them. For this act she was fined 5/-. The Mission have a system of fines. One play hour is valued at one penny. If a girl is fined she has to work during the play hours. In this particular case the girl had to work during sixty play hours. As they only get a couple of hours or so a day for respite the sixty hours would take some paying off. In a signed statement a male half-caste alleges that girls have been chained up to a tree in the compound, put in the cell and chained and kept for a fortnight on a diet of bread and water and not allowed out for exercise. One girl had to pump water with a hand pump from the creek to a tank at the Mission. She kept at it for a while and came and complained to Warren and Miss Dove that she could not pump any longer as her arm was aching too much. Warren, it is alleged, gave the girl a blow in the face and then grasping her by the back of the neck dragged her back to the pump and forced her to pump. When Warren left the girl she ran away into the bush. Missionary Buckley and some of the girls chased her and caught her about two miles out. She was brought back and chained up in the calaboose and fed on the usual bread and water.

Pages could be filled on matters of like nature. From our observations it is only too apparent that the half-castes are the drudges of the mission. On two occasions we were forced, on the grounds of humanity, to interfere and remonstrate with the missionaries. Once when a girl was locked up in a tiny iron shed. This was during a period of particularly blistering weather. It was unendurable in the shed and amounted to torture. The girl was punished thus because she had called one of the other girls a 'stinking cat'. Not very elegant but still it was not any heinous offence. The other occasion was when the girls were kept working in the rain. They were in their bag dresses. . .water was streaming down their backs and they were wet to the skin. The bags were acting as a cooler on their bodies. They were only digging weeds off the path—it was a job that there wasn't any necessity to do at all really. They complained that they were cold. They certainly looked objects of abject misery and discomfort. We saw the missionaries about it and they said that it had always been the practice of the mission since its foundation to work the inmates in the rain.

At that time Japan was Australia's second biggest wool buyer; imported goods from Japan were cheap and as a consequence Japan had replaced Britain as the largest supplier of textiles to Australia. In view of the trade agreements it is not difficult to see why the Lyons' government turned a blind eye to the casual transgression of a few stray Japanese fishermen illegally fishing Australian waters. It is possible that the government was indifferent to bringing the killers to justice. Perhaps a band of Aborigines roaming the northern coastline was the most effective deterrent against illegal entry the government could hope for at that time.

In light of the efficient police record there is little doubt that the police would have brought back the killers. Therefore by stationing them on guard duty at the Groote Mission the possible capture of the wanted men was unlikely. The offer by the missionaries to bring the Aborigines to Darwin may have been seen by the Government as an opportunity to placate both the Japanese Consulate and the general call from the southern states for reform of the treatment of Aboriginal people. At the same time it was probably assessed that the chance of the missionaries succeeding was slim, or none at all. However, the government had not counted on the Reverend Warren's grab-bag of dirty tricks.

The missionaries did bring back the killers who had to be brought to trial. To keep faith with the Japanese, the killers had to be seen to be punished, while McColl's murderer, Tuckiar, was reprieved to keep faith with the reformists.

Morey's observations and material gleaned from other reports produced over sixteen closely-typed foolscap pages, some 14,500 words which would be the equivalent of four good sized short stories. Almost every paragraph was a story in itself. Morey covered every aspect of the situation on Groote, Warren's duplicity, the complicated questioning procedure of the natives involved in the Trynor and Fagan murders, and the precautions taken by the police on Groote Eylandt against attack from the Balamumu.

Considering the amount of material, its scandalous content and Jack's respect for the Mounted Police of the Northern Territory, it must have been an enormous temptation for him to write a book which presented the other side of the Caledon Bay story. Instead, in deference to Morey's request not to reveal the source of his information, and without inference to what, at the time, could have been explosive material, he closed one of the *Man Tracks* chapters, 'The Law of the Assagai', which dealt with the ambush, the spearing of McColl, the attempt to kill Constable Mahony, and the finding of McColl's body, with: 'Events that immediately followed this tragedy, too long for inclusion in this already long book, led to the formation of the Missionary Peace Expedition.'

McColl's murder was eventually revenged by 'Big Pat', a tracker who could not accept the leniency of white man's justice. The story of how he left police employment relentlessly to track and kill Tuckiar is told by Jack in *Outlaws of the Leopolds* published eighteen years later in 1952.

Attorney General Judge Latham relinquished politics in 1934 and by 1935 was appointed Chief Justice of the High Court. He acted as Australia's first Minister to Japan during 1940 and 1941. The *Australian Encyclopaedia* notes that McColl's murderer, Tuckiar, was released due to intervention by 'interested parties'. Were those interested parties politicians seeking to dismiss the matter in consideration of Australia's burgeoning trade with Japan and the pursuit of peaceful political relations with church and protest groups at home? Unable to find a reason for Tuckiar's reprieve, Jack decided, as had most Darwinians, that the missionaries were responsible and not to be trusted.

Jack had gathered all the material he could on the Caledon Bay Massacre. There was no valid reason for him to stay longer in Darwin.

Chapter Twenty-seven
THE CENTRE

JACK left Darwin on 26 September on his way to Tennant Creek. Unlike the men who had urged him to leave with them for the Creek a few weeks earlier he was not bent on searching for gold; he was on his way home.

The train, the *Birdum Flyer*, made its first formal stop at Brock Creek. The passengers trooped off the train and sauntered across to Fanny Haynes' Hotel, the Shanty. The colourful Fanny was a 'square built old girl, short and preposterously nuggetty' and well able to take care of herself, which was just as well, for apart from the naked Aborigines who tried to gain entry to her establishment, her male clientele of miners, cattlemen and the like were 'pretty tough old characters, blokes who could eat a tiger without troubling to spit out the teeth.'

'Train day' was a big event at Pine Creek, the next stop and one of the very few townships in the Territory. The pub was the meeting place for settlers from hundreds of miles around. Jack and his fellow travellers arrived just in time to wash up before the evening meal and breast the bar for a chat with the men who had come to town, in a dozen or so trucks, to meet the train.

The bar of the Pine Creek Hotel was built of bare iron. Behind the bar three men served the booze at a furious pace. All the men disgorged by the *Flyer* were in possession of a thirst that soaked up the amber fluid like the surrounding arid country soaked up water. The first glass of warm beer, 'for openers', was to wash the dust away, the second to assuage the thirst, while the glasses which followed had more to do with promoting general conviviality.

After their whistles were sufficiently wet, the noisy, laughing crowd jostled their way along the narrow corridor to the dining-room. The iron 'eat-up' room was long, low and painted green. The pub building, built entirely from iron sheeting, stood on a solid concrete floor. It was hardly elegant but definitely utilitarian and most practical. Virtually collapsible, the building was designed so that it could be quickly reassembled at the site of another goldfield should a new strike be made. The Creek Hotel, however, had been there long enough to have acquired a tree-shaded verandah which was set with additional tables to accommodate the hungry crowd.

Lifeless punkahs hung from the ceiling of the dining-room and Jack wondered who the pukka sahib was who had been struck with the brilliant idea of installing them. Whoever he was he had overlooked the need for manpower to pull the cord. Perhaps he had thought that the Aborigines, like the Indians, would dutifully toil, patiently and mindlessly, hour after hour to create a cooling, swirling breeze for patrons of the pub to enjoy.

Everyone wanted to eat at once. Apart from the passengers who had arrived on the train there was also the 'mob from the bush' who had come to town for a change of scenery and in expectation of 'a bit of fun'. Train day was also time to pick up supplies, perhaps pick a fight just to let off some steam, share a joke or two with old friends, see some new faces and, most importantly, to collect any precious mail that may have come for them on the *Flyer*.

Even though he wanted to get back to Sydney, Jack was sorry that as usual he couldn't stay to get at least some of the stories from these hard-bitten pioneering men whom he admired. Jack's father, who held both explorers and pioneers in high esteem, regularly described these men to the young Jack Idriess as 'men who did things, my boy'. Perhaps it was this simple statement, repeated often, which provided the impetus that compelled Jack to keep travelling through a land which was harsh and almost unknown to white men.

At Pine Creek Jack found himself surrounded by the real old timers who were not only doers and finders, they had stayed and taken up cattle holdings; only a small number of those gathered in the Creek dining-room were buffalo shooters, miners, and itinerant workers. Jack wanted to stay, not just to record a story or two, but to understand what kind of men these were who could withstand the fight for survival in this unforgiving land.

However, he was on his way to Adelaide to meet another man 'who had done things', the Cattle King, Sidney Kidman.

◆

AFTER Pine Creek the *Flyer* stopped at Katherine, two hundred miles south from Darwin. The town was nothing more than a line of twenty-five or so houses constructed from iron; a line that staggered along a creek flat, lightly timbered and covered with tall dry, brown grass. Two pubs provided a choice of venue for the morning break and a 'spot or two'; these were Mrs Kate Barnhard's Sportsman's Arms and O'Shea's Railway Hotel. Jack chose O'Shea's where he and the others were greeted as 'Furriners!' by some 'sour-faced grump' who was already there holding up the bar. The cantankerous 'old coot' treated them to a story or two about how the Territory had gone to the dogs with the advent of 'motor trucks, aeroplanes and flash women!'. He also complained that the Territory men had gone soft, because they were being buried in coffins made from beer cases, instead of a moth-eaten blanket.

The lunch stop was made at Mataranka which was then nothing more than 'four or five houses under the trees ... and, of course, there was "the pub", a low-built place of iron, suffocatingly hot on that summer day'.

However, here, in this most unlikely place, was an unexpected oasis of ferns on the pub's verandah. The small grotto, walled off from the scorching outside inferno by wire netting, was damp and cool and deep with ferns and palms. It smelt of jungle dampness and reminded Jack, for one haunting second, of the Cape York Peninsula. He wondered what the hell he was doing there in the middle of nowhere, and more to the point, he wondered how the little old lady who ran the pub managed to keep the little fernery alive.

In a pensive mood he boarded the *Flyer* for the last leg of the trip across the flat, dry country to Birdum, the end of the line. The Territory's only railway line had been built mostly by Chinese labour during the 1880s and 1890s. Birdum was then, and still is, the end of the line. The railway had done no more to populate the Northern Territory of the State of South Australia than the other questionable efforts of its various Governments.

Birdum comprised six houses and, dwarfed by the vast area of flat bushland that it stood on, seemed very lonely at sundown. It too had a pub. This one was a pretty white-washed iron construction and had green-painted lattice-work. The atmosphere inside was comforting and cheerful and seemed to provide an invisible barrier against isolation and a loneliness that went on forever.

Sheila O'Shea's watering hole was built along the lines of her father's Railway Hotel at Katherine. Like most of the Territory hostelries it had been built with a view to quick and easy dismantling and fuss-free transport. It, too, was made of iron and stood on a large cement floor. The walls between the rooms were iron partitions, which cleared the floor by a gap of six inches and finished anything between four and six feet below the roof. This simple construction provided the best and only form of air-conditioning but offered very little in the way of privacy.

The following morning Jack joined the small group of travellers assembled outside the pub to wait for Sam Irvine's mail truck, the only transport to be had between Birdum and Tennant Creek. The truck arrived shrouded in a cloud of swirling red dust. After throwing their swags, bags, and cases onto the mail truck, the passengers clambered aboard. Within minutes they were headed for the newly-found goldfields at Tennant Creek.

Jack found himself rubbing shoulders with Nelson, the first Federal Member for the Territory, and Police Inspector P. A. Giles. Jack was interested in both men but for different reasons. He would have liked to have quizzed Nelson about the government's intervention in the Caledon Bay murder trials, but fearing a rhetorical political dissertation he decided to chat with Inspector Giles instead. During the course of his spasmodic conversation with the quiet Giles he discovered that Giles' father was one of those men Jack admired most, an explorer and pioneer. The elder Giles had spent much time with John Ross, himself an explorer and pioneer, opening up new lands in the north. Giles had also been the pilot for the construction gangs building the Overland Telegraph Line. It was this conversation with Police Inspector Giles that set Jack researching the history of the building of the Overland Telegraph Line, a project which he was never to complete.

This trip to Tennant Creek is recorded in *Tracks of Destiny* published in 1961. Jack draws upon some of his vast collection of tall stories which demonstrate the dry, wry humour of the bush people. It is doubtful that the characters who are accredited with the witticisms actually voiced them at that time and place, for often the narrative is strained and the humorist not one of the assembled party, but like most of Jack's works it is a delight for all who enjoy delving in Australian history, mythology, folklore and obvious tall stories.

The mail truck rolled into the yard of the Tennant Creek Overland Telegraph Station, which was seven miles from the new goldfield: 'Just two long low buildings of whitewashed stone, iron roofed, standing solidly one behind the other, a scullery, a meat-house, half a dozen tiny shacks, all enclosed within a fence.'

Jack observed that it was most likely the same as the other telegraph stations which punctuated the two thousand miles of line between Adelaide and Darwin, 'every smoke blackened stone and beam would have a story to tell.' Rolling a smoke, he leaned back against the sun-heated wall of the station staring at the two wires which performed such an incredible feat. Jack could never look at those overland telegraph wires without a vague feeling of disbelief. It seemed impossible to him that the two wires strung on poles, primitive in appearance, were zapping words across the continent even as he watched.

Tennant Creek ran in front of the telegraph station. The big old trees which lined its banks and clustered around a water-hole proved that the desert could grow anything, given water. Looking south the land continued for vast distances. The red earth was clothed in a grey, low-growing bush known as spinifex. Here and there in the distance could be seen the tops of low hills. With the exception of the immediate area surrounding the creek the land was waterless, desperately barren and sun-scorched.

Camped down by the water-hole a small band of the local Warramunga tribe were entertaining visiting members of the Warramulla tribe. The Warramunga Aborigines were accustomed to the sight of the white man working himself into a lather of sweat as he dug holes in the earth; it was a sight they found both amusing and incomprehensible. Jack would write in reference to the Warramullas: 'The Stone Age man appealed to me in his primitive state. I could not help hoping that these wild visitors, who now could not speak a word of English, would not carry to their wild tribesmen the urge to come a-visiting the Warramungas, and be introduced to the "white-feller man"'.

The group once again boarded the mail truck to cover the remaining seven miles that lay between the overland telegraph station and the embryonic town of Tennant Creek.

Jack finished the trip in brooding concern over the inevitable fate the future would bring to the Warramulla, whose tribal grounds extended approximately two hundred and forty miles to Wave Hill Station north-west of Tennant Creek and out to the west: 'We could not wait to help, in one way or another, the destiny of the Warramulla.'

Jack came to the Tennant Creek goldfield covered in a fine red dust that clung to his clothes. The same dust ground between his teeth, coated his tongue, and choked his throat; it irritated his eye sockets, and set like red cement around the rims of his eyes. Each passing mile brought him closer to home and decisions to be made. He was tired, and pre-occupied, and hoping for something unusual to divert him from the introversion which had slowly taken root since leaving Darwin.

Many times throughout the trip he had been relieved to find a pub at sunset. Here he had not expected to be so fortunate, but sure enough there, in the distance, a bright new iron roof winked a welcome above the grey, low-growing brush—the pub!

> With a quickening of interest I saw the gleam of several other new roofs, half a dozen shacks, a few tents. Fronting the pub was the 'street', merely the overland telegraph line running down the centre of a broad path of dust churned up by motor vehicles and horse traffic through the spinifex. At regular intervals on either side of this 'street' stood, or rather leant, a wobbly iron shack. There were others made of hessian and saplings, and tents reinforced by mulga branches. The butchers shop run by young Nelson (son of the Member for the Territory), the boarding house where you didn't board and could get 'only tucker', the bakery, several 'stores' and a half dozen rough camps made the settlement, with a few scattered beehives of dull grey-green, gigantic things, these.

The Tennant Creek buildings were the epitome of the Australian craft of making-do, and the architectural style as indigenous to the Centre as igloos are to the Arctic. Since timber in the Centre is sparse and poor, with the exception of trees that line the rare waterholes, it is virtually impossible to use. The 'beehives' Jack saw were spinifex houses, shelters built by forming frameworks of saplings covered with coarse, dense tufts of spinifex grass, the only natural building materials available in the Centre. However it wasn't the spinifex beehives that took Jack's attention, it was the pub. In the growing darkness it appeared to be built of cement. Finding a cement pub out there on the devil's front lawn made Jack wonder if the dust which had got into his eye-sockets had, now, irreparably damaged his eyesight.

Here was an unbelievably modern pub which had been built of cement poured into flat block forms and moulded right on the spot. And wonder of wonders, a small generator huffed and puffed away at the back of the building, supplying the power for electric light, and most importantly, power to keep the beer cold. Light was one thing but cold beer was something else! Had there been a choice between seeing and drinking cold beer Jack would have drunk it in the dark, as would any of the other travellers who gratefully climbed down from Sam's mail truck as it lurched, groaning and squeaking, to a complaining stop outside this cement desert palace.

This edifice of modernity sported a walled-in iron verandah which was fully netted to keep out the persistent bush flies, which, even after dark, were dedicated to inflicting ceaseless torment.

Jack swung his now battered felt hat in an attempt to dislodge both the red dust and clinging flies from his clothes and person. All he accomplished, however, was a rearrangement of the two.

The trip had been long, hot and dirty and Jack was in no mood to cope with the handful of drunks who rose 'hitching up their strides' to follow Sam and himself across the verandah and into the pub:

> Some were brazen beer-bums who came butting in between us for their drink. They were noisy and hoarse-voiced. Two of them flung their arms around Sam's neck in howling joviality. Sam gave a heave, threw out his big arms and the two fools were flying back through the door. The deck thus cleared for action, Sam glared around like an angry bull. But not one of the he-men accepted the challenge.

Having disposed of the bar-flies the sanguine Sam nodded towards the modern, horseshoe-shaped bar, which was 'armour-plated' with strong wire netting, and the bartender caged safely behind it. Above the bar was a large notice which bellowed NO TICK at the milling crowd, proclaiming to all and sundry that credit would not be marked up on the board of this pub. Despite the existence of the generator which promised cold beer, the beer was warm and no amount of geniality from Joe Kilgariff, barman and owner of the pub, could change Jack's humour:

> Sipping that hot beer I gazed at the armour of heavy wire netting. From about twelve inches above the bar it stretched up to the roof. Thus you shoved your money under the wire, and Joe pushed the beer across the bar out under the wire to you. No hand could snatch out across the bar should gold or a wad of notes lie there. Also, in a brawl, no one could leap over the bar to take piratical charge, that tough netting was solidly built into the bar and walls.

Jack could see how the netting would be effective against a bodily attack but after watching an impatient, trigger-happy, gun slinger thumping the bar with the butt of his revolver he was moved to enquire about its effectiveness against bullets should anyone attack.

It was Sam who told him: 'He can duck down anywhere inside, the bar is built so that he's covered from any angle. When the storm blows over he just pops up and whistles for the abo house-boys to carry out the corpses. Otherwise there is very little wreckage to be cleaned up.'

Of course Joe did not rely solely on his agility to avoid a personal disaster. In a strategic spot tucked under the bar he kept 'a blunderbuss that could blow daylight through a camel'. Joe, however, solemnly assured Jack that he was a man of peace.

Tennant Creek was a wild town. Apart from the genuine, hard-working miners trying to strike pay-dirt, there were a number of young drifters from the southern cities who had been attracted to the field by the scent of gold. These would-be he-men wandered around with .45 revolvers, 'young cannons' Jack called them, in open holsters strapped to their legs ready for instant action. Broad belts heavy with cartridges hung around their waists. Assuming the bow-legged stance of men born in the saddle and with thumbs stuck loosely in their belts, they did their best to strike aggressive poses. Drunk or sober, most of them didn't hesitate to pull a gun and fire off a round or two.

Most people took the gunmen seriously. Jack, however, found it difficult to suppress a guffaw or two at dinner time when two of the Tennant Creek terrorists appeared in the doorway of the dining-room and stood coldly eyeing the diners. Jack was stopped from laughing by Sam's frown and by someone rapping him on the shin under the table. Evidently the one hundred and seventeen men on the field knew better than to provoke these trouble-seeking young swaggerers.

While Jack was at Tennant Creek things did get out of hand when a fight between two rival camps broke out over a rifle. In the fracas a man named O'Brien was shot twice in the stomach. O'Brien was known on the goldfield as the 'drover of goats'. He had survived the 1914–18 war and had taken employment driving a herd of goats across the desert from Mount Isa to Tennant Creek for an Afghan as a means of reaching Tennant Creek to search for gold. O'Brien was reported to have said, 'I'd go hopping to hell along a road of criss-crossed swords to reach a new goldfield, let alone drive a mob of goats across a desert.' Sadly, his effort was to be rewarded not with a weight of gold, but with two ounces of lead, in his stomach. Fully conscious, O'Brien lingered on for nearly two days before he died.

Jack withdrew into himself on this occasion—as he had done on previous occasions during the Great War when pointless death had distressed him, and said very little. Graphically he recorded the fracas in *Tracks of Destiny*, wherein O'Brien is attributed with a line or two which could be called sentimental, if not classic corn:

'"I've had it!" he gasped. "There's not much you can do for me 'cept keep the flies away. And give me a smoke!"'

O'Brien is immortalised by Jack as a man of great fortitude and forbearance with, seemingly, a great sense of drama. Battling against great pain and the intolerable thirst of a gut-shot man O'Brien calls for the man who had shot him. As water poured through holes left by the bullets, he is reported by Jack as saying: 'Well, I'm going now. If it does you any good, I tell you you're not the man who shot me. Well, I'm going now, lads. And with an easy conscience. I never squealed'.

Notwithstanding O'Brien's claim that his killer was innocent, the man who fired the fatal shots was taken into custody by the policeman who had been camped down by the creek and who, as the miners had observed sagaciously, had been of no use at all.

There was no lock-up at Tennant Creek so the policeman and his prisoner slept on the pub verandah and strolled around together. The man was eventually acquitted.

Not only was Tennant Creek lawless and almost waterless, it was roadless and crying out for organised transport. It also needed police protection and planned development. The Member for the Northern Territory found himself in great demand from the miners and cattlemen of Tennant Creek. It wasn't, however, Nelson or the need for development which finally opened up the Territory and brought the road through to Tennant Creek. It was the Japanese and their bombs which devastated Darwin in February 1942 and the need of defences for Australia's northern coastline that brought roads, for rapid military transport, and the building of the Stuart Highway from Alice Springs to Darwin as well as the Barkly Highway from Tennant Creek to Camooweal in Queensland.

In 1934 Jack could have no idea what the future held for Tennant Creek. It was the only new goldfield Jack had seen in a trip of eleven thousand miles. As it was a reefing goldfield it was not exactly his cup of tea. The gold was locked deep into solid rock, difficult to discover and difficult to extract. It required men who had a little money to enable them to hang on, and men with even more money to take it out from that isolated place.

Jack believed that the Tennant Creek field was then the most difficult field to mine in Australia. Years later he wrote:

> To seek gold at Tennant at that time, even for the experienced miner, was like going to school to learn all over again. Geologists were to be tricked again and again by the unusual conditions on this

265

field. No wonder that before its peculiarities were really understood the seeking of its gold had made a ladder of broken hearts reaching to high heaven.

But find it they did, by sheer hard work. Today, fifty or more years after the first bent-backed old miner scratched a bit of gold from those iron-bound hills, Peko-Wallsend still takes a healthy weight of gold and copper from the Warrego and Gecko mines at Tennant Creek.

Jack uncovered one more surprise on the field; it was a ginger-beer shop selling glasses of the biting drink for sixpence a glass. The brew tasted good and was colder than the beer at the pub. Jack couldn't understand how these men could buy the water and ingredients and sell it so cheaply. The shop was a cool lattice shelter of saplings which housed the kegs, some of which stood on boxes. Young and old men dressed in shirt sleeves, singlets and flannels, assembled around the rough tables, pint pot in hand, talking very seriously about gold. There the 'ginger-beer man' and his assistant, both wearing Jacky Howe singlets, carried on a thriving business.

In the dusty half-lit atmosphere of the ginger-beer shop, surrounded by wire-bearded men, Jack experienced a sense of being transported back to the goldfields of a hundred years earlier, but out in the darkness there was the whirr of a generator and music from a radio.

As he left Tennant Creek Jack remarked, 'I'm for the gold of Pitt Street, I've had the spinifex and the mulga and the witchetty grubs, for the time being anyway.'

◆

I took the road again to Alice. Heavy skies, red earth, anthills. The truck buzzes along through the waving, now yellowing stalks of the drab grey spinifex. Past lancewood, stunted ironwood, and the startling white trunks of the stunted ghost-gums. The haze makes the sky appear so low that to the south-east it seems to rest upon a long string of hills, so far away that the line of the range-top shows as grey as the thin grey leaves of the lancewood trees.

ALICE Springs is often referred to as being in the 'dead heart', which has nothing to do with being dead, but rather of being in the 'dead centre' of the continent. It would, however, be better described as being in the 'red heart', for the red earth there is found nowhere else in Australia. Jack observed that, from the hills,

Alice Springs seemed to be a pretty little town of white roofed bungalows built of grey or dull green cement blocks.

Jack noted gratefully the railway station as they drove through the town—the end of the line and the beginning of his last run into Adelaide. He also made note, as they continued across town towards the inevitable Joe Kilgariff watering hole, the Stuart Arms Hotel, that the hotel was 'a nice modern little place' and that the town was very quiet.

Before leaving Alice Springs, he picked up another story from the police which he planned to use in the 'mounted book'. The story of Terry, a renegade Aboriginal caught between two cultures, was not, however, used in *Man Tracks* but eventually published in 1961 in *Tracks of Destiny*.

Published in the same book are some asides from Mrs Joe Kilgariff. The wife of the enterprising publican had earned herself the reputation in the Alice of being the maker of 'beaut boxes'—the 'boxes' being coffins. Mrs Kilgariff had acquired this skill when the town was very young because, as Jack put it, 'the boys would bring in the stiffs to the pub for a beano before they planted them', and Mrs Kilgariff, believing that it was scandalous to 'plant' them in a moth-eaten blanket, made them coffins lined with unbleached calico for the send-off.

Two letters from Cousins addressed to him care of Post Office, Alice Springs, caught up with him on 14 October. In the first, dated 25 September, Cousins wrote:

> The Sydney Agent of RKO Pictures has asked us for books likely to interest their people in USA They are the biggest producers in USA at the present time, doing pictures at the rate of one per week. I have sent the agent *Gold Dust and Ashes* and *Drums of Mer*, thinking these two the most likely books to interest them. I have told them that we already have an inquiry for *Mer*, but there is no reason why they should not make an offer if interested.

The second dated 26 September:

> Since dictating my letter to you yesterday's date regarding *Drums of Mer* the RKO people telephoned me not to close with the *Drums of Mer* film offer until their American people had a chance to look at it. I have a feeling that these people will do the right thing with *Mer* if they take it up, and I think they will take it, providing satisfactory arrangements can be made with you.'

Jack's trip had been virtually spent in a type of isolation without verbal communication at a personal level. His long conversational letters to Cousins, repeatedly returning to a single personal topic in each letter, seem to have been his method of working his way through a problem. At that period of Jack's life there was not one person, apart from Cousins, to whom he could talk on an intimate basis, or use as a sounding board. Cousins, however, does not appear to have perceived this need, for his responses never acknowledged an awareness of Jack's obvious concerns.

Jack answered both the Cousins letters the day following their arrival, but his reply did not contain the usual chatty material and was generally somewhat terse. The opening paragraph was extremely cryptic and displayed the word economy of the practised telegram writer, a skill that he had no doubt acquired during the trip; 'I leave for Adelaide tomorrow. Will wire you there. Will see Kidman's secretary. Have a dozen necessary police calls to make then will hurry on to Melbourne.'

In his reference to RKO he failed to comment on the company's claimed prolific output of 'a film per week'. Maintaining his newly polished brevity he wrote, 'Very interested re RKO people and *Mer*. Will not see that Melbourne man but leave the matter entirely in your hands.'

Throughout the trip when writing to Cousins he had referred again and again, often several times in a letter, to specific people and subjects—these were Eta, the ten-volume set, the lack of a book-buying public, and Terry ('The Main Roads' Explorer'), together with the fact that he, Jack, should not be known as an explorer. Now, in this, his only letter to Cousins from Alice Springs, the repeated reference was to the police material. 'I am beginning to think the police book will be a winner, but it bristles with all sorts of complexities. However, will explain when I see you.' And in the closing paragraph, 'I've a lot of worrying to do re this Police book. However, better not start on that or I'll never finish the letter.'

Chapter Twenty-eight
KIDMAN

JACK had followed Prince Henry, Duke of Gloucester, to Adelaide. The Duke, who was gracing Australia with his royal presence for the Melbourne Centenary celebrations, had passed through Adelaide on his trans-continental journey from Perth to Melbourne a few days before.

The day after the Duke had declared the Centenary Celebrations open in Melbourne, Jack arrived in Adelaide. The city was still bubbling with the excitement of having received many nods from the royal personage. Jack was not impressed or interested in all the doffing of caps and tugging of forelocks; he had one purpose in mind—visiting Sir Sidney Kidman. The ten days that Jack spent in Adelaide were given over to coming to a satisfactory conclusion for the research and writing of Kidman's biography, making the rounds of the newspaper offices and calling on booksellers.

Cousins wrote to him reporting that the Australian Inland Mission had requested permission for a radio reading of *Flynn of the Inland* as part of a drive to raise funds. Permission had been granted on the understanding that a Captain Stevens would be the reader. Cousins hoped that the reading would both stimulate sales and raise funds for the mission.

As usual Cousins was cracking the whip. Satisfied that Jack had the police book well in hand, Cousins wrote him one of his now customary incentive letters. He observed that the publication of *Man Tracks*, a book which covered a subject of national interest, would accelerate the sales of the other titles and reiterated that it must be off the press by March. He expressed the belief that the book 'was sure to be winner'. Obviously he was already regarding it as a *fait accompli* and was setting his sights on other titles. With the future in mind, he popped yet another idea for a book on Jack's 'back-burner'. He wrote, 'A successful Abo. book must be different from anything so far done, and I'm sure you are the only one who can do it.' But keeping the priorities in perspective he observed that, 'the Kidman one is more important'.

Not quite thirty years later in 1963, after a prolonged simmering gestation, the idea for the Aboriginal book reached fruition with the publication of *Our Living Stone Age*, the life of the Australian Aborigine, from birth to marriage. This book was to be closely followed a year later by the publication of *Our Stone Age Mystery*, the life of the Australian Aboriginal from marriage to death and broadly addressing Aboriginal spiritual life.

Neither is a dry treatise, nor do they pretend to be anthropological or critical works. Both books are drawn from Jack's diaries and the innumerable records of his personal experiences and observations of Aboriginal tribes and customs right across Australia—from the Cape York Peninsula in the north-east to Western Australia and Arnhem Land in the north-west.

The title of 'Boswell of the Bush' that Jack earned for *Flynn of the Inland* is perhaps better deserved for his recording of the Aboriginal way of life as he experienced it during his time with these people.

Walter Cousins did not see the results of his influence, for he died before either of the two Aboriginal books were to be written.

From Adelaide in that October of 1934 Jack kept Cousins up to date with telegraphed reports of the Kidman biography negotiations. He wired Cousins on 23 October—the same day that the English aviators, Scott and Black, crossed the finishing line in Melbourne to win the Victorian-sponsored Centenary Air Race for England. England was now only three days away from Australia. The 'greatest race in history' had captured Jack's interest while he was in Darwin but now his full attention was on Kidman.

♦

WHEN Jack arrived at the Royal Artillery Hotel on Elizabeth Street in Melbourne he found a letter from Cousins reminding him to call and see Claude Flemming about the filming of *Drums of Mer*. Cousins wanted to keep a foot in both camps while he waited for RKO to indicate more than an interest in buying the film rights to the book.

Jack made a number of enquiries and found that various business sources seemed to doubt that Flemming would be able to finance the film, but he wrote that he would still call and discuss the matter with him if Cousins wanted him to do so.

In Melbourne, as in Adelaide, Jack did the rounds of the newspapers and Melbourne booksellers. Captain Peters, manager of Robertson and Mullens bookshop, unable to convince Jack to 'stand' autographing books, agreed to a compromise whereby Jack visited the shop occasionally to autograph books left by customers. The same Captain Peters also sponsored Jack as an honorary member of the Melbourne Savage Club for the duration of his visit; however, the sponsorship did not induce Jack to acquiesce to the autographing sessions. He continued to maintain his position, refusing to 'stand like an ass on exhibit'.

While visiting the Robertson and Mullens bookshop he was introduced to the poet laureate, John Masefield, and his wife. Masefield, a guest of the Victorian Centenary Committee, had come from Boar's Hill, Oxford, England to lend a little English culture to the Centenary Celebration by lecturing young university students on English poetry. Jack reported to Cousins, 'I like him. He is very much taken with *The Desert Column* but knows nothing about the other books.' Masefield's lack of knowledge was remedied by a presentation copy of *Flynn of the Inland* by Robertson and Mullens.

Cousins responded to the news somewhat dourly but with his marketing view to the fore. 'I wish this man would tell us what he thinks of *Flynn of the Inland* and yourself as a writer. If we could get something out of him it would carry a lot of weight.' Jack declined to comment, as, it would seem, did Masefield.

Jack was not really concerned about gaining Masefield's opinion; the booksellers were making sales, and that was all that counted. The praise he received from the Adelaide and Melbourne booksellers did much to revive his faith in the marketing ability of booksellers, which he had lost in the west. He reported to Cousins that booksellers in both Adelaide and Melbourne had told him that his books had saved them during the Depression, 'which was flattery of course. What they meant to convey was that an impetus was given to other Australian books and the sales at that time proved a help.'

Jack's faith in a strong future for the Australian book never wavered and he did everything that he could to promote public awareness and sales of Australian books above imported works. He was the publishing industry's self-appointed ambassador. While he was in Melbourne he preached the gospel of the Australian book with an ardour approaching religious fervour. He did not pontificate on the creation of Australian culture through literature as would Vance Palmer in his lengthy article 'Future of Australian Literature' published in the *Age* on 9 February 1935. Neither did he expound on the discovery of the Australian character or the character of the country 'through the searching explorations of literature'.

He knew that the so-called 'character' began its creation from the moment of colonisation. As far as Jack was concerned, people like Vance Palmer were out of touch with reality, and he thought that they were far more uncertain of their own identity than the average man on the street or in the bush. Neither did he patronise his fellow countrymen in witty but cruel comments as did Norman Lindsay. While the brilliant doyens of culture put forth an almost unbroken diatribe lamenting the lack of understanding of the Australian character, Jack Idriess was showing Australians who they were. Yet somehow he has never been recognised as doing so by the so-called 'establishment'. Of all the people I have spoken with about Jack Idriess during the research of this biography, only one man, John Ferguson, George Robertson's grandson and one-time publishing director of Angus and Robertson, expressed the view that it was Ion L. Idriess who put the Australian book on its feet and into the homes of millions of Australians at a time when Australian 'literature' was clawing its way to acceptance.

Obviously Jack was an accepted voice in literary circles during his Melbourne sojourn, for he was introduced to the Victorian Director of Education or 'something or other of education' who 'thanked him' in front of a crowd of friends. Although they were quite sincere they properly succeeded in embarrassing me, and I am now well used to this sort of thing,' he wrote to Cousins, 'however, big business may result.'

Jack was on everyone's guest list; if he couldn't be coaxed to give public lectures he was invited to lunch or to dinner. If people wanted to hear him talk about the places he had been to and the curious things he had seen, they had to listen to him talk about Australian books.

He attended his second Melbourne Cup, the Centenary Melbourne Cup. The year before he had backed the winner the day prior to leaving for points west. So much had happened since that time that it seemed to him the event might have taken place a lifetime ago.

To celebrate his return to civilisation the Melbourne *Herald* engaged him to write an article about Cup Day and the running of the Cup as he saw it. As far as Jack seems to have been concerned the magnificent horses ran second to the chattering flocks of colourfully dressed ladies which swept across the lush green Flemington lawns. Attending the Cup was only part of his social round, for many of his friends and acquaintances had been drawn to Melbourne for the Centenary Celebrations. Among the visiting New Guinea celebrities was Mrs Levien, widow of C. J. Levien, the founder of New Guinea Airways. And he visited his old friend and staunch supporter, Alec Chisholm, who was resident in Melbourne at the time.

The Melbourne newspapers had a surfeit of interesting copy but they managed to find space to run a number of interviews with Jack accompanied by photographs of a tooth taken from a crocodile Jack had shot while visiting Arnhem Land. The grisly thing was twice as long as a match box and Jack had kept it as a souvenir.

Appearing in the press at the same time was a small article entitled 'We're Fools to the Abo'. The heading and its contents simultaneously irritated and amused him. It was not the first time that he had been quoted out of context nor was it to be the last. The article, widely syndicated, inferred that Jack had said the West Australian Department of Health doctors were inefficient in their administration of medicine and treatment of diseased Aborigines in the north of the state. Jack found it ironic that this mutilation of his original statement was actually the truth, for in his opinion the doctors were 'shockingly' inept. What irritated him was that he had been misreported. Furthermore he found nothing to justify the careless choice of the heading, which to him implied the white population was being made a fool of by the Aborigines. But try as he might he couldn't get back into print with his full statement, for the papers were full of Kisch the Czech journalist and his fight to overturn the federal government's ban on his entry to Australia.

The misquote was not the only thing which proved to be an annoyance. Jack had missed the Exhibition of Australian Frontier Pictures arranged by Charles Barrett. Although Barrett assured Jack that the Aboriginal artefacts, which Jack had collected and so carefully packed in Wyndham and shipped from Darwin, had formed an exhibit on their own, he felt instinctively that something was not quite as it should be. Barrett was bending over backward to do anything that he could for Jack and his extreme geniality put Jack on his guard. By asking a few judiciously placed questions he found that no one could remember having seen the collection. It wasn't until he dined with Alec Chisholm and his wife that his suspicions were confirmed. Neither Alec, who had been sent by the press to report on the exhibition, or his wife, 'who appears to be a keen woman', had been able to find Jack's artefacts at the exhibition.

Oddly, in the face of confirmation by his friends that the collection had not been on exhibit, he did not directly ask Barrett what had happened to it. Instead Jack wrote to Cousins to ask if the collection had been forwarded on to him after the exhibition as Barrett had agreed. His ire grew when the 'smug Church people for whose benefit I now believe this exhibition was arranged' said not a word in appreciation of his trouble and expense.

'I feel annoyed,' he wrote to Cousins. 'I have thought there might be cause for some time but have smothered the feeling and asked no questions.' He found himself further confused when Chisholm, who claimed not to have seen the collection, and Barrett, who hadn't displayed it, asked him if they could have the pieces for their museum. Confounded by the incomprehensible actions of both Chisholm and Barrett, and unable to discover the truth of what had happened, he was prepared to believe that both men were a little eccentric. 'Of course Charles and Chis are, well, naturalists or scientists. As you probably know, all of this species is poison one to the other, though they may be very good fellows to the outside public.' Though it explained nothing to Cousins, this was good enough reason for Jack.

What actually happened to the Aboriginal artefacts is anyone's guess but, given that a major number of the pieces were weapons of the type used for killing both man and beast—especially the shovel-nosed spears—and given that Jack had written show cards to be used with the display which described the use of the lethal weapons, and which also referred to the recent killings in Arnhem Land, it is possible that the collection was withdrawn because no one wanted to revive a controversy which, a few short weeks after the event, was being absorbed into the great Australian Silence.

The following legend describing a shovel-nosed spear and its uses is taken from one of the cards that Jack prepared for the exhibition:

> The type used in the recent spearing of Mounted Constable McColl at Woodah Island, Arnhem Land, of Cook and Stephens killed on the Fitzmaurice River, of Traynor and Fagan killed on the Arnhem Land Coast, Herb Watts killed west of Daly, Nicholls in the Eastern Territory; used to kill bullocks. The wound is a terrible thing. Numerous cattle are killed annually by natives using these weapons in the Kimberleys and Northern Territory.

It is likely that Barrett decided not to upset the Australian Inland Mission personnel's sensitivities by reviving the contentious issue of the death of McColl and others. Or perhaps the missionaries themselves threw up their hands in horror and vetoed the display. Jack's remark, however, that the 'smug Church people' did

274

not acknowledge his effort seems to indicate that it was Barrett who made the executive decision. While Jack seems to have dismissed the loss of the collection without too much fuss, he often recalled that the pieces could never be replaced, and that had it been preserved the collection would have been of historical value for future generations.

By 2 November, one day after arriving in Melbourne, Jack was writing to Cousins. Once again he was using his letters to help him think through his problems. He had made two major decisions: the direction to take with the police book and, because Sidney Kidman seemed to him to be very frail, 'to somehow write the Kidman book at the same time'. Throughout this letter to Cousins, just as in the others, he returned repeatedly to the subjects that worried him the most. Now that he was within shouting distance of Sydney and knowing that the time to decide about Eta was fast approaching, he hovered between confusion and anger over the whole affair. Perfecting the art of procrastination, he found good reasons, and every unreasonable reason, to delay his return.

'I won't be leaving here for a while, I think I'll stay until this presentation to Masefield on Friday or Monday,' he wrote to Cousins. 'I have numerous appointments, some re Kidman, and anyway, though I wish I was in Sydney settled down again, I hate going back.'

Then, on the last page of the letter he wrote the most direct statement: 'I wish the Morris business was completely finished. If it was my own fault I would not mind, but I'm blessed if I see why I should keep the families of other people for the rest of my blooming life.'

So a vacillating Mr Idriess, torn between wanting to go home and the desire to remain free of complicated personal circumstances, stayed in Melbourne.

At forty-five, exactly half-way through his life, he had enjoyed more personal freedom than most men and had survived an exceptionally bloody war. He had seen the harsher side of life, living the virtual hand-to-mouth existence of a prospector and Jack-of-all-trades, while at the same time laboriously polishing the art of penmanship.

In just four years after the publication of *Prospecting for Gold*, and especially *Lasseter's Last Ride* and *The Desert Column*, he had been catapulted into the spotlight of public acclaim to become the darling of wide-eyed ladies, to converse with, and be praised by, politicians and educationalists, and to dine with titled personages.

His world had moved slowly but now he was experiencing

the high life. He had come from isolated campfires, bark lean-tos, and five shillings a week rented rooms to his own flat or hotel accommodation. His companions were no longer the remittance-men, prospectors and men on the track humping the bluey; now they were sophisticated and often drawn from the 'upper-crust'.

He stayed on in Melbourne until the end of November. He continued to write to Cousins but his letters never again held anything of a personal nature. It would appear that he was stalling for time—time to come to terms with his decision.

For twenty-six years, since the death of his mother, Jack Idriess had remained emotionally unattached to any one person. Not only was he facing a mid-life crisis, he knew that returning to Sydney meant assuming responsibilities that would totally change his life.

No one would have guessed this quiet, wiry, slightly balding man had a concern in the world. Only the long, sensitive, deeply nicotine-stained fingers, which habitually played across his high forehead and slid down the sides of his cheeks to progress along the elongated jaw to meet at the chin tip—fingers which rolled cigarette after cigarette—betrayed the man hidden behind the huge, veiled, grey eyes.

♦

AMONG Jack's papers I found an undated note in an envelope marked 'Private':

Dear Idriess
I particularly want to see you. I have a proposition to make.
I will call tomorrow about 7.
J. Gibson

It seems certain that the writer of this note was Jesse Gibson, Eta's husband.

Given Jack's often repeated instructions to Cousins to pay Eta weekly amounts of money while he was travelling though Western Australia during 1934, and his repeated references to the 'Morris affair', I can only conjecture that Gibson's 'proposition' amounted to blackmail.

The note and Jack's numerous complaints written to Cousins throughout 1934, when coupled with the story told to Wendy Idriess by her mother, Eta, of Gibson confronting Jack in the bar at the old Hyde Park Hotel where Jack was drinking, and of the resulting fight between the two men ending with Jack being thrown down the stairs and out on to the footpath by Gibson, seems to confirm that the fight was not based purely on accusation or revelation, nor the outrage of a jealous husband.

In October 1933 Jack had written to Farmer Whyte, a friend and Canberra-based journalist, mentioning that he had an 'enemy'. This is borne out in a letter dated October 1933 from Farmer Whyte, who, apart from his 'Canberra Correspondent' articles, wrote widely syndicated reviews of Jack's books over many years. After receiving the just-published *Drums of Mer* Whyte wrote to Jack highly praising the book and asking Jack to forward—if he could find the time—the story of his life in order that he could write up an interview with Jack. Toward the end of the four-page letter Whyte made perplexed reference to Jack having an 'enemy': 'Can't understand what you say about an enemy. Didn't think you had an enemy in the world. Have you any idea who he is and why?'

Jack knew only too well who his enemy was, although the disclosure of Gibson's existence would have staggered him when he first heard. I can believe that Jack sincerely did not know that Eta was married, nor that she had a two-year old son, when their relationship began in 1931.

Obviously Jack was in possession of the truth when he left Sydney for Western Australia in November 1933. Given this knowledge it is not difficult to understand his reluctance to accept that the child Eta was carrying was his; nor is it difficult to understand his refusal to write to her, leaving Cousins to be the go-between.

This was a time when you could be sued for breach of promise, when adultery was almost the only grounds for divorce and a paternity suit a disaster. If any such action had been brought against Jack, an author whose image was more than squeaky-clean, whose books sold to readers of all ages in phenomenal numbers, both Jack, and as a consequence Angus and Robertson, would have sustained heavy financial loses as a result of scandalous publicity. Cousins' role of agent in this delicate situation would have simply constituted sound business practice.

I believe that Gibson, too, had an eye for business and saw in Jack, the successful author, someone whom he could either outright blackmail or at the very least foist his responsibilities on. In this he was successful.

Exactly what Eta's role was is difficult to say. She was either very artful to be able to keep two men unaware of the existence of each other, or she and Gibson enjoyed a so-called 'open' relationship. How was it that she was able to carry on what appears to have been a close relationship with Jack, even to the point of spending a two-week holiday with him at Katoomba in November 1932, without Gibson knowing or suspecting that she was involved with another man? Further, Eta's timing must have been exquisitely precise for Jack not to have known that she was pregnant with Judy, her first daughter, when she and a girlfriend vacationed with him that November. Where was her three-year-old son, Maurice, during that two-week period?

Perhaps it is possible that Eta, who stated to a close friend that she found Gibson physically abhorrent, used her pregnancy to rid herself of Gibson, never expecting him to make Jack a 'proposition' in order to profit from their liaison.

Eta's affair with Jack had continued over a two-year period. Doubtless there had been protestations of love between the two and therefore Eta, confident that her charm would hold Jack, would never have expected her plan, if indeed she had one, to backfire.

What actually occurred, and why, will never be known. We do know, however, that Jack, motivated by a sense of honour, or because he had no other choice, accepted full responsibility for Eta and Wendy, the child born while he was travelling in the Kimberley. This was the beginning of a very uncomfortable and, at times, painful relationship.

That January 1935 found Jack back in Sydney, where he declined a meeting with Frank Clune and Jonathan Cape, the British publisher. Clune was attempting to have his work published by Cape in England and felt that Cape would be interested in adding Jack to the Cape stable. Jack, dedicated to expanding the future of Australian publishing, felt this to be a traitorous act and, further, not good business. In view of the ethics involved he suggested that he would attend such a meeting only if it was convened at Angus and Robertson's.

At that time English publishers were only producing on average editions of ten thousand copies, while the author of a runaway best-seller could, perhaps, look forward to three editions and a royalty of a mere five per cent. Australian works of Australian content were basically published for sale to the 'colonial market'; at a cover price of six shillings and sixpence. Authors received three pence per copy royalty payment. Even if the book was well received Australian authors could anticipate no more than a pittance in reward for their efforts. Unprofitable as it was, for many Australian authors acceptance by an English publisher was the ultimate seal of approval. Despite the obvious competence and marketing efficiency of Australian publishers in which Angus and

Robertson led the way, this attitude persisted well into the 1950s.

Jack also declined a luncheon in his honour with the Fellowship of Australian Authors in view of the Fellowship's attitude to the Kisch affair:

> If I said 'yes' I would feel like I was sailing under false colours. Some other time with pleasure, if the Fellowship still think the same way about it [the lunch]. I am also very busy trying to get twelve months' work done in three months and by Jove every hour counts, I can only work when I feel like it and I've got to go hell for leather then!

While he had been out of New South Wales personal relations within the Idriess family had deteriorated still further. A letter from his sister Ildyce brought Jack up-to-date on the continuing wrangle between their sister, Esmé, and their father, Walter Owen Idriess.

The enmity between Walter's second wife, Amy, and his children had continued to simmer over the years. Amy had virtually reared the youngest daughter, Katie, after Julia had died. As the only mother she had ever known, Katie accepted her without antagonism. Jack had very little contact with Amy, probably by design, for no one could have replaced Julia in his heart; in fact he seems to have ignored Amy's very existence. However, the overbearing Amy was a very tangible presence in the lives of Ildyce and Esmé. Ildyce had come to treat her with patronising indifference, while Esmé made no attempt to conceal her overt dislike for the second Mrs Idriess.

Ildyce wrote to Jack telling him of Esmé's intention to continue her district court action between the family and Walter in the hope of obtaining a ruling in their favour on the rightful distribution of their mother's estate. Kate Edmond's will had provided for the daughters of Julia Matilda Idriess the sum of six hundred pounds which was to be held in Trust until each reached the age of twenty-one or married, whichever came first. It would appear that the bequest was mal-administrated for the money, now the sizeable sum of eight thousand pounds due to compounding interest, remained in the hands of Walter and Amy Idriess.

At the end of 1935 Esmé and her family were suffering the effect of the Depression and in desperate need of financial assistance. Esmé hated the country and wanted to go to Sydney to start a business; therefore she was not prepared to stand by and have what she believed to be their rightful inheritance dissipated by Amy or to have it go to 'all her side'. Ildyce also reminded Jack in the same letter that he had signed away to his sisters any claim to the inheritance for a sum of one hundred pounds. Just how Jack responded to the news of the impending court action is not known.

It is doubtful that he concerned himself with the angst between his sisters and their father or took any active part in discussions relevant to his father's hold on Julia's estate. Given that Jack had experienced very little contact with his family since the age of nineteen, his loyalty probably lay mostly with the father with whom he had spent many of his formative years, and from whom he learned to love the bush and how to survive its capricious moods. Apart from emotional ties with Walter he also respected him. Walter was a person who had lived an arduous and often dangerous life and was basically the type of man whom Jack held in high esteem.

Walter was now seventy-three years old. In 1889, the year of Jack's birth, he had begun service as a Sheriff's Officer with both the Department of Justice and the Department of Mines and Agriculture. In the service of the Department of Justice he acted as District Court Bailiff, Small Debts Courts Bailiff, Inspector of Shops and Factories; as Warden's Bailiff with the Department of Mines and Agriculture he carried out the orders of the Warden, the government officer with magisterial and executive powers in charge of a mineral field. As Warden's Bailiff he was responsible for the issue of miners' rights, for serving writs and summonses, making arrests, enforcing court orders and collecting payments of adjudged debts.

In Walter's day Broken Hill, isolated as it was from mainstream Australia, was a virtually lawless town of thirty thousand people who suffered from endemic debt. His work often exposed him to physical danger: many times he found himself arbitrating between hot-blooded Afghans locked in passionate disputes, and settling angry miners' claims. Walter, however, enjoyed the reputation of being a fair man, but the profile of his office condemned him to a degree of exclusion from the community.

In view of the often difficult life that his father had lived, it seems most likely that Jack would have felt that the old man should be left in peace, and he may have resented the attack upon his father's integrity by sisters whom he hardly knew. The question of Julia's inheritance was of no concern to him. Through incessant work he had maintained a constant income throughout the Depression; this hard-won financial position was the reason he had declined his share, preferring to have it shared between his sisters.

◆

I N 1935 over thirty articles written by Ion L. Idriess were published in newspapers and magazines around Australia. The sales of *Lasseter's Last Ride* and *Flynn of the Inland* were breaking records; *Lasseter's Last Ride* was in publication in Swedish, Dutch and French editions and *Prospecting for Gold* was selling well, while the New Guinea epic, *Gold Dust and Ashes,* was up and racing and still drawing the attention of film-makers. Cinesound's General Manager, Ken Hall, lamented the fact that Jack did not have the time to write a movie script for the company, subject to be nominated, while Mr Cecil Marks, General Manager of United Artists (Australia), was sailing for the USA to confer with his 'New York Chiefs' about acquiring the movie rights to *Gold Dust and Ashes* and *Man Tracks.*

Due to Jack's previously published successes and based on his popularity and Sid Kidman's failing health, the Kidman family urged him to return to Adelaide to start work on the Kidman biography before he began another book. Angus and Robertson also urged him to start the Kidman biography, which would ultimately be published as *The Cattle King.*

Jack wrote to many of Kidman's station managers in the hope of getting some answers to probing questions relevant to Kidman and his pastoral operations. He hoped their answers would shorten the research time he would have to spend when he eventually was able to return to South Australia. However, the answers were not forthcoming.

On 23 January the Kidman Company Secretary J. H. Bird wrote to Jack:

> Our General Manager, Mr Sydney Reid, is now home from England and I have discussed this matter with him. He is of the opinion that if you are able to come over in March you would be able to gain a lot of information by interviews with Sir Sidney and then taking a trip with our Pastoral Inspector who has been with Sir Sidney for nearly forty years and who will be visiting the South Western Queensland properties and the Barrier District where all Sir Sidney's operations took place.

Early in April Jack returned to Adelaide. All was going well with *Man Tracks.* Cousins wrote to advise that the second edition had sold out and that Angus and Robertson hoped to 'clean up third and fourth before end of May'.

On 10 April Jack wrote to Cousins outlining the difficulties he was experiencing in getting material for the Kidman biography. He had just returned to Adelaide after a seven-week trip, covering three thousand miles through south-western Queensland, with Kidman's travelling station inspector, Edward Pratt. Although Pratt had been with Kidman for thirty-seven years he had not proved to be a fount of knowledge. Jack was concerned that 'the Kidman men knew very little of Sid Kidman'. He further observed that Kidman was 'not a pioneer type' but added that he had undoubtedly 'been a wonderful man'.

Four notebooks, the numbers one to four carved into the cloth and cardboard covers, are crammed with close pencil-written notes documenting the trip. Attached to many pages by rusted paper clips are tags identifying the material he ultimately used or intended to use in the book. Many of these pages bear a single pencil slash across the notes to indicate the used material. The notes record an arduous trip and show the country to be suffocated by drought.

These notebooks are also crammed with minute descriptions of birds and animals, some of which he noted in later years as possibly being extinct. They also contain descriptions of the passing terrain, the type of trees growing in each area they rode through, the colour of tree trunks, the small bushes, the species of grasses native to each district and a multitude of observations that the average man would never notice, much less commit to paper.

There are many fascinating accounts contributed by the Kidman managers who, while not overburdened with personal Kidman stories, supplied details of the humanistic dynamics involved in the successful management of an outlying station. They also hold notes of conversations with some of the station managers' wives. These women were overjoyed to see a new face. To talk with someone who was eventually going to make contact with the 'big boss' prompted some to try to have him put in a word or two for them in the hope of obtaining some small extra comfort. Life for them was not easy but, by comparison, working for Kidman was far better than employment elsewhere.

The country was in the grip of a drought—the waterholes were drying up. The notebooks also contain a series of pertinent conservation observations—for Jack was a conservationist long before such a practice was thought of.

Miles and miles of ringbarked trees, all have rotted away. Without living roots to hold it, the top soil is blowing away. Drought, everywhere is dry and dusty, drought and man have made waste of this land of ours. If we tried to plant trees in good times we might get it to regenerate. I wonder how long it would take? But we won't, rather ringbark more areas and continue making more deserts... The land is dreadfully overgrazed, where ten sheep would fatten, five only are lucky to survive.

On 11 April Cousins forwarded Jack's mail to him at Piper's Hotel Richmond on Rundle Street in Adelaide. The package contained copies of *Man Tracks* to be autographed for customers of the New South Wales Bookstall Co. and a letter from Walter advising him that Esmé was suing for part of Julia's estate. Walter's letter also contained information about Kidman which Jack had requested. Walter supplied what he could recall of Kidman from his days of service at Broken Hill when Kidman and his operations were well known.

Still using the formal mode of address, Cousins wrote on 8 May 1935 to Jack c/o the Marree Post Office, South Australia:

Dear Mr Idriess,
No doubt you have seen notices in the papers that the following authors are to receive the King's Royal Jubilee Medal. These names are in the Federal List. Some other authors are in the State list but I am very glad to see they have placed you as a national author.
Dr C.E. Bean
Mrs H.R. Curlewis
F.M. Cutlack
Hugh McCrae
A.B. Paterson
Ion L. Idriess

Not a word of congratulation!

♦

THAT August of 1935 Jonathan Cape began the English publication of *Lasseter's Last Ride* with an introduction by Field Marshall Sir William Birdwoods, Commander of the AIF.

On 2 August in a letter c/o S. Reid, Kidman Buildings, Adelaide, Cousins empathised with Jack: 'It must be an awful job having to write a story like you are now and not being able to verify dates from Head Office. Anyhow there will not be many people who can challenge anything if Kidman can't.'

This was a non-academic, highly simplistic view taken by Cousins and one not endorsed by Jack. Throughout August he continued the battle to have dates verified by the Kidman Head Office. A letter to Cousins from Mary Gilmore, who was greatly interested in the book, caused him to write urging Jack to 'hang on and do his utmost' to obtain even simple details and dates.

On 2 September 1935 back home in Sydney, Jack received a telegram: 'Regret to inform you Sir Sidney passed away midday today funeral tomorrow. Sid Reid.'

On 3 September, the day following Kidman's death, the *Sydney Morning Herald* published Jack's memorial article, 'Bushman to the Last'.

Jack continued to try to pull the biography together. The problem of obtaining confirmation of dates continued to dog him and the size of the book became a continual worry. On 7 November he wrote to J. H. Bird requesting more concise information to verify the time between Kidman's departure from Mount Gipps and when he met Lady Kidman. 'I cannot put in all his trips because the book is now thirty thousand words longer than is allowed for a book. It would take at least three large volumes to fill in Sir Sidney's life in detail, the bringing of the main events in cameo is rather a job.' The letter closes, 'Yesterday I wrote the last line of the book, for which I am deeply grateful. It has been a harder job than any three of the others.'

Cousins wired Jack to go ahead with press publicity to promote the Cape edition of *Lasseter's Last Ride* in Adelaide, and further advised him that Cape would come out with one of Jack's books a year. The wire also carried the news that a Swedish edition was in preparation of 'Jungle Drums' which one must assume to have been a translation of *Men of the Jungle*. *Lasseter's Last Ride* was published in Sweden on 26 August 1935.

Jack wrote two letters to M. C. Rice, Kidman's son-in-law, on 9 January 1936 telling him that coming to Adelaide was out of the question as he was right in the middle of the 'pearling book' (*Forty Fathoms Deep*) which had been held up due to difficulties in writing *The Cattle King*. He further stated that if he were to come to Adelaide the Kidman family would have to pay his expenses of forty pounds as he simply could not afford the outlay. In both letters he reiterated that the Kidman family were to proof the book and make the necessary corrections, and promised that any corrections or alterations to the manuscript would be carried out. The second letter of 9 January contained a very detailed explanation of why he wrote the book as he did, and why certain aspects were not mentioned, especially the two properties—one on each side of the Queensland border—which were used to transfer cattle to avoid payment of one pound per head duty:

> Re the border fence, and S. K.'s station, one on each side. This gave me a first-class chance of pointing out the astuteness of Sir Sidney. I purposely did not avail myself of it because I thought it just possible some unpleasantness might arise from it. Sir Sidney brought some thousands of cattle in Queensland and passed them through his Queensland station into his NSW station, thus obviating the difficulty of paying £1 per head. Even at this late stage I thought it best to let 'sleeping dogs lie'. I thought it best not to point out the astuteness of S. K. in evading those Customs dues. However, if on consideration you write me to go ahead with the particulars of the station on each side of the fence I will willingly do so, for it was a shrewd move and would excite some comment in that chapter.
>
> Re the shearers strike. I got a fair amount of copy re this from the office and Sir Sidney, also from some of the station managers. I have refrained from using it because of lack of space. The book already is of 113,000 words, and the ordinary length of such a book is 80,000 words. Also this verges closely on political matters, and such incidents rankle, even after the course of years. I would suggest that it is best, from every point of view, not to stir up incidents of this kind...
>
> As I do not know the exact words any person would use under any given circumstances, you must help me out in this. Wherever you pencil any phrase that could be used by a person in conversation I will use it... The book is woefully short of brighter touches. Too much detail of buying mob after mob, station after station would drag with the reading public so help me out with lighter patches when you are making corrections.

These were not the only difficulties. Kidman employees gave him information and stories which others denied. During his interviews in 1935 Sir Sidney told him that he had partly financed the purchase of the Warrenda and Tinapagee stations in 1911 with the sale of fats from Durham Downs purchased in 1910. Bird, however, gave him a list of stations and their purchase dates which showed Durham Downs as being purchased in 1911. It was eventually established that Kidman was correct. Controversy between Kidman and Bird over the size and price of two horse teams purchased at

285

Cobar could not be resolved, with the result that he could not go into details.

Problems with *The Cattle King* compounded and continued. Few of the photographs supplied by the Kidmans could be reproduced and eventually most of the illustrations which appeared in the published book were supplied by Dr MacGilivray. Instead of information about the purpose and the number of trips Kidman took overseas, Jack was supplied with a list of stations and the number of sheep shorn on those properties from 1924 to 1935.

The Cattle King was finally published in March 1936.

Academics and critics have always criticised Jack's work and no doubt will continue to do so, some rightly but most without knowledge of the constraints laid upon him. Stylist he might not have been; however the economic restrictions placed upon publishers during the 1930s Depression restricted the size of their publications, forcing authors to truncate their work. Angus and Robertson wanted a 'good read' that would sell in high numbers to a largely uninformed populace. To the detriment of his reputation as an author Jack wrote very much to a market dictated by both publisher and consumer demand.

Sadly it is *The Cattle King*, more than any other of his works, which has received the most condemnation. It is Ion L. Idriess who is blamed for producing a work identified as 'faction', not the other culprits: Angus and Robertson, the Kidman family, the 1930s Depression, the level of general readership, or the prevailing state of Australian publishing.

Australian publishing, basically in its infancy at that time, was making a valiant attempt to compete against imported British books which sold, on average, for two shillings a copy. Public lending libraries were, understandably, heavily patronised; many people could only afford to spend sixpence, as opposed to six shillings, to read a book, with the result that Australian publishers were continually on a tight budget.

The publishers were not alone in their economic circumstances. Jack had no secretary, no financial research help, neither was he fortunate enough to have a financial backer, nor did he receive a publisher's advance.

At the same time as he researched and was writing *The Cattle King* he finished and proofed *Man Tracks*, and wrote endless newspaper articles to keep both himself and the family he had acquired. At that same time he drafted *Forty Fathoms Deep*. Obviously he did not have three years at his disposal to write the book. If he had been fortunate enough to have had such advantageous circumstances the work would not have been published, as Angus and Robertson were in no position to indulge their authors.

While Jill Bowen's work, *Kidman: The Forgotten King*, published in 1987 also by Angus and Robertson, is undoubtedly the definitive Kidman biography, the comments made by her about Ion L. Idriess and *The Cattle King* are at best uninformed, and at worst patronising.

In an interview with Jill Bowen, Muriel Kidman, Sir Sidney and Lady Kidman's daughter-in-law, is reported to have said, 'Because of deafness he [Kidman] found it hard to hear what Idriess said. Walter sat on the chair and prompted his father. It was an awful book and everyone said later "What a pity someone else didn't do a book while Walter was still alive".'

Muriel Kidman was right; if Kidman was deaf, he would have been hard-pressed to have heard Jack's questions, for Jack was very softly spoken. However, even those who did hear, did not, for whatever reasons, supply the correct answers to his questions and they were often prepared to argue with Kidman over facts in which he was proved to be correct.

An awful book? Despite all the obstacles and constraints previously mentioned, *The Cattle King* was a success. After all the trouble Jack had experienced I also know he would have heartily agreed with Muriel Kidman on one point '...it is a pity that someone else didn't do a book' at that time. Jack and that 'awful book' did have one fan, however: Mary Gilmore, later Dame Mary Gilmore. He received a letter from her dated 29 December which read:

> Your book has just come to hand and I have been turning the leaves unable to read because of half crying over familiar names, remembrance of years gone and people I shall never see again. My dear, what a work you are doing for Australia, and what a darling you are to give me the inscription you did! And how little Kidman altered in appearance! He always stood, was framed and looked of the same breed as my father. That was the first thing I said of him when, in the distance, I saw him first in about 1887 at Silverton ... may the Kidman track to fortune be yours. The horns are on the right end of the bullock there!

◆

IN June 1936 *Lasseter's Last Ride* received the London Book Society recommendation: one of the six best books published during

April 1936. May had seen a review in the *London Times* which stated, 'Ion L Idriess, the Australian author, is receiving recognition in England as the foremost example of an author deserving fame outside his own country'. The *Times* praised the 'epic-like' quality of the book, saying that 'Idriess has again brilliantly exploited the field of literature which allows a blend of fact and imaginative reconstruction. Some reviewers qualify their eulogies by regretting the degree of incoherence in the author's narrative style, but the *Times* congratulates Idriess on his 'coherence and romance solidly based on knowledge of the wild country and the wild people of which he is writing'.

This is fitting praise and shows that Jack's efforts were appreciated when he was allowed a free rein with his writing.

Chapter Twenty-nine
OF 'JAPS' AND 'ABOS'.

1936, and the wandering Ion L. Idriess had settled into a working routine. Every morning including Saturday he could be found working at his desk on the mezzanine floor at Angus and Robertson in Sydney. All his work was still written in pencil on loose sheets of quarto paper. In contrast to the almost microscopic handwriting and the closely-packed lines he used when recording his war diaries, the writing was now large, perhaps best described as square and easy to read. Wide spaces between the lines allowed him to easily revise his first drafts and to replace any words he crossed out, sometimes adding an entire line.

There was always a pile of quarto typing paper on the desk in front of him and two or three larger piles ready nearby. Piled around him would be notes, diaries, photographs, letters, maps, pencil sharpener, tobacco and paper and his pipes, not to mention the pins and paper clips which he used to clip together the multitude of newspaper clippings, drafts of his own letters, or letters received by him. As Jack filled a page he would move it to his left and turn it face down, while the right hand went on writing. Then, after he had read, corrected, selected photographs and clipped them to the material, he would read the work again and consider the whole, photographs and written work, and if necessary make more corrections. Then, content with the work, he would hand it to Bess for one of 'her girls' to type.

As an author Jack could be said to have had a very unusual relationship with his publisher, Angus and Robertson, wherein he was almost regarded a member of the Firm. The close association between him and Cousins, which had its beginning in correspondence during the West Australian trip and his extended periods of absence while researching *The Cattle King*, continued, and, according to Jack, the two could be found 'meeting every afternoon at three o'clock' to 'discuss business and various questions'.

This statement is contrary to the memory of his nephew, Dr Ion Morrison, the eldest son of Jack's sister, Ildyce, and George Morrison:

Jack worked from 9.30 each morning until 1.30 every day, then he would go to the hotel across from David Jones, the St James, there he would have a counter lunch and steadily drink all afternoon until closing time and take a taxi home about 6.30. He used to sit on a high stool like a Guru with his legs crossed, you could always hear his laugh when you came into the room because he had a high pitched, infectious laugh. He would introduce his nephew who was going to become a doctor saying 'get on to him for a free consultation'.

At the time Ion Morrison was studying medicine at University. He recalled that, although the Depression was almost over, he was usually strapped for cash after his fees were paid. Somehow Jack seemed to know when Ion needed money, which he gave him without ever being asked.

Jack's interest in Ion was motivated by more than the desire to assist his sister's child obtain his medical degree, for, given a suitable education, Jack's chosen field would have been medical research. Ion Morrison, who declared himself to be a depressive, stated that he was forever threatening to give up his study to return to Grafton, and had it not been for Jack's motivational encouragement, based on his belief that medicine was the most important field a man could give his life to, he would never have graduated.

Ion said that Jack's desire for greater medical knowledge originated at Broken Hill with the death of Julia. The fact that Julia had died because he had contracted typhoid preyed on his mind. The Morrison children all make mention that he regarded himself as the direct cause of her death, and his sense of guilt, rather than diminishing, grew with the years.

As a regular visitor at Angus and Robertson, Ion Morrison remembered the tension surrounding the release in March 1936 of *The Cattle King* and the relief when the glowing reviews began to stream in.

The *Bulletin* stated: 'This is the greatest real romance in the business life of Australia. Only the author of *Flynn of the Inland* could have done it.' The *Bulletin* reviewer went further and compared Jack to Kidman. Alec Chisholm contained himself to stating in his Red Page *Bulletin* article that it was 'unbeatable', while the Perth *West Australian* printed, 'No other Australian writer has done better work in way of a vivid portrayal of the Australian Outback and the men who made it'.

C. H. Holmes, editor of *Walkabout* magazine, urged Jack to write a digest of *The Cattle King* for publication in the magazine, but

Jack replied that he had never written a digest of a book before and added, 'Besides, between you and me, the writing of the book was such a devil of a job that I got heartily sick of it.' In its place he sent him an article entitled 'The Blood Hole of Wyndham'.

Cousins had breathed a sigh of relief with each review praising *The Cattle King*. He had been particularly anxious about this book. Cousins had even counselled Jack to give up trying to 'put the man on the map'. There had been so many delays during the writing and verifying that Cousins, like Jack, had come to believe that the book was going to be the publisher's nightmare: 'a monument in the warehouse'. Jack's negative attitude about the book's lack of human interest and his fear that it would have only limited appeal had affected Cousins. Despite the fact Jack had reduced the book by two chapters, as directed by Cousins, it was still the largest A&R had published for the general market. Although the Depression was easing, Cousins was understandably apprehensive.

Finally, content that *The Cattle King* had been well accepted in Sydney, Cousins turned his attention to South Australia, Kidman's home state. The South Australian reviews couldn't get to Sydney fast enough for Cousins. On 1 April 1936 he could contain himself no longer and wrote a letter to Dr Angus Johnson at the Town Hall in Adelaide:

Many thanks for your letter. I am particularly anxious to learn how the Adelaide Press treat *The Cattle King*. It received an ovation in Sydney. The *Sydney Morning Herald* not only gave it a review, but a leader as well. All class it as the author's best. We have not seen any reviews from other states yet, but expect them to trickle through in a few days. In the first week we sold twice as many *Cattle King* as any other Idriess title in the same period. Whatever success comes to Idriess, here or abroad, it will never go to his head. He is the most unassuming and likeable author I have ever had dealings with, and I have never in all the years I have known him heard him speak unkindly of anyone—no matter how great the injury.

The Cattle King received the same accolade in Adelaide as in Sydney. With the Kidman epic behind him Jack set to work to finalise *Forty Fathoms Deep* and *Over The Range*. At the same time he worked on a series of 'Believe It Or Not'-type illustrated articles which were published that year. Titled 'Strange Things I Have Seen', the series, featuring odd and exotic Australian flora and fauna, and illustrated by E. A. Holloway, was offered to the provincial press in Australia and New Zealand by Angus and Robertson.

That year Jonathan Cape published *Lasseter's Last Ride* in England. *John O'Londons Weekly* gave it a rave review and sent Jack a copy of the magazine. Jack, the frustrated marketer, couldn't resist writing to the editor to let him know how difficult it was to get a copy of the magazine in Australia and gave him details of how to market it and to whom, including the population of each capital city: 'Sydney 1,250,000; Melbourne 1,000,000; Adelaide and Brisbane 35,000; Perth 25,000; New Zealand 2,000,000'. He dismissed Hobart as 'smaller'.

Then, as if he didn't have enough to do, he launched himself into promoting his concept of the first Around Australia Endurance Rally together with the National Road Motoring Association (NRMA).

In August he wrote to the Reverend MacFarlane, who had left the warm climate of the Coral Sea islands to live in chilly Tasmania:

> The Round Australia Car Contest will be the 'Big Thing' here in the very near future; we hope to intrigue the world. My real idea was that it would probably develop world tourist traffic which would mean the manufacture of cars in Australia, enlargement of iron and steel works and employment for many thousands of people.

The letter had been written in reply to one from MacFarlane which he had written from hospital suggesting that Jack should take a holiday in Tasmania. Jack didn't find the idea of taking a holiday appealing but he did fancy looking over one or two nurses: 'As long as they are the right shape and size I'm their slave. Between you and me Mac, let me know what sort of figures they've got and I might find it convenient to get quietly sick in Tasmania. A holiday wouldn't hurt me, especially if they tucked in the sheets right.'

Jack and MacFarlane continued to correspond for many years until MacFarlane's death. Throughout their long association Jack obviously never mentioned Eta or the children, for MacFarlane's letters regularly urged Jack to take a wife and settle down. Occasionally he attempted to play matchmaker, suggesting one or two ladies of his acquaintance who were 'enthralled that he knew the famous author and were dying to meet him'. Jack's standard response on these occasions was to ask about age, proportion, hair colour and imply that he was interested.

That year Cousins wrote to E. T. Fisk, chairman of AWA (Amalgamated Wireless of Australia) suggesting that Jack should do one or two broadcasts to America to promote the Car Contest: 'We have good reason to believe that a series of talks from Ion L. Idriess would soon create interest in America to such a degree that Australia's tourist and commercial business would benefit appreciably.' Jack's and Cousins' concept to promote Australia was about forty-five years ahead of Hogan and Cornell and just a shade more sophisticated than 'throwing another shrimp on the barbie'— which simply demonstrates that there are no new ideas, only old ones up-dated.

The year rolled on and the letters rolled in, in ever-growing numbers. The *Sydney Morning Herald* carried a report in August which said that Jack had received four thousand letters and that the stamps to answer them had cost him one hundred pounds. He said that ninety-eight per cent of the letters referred to something in his books, or were letters of appreciation, and that two per cent were crank letters, including suggestions to build a monstrous tower in the centre of Australia with a view to making contact with other planets to demand the 'Messiah of Peace' to appear. One of his devoted followers insisted that Jack dig a tunnel right through the centre of the earth, and after having done so, demanded that Jack take him to London for the Coronation!

Walter and Amy had left Grafton some years earlier, moving to Sydney to take up residence at Mosman. They had bought a block of six large flats close to the Mosman Ferry, a very choice piece of real estate.

The pace of the city and all the demands that came with being a public figure, coupled with his enforced domestic arrangement, created in Jack the need to renew his relationship with Walter, and he began to visit his father every Sunday afternoon.

Ildyce Pike, Ion Morrison's sister and Jack's niece, recalled attending one or two of those family gatherings at that time:

> I remember Grandfather had beautiful skin and blue eyes, silver hair and bald on top. All of Amy's relatives arrived in droves. Those Sunday afternoons were a scream, culminating in a 'High Tea'. The Scotts never stopped talking, laughing and to my child's mind, arguing with one another. In the midst of this, by a window, sat Ion and his father, smoking their pipes and apparently saying nothing to one another but enjoying each other's company enormously. They seemed to be in their own little island of peace whilst the stormy sea of the Scotts' chatter raged all around them.

Ildyce also recalled her memory of Jack at that time: 'Ion always looked like a countryman. He was about five foot ten inches with nice features, the most outstanding of which were his beautiful expressive eyes. I think they were a hazel-grey in colour.'

Oddly, no one accurately recalls the colour of Jack's eyes, although everyone mentions his eyes as being his most commanding feature and makes comment on how expressive they were. For the record his eyes were grey, not hazel or blue, the most commonly held misconceptions. Obviously Jack found it irritating when the colour his eyes were reported as being other than grey, for he would cross out the wrong colour and write 'GREY' in capital letters over the top.

After leaving 42 Bayswater Road, Kings Cross, where he had been living since late 1930, Jack had moved to 111 Cottenham Road in Kingsford. Ion Morrison recalls that Jack lived at Bayswater Road until his return to Sydney in the December of 1934 and was still there for a period of time during 1935 while he concluded work on *The Cattle King*. Ion also recalled that Jack and Eta did not live together during that time. As it is not known just when he moved to Kingsford, I assume that he finally took up permanent residence with Eta and the children either late in 1935, or early in 1936.

Now, at forty-seven, Jack the separatist had been forced to conform and assume the role of a family man. Obviously he didn't accept this easily. Not only was he a compulsive writer, bordering on being a workaholic, he was now verging on becoming an alcoholic.

Life at home in Kingsford would have been far from the proverbial bed of roses for either party. Theoretically, although he drank his way through each afternoon, Jack worked five days a week, not returning home before seven each night. He also worked Saturday mornings at A&R and spent the afternoon at the races; each Sunday afternoon he visited his father. Consciously or unconsciously, he appears to have done everything he could to avoid being at home, and when he was there his senses would have been dulled by alcohol. One would anticipate that this routine would have affected his work output; however, he didn't even slow down, much to the amazement of many people, including his nephews Ion and Terry Morrison. Terry commented years later, 'With all the drinking I wonder how Ion found time to write but I don't think there was ever a lapse in his productivity.' And indeed there wasn't.

Times had changed since he wrote to D. H. Souter in August 1933, 'I have carried my swag and dined in state in cities. I have smoked Nigger-Twist tobacco and the best brand of cigars. I have had to go without a pair of boots, but now have them made to order. I think the world is an interesting old place to live in.' His world was no longer such an interesting old place to live in.

Suddenly he developed an ability to talk on request to various groups such as Rotary Clubs. He flooded the press with articles and letters and more than fully answered all his fan mail, responding in detail to the questions asked.

In February 1937 he addressed the Agricultural Bureau Conference at Narrabri on the serious problem of soil erosion. It was a graphic address in which he took the audience over terrain he had traversed in his wanderings from Adelaide to the Kimberley.

Addresses by Ion L. Idriess were popular that year. In May he spoke to the Katoomba Rotarians about the problems facing half-caste Aborigines and his concern for the fate of their descendants, and further spoke on how white Australians could profit from the knowledge that the Aborigines had in using the medicinal properties of plants, in which he claimed to have extensive knowledge.

On 8 May he received a letter from Government House in Canberra, signed by L. S. Bracegirdle, Captain RAN, Military and Official Secretary to the Governor-General. The letter informed Ion L. Idriess that he was to be the recipient of a special medal to commemorate the Coronation of Their Majesties, King George VI and Queen Elizabeth. Jack's response to this news is not recorded but I suspect that he would not have been overly impressed—nothing in the way of pomp and circumstance, flag waving and the like, cut much ice with Jack.

After his Katoomba appearance he travelled to Tamworth, addressing several schools where he drew upon his memories of going to school there as a very young child.

Jack, the man who hated public speaking, must have impressed the Katoomba Rotary Club, for the following month, June, after his return from Tamworth, he accepted a second engagement to address the club. This time he spoke about 'Yampie Sound Country' which was reported by the *Blue Mountains Courier* as being both interesting and informative.

Throughout the year he continued to be in demand as a speaker, undertaking a series of lectures for the YMCA under the title of 'Experiences of an Australian Author'. 8 November found him in Young where he addressed a crowded meeting on how the Japanese were stealing pearling grounds from Australian pearlers. Then he switched to pre-historic monsters, an odd combination but one the people of Young found 'enthralling', according to the report in the *Young Witness*.

Somehow during all the travelling he managed to continue to promote the Round Australia Motor Contest as a tourist attraction for the 1938 Sesqui-Centenary, undertake several radio broadcasts over radio 2KY, write a number of articles, launch *Forty Fathoms Deep*, and finish *Over The Range* in time for the 1937 Christmas market.

On 4 November 1937 Jack received two letters from Captain Cochrane of the *Swannie*, whose home port was Darwin. Jack had sailed with him during his Darwin sojourn in 1934. Cochrane and Jack had dealt extensively with the Aborigines and both men were deeply concerned over the spread of venereal disease and leprosy among the northern tribes. Cochrane, worried about the exploitation of the Aborigines by Japanese pearlers, wrote to Jack:

Dear Edriess [sic],
Enclosed herewith you will find a letter to yourself from me going on about the use of Abos by the B. Japs here which I should be glad if you would use in your efforts to improve the lot of the Abos.

It really is a dashed scandal to realise that Japs are still allowed to GO INTO THE NEW ABO RESERVE AND RECRUIT and the Govt blokes here—Cook—the Chief Protector and the Police & even Abbot refused me permission to go into the croc rivers here to carry on the good work in the Goulbourne District [King River] yet Indented Japs from Singapore have a free hand. It takes a place like Australia to put that over and Particularly the Territory Gov. Official's Fancy. I have been in existence here as a Trepanger Pearler Timber getter—Crock [sic] hunter for over 10 years and yet the[y] Block me and allow the Pearling Japs to carry on. I have a plant and a complete outfit for the Crock [sic] hunting game and when they heard that I was going down to carry on they warned me that my boat would be pinched and myself fined if I put my nose into the reserve where I have been operating since 1929. Gawd...

Page two of the letter is missing from Jack's collection, but page three continues:

Things here are middling. Lots of Govt. monish [sic] money floating around for building and improvements and more to come if this is to be a second S/pore.

Briefly setting aside what appears to have been a government

296

protection policy in favour of the Japanese, which discriminated against the Aborigines and turned a blind eye to the Japanese exploitation of Aborigine labour while condoning the sexual abuse of the women, I am forced to question the naivety or the crass stupidity of a government which allowed the Japanese free access to the Northern ports, bays and inlets, especially when there was talk of making Darwin 'a second S/pore'!

On 12 November 1937 Jack received a letter from the New South Wales Parliament notifying him of the calling together of the Parliamentary Select Committee on the Administration of the Aborigines Protection Board for the purpose of electing a chairman and to decide what procedure to take with regard to their inquiry into the conditions of the Aborigines.

Mr Davidson, the writer of the letter, asked if Jack would be good enough to attend the inquiry and address the committee and if so would he please notify him as soon as possible. Jack agreed without hesitation.

A second letter dated 18 November 1937 read:

> Following upon the conversation between yourself and the chairman of this Committee, Mr M. A. Davidson, MLA, I am desired by the chairman to ask that you will be so good as to assist the Committee by such means as may lie in your power in connections with the forthcoming inquiry into the Administration of the Aborigines Protection Board.

Jack's statement before the Select Committee on Wednesday 24 November 1937 was extensive. Extremely truncated press reports of his statement generated an avalanche of angry letters from the North. White pearlers, both friends and acquaintances of Jack's, read mangled reports in the local press which appeared to state that he had identified all pearlers as being responsible for infecting the coastal Aborigines with venereal diseases.

The entire episode was a distressing experience for Jack. Just as he was about to give his statement before the committee an Aborigine present had jumped to his feet and said, 'We would like to ask, is the author using the Aborigines' cause to get publicity for his latest book?'

The *Sunday Sun* of 28 November named this 'as a mean, nasty piece of work', and continued, 'Don't blame the Abo. He was primed by a woman, a well-known woman. Motive: Jealous intellectual snobbery. "Jack" Idriess, who was deeply hurt was induced to ignore the insult and gave his address.'

The columnist went on: 'There isn't a streak of guile in his make-up. And what would a man want to "get publicity" for a book that has sold ten thousand copies in twelve days, anyway?'

The book was *Over The Range* which was claimed by Angus and Robertson to have set a record in popularity for best-sellers by Australian authors. *Over The Range* is Jack's account of the twelve-hundred-mile police patrol in the north-west Kimberley. Angus and Robertson announced to the press that ten thousand copies had been sold in twelve days, sales which they estimated would be the equivalent of some eighty thousand copies in England and two million in America on a comparative population basis.

The incredible sales of *Over The Range*, however satisfying, did little to assuage Jack's hurt. Stung by the criticism from the North he wrote a long letter to the *Sydney Morning Herald*. However, only the paragraph of correction was published. The castigation of his unnamed female accuser he left to members of the press; disgusted by the underhand attack on their favourite they rallied to his side, defending him with cries of 'Shame!'.

The *Sun*, however, published a large article written by Jack in December 1937 entitled 'Rescuing The Aborigines From The Grip Of Disease'. This incorporated the main thrust of his original letter to the *Sydney Morning Herald*. Far from being only a clarification of his statement, the article contributed more constructive and practical advice than his address to the committee.

The article dealt with the real handicap—the need to provide adequate provision for medical treatment to Aborigines who were precluded from obtaining effective medical attention because of their beliefs, superstition and the size of the continent. He saw the very widely scattered medical posts as useless unless there was a coordinated effort to gain the confidence of the Aborigines in order to treat them successfully. In his opinion there was a vital need to train people, who understood the Aborigines, their life and their customs, to administer their health care. Most importantly again he urged the government to treat the Aborigines in their own country, further pointing out where such medical posts should be established:

> ...in Western Australia in the well-placed Government Native Station of Moola Boola, near Hall's Creek, and at Munja, Walcott Inlet Government Station, or the coast for instance. Similar Posts, but equipped thoroughly medically, would be a humane objective to establish throughout Northern Australia in such areas yet remaining where native life is still fairly plentiful.

He wrote that his greatest distress was witnessing the detrib-alisation of the Aboriginal race, which had accelerated rapidly during his lifetime. He saw the race at that time as existing in three stratas—the first and most lamentable, in his opinion, was the 'township natives which hang around the outskirts of a settlement. These have lost most of what there is generally to be admired in a native.' Ready access to medical treatment for this group came at the high cost of racial degradation.

The second group, 'those Aboriginals in employment at camps or stations', were generally sent by their white employers to the nearest native medical centre for treatment of venereal disease or, in the case of leprosy, to the nearest leprosarium. The largest deterrent in obtaining treatment for the infected station Aborigine lay in the hundreds of miles between station and medical assistance. This meant that treatment was often left in the hands of the station owners or managers. The alternative to this lay treatment was to have the sufferers taken to the nearest hospital. This usually involved the traversing of tribal grounds peopled by Aborigines hostile to the sick person, usually from another tribe. The sufferer would run away, fear condemning him to death, but not before spreading the disease still further.

Jack saw the station owners, managers and 'book-keepers who often prided themselves on their rough medical knowledge', people who usually took care of the health of their stockmen, as a ready-made front line in the battle to wipe out venereal disease, influenza and tertian malaria. His idea to provide them with medical supplies at no cost and the relevant training to recognise the early symptoms of both types of venereal disease and leprosy was never officially recognised or adopted.

The third and remaining group, the 'semi-wild' and the 'wild' tribes, unfortunately the worst sufferers, presented the greatest problem. These could have been treated effectively but only through careful organisation beforehand of men familiar with the Northern Australian terrain and versed in the customs and beliefs of the remnants of the tribes scattered there:

> In such areas, among the few wild and more numerous semi-wild tribes, treatment is needed most. With doubly good effect. For detribalisation could be at the same time discouraged and checked. Thus the painful sight of a once fine type of free upright Stone Age man clad in rags around the fringe of a settlement might disappear.

He went on to outline the possible service that could be established:

A few small hospital posts with, say, one travelling doctor familiar particularly with VD and a knowledge of tropical diseases, to supervise a division holding five such posts. Two medical assistants to each post, not necessarily qualified men but men with excellent practical experience in their field. A few such divisions would cover the continent from coast to coast.

His article closed with:

Now that Science is familiar with the cure for VD, now that there are men throughout Australia familiar with native custom, and now we fully realise the plight of the remnants of the Aboriginal it is only humane of us to give him all the aid we can. It is only because I have so often seen the sick Aboriginal and his missus and youngster in their haplessness that I write thus.

The article brought him more trouble. The West Australian Government Health Department saw it as an attack on its integrity and generated a dismissive press release. The Darwinian pearlers however were appeased and accepted him back into the fold. Captain Cochrane felt that Jack had 'made good the marbles' of all the good, clean-living white folk at the top of the West Australian coast, Jack's included. Cochrane also reported that a flurry of activity had taken place throughout the northern end of Australia and that doctors were now travelling to the most accessible areas in motor transport which of course did nothing to help those Aborigines off the beaten track, the ones who needed help most.

In Sydney and Melbourne statements made by anthropologists unconnected with the committee appeared in the press. These ranged from advocating the setting aside of half a million acres of land reserved for Aborigines to continue their nomadic lifestyle, to the theory reported in the *Times* in London of Sir Hal Colebatch, Agent-General for Western Australia, that 'The aborigines were already a decaying race when colonisation of Australia began'. Sir Hal Colebatch, defending the treatment of the Aborigines by Australians, based his theory on what he believed to be low numbers—three hundred thousand Aborigines—inhabiting Australia in 1788. Sir Hal further defended the disgraceful genocide which had taken place in Tasmania with a back-handed swipe at Mother England: 'It must be remembered, when considering Tasmania's treatment of the Aborigines, that England then still employed women and children in coal mines and that Tasmanian convicts were not gently treated!'

As evidence of the impeccable administration of the care given the Aborigines Sir Hal rested his case on the findings of the West Australian Royal Commissioner. Mr H. D. Mosely had concluded at the closing of the Aborigine Royal Commission, held in 1934 while Jack was travelling through Western Australia, 'that there was no justification for the charges against officials and settlers of cruelty, slavery or neglect'.

Of course the missionaries hotly defended their treatment of the Aboriginal people. One of them, aflame with religious passion and obsessed with his divine desire to save souls, declared (to the mortification of his fellow missionaries) 'that the salvation of even one native soul was worth the death of the remainder'!

The newspaper journalists added their two cents' worth. The *Times* of London pontificated from afar, ignoring the fact that the desecration of the Aboriginal race was cast in bronze when England, no longer able to 'sell' shiploads of convicts to the American colonies, established penal colonies in Australia and Tasmania. The *Times* commented in a leading article under the heading 'Deplorable State of Affairs', 'The immediate cause of a deplorable state of affairs has been the lack both of trained administrators and funds.' It added that 'Professor Wood Jones ascribed the ultimate cause to official and popular indifference', and that the Professor of Anthropology's address was a scathing indictment of official neglect. The article concluded with the hope that 'the Australian Governments and people will support a more constructive native policy than that of laissez faire'.

The *Daily Telegraph* editorial harassed, harangued, and accused its readers but, in closing, justified every preceding vile act: 'it was all right for the pioneer to hate the black. He had to fight with him for existence. But the fight is over. We can afford to be humane.'

The extensive file of newspaper cuttings on Aboriginal affairs which Jack kept over the years shows no record of the committee's findings or recommendations; it seems to have achieved nothing. Most speakers were prepared to offer much intemperate condemnation but no comprehensive policy for the future.

The only person throughout the entire proceedings to offer sound, practical plans for the betterment of Aboriginal health administration was Jack. Never once was he negative. He never criticised, accused or abused. A born diplomat and manipulator, he commended the government of the day, and governments past, for their work in the field, suggesting only that the adoption of advances in medicine would improve government performance.

It was all wasted time and effort. The entrenched bureaucracy, after requesting that he 'assist them materially', either couldn't or wouldn't, dignify Jack's contribution with public acknowledgement of its worth, much less put even some elements of his outlined plan into operation.

It is ironic that in the end it will be the Kooris who will save their race, not politicians, social workers, missionaries or anthropologists. If Jack were alive today he would be delighted, for that he knew and admired the courage and intelligence of the Aborigines is clearly evident in his books.

At the same time that Australia deliberated over who should financially support Australia's Aborigines—commonwealth or state governments—in November 1937 Hitler was demanding the return of the colonies lost to Germany by the Treaty of Versailles. Lord Halifax had whipped over to Germany and had a chat with him and the general opinion was that Germany had made a great mistake in the manner in which the colonies had been demanded back. Goebbels, the Minister of Propaganda, claimed that the conversion of the German colonies to mandates amounted to theft. Displaying razor sharp insight a *Sun* analyst dismissed Goebbels as being 'all froth'.

The Japanese had invaded China. The Chinese defence forces were moving ahead of the Japanese, systematically blowing up and burning buildings, ammunition dumps, and hangars, vowing to leave the conquerors nothing but an ash-heap to occupy.

The Sydney *Sun* on 8 December 1937 carried a gung-ho front page report of how Marshal and Madame Chiang Kai-shek and Mr W. H. Donald, their Australian-born adviser, had won a 'thrilling air race from Nanking in a three-engined high-speed airliner pursued by Japanese planes'.

The drums of world war were sounding then, but the world seemed to have been deaf to their beat.

Somehow between attending the Select Committee and writing the extensive articles related to the plight of the Aborigines Jack found time to write 'The Sniper' for *Man Magazine*. On the original typescript is a note written in Jack's hand: 'The best short story I ever wrote.' 'The Sniper' was to appear many times in other publications over the following years.

That December was pretty hectic for Jack. Sometime after refusing to autograph his books in bookshops while in Perth in 1933 because it 'cheapened a man's work', he had undergone a change of heart. Due to popular demand he was to be found in Anthony Horden's book department where he autographed his latest best-sellers, *Over The Range* and *Forty Fathoms Deep*, each priced at six shillings, postage threepence. He recalled that it was in this same place that he had seen *Madman's Island* on remainder sale at sixpence a copy in 1927.

Jack carried over his autographing sessions into 1938. That Easter he found himself in the Sydney Showground's Horden Pavilion. The Anthony Horden four-page lift-out advertisement advised their customers that the 'Famous Author Ion L. Idriess would be in attendance between ten a.m. and twelve p.m. each morning and between two p.m. and four p.m. each afternoon'. The advertisement also stated that he could be seen at work writing! A photograph of Jack smoking a pipe, and looking very much like Bing Crosby, appeared along with advertisements for smart Easter chapeaux, the latest in women's wear, and various other items of apparel. There was also a message urging Horden's customers to order their Easter Hot Cross Buns—Horden Bakery's Deluxe mix, one shilling and twopence per dozen and the Public Service mix, one shilling and sixpence per dozen.

That year the education authorities recognised Jack's works as a useful education tool. In May 1938 the New South Wales Department of Education used an excerpt from *Men of the Jungle* in its school magazine readers in the fifth class. This appears to have been the first of these items. There is no record of a fee being paid.

Then in September the ABC approached him requesting permission to utilise *The Cattle King* in the preparation of a school broadcast on Sir Sidney Kidman for Victorian third-term students studying the Australian History Series.

Still the darling of the press reviewers, and enjoying his popularity, Jack received a letter from *Burke's Landed Gentry* asking him to supply his 'Pedigree Form' for inclusion in their forthcoming Coronation Edition. The uncompleted 'Pedigree Form', still in the envelope with the letter, bears silent, yet eloquent testimony to Jack's response to the offer. It is a wonder that he didn't write some scathing remark on it, as was his usual response.

At that time he was also working on *Cyaniding for Gold* and editing the 'Australiana' section in *Man Magazine*. Faced with the approach of war he put *Cyaniding for Gold* aside and began work on *Must Australia Fight?* which would be published as *How Must Australia Fight?*.

Jack was taking the threat of war seriously, as was Gus Gaunt. Dear Gus, the link between Jack, Morry, Stan and Bert over the intervening ten years between 1918 and 1938, was desperate to enlist again. That September he wrote to Jack begging him 'to pull a few strings' to get him 'into this scrap'. Jack was appalled—he believed that Australians should be training to defend their own shores, not going overseas to fight someone else's war again. About the same time that Gus was champing at the bit to get back into uniform, Jack's nephew, Ion Morrison, declared his intention to enlist as soon as he had graduated from university. Jack was angry and refused to believe that he was serious. The memory of his own war experiences had left him soured; he believed that the government had treated him and all returned men badly. He never made any specific claims except to say that the only people who got anything out of war were those who didn't go.

Around this time Jack appears to have settled into something bordering on an acceptable home life. Among his souvenirs are dance cards saved from balls which he attended with Eta in that pre-war period. Apart from the famous Trocadero Artist Balls— tickets ten shillings and sixpence— and the Theatrical Midnight Ball at the Mark Foys Empress Ballroom, they attended the second Grand Annual Ball of Household Brigade of Guards Association and other glittering occasions.

There were many parties at Kingsford, which were carried out on a grand scale. A portable dance floor would be set up in the back garden which was decked out with coloured lights and a dance band hired for the occasion. These gay Bohemian gatherings were attended by Sydney's well-known artists and writers. Evening dress was mandatory! The Angus and Robertson group was led by Walter Cousins and Bert Ritchie (always known as Ritchie, never Bert), one of the directors of the company.

Wendy Idriess recalls her childhood memories of both Cousins and Ritchie: 'Cousins was a big, black-bearded man, he later removed the beard. He was a man who radiated quiet confidence, he was also very caring and beautifully mannered.' In her opinion Cousins was 'a true gentleman of the Victorian school'.

Of Ritchie: 'He too was big and black-bearded—a vital, hearty, jovial, hard drinking energetic man.' Ritchie reminded Wendy of a roistering pirate. Obviously he captivated her. He was courteous and charmed the ladies—a hand-kissing, door-opening dandy, and much adored by Jack's sisters, Ildyce and Esmé, who always visited the Angus and Robertson offices when in Sydney.

When the Kingsford parties were in full swing, late in the evening Ritchie would creep into Wendy and Judy's bedroom. While the small girls pretended to be asleep he would slip two shillings under each pillow, whispering something about fairies, and that the little girls would never guess who the 'fairy' was.

Ildyce Morrison also remembered Ritchie as being a handsome, big, charming man with thick greying hair and beautifully dressed. She felt that Ritchie was very fond of Jack and that they shared a good relationship.

Life was not all parties and balls. Jack's ever-lively mind and desire to see the inland desert bloom set him to devising a plan to increase the rainfall over the desert. To this end he wrote to the Department of the Interior outlining a plan which would increase rainfall in the Northern Territory. The Department took him seriously and had the plan analysed by the Commonwealth Meteorologist. After receiving the meteorologist's report, Mr T. H. Garrett, Acting Secretary, Department of the Interior, replied with an eight-point letter clearly explaining the reasons why Jack's plan would not work. The pivotal point of Jack's scheme was the building of a massive mountain. Mr Garrett's closing point that the proposed mountain would 'probably take a century at least to construct' put an end to that idea.

A report on Australian literature compiled for Book Week in 1938 appeared in the *Sydney Morning Herald* and read: 'It appears that the magical atmosphere of the Australian Hinterland when enshrined in literature makes a moving appeal to Australians, despite the present large concentration of the population in the cities. The writings of Ion L. Idriess are in the front rank as best-sellers and appreciation of his lively books remains undiminished.'

Odd that the writer of the report didn't recognise that the reason for Jack's popularity lay in his ability to project to the largely education-starved population trapped in the cities the image they held of themselves—the bushman.

Chapter Thirty
EDUCATION AND WAR

1939 and the die was cast—there was no avoiding the horror of yet another war. In Australia veterans of the 'war to end all wars' and non-combatants alike recalled with pride the sacrifice of their golden youth and their shining hours of glory at Gallipoli, Beersheba and in France. Steeped in the mystique of Anzac the majority of men saw the coming war as an opportunity to carry on the Anzac tradition—not so Jack.

Attempting to ignore the war he was hard at work completing the manuscripts of *Must Australia Fight?* and *Cyaniding for Gold*. At the same time he was also drafting *Lightning Ridge*, *Headhunters of the Coral Sea* and *The Great Trek*. Ion L. Idriess was cruising along on the crest of popularity.

At the beginning of the 1930s the Australian education system, was, by today's standards, extremely backward. Three-quarters of Australians had no secondary education. It was true that everyone, politicians, union leaders, captains of industry, gave no special thought to education. In fact, the need for a higher education was considered largely unnecessary. Without the provision of an evolving education programme, the ability to read, write and manage elementary mathematics together with a well-developed sense of the Protestant work ethic was all that most people required.

Crowded in dismal slums and in the sprawling suburbs clustered around the cities on the narrow coastal fringe these Australians considered it a miracle just to have survived the Depression. Much of that survival in the suburbs was due to the street community combining to grow and swap their produce and the strong support system of family and friends. Their restricted social life revolved around the street. Women wearing hats and gloves in an effort to maintain a degree of dignity exchanged formal visits with their neighbours. The people in tent cities and the hovels around Port Kembla and in other shanty towns survived by dint of making-do, just as their forefathers had done—and they were proud to have done so. All of which served to confirm who they were and where they had come from.

They had survived an economic disaster, which had stolen six years of their lives. Three-quarters of the Australian population which had entered the Depression with only the barest education, emerged as they had begun—uneducated.

Constricted by mental stagnation and relieved to be working again, the average family, driven by the memory of abject poverty, urged their children to find work as soon as possible. The possibility of their children gaining a better education was never a consideration.

These people formed the greater part of Jack's audience. During the Depression he had entertained them and brought them relief from ugly reality. He showed them in vivid word pictures the windswept deserts of Central Australia and jungles of the Cape York Peninsula. He wrote of wild seas, cannibals and headhunters; took them pearl diving and crocodile shooting; and gave them heroes like Kidman and John Flynn.

Through his books his readers felt they knew Australia and Jack Idriess, and they identified with him. During the Depression years he had become a hero of a culture that urgently needed to fulfil its own ethos. Now, with the Depression past some three years, the society they were part of offered no goal other than the need to work hard if they wanted to continue to survive, which was the way it had always been.

Clearly the incredible popularity Jack enjoyed was the result of a combination of a number of factors. However, adverse national economic circumstances, coupled with an education system which did not encourage the nation with the stimulation of new ideas, provided the right climate for the works of Ion L. Idriess to flourish. In 1939 Jack was still their man.

Once again Jack was writing to the press, only now he was acknowledging that a war was in the offing. He was concerned that the Japanese might blockade Malaya and what was then known as the Dutch East Indies. Jack felt that it was time Australia tried to grow rubber, hemp, kapok, tea and coffee and other tropical products before the need arose.

He was back in print again in the *Sydney Morning Herald* of 6 April to cry out in outrage against the intention of a group of Harvard and Adelaide researchers, sponsored by the Carnegie Corporation of New York, who were mounting an expedition to 'ascertain whether half-caste Aborigines can be adjusted to modern civilisation, or must remain a group apart.'

Jack couldn't believe the Australian Government would

allow Americans to treat the half-caste Aborigines in such a patronising fashion. He wrote at length on his own experiences working with half-caste stockmen and fighting beside half-caste soldiers during the 1914–1918 war. These were people who worked as well, in some cases better, than Anglo-Saxon whites, and during the war had died for another country. Jack was incensed over the entire proposal and would have personally tarred and feathered the lot and sent them packing back to the States.

The European situation was rapidly coming to a head. On 1 April Chamberlain pledged Britain to defend Poland in the event of an attack by Germany. In view of such simmering unrest and the inevitability of war in Europe, and Jack's attitude to war, he did something that seems completely out of character. After receiving a letter from the Swedish Crown Prince Wilhelm, and a review written by the prince of *Men of the Jungle*, which had just been published in Swedish, he wrote to Robert Menzies, who was enjoying his first brief term as Australian prime minister, requesting permission to go to Sweden as guest of the Prince. This was to be a goodwill mission aimed at cementing Australian and British ties with the Swedish people and to promote 'trade between the two countries'.

Menzies refused him permission on the grounds that his presence in Sweden might prove to be an embarrassment to the Swedish government and further, it was much too dangerous. As indeed it was, for on 3 September Robert Menzies solemnly broadcast to the nation that it was his 'melancholy duty to inform the nation that Britain is at war and as a consequence, Australia'.

Jack continued on as if nothing had happened. 'The Sniper' turned up again in the *Sunday Telegraph* Christmas Magazine while 'The Squatting Devil of Samarai' made its first appearance in the *Australian Telegraphist*.

A letter from the Pan-Pacific *Who's Who* published by the *Honolulu Star Bulletin* in Hawaii asked him to check the biographical data he had supplied before they went to press. As usual the year of his birth date was wrong. Jack never did get it right.

In May 1940, partly in an attempt to stop young Ion Morrison from enlisting, Jack decided to mount an expedition to search for the lost Lasseter reef. It wasn't too difficult to persuade his nephew to postpone enlisting for a month or two, Ion was also badly bitten by the gold bug. Jack had nominated him as the expedition's medical officer. However the government introduced petrol rationing, all surplus aircraft was confiscated and the expedition's rolling stock became army property. Lasseter's reef or the myth of the Lasseter reef was safe from exposure once again.

Both Jack and Ion believed that they knew where the reef was to be located. Years later Ion Morrison flew over the area where the reef was supposed to be. Ion said that Lasseter must have had the wrong latitude for there was nothing but razor-back ranges in that area. How odd!

Many years later after Jack had suffered a stroke which left him badly disabled, he insisted that Ion should get a four-wheel drive vehicle and hire men to take them out to where he believed Lasseter's reef to be. Ion refused to do this because of his own war injuries and, speaking as a doctor, he believed that Jack wouldn't survive the trip. Jack was furious and shouted about how they were letting the Idriess name down because he (Ion) wasn't man enough to 'give it a go'. This was the only time Jack and Ion ever fell out.

All hope of attempting to find the reef and getting away from Sydney and back to the outback gone, Jack settled back into his writing routine.

Gus Gaunt wasn't the only one to believe that Jack had enough clout to persuade the army to accept his services. Stan, one of the section of four from the Desert Column, wrote to him from Kavierg in New Guinea, where he was employed by the Department of Agriculture, Rabaul. He enquired if Jack had received the 'Fiver' which he had returned to him some time back. The letter was dated 20 January 1940, approximately a year before the Japanese invaded New Guinea.

'This war is getting on my nerves,' wrote Stan. 'The news of the crowd going away and joining up has made me restless. So far as I can tell I have no chance of getting in here and am wondering if you could help me at all if I chucked the job here and went down south. Do you think that you could get me into something going overseas? I don't want any of this keeping the home fires burning stuff. I'm still in good nick and know what I'm going to.'

Jack thought that Stan needed to have 'his head read'. After the disbanding of the 5th Light Horse Regiment Stan had been given a public service job—public service jobs had been reserved for returned soldiers since the 1914–1918 war—and Jack could not understand why Stan, who was no longer a young man, would give up his well-earned patch of peace.

Jack tried to maintain his distance from the war but every time he saw a report in the press which he thought to be wrong he couldn't resist correcting it. In response to a report which claimed that Australia did not have enough white metals to use in the manufacture of defence aeroplanes he wrote an article entitled 'White Minerals In Australia'. Calling on his extensive academic and practical knowledge of mining and minerals he wrote that there were vast deposits of manganese and aluminium scattered right throughout Australia.

That February he received a letter of appreciation of his work from Canon Frank Madell. The Stanton Chaplain to the Diocese of Newcastle wrote, 'Your books are listed I believe as novels; but to me they are ethnological studies; and in the writing of them I note that you have made them also narratives of adventure with a fine flavour of sympathy and understanding for your fellow man'.

Bravo Canon Madell! His letter was the first written evidence I found which recognised Jack's work as fact. Reviewers and literary critics alike either didn't classify his books, or referred to them as novels, which leads me to question the qualifications of the literary doyens of the day.

In the same letter in reference to the war and the madness that possessed men's minds Canon Madell quoted a passage from *Forty Fathoms Deep* concerning Conard Gill, 'Con' the West India man, bosun of the Alma, suave-voiced, hoodoo man, worker of pourri-pourri and black magic:

> Con spoke of Lucifer and surprised me with his knowledge of the Bible's chief, with power unbelievable, whirling through the universe, leading armies of cavalry defying God and every now and then breaking through some gigantic heavenly cordon, to stir up trouble in the hearts of men. This malign influence working through the minds of men caused the Great War!

Jack replied to Madell:

> It is our sons and money which are sacrificed, not the blood and money of the few original schemers. It is not they who produce the armies of sons, the thousands of millions of pounds. Yes it is time Mankind woke up. Finish this war, make it the last. Then use this vast, world-wide propaganda machine. Make it blare to peoples of all countries to add their voice to an insistent 'No!' to any other war. Humankind can then save its tears, can then use those thousands of millions of pounds in the ceaseless war against disease and distress.

Throughout 1940 Jack continued to write and be published. 'The White Witch' appeared in the *Sunday Telegraph*. Articles and letters were printed in other publications. In April he wrote to J. M. C. Forsyth at Vaucluse Hall in Sydney to ask for a meeting to discuss the writing of a book about Queen Emma of the South Seas.

Where Jack would have found time to work on a new book is hard to say because at that time he was working on the story of Nemarluk the Aboriginal chief, to be published as *Nemarluk— King of the Wilds*. At the same time he was writing *Fortunes in Minerals*, describing minerals people had mostly never heard of. He was also burning the midnight oil working on *The Great Boomerang*. Jack had never given up on the idea that the inland deserts could be fed with water. *The Great Boomerang* explained his plan to turn the great rivers of the north that run to the sea back into the desert by using a system of tunnels. In its death throes the Fraser government, strapped for an innovative concept with which to woo votes for a government which had clearly lost support, briefly ran the idea up the flag pole. All too late; the electorate didn't have time to assimilate it, nor did the project benefit from a feasibility study applying contemporary technology. The concept seems to have sunk without trace. Maybe it isn't possible to turn the waters inland, and if it is, perhaps any benefit would be negated by the damage to the ecology. However, if sometime in the future the project becomes a reality, I hope that Jack will be acknowledged as the man who had the vision to dream of a way to water the desert.

◆

REGARDLESS of the position that Jack had adopted toward the war his ego would not allow him to ignore what he considered to be a stupid suggestion to establish a Camel Corps to defend Australia's north. The proposal had come from Major General Rankin in the House of Representatives. Jack responded in the *Sun* on 25 August 1940: 'Forming a Camel Corps in the Kimberleys is foolish. A Camel Corps as a defence unit in the Kimberley country would be a good idea if you could persuade camels to walk up sheer cliffs and scale mountain peaks. Unfortunately, the camel is not built for it. The General is weak on his geography.' To reinforce his argument he closed with, 'the mounted police with pack mules never thought of using camels'.

On 1 September Mr A. M. Blain, the member for the Northern Territory, disputed Jack's statement by citing camels as beasts of burden and how, for millions of ages, they had scrambled over the high Persian and Afghan ranges through to Constantinople over very rough country and back again.

If the member for the Northern Territory might have thought he had the last word on the subject he was wrong. On 5

September Jack was back in print, interviewed by the *Sun:*

> Idriess presses his point by example of swiftly moving Light Horse
> in World War I being superior to camels and further forces home his
> knowledge of warfare and the needs of modern fast transportation
> to meet the enemy; citing Mussolini's successful campaign in
> Somaliland the week before. The Somaliland defence was, in good
> part, dependent on Camel Corps defending a mountain range.
> Aeroplanes, cars, tanks, with machine-guns and infantry units,
> were rushed to the front by the Italians. 'We know the result of that
> encounter,' he said. 'That recent campaign was fought in country
> that had been the home of the camel for ages. Australia is littered
> with wild camels in camel country because they have been replaced
> by trucks and motorisation—one would hope that Australia would
> be defended by utilising the same'.

That appears to have put paid to the Camel Corps argument.
Jack had the last word.

A few days later Jack received a letter from Gus Gaunt telling
him that Bert Card had died. Bert had been battling the after-effects
of a stroke which he had suffered towards the end of the
Depression. After each of his visits to see Bert and his wife, Gus
had written to Jack describing Bert's faltering state of health.
Although he was depressed at the news, Jack was not surprised to
hear of his death. This first death of a member of the section of four
made the others acutely aware of their own mortality.

Jack had lent Bert thirty pounds to help him establish a small
store, a large sum of money at that time. Shortly after her husband's death Mrs Card wrote to Jack telling him that she would
return the loan when Bert's affairs were settled. Jack refused to
accept the return of the money.

Lightning Ridge, the biographical account of Jack's opal mining days and one of the very few books ever written about the early
days on the opal field of Lightning Ridge, was published in October
1940. As usual the reviews were excellent, and Jack continued to
hold his exalted position.

In August 1941 the *Barrier Daily Truth* of Broken Hill carried
a reference to the Idriess multi-volume set on its front page.

On 5 September George Morrison died in St Luke's Hospital
in Sydney after a protracted fight against cancer. George's daughter Ildyce recalls that Jack used to visit George as often as he could;
she also remembers the distress he felt over not being able to do
anything for George to ease his pain. After one of these visits he

was moved to say to Dycie that he wished he were able to give George something so that he would not suffer on.

Sunday 7 December 1941 the Japanese attacked Pearl Harbour, and on Monday 8 December Australia declared war on Japan.

It was all too much for Jack. Now sure that the Japanese would attack Australia he offered to place his knowledge of Australia and the surrounding islands at the disposal of the Commonwealth Government. His offer was rejected.

On 12 December 1941, C. J. Cosgrove, General Secretary of the Police Association of NSW and a close friend of Jack's, wrote a passionate letter to the Minister for Supply, the Hon. J. A. Beasley, MHR:

> I am taking the opportunity of our acquaintance to approach you on a matter which I consider one of importance to Australia, apart from the fact that it has a personal aspect in relation to a very particular friend of mine. The position I wish to place before you concerns Ion L. Idriess, the well-known Australian author, who desires to place his extensive knowledge of Australia and the surrounding islands at the disposal of the Commonwealth Government. Mr Idriess served with the 5th Light Horse, and is now fifty-one years of age and in good health. Mr Idriess's knowledge of the Australian coastline and the surrounding islands, including those of the Coral Sea and the Great Barrier Reef, is so extensive that I venture to suggest there is not another Australian whose learning could even compare with it.

In Beasley's response to Cosgrove, he wrote:

> I was advised some weeks ago that the Department of Information was seeking experienced journalists, and in this connection I feel that Mr Idriess would suit admirably, particularly with the knowledge he possesses of the Islands. I suggest that he might write to Mr R. Dawson, News Editor, Department of Information, Collins Street, Melbourne, who will be pleased to advise him along the right lines.

One has to wonder at the level of intelligence possessed by those people in government at the time. Not only had the government allowed the Japanese free access to the north-west coast, given them total freedom to roam at will, to chart every reef, map every bay and inlet, sanctioned their abuse of the Aborigines, men and women alike, turned a blind eye, especially when it was obvious that the Japanese were arming for war, they didn't have the wit to see that Jack's knowledge of all points north was detailed and priceless! Jack wondered if he was speaking the same language or if his intention was being deliberately misinterpreted.

However, he had no trouble in deciding what he wanted and did not want. Jack wanted to contribute in some useful way to the defence of Australia. His intention was not to be locked in a government office with government men who would most likely attempt to alter his work, confine his style and direct him in a way he had never been directed before. This was definitely not for Jack.

It had been his hope that, as well as offering his knowledge, he would be used as a coastwatcher. The solitary life would not have bothered him. Between watching stints he could have written a book or two about his experiences.

◆

UNABLE to resist the call to arms Ion Morrison enlisted to serve as a doctor with the Royal Australian Air Force. When Ion visited Jack to tell him he had enlisted he was wearing his uniform. Ion dreaded the encounter for he knew what Jack's reaction would be. Jack greeted him in anger born out of his fear that his nephew might be killed. Ion said that it was an emotional encounter made more intense because he shared a relationship with Jack which in many ways was closer than the bond between himself and his own father; he also felt that he and Jack were rather alike. By the time the two parted Jack had accepted the inevitable. Fighting mixed emotions of sorrow and pride, he farewelled his nephew, who would eventually be stationed at Bougainville.

Shortly before Ion enlisted, Ildyce, Jack's niece, enlisted in the Australian Women's Army Service. Obviously Dycie's daughter was the apple of her mother's eye and her father's delight. Every one of the numerous letters written to Jack by both Morrisons over the years contained loving references to Ildyce, each parent independently describing her beauty and her wonderful nature.

Dycie's letters were bright, frank, confident and full of humour. To Dycie her sons were a pair of adorable tear-aways while her daughter was a beautiful young woman, once seen never forgotten.

George Morrison's letters which Jack had kept since the beginning of the Depression show him to have been a very steady, perhaps reserved, man. Through the letters runs a tone of quiet desperation. At first this was the product of the Depression which had hit his Grafton real estate business and then, in 1940, the letters convey a sense of desperate urgency that young Ildyce should find a secure niche or at least a profession. He often wrote, 'She is so wonderful she should have the best.' George's concern for his seventeen-year-old daughter's future was no doubt based on the knowledge that he was dying of cancer.

Ildyce Morrison must have resembled her grandmother, Julia, for she remembers visiting Walter Owen Idriess shortly before she enlisted and that her grandfather repeatedly kept looking at her, saying over and over to Amy, 'Julia', which didn't seem to please Amy.

Over the war years whenever Ildyce was on leave she would call in to Angus and Robertsons to visit Jack.' Usually she would take a friend along with her. Jack loved these visits; he really couldn't resist paying a pretty girl a compliment, especially a pretty girl in uniform!

As the Commonwealth Government wouldn't accept his help Jack decided to do the next best thing, the thing he did best: he wrote. During 1942 he wrote and had published The Guerrilla Series: *Shoot to Kill, Sniping, Trapping the Jap, Guerrilla Tactics, Lurking Death* and *The Scout*. These little books proved to be very popular with young soldiers in training during war time.

On 19 February 1942 the Japanese devastated Darwin with their bombers. As they knew the coast like the back of their hands courtesy of the government this would have posed no problem to the Japanese.

Jack believed that if Australia should be attacked, by any country, every able-bodied Australian should be given a gun to defend themselves and to defend the country. That hypothetical attack was now a reality. Immediately after the attack on Darwin he wrote an article which also mentions the necessity of mounting a 'Stock Evacuation' programme which was Jack's equivalent of the Russian scorched earth policy, but not as drastic. He was concerned that first-class breeding stock should be selected and moved to a safe area in order to replenish the herds after the war. He just didn't elaborate on where he planned to secrete the herds. The government was more concerned that the herds were moved so that the beef wouldn't be on the Japanese menu.

Of course there was no question in his mind that Australia would be defeated. The task of arming the people and the herding and hiding of the stock he felt belonged to the Voluntary Defence Committee. The VDC was more concerned about how they were to obtain guns and ammunition, especially when the government was having enough trouble arming the troops.

Early in March 1942 the Japanese landed at Lae on the north coast of New Guinea. Jack was extremely worried about the fate of many of his friends living in New Guinea; a number had left for the south after the fall of Pearl Harbour, but some had stayed behind for different reasons. Like all Australians he was concerned that if the line wasn't held in New Guinea and it fell to the Japanese then clearly Australia would be the next country to be invaded.

Jack was still very keen to do something for the war effort. The Commonwealth Government continued steadfastly to refuse his offer. Jack's rare knowledge of New Guinea and the islands north of Australia is clearly evident from a letter to Joe Bourke.

On 14 May 1942, Joe wrote to Jack from Port Moresby. 'As you can imagine things have been pretty mixed up here during the past few months, the towns about the district have been pretty well bashed about, but circumstances generally could be a lot worse, anyhow the sons of Nippon have paid dearly for their rather slippery hold on the mainland.'

Joe goes on to describe how he and his partner erected a 'battery' on a lode formation up in Eddie Creek. Apparently it went quite well and Joe was ready to start on the first 'vat' but had to 'shoulder arms instead'. Joe concluded his letter by writing:

> We are all interested in the Coral Sea scrap and wondering when the next round will commence; if ever they try to invade Australia I would like to get home, if it does happen I will try and get permission from here to do so, in that event N.G. will most probably be cut off from Australia, I know the track from here to Daru, and I have an idea how to get there to T.I. [Thursday Island]. Can you supply any information as to the route from there to, say, Cooktown? What is the country like? What are the possibilities of food and water? If you can supply this information I'll be very grateful, but you too will have to keep the censor in mind.

Jack's reply to Joe was dated 27 May 1942. After the usual friendly preliminaries Jack carries on:

> And now Joe, if ever you should be forced to make that trip. You know the track to Daru. Be very careful that the Japanese are not in possession of Daru if the time comes to make the trip. Say the coast is clear. From there to the tip of Cape York Peninsula is one hundred and twenty miles. That is straight line of course. That line would take you to the east of T.I. You would be travelling south-

west. If you set out in that direction from Daru so as to strike the west side of the Warrior Reefs (only about fourteen miles from Daru) you could travel along the western side of the two reefs, pass Dungeness Island, then carry on along the Dungeness reef right to Long Island. That would take you seventy-two miles (straight) by the reefs. You could carry on approximately SW to Cape York Peninsula, islands every twenty or so miles apart. You couldn't go too far west for if you did so you must strike big Moa and Badu Islands, or lower still the Prince of Wales and T.I. group.

Well now, say the Japs had Daru. You could make your way forty-five miles (as the crow flies of course) west along the coast until opposite Saibai Island. It is only about five miles off the coast. If you travelled south from there you must hit Cape York Peninsula. If you veered a little S of W you'd strike the T.I. Group, they're only sixty miles nearly SW.

If Japs had Saibai then W a few miles along the coast is the mouth of Mai Kussa river. Opposite is Boigu island. From there, fifty-five miles direct south is the large Moa and Badu islands adjoining one another. The T.I. group are a few miles directly south.

If enemy still blocked you'd have to sail south at night, leaving the line of islands to your east. You'd thus sail down into the Gulf of Carpentaria. Cape York would be on your left. Land there and walk directly east, if you did not land near a Mission Station. It is in general fairly scrubby country, the walking over a range would be rough but in forty or less (rough) miles you'd strike the O.T. [overland telegraph] line. The west coast is much less inhabited than the east.

And now Joe, from T.I. to Cooktown. It is only about thirty miles from T.I. to the tip of Cape York. Get there, and the rest is simple. Some of our lads are bound to be there. If not make for the O.T. Line, and simply follow it down. The O.T. line follows straight down through the centre of the Peninsula.

If you landed lower down than the Point and met no one, say you landed on the east coast you would simply head straight west. If you landed on the west coast you'd head direct east. The rest is simple. Plenty of water, stations every here and there etc.

Well Joe, I've done the best I can, could write more fully but am doubtful what the censor would allow. Am going to try and trace out a copy from my old chart. If I can manage it, will enclose it. Don't be so long in writing in the future.

Cheerio and good luck

P.S. Some Strait Islands inhabited, others not so. All islands speak English. Good class Islander, very loyal to us. But be very careful Japs are not among them.

Who would ever contemplate such a journey today and who could you turn to for such explicit instructions? Both men treated the hazardous trip like a weekend excursion.

Joe Bourke was just too late to leave New Guinea before the Japanese invasion; he joined the New Guinea Volunteer Rifles and stayed to harass the Japanese forces occupying Salamaua and Lae.

Chapter Thirty-one
AMERICANS IN THE KITCHEN

SYDNEY'S beautiful beaches were barbed-wired and sandbagged. After the Japanese attack on Darwin a full-scale invasion was expected in the north by April and a further invasion of the east coast by May.

By 21 July the Japanese had landed on New Guinea and captured Gona and Buna, forging on to take Kokoda on 29 July, Port Moresby being the next objective.

The Japanese mini-submarines had made their historic run into Sydney Harbour a few weeks prior to the landing at Buna. The people of Sydney had experienced what proved to be their first and only attack by the Japanese. Some people who had remained in the city throughout April and May after Darwin now left for country areas considered to be safer than the harbour city. Many men, employed in protected industries, sent their wives and children as far out of the reach of potential danger as they could. Wendy and Judy were sent to Merriwether for safety. Maurice was already out of harm's way, everyone's way in fact; he had been placed in the Marist Brothers' College at Springwood on the lower Blue Mountains some years earlier.

Immediately following the Darwin raids General Douglas MacArthur arrived from the Philippines. MacArthur's appointment as Supreme Commander in April, and the American contribution of eighty-eight thousand men to swell the ranks of approximately half a million of our own uniformed men gave morale a boost and Jack the idea to write to MacArthur offering his services as a coast-watcher. The letter ran:

> I venture to submit for your consideration a plan for destroying enemy planes and reporting on enemy activity in New Guinea, the Rabaul district in particular, with very light cost to ourselves. The objective being that, if landed on the coast with twenty picked men at a spot to be agreed upon and as circumstances permit, a hideout could be found which would overlook enemy operations around Rabaul, or in any enemy occupied country you chose. If one of the

319

party was a wireless man with a small portable transmitter valuable information could be sent to Moresby or Cooktown. Probably also advise planes while in the air during bombing operations, meanwhile, would spy out enemy dromes. On any suitable night, or opportunity, a large number of planes could be destroyed by means of grenades or by small time-bombs or other means to be decided upon.

I am convinced a determined party could get away with it. Certainly it would be possible to do a lot of damage, and the greatest cost to Australia could not be more than twenty-one men. But there is a good chance that a number of the men would come back...

I would very much like to lead such a party. The men, if possible, should be New Guinea men, knowing the country. There are a fair number in Sydney at present. Almost all are certainly sufficient and would volunteer should you approve the scheme. I know the risks. So would the men when the scheme was explained to them. Even from the point of view of information alone the idea may appeal to you. A few men well hidden for instance in a spot overlooking the harbour at Rabaul could wireless word of all that comes and goes.

There doesn't appear to have been a response from MacArthur's staff, or MacArthur for that matter, to Jack's sound proposal. It is interesting to note here, however, that such tactics were eventually put into practice in New Guinea and the surrounding Coral Sea Islands.

Jack laid the Singapore fiasco directly at Churchill's feet. As far as Jack was concerned Churchill was performing true to form; he had misjudged the strength of the Turks in the Dardanelles and had been responsible for the Gallipoli debacle. Again, in Cyprus and Crete in 1940 he had been responsible for the ignominious retreat and defeat of the Australian and New Zealand forces—sentimentally named 'Anzacs'.

Three times now Jack had seen Australian, New Zealand and British troops used and wasted by Churchill. Totally disillusioned, he viewed the coming of MacArthur and the Americans as the first sign of hope. Like many other Australians he felt that Churchill, only concerned with the defending of the Empire in the Middle East, had paid scant attention to Singapore, Australia's outer defence post. In this instance Jack did not display one iota of his usual even-handedness.

Who needed Churchill and Britain anyway when we now

had MacArthur and America? No more could General Tojo taunt Australia as 'the orphan of the Pacific, helplessly expecting Japan's attack'.

The Japanese suffered their first land defeat at the hands of the Australians when they landed at Milne Bay, New Guinea—the myth of Japanese invincibility was shattered. This was purely an Australian operation and Jack was so proud of the 'lads'.

The Australians fought for every muddy foot of the Kokoda Trail, and inch by inch took back the steaming jungles, towering mountains and the swamps finally to win back their two bases in New Guinea in 1943.

At home Australians began to breathe a little easier. Women and children came back to their homes, the war effort continued at a furious pace and Jack began to write *The Silent Service* with a co-author, torpedo-man 'Taff' Jones, himself already an author of two naval books—*Watchdogs of the Sea* and *Sons of the Sea*.

The Silent Service is the story of the Royal Australian Navy. A rush edition of four copies was printed in 1944 so that one could be presented to Vice-Admiral William Halsy prior to the sea attack on Japanese-held Bougainville.

By March 1943 only the Guerrilla Series and *The Great Boomerang* were in print. The others were out of print due to war-induced shortages of manpower and paper. The demand for the Guerrilla Series was significantly high to maintain a profitable and patriotic production throughout the war.

Unsighted readers, however, had access to *Forty Fathoms Deep, Men of the Jungle, Flynn of the Inland, Gold Dust and Ashes, Lightning Ridge, Lasseter's Last Ride, The Cattle King, Drums of Mer, Over The Range* and *The Great Boomerang*. These ten titles were available from the Braille Library.

Very few Australian authors were able to find their books in print during the war. Many were irate over reports that Melbourne printers had commandeered the scant paper quota and were producing 'many thousands of English novels'.

Australia, the only country to have built a combat aircraft before an automobile, became a base for two American divisions and eight air groups. A great deal of anger was felt and often expressed, about 'our boys over there' underpaid, fighting to keep Australia safe while the Yanks, 'over here' were armed with chocolates and silk stockings, bought with what the Aussies believed to be excessive pay. What's more they were stealing their women. All the animosity was directed at the Americans, very few seem to have pointed the finger at the women.

Many Australian families nonetheless answered the call to make the American soldiers feel at home, inviting them into their homes to share meals or by providing accommodation for the 'family' boy on brief leave.

Jack, being Jack, saw in these Americans an opportunity to promote his books to the American market. To this end he made contacts among American recreation officers who were responsible for stocking the libraries aboard transport ships, army camps and the air bases. These men usually found their way home with Jack. This was a good try which didn't come off, for the books of Ion L. Idriess never did find their way on to the American market.

Jack wasn't the only person in the Idriess house who invited the Americans home; Eta, often referred to as 'lively' and described as a 'party girl', made her contribution to the war effort by providing an open house for the American armed forces personnel. During those years the house at Isaac Smith Street in Kingsford, where the family had moved in 1942, was filled with men in American uniforms; the kitchen smelt of food, Camel cigarettes, whisky and sweat.

The Americans would have found a visit to the Idriess household a novel experience for, by Australian standards, they were unconventional people. Jack found most of his company and his pleasure outside of the home while Eta, who enjoyed dancing went out alone or with her next-door neighbour and friend. Never Jack!

Jack was a heavy drinker, perhaps an alcoholic, who drank a bottle of whisky a day with beer chasers. His habit of drinking steadily from 1.30 each afternoon until 6 p.m. closing, the 'six o'clock swill', hadn't changed, it had actually accelerated. Family, friends and neighbours attest to this. Each night Jack could be seen making his way home, literally sloshed to the eyeballs. Dressed in a blue suit and with deeply nicotine-stained fingers raising the grey felt hat he always wore to any ladies he passed on the street, he would wish them a gallant 'goodnight'. I suspect that this was a larrikin gesture, not a truly chivalrous one.

How Jack managed to arrive home safely in his inebriated state is a mystery. There are two stories of Jack, drunk, playing fast and loose with trams and buses. Jack loved Sydney's trams and the 'trammies' (the ticket collectors) and he hated the red double-deck government buses which replaced them. When he was drunk, which was most nights, he would jump out in front of buses, hurling abuse at the drivers. No doubt the drivers would be hurling abuse back at this madman bent on killing himself. After an argument with one of these red monsters he was badly hurt and had to be taken to hospital. On another occasion he was coming home—drunk again—ambling from one side of the road to the other when he slipped and fell into a ditch between tram tracks where work was being undertaken at that time. As he lay there a tram passed over the top of him. After the tram had passed, he climbed out of the ditch, raised his hat to the horrified onlookers and continued on his way home!

Obviously when Jack left the hotel and when he was in the street he was a happy drunk, or he maintained the appearance at least of being affable (except when he was attacking government buses) for there are people who claim never to have seen him in a bad mood. Once inside the front door, however, for whatever reason, his mood changed. The intensity of his aggression was alcohol-driven because Wendy states that she could tell by the way he put his key in the door whether he had been drinking whisky or beer.

It is about now that personal accounts of Jack and his temperament begin to differ. There are those, like Wendy Idriess his daughter, who knew him better than anyone, who describe him as 'street angel and a house devil'; and Ion Morrison, who said that under normal circumstances, Jack spoke in a soft, superbly modulated voice, but he could change to mouthing vulgar language in a coarse, uncultured tone with lightning speed, 'like flicking on a light switch'. There are others, such as Wendy's half-sister Judy, who only recall, or prefer to recall, that he was a quiet, warm and very human man. His niece, Ildyce Pike (née Morrison) compared Jack to her grandfather: 'I would have liked to have known him [Walter] better but he was a shy man like his son.'

As children the girls, Wendy and Judy, did not know Jack well. Very rarely did the family take outings together. When he was at home Jack isolated himself in the lounge-room writing, or in his bedroom reading, sleeping or thinking. It was absolutley forbidden to disturb him, especially when he was thinking:

> At those times he would lay on his back, propped up by a couple of pillows, stroking his head with his left hand, running the fingers gently from the back of his head, down the centre and lifting them off as they reached the top of his forehead, over and over and over, hour after hour, completely oblivious to all else around him. As if he was stimulating his mind to take him back in time to the country and the people he knew he had to write about.

The best that could be hoped for when Jack came home was that he would only be irritable; however, in this touchy mood he could switch to explicit obscene insults directed at Eta, Wendy and Judy. Engaging in conversation with him at this time was akin to walking through a minefield.

Terry Morrison witnessed this tense ritual each evening when staying with the Idriess family for a short period in 1945 while his family were visiting friends in the country. 'When Ion L. came home the girls and I kept a low profile. I recall Eta warning us to steer clear... I got the feeling from the girls that the marriage was not a very happy one.'

When Jack worked at home the children were not allowed in the room. The blinds were always drawn but Judy used to go outside the house and watch through the window if they hadn't been fully drawn. She remembers that it was always: 'Don't disturb your father, he's writing' or 'Don't make a noise, your father's working.'

The missing member of the family, Maurice, who was supposed to have been intensely disliked by Jack, had been banished by him to boarding school at a very early age. As evidence of Jack's aversion to the child there is a story of Jack regularly bringing home sweets for the girls when they were small, but none for Maurice.

Once again the stories are conflicting. Val Pepper, next door neighbour and Eta's friend, says that Maurie was an asthmatic and that was the reason why he was sent to live, at first in the clean air of the Blue Mountains, and then in the dry outback.

By that time the war between Jack and Eta had escalated to such a deadly level that he seems to have wilfully intensified his monstrous image. That Eta was unhappy is unquestioned. Doubtless she had paid, and was continuing to pay dearly, for the concealment of her marriage to Gibson and the existence of his children.

If, out of kindness, one were to romanticise and assume that Eta had seen in Jack, the successful author, a better provider for her children than Gibson and that this had been her motivation when she proceeded to ensure that he assumed their responsibility, then the price of their care came high.

It is possible to understand that Jack would not want to be reminded that he had been trapped into 'taking care of other people's families for the rest of his blooming life' each time he looked at young Maurice and, as much as anyone of us might moralise or condemn him for it, this child, representing a constant source of irritation or anger, had to be removed from his sight.

Sending Maurice to boarding school would have been costly at that time; yet while Eta lost close contact with her young son, she achieved one thing: Maurice did receive a good education, which she and Gibson probably could not have afforded to give him.

Maurice is said to have qualified as a mining engineer and his first employment was apparently at Wauchope on a Vesty property. From there he went to Tennant Creek to work as a battery manager at Noble's Knob.

Even when Maurice had grown into a young adult Jack apparently steadfastly refused to have him in the house. The last time Jack saw Maurice was when the young man visited Eta and the girls at the age of twenty. There ensued a loud argument between the two and Maurice was told never to come to the house again. Maurice is said to have left vowing to come back after his twenty-first birthday to take his mother away, which would have been a natural reaction, especially as Jack would no doubt have been very drunk at the time and Eta hysterical.

Towards the end of 1943 Jack managed to get away from both the family and the Americans by heading north again, possibly to attend the 5th Light Horse Regiment Reunion in Brisbane. This he tried to do each year but because he was so busy he wasn't able to make a regular appearance.

The year before Gus Gaunt had written to tell him that a new regiment, the New Light Horse, had assembled and was comprised of younger men. Describing a young member of the new regiment he wrote:

> He arrives at the table for his first meal and to my great and glorious surprise a full blown Light Horseman with colours up and everything. Well, I can assure you I was pleased to see the emu feathers and the badge with the emu in it and the red and blue colours—well I put his bandolier over my shoulder and around me and put his hat on and done (sic) a little drill with the rifle...you can guess how I felt. He says the New Light Horse camps ring with your name and the tales of *The Desert Column*. What a young solider he is and what soldiers we were!

On his way north Jack visited Ildyce and Terry, who had returned to Grafton after George's death in Sydney. Jack had an unnamed friend with him and there was much excitement and a bit of heavy drinking, for sister Dycie was not adverse to a spot or two—or three or four. Terry recalls: 'The drinking bit I remember well as I was packed off up the street on my bike to collect a rare [war time rationing] bottle of spirits.'

At the close of 1943 Jack was still trying to have his help accepted. He again wrote to Major J. Prentice at the Intelligence Department in Sydney, and offered to undertake intelligence work in Japanese mandated territory and throughout the Coral Sea. The plans which Jack outlined to the major were very detailed but his offer was never taken up. This appears to have been his last desperate effort to get involved in the war which he tried to stop everyone else from getting into.

It was all too late anyway for Jack and his New Guinea mates to become actively involved. They felt that the Americans were glory-seeking in the Pacific while the Australians were relegated to the inglorious but dangerous task of beating the bush and despatching those Japanese whom the Americans had missed.

1944 brought another distinction for Jack. On 14 April he accepted the Fellowship of the Royal Geographical Society of Australia. Originally Jack refused to accept his nomination. However, just before offering the fellowship, the society had made Frank Clune a life member. Frank contacted him and after much persuasion managed to get Jack to accept the diploma of fellowship. Now Ion L. Idriess was a life member of the society and entitled to put FRGSA after his name—he never used this 'tomfoolery'.

As well as being a Fellow of the Royal Geographical Society of Australia he was made an honorary member of the City Tattersall Club. He was also a member of the Australian Journalists' Club, donating as raffle prizes for the AJA Benevolent Fund: 1st— a set of twelve Idriess works. 2nd—a set of four Idriess works. 3rd—a set of two Idriess works.

The first full edition of *The Silent Service* was finally published and he was working on *Horrie the Wog Dog* which was written from the diary of J .B. Moody, Private VX13091, AIF.

The 1945 files are full of letters from soldiers both Australian and American, serving in New Guinea, many of whom Jack obviously knew well, and from others who were fans. The price of alcohol is reported on regularly as a common cause for complaint; whisky ranged between five and ten pounds a bottle, while beer was a staggering thirty shillings a bottle! Getting drunk would have been either impossible or a highly expensive pastime.

Horrie the Wog Dog was published that year and with its publication the controversy over the death of the little dog began again. Horrie had been responsible for the saving of many lives during the Middle East campaign because the little bloke had extremely sensitive hearing and was able to pick up the sound of incoming bombers and accordingly warn the men a long time before they were able to detect the approach themselves. Because of Australia's strict quarantine laws the dog was ordered to be destroyed, but it was smuggled back to Australia. When that was discovered much impassioned pleading by soldiers and citizens failed to save the dog. The sad destruction of the poor animal vividly reminded Jack of the horror and sorrow the mounted men had experienced when, at the end of the 1914–1918 desert campaign, they were ordered to shoot their own horses which had served them faithfully—horses which they loved.

With the end of the war publishing was starting to make a slow recovery. It appeared that Australia was about to be invaded yet again, this time by American writers and publishers. In reference to the position of Australian authors and the predicted attack by American publishers on the Australian market, the *Journalist* reported the statements made by Dr Henry Seidel Canby: 'This is just another nail in the native writer's coffin.' Dr Canby was a noted American critic who had come to Australia to lecture on American literature for Melbourne University. The *Journalist* went on:

> Dr Canby speaks of anomalies. The tragic anomaly is that American authors are more widely read in Australia today than are our own writers, Australian writers are hardly, if ever, read in the USA...There are few writers in the Commonwealth to equal Ion L. Idriess, who has become a classic in his own lifetime. Yet thirty-two of his books are out print. Will Lawson, one of our best writers of historical romances, and the last of the old school balladists, has ten books out of print. Where are the works of William Hatfield, Arthur Upfield, Alec H. Chisholm, Katharine Susannah Prichard, Mary Gilmore, Frank Clune, Henry Lawson, Banjo Paterson, E. J. Brady, Roderick Quinn, and others? Of two hundred or so recognised writers only about ten have any books in the shops.

The article closed with a plea printed in bold type demanding government intervention: 'Only immediate government intervention can save the day for our writers. Restrictions on the importation of books from overseas have been of little use because these overseas works are being printed and published in Australia to the detriment of our native writers.'

As a result of the continued outcry against imported books the government responded with a Tariff Enquiry on 21 November

1945. To the surprise of everyone the publishers gave evidence to the effect that excessive tariff on imported books would only penalise the booksellers.

♦

THROUGHOUT the years a lady kept writing to Jack. She appears to have been a nurse during the 1914–1918 war and had later married Allen Innes of New Guinea. While her husband ran his businesses she ran and managed their hotel at Salamaua; it was here that Alice held the wedding reception for Jack's sister, Katie, after her New Guinea marriage. Allie, as she signed herself, was also a writer and quite a lady.

While their affection for each other was not overt it was certainly obvious. If Jack didn't enjoy Allie's letters and smile as he read them, I did; in fact I really looked forward to finding another Allie Innes letter while going through his files. The following excerpts are a small sample of her correspondence with Jack: 'Your reference to me as "Lady" made me smile, God meant to cut me out so, but the devil ran off with the pattern. Regards Allie.'

And this, commencing with a barely decipherable word that looks like 'Funnyone':

Is the [literary] Lion still working or is he a nice tawny tame beast with social circus tricks? I wrote to you—along sanely sober lines and told you of all things ... but left the letter on my desk and Himself read it—tore it up ... He pointed out—that a perfect lady does not mention her [...? foundation garments] giving her prickly heat and causing her to terminate the letter abruptly...I agree of course —so I won't end this letter as I did the last...but it was hell trying to write in a compressing slendering Thingummy—unmentionable... so I am compelled to write you all over again, with all bulges comfortably relaxed in a pyjama suit!

Allie and Allen left New Guinea to live first at Vaucluse in Sydney, then Dee Why, and to end their days at the Mowell Retirement Village. I missed speaking with the charming Allie by only three weeks. I cannot help but wonder if she would have spoken to me of those memories of Jack which she kept enfolded with the lavender and lace.

Allie wasn't the only lady to write to Jack. Mary Gilmore usually wrote to Jack after a new Idriess book had been published. On 21 October 1946 she wrote to him one of her emotional letters:

There is something I very badly want you to do before you tie yourself up with another book, and that is to see Sir Donald Cameron,
and arrange to write his life and his people. He himself has done
things that should be recorded; and his people did big things in
early Queensland. There are two reasons why I ask you to see him
and that will be easy as I have told him I am writing to ask you to
do this. I did not say this to Sir Donald, but I am on my knees to
you, in my anxiety for this to be done.

I know you think the world of Sir Donald; you know
him as a soldier and as a man; you know Australia and her need of
such historical recording as this; and you, as no one else can, can
write this man.

You won't slight Sir Donald, you won't disappoint me,
you won't rob Australia, will you? You know I have always believed
in you, Ion, from the first time I met you, and for long enough
before. This thing needs doing, and you are the man to do it. You
won't, you can't, you mustn't say no—you'll break my heart if you
do—for you know what the history of this country and its makers
mean to me—my heart is with you for this.

Obviously Mary's plea from the heart wasn't enough to
entice Jack to grant her desire for Jack didn't write the Sir Donald
Cameron biography.

Mary Gilmore's letter came while he was researching and
working on *Isles of Despair* which could be classified as a biography
as it deals with the life of Barbara Thompson, a shipwrecked
Scottish girl kept captive by the headhunting warriors of
Murralug—now Prince of Wales Island.

Barbara's story is a harrowing tale of how she was captured,
spared at the last minute and finally taken to the hut of an under-
chief of Murralug. It also takes in part of the story of 'Wongai' as
set out in Jack's book, *The Wild White Man of Badu*, published in
1950. This true story came from the ship's log of the HMS
Rattlesnake under the command of Captain Owen Stanley, after
whom the Owen Stanley Ranges in New Guinea were named. At
that time Stanley was searching for the Kennedy expedition and
'Jacky Jacky', the Aborigine who had accompanied the expedition
to guide it through the rugged tropical Cape York Peninsula.

While Kennedy and his company were hopelessly lost, and
Captain Owen Stanley was sailing the Coral Seas searching for the
men in pensinsula jungles, and Barbara Thompson was captive on
Murralug, Billy Winn, an escaped prisoner from Norfolk Island,
had, through a reign of terror and treachery, cowed the most

fiercesome of all peoples—the Coral Sea headhunters. He had taken power on Badu as the feared demi-god Wongai. Hearing that a white woman was to be found on Murralug, he gathered the Badu headhunters to raid Murralug, where he planned to take Barbara. However Barbara, after being held on Murralug for five years, succeeded in escaping from the Murralug people and Wongai and, incredibly, was rescued by Captain Owen Stanley and taken back to Sydney.

In Crocodile Land, one of the books Jack had gathered material for during his visit to Darwin as part of the 1934 trip around Western Australia, was the first new Idriess book to be published after the war. The book was published towards the end of 1946. Jack, however, was not working to full capacity; throughout the year he had been plagued by recurring bouts of malignant malaria.

The personal war at home between himself and Eta hadn't abated but it seems to have reached a stalemate. On the surface things appeared to be normal. The girls were members of the Junior Air League and Eta, Judy and Wendy enjoyed impromptu musical performances in the backyard, Eta playing the banjo, Judy on the mouth organ while Wendy played anything that would pass as a drum.

The girls were learning to swim at the Ramsgate Swimming baths. Although Judy hadn't told Jack that her progress was almost non-existent Jack knew she wasn't learning at all. With what Judy describes as incredible patience he taught her to swim in one afternoon in the lake in Eastlakes Golf Course, which was immediately opposite their home in Isaac Smith Street. The lesson, however, culminated in Jack leaving her alone on the small island in the middle of the lake. With no other alternative to get home she had to swim back to the lake shore. At first she was frightened, then fear turned to hate. All she could think of was that he knew she couldn't swim and that he was 'a horrible cruel little man!', and how much she hated him.

Of course she did swim, remembering all the things he had spoken to her about previously such as buoyancy, not panicking, breathing easily, cupping her hands, coordinating her efforts and not wasting her energy splashing.

Jack never mentioned the incident then or ever again. Judy says that she felt that as far as he was concerned he had done his part, and it was up to her to reap the benefit of his knowledge; and that Jack had shown that he had confidence in her—the most important thing that he could have done for her.

Wendy believes Judy's interpretation of this incident is pure sentimental nonsense and that Jack would have enjoyed Judy's distress.

Jack appears to have developed a somewhat perverse streak; on one hand he could be gentle, caring and intuitive, sensitive to the needs of others. Then, for no apparent reason, he could be difficult, totally self-centred, careless, as if he enjoyed hurting people.

This callous streak came to the fore when Ion Morrison invited him to his wedding. Jack refused to attend. Ion couldn't understand why, particularly when the two shared such affection for each other and had done so since the younger Ion had been a small child. Jack knew how much Ion wanted him to be at the wedding but he only laughed each time he was asked and declared that he preferred to write. Because Ion was quite upset Jack made one concession—he would have a drink with him and Ildyce's husband John, before the wedding. The two attempted to get young Ion drunk and failed, but Jack got very drunk and kept threatening to come and disrupt the wedding.

Ion endured the service in a state of nervous tension because he knew Jack to be capable of doing anything he said he would, especially when he was in one of his surly moods. He fully expected Jack to come weaving down the aisle at the crucial moment when the minister asked the standard question. Of course Jack didn't appear but Ion said that the spectre of Jack cast a long shadow on what would otherwise have been a happy day.

After his marriage the relationship between Jack and Ion changed. Ion and his wife lived at Campbelltown before they moved to Brisbane in 1953. During their seven years at Campbelltown Jack steadfastly refused to visit them. Ion never knew what motivated Jack's stubborn resistance. This also hurt Ion, but it did nothing to change his opinion that Jack was as close to him as a brother, or a father, or that Jack was a wonderful man.

In my opinion Jack simply couldn't cope with Ion's changed status. In his relationship with Ion he had allowed himself to come close to loving another person, a relationship which demanded nothing of him except to give the occasional pep-talk, to share the odd prospecting trip and sometimes get drunk with. They had been mates! Now those days were gone for Ion had willingly done the one thing that Jack's fear of being hurt stopped him from doing— he had wholeheartedly committed himself to another human being.

I believe the aloofness which Jack had cultivated since Julia's death had, by that time, become distorted. In the beginning it had purely been a survival technique which he used to shield himself from the emotional pain that came with close human relationships.

Now, reinforced by his war experiences and his obviously unhappy relationship with Eta, it was destroying his relationships with those people like Ion who genuinely loved him.

Jack's early days in the bush had provided him with a certain degree of isolation—every word written about him by those who knew him makes mention of his reserve and that he was always an observer who rarely made comment on anything. The men who fought beside him make the same observations.

His chosen career of writing and researching had become his final hiding place. What other profession, with the exception of being a long-distance swimmer or runner, provides and requires such isolation?

Living in his head, in his own world, and avoiding emotional attachment he had managed to observe the world with tolerant, even-handed, amused detachment. He could be passionate about Australia, the Aborigines, Australian authors and Australian publishing, but never individuals.

His entire life seemingly revolved around avoiding the home and the family and he achieved this by working at Angus and Robertson, drinking for hours with his mates—the alcohol providing yet another hiding place, his mates demanding nothing of him except company—shutting himself up in his room to think and write for hours on end when he finally did come home.

Whatever problems lay between Jack and Eta it couldn't be solved by this man who was virtually unskilled in personal communication. Without the ability to verbalise, a problem intensified by alcohol, he resorted to crude abuse which isolated him still further from the understanding of those closest to him.

Jack was so caught up with his past that he couldn't now change. One cannot but feel a desperate sorrow for the boy who had worn sackcloth and ashes since the age of nineteen and wonder how different his life might have been if he had not drunk that typhoid-infected water, an action which he believed had directly caused the death of his mother.

Chapter Thirty-two
MÉNAGE A TROIS

JACK and Eta continued to lead almost separate lives. Jack's daily routine remained very much the same; apart from his giving up the unequal contest with buses by taking a taxi home each night from the St James taxi rank, little had changed. The taxi drivers knew him so well they didn't have to ask for his destination.

Eta maintained the home, looked after the children and each week played tennis, a game she enjoyed. Ballroom dancing however remained her first love. History repeated itself in 1946 when Eta, who attended dances alone each week, met Frank Lax.

Frank, twenty years younger than Eta, was a dedicated ballroom dancer. Frank found Eta most attractive, beautifully dressed in rustling taffeta gowns and long gloves, with an elegant hair style. He also found it curious that she was always alone. Naturally, as he didn't have a regular partner, he eventually asked Eta to dance with him; the relationship developed until the two became closely involved.

Over a period of time Frank virtually became a family member without actually taking up residence at Isaac Smith Street. Whether this was with Jack's understanding and knowledge at this time I do not know.

At night Eta would cook the family meal; putting Frank's dinner aside she would keep it warm. After Jack had come home, eaten and gone to bed, she would take Frank his meal where he would be waiting for her in his van parked a block away from the house. She would sit there and talk with him until he had finished eating. This nightly event became the talk of the neighbourhood.

This ménage à trois would continue until 1954. Certainly by this time Jack was fully aware of the situation.

Between 1946 and 1954 Frank appears to have become both Eta's companion and surrogate father to Wendy and Judy. In this role he took the girls ice-skating and in the summer he would meet them after school and take them and Eta to Maroubra beach to enjoy the surf.

The situation that had developed certainly took some of the

pressure off Jack, in as much as it released him to work and maintain his own lifestyle knowing that someone else was taking care of those mundane duties which he was not able to fulfil for whatever reason.

However, the stormy nightly fights continued to intensify. Talk of divorce was regularly flung about. As Jack and Eta were not married one has to wonder why, for neither one could threaten the other with what was then something of a disgrace. Perhaps Jack wanted Eta to divorce Gibson, or Eta was threatening to divorce Gibson and create a scandal. Whichever way it went, both seem to have been hell-bent on hurting the other as deeply as possible.

Unable to contend with Jack's ire when he returned home each night Eta would go out as often as possible, leaving Wendy, the only person who could handle him, to give him his evening meal. On one of those occasions Wendy remembered being so angry with him that she tried to poison him. However lamb chops which could only be identified as 'over-ripe' have never been known to kill anyone. She had carefully smothered the food in a mixture of onions and every other sauce she could find in the cupboard, a spicy concoction prepared in the hope of disguising what she believed to be poisonous food. She recalls clearly how distressed she had been when he fell asleep after eating the chops and she thought that she had succeeded.

Somehow, through the constant unrest, Jack continued to write and research and keep up his letters to editors. During 1947 and 1948 he worked on *The Opium Smugglers*, based on his travels with Dick Welch along the Queensland coast prior to the 1914–1918 war. This would be identified as a 'boy's book', a tale of adventure Australian style. At the same time he was researching and working on *Stone of Destiny*. The idea for this book had come from Jules Jorris, the diamond merchant. It is a little-known work of Jack's which traces the history of diamonds in Australia up to the date of publication in 1948. The first editions were earmarked for sale through the Jules Jorris jewellery stores. The numbers sold were not sufficiently large to maintain the book in print over a period of years and it eventually ceased to be published and it seems to have disappeared.

The war years over, Jack's books were slowly beginning to come back on to the market. He was desperately trying to keep up a steady work effort. However, a record of his activities and expenses which he kept from 1 July to 31 December 1947 show that he constantly suffered debilitating malaria: 'Sept. 2nd Blasted fever. Expenses 30s. Sept. 3rd Blasted fever. Expenses 1 Pound. Sept. 5th

Fever still hangs on. Expenses 25s and Nov. 3rd Malaria still. Nov. 4th Blasted fever in bed on cup day! Stone the flamin' crows! Nov. 5th fever. Nov. 6th fever.' These records show over the years that the length of this bout of malaria was not unusual; in one particular year he was unable to write for fifty-three days.

These tax records contain some amusing asides, which perhaps were meant to soften the stone heart of the Taxation Department: 'Cost me a fiver to help a young woman writer out of a lame patch. Don't suppose I'll get an allowance on it for tax but it cost me a fiver to help her pay her rent anyway. Exp 5 Pound. P.S. I got nothing out of it.'

Dycie had remarried in 1944—at that time she wrote to Jack saying that she was not meant to live alone— and now she was the wife of an English Lieutenant Colonel, John Rena, serving with the Australian army.

Late in 1944 Dycie, Terry and her new husband moved to Sydney. Accommodation was difficult to find in the war years so the family had stayed at the Hotel St James, on the corner of Market and Castlereagh Streets. The building is still standing and is now a bank. The St James was just a stone's throw from Angus and Robertson. Several days a week Dycie would take Terry around the corner at about 10.30 a.m. to visit Jack. It appears that this was just an excuse to have a whisky or two with Jack and Bert Ritchie and on occasions Colin Simpson the journalist, later to become better known as a travel writer.

Terry Morrison recalls those drinking sessions:

With hindsight they would really get stuck into it. I remember that around the picture rail there were hundreds of McCallum Whisky Silver Bottle Measures, evidence of many a 'working' day. This went on then until Easter 1945. At that time we got a flat at Darlinghurst and moved there though Mum continued these visits every time she went to town (twice weekly). Each session would last two to three hours and I would guess six whiskies minimum.

Fortunately, in respect of establishing some form of sobriety at Angus and Robertson, Dycie and Terry's stepfather moved back to Grafton in 1947. However, the two would make a twice-yearly visit to Sydney when Dycie, John, Jack and Ritchie continued their long established drinking ritual most mornings in Ritchie's suite.

The year before, the Labor Party had been elected to a second term in office under the leadership of Ben Chifley. The Australian Communist party had gained quite a hold. By 1947 people were writing to Jack, whom they identified as being non-Communist. Many asked him to speak out against the Communist movement in Australia, while others wrote to ask if he was a Catholic; these people expected him to be aligned with the anti-Communist organisation, the 'Catholic Social Studies Movement' better known by some Catholics as 'the Movement'. Jack, being basically apolitical and non-sectarian, was opposed to any fanatical groups, which he identified both the Catholics and Communists as. He joined those people who were fearful that Australia, and indeed the world, was being threatened by the Communist armies raging out of control in seven European countries. It was also obvious the Communist army would take control in China. Closer to home the Communist-led guerilla war in Malaya, in Jack's estimation, posed an even greater threat than the handful of Australian Communists.

Like many other Australians, Jack felt that before too long there would be another world war. It was his perceived prospect of war, not the threat of Communism breaking through, which concerned him the most. Though not politically aligned he was moved to condone the Labor Party's swift action when it put down the Communist-instigated miners' strike in 1949 by sending troops into open cut mines in New South Wales and gaoling eight of the miners' leaders under emergency legislation.

Having had enough of all the Communist letters and tired of the quarrelling at home Jack decided to take a protracted trip on his own in search of material for a new book. On 3 August 1949 he started out with a view to covering north-west New South Wales. The route he planned went first to Brisbane and on to Toowoomba, Warwick, Goondiwindi, Mungindi, Garah, Moree, Narrabri, Boggabri, Gunnedah, Quirindi, Murundi, Scone, Singleton, Maitland, Newcastle and ending back in Sydney.

Notes in the diary which he kept to record his day-to-day expenses for the 'taxman', dated 3 August to 4 September, read: 'The trip came to an abrupt ending as word arrived that the stepson was killed in a motor truck accident. In the resulting distress at home all my records of the trip, including my expense accounts, were mislaid, or somehow lost. The trip cost me 130 Pounds.' He didn't record where he was when he received the news.

Maurice was killed on 17 August 1949 at Tennant Creek, Northern Territory. The death certificate shows that Maurice Beresford Gibson, age twenty, was not a mining engineer as claimed, but a mechanic. It shows also the cause of death as a fracture at the base of the skull, and it confirms that Gibson, declared to be Maurice's father, was a gardener.

It was Frank who went to the school to tell Wendy of Maurice's death and to take her home to Eta. Eta was in shock, her grief was intense. Retreating into her sorrow she didn't shed a tear, but sat for days, dry-eyed, never speaking to anyone.

Eta used to say that the 17th day of the month was her day for momentous events ...she had been married on the 17th, Wendy had been born on the 17th and now Maurice had been killed on the 17th.

♦

I N the following year Jack and the Angus and Robertson sales representative, Colin Smith, left Sydney for Perth.

Somewhere over the years someone, perhaps the Taxation Department, had managed to convince Jack that no matter what, no matter where he travelled, the tax man would always be waiting for him when he returned. On this trip Jack kept a fairly detailed record of his expenses, and of his movements: 'A trip of nine thousand miles, visiting just over one hundred towns, meeting—on business—three hundred booksellers and newsagent booksellers.'

Ten more pages follow detailing visits and expenses incurred, to conclude with: 'Expenses for the trip east to west and back: 355 Pounds 16/9.'

Eta wrote to Jack on 18 August 1950 while he was on the Perth trip. The letter began by saying that she was pleased he had stopped drinking and that, if he had stopped drinking earlier, things would have been happier at home. She also went on to say he would probably be looking much better and observed that he had been looking old and 'dreadful', which wouldn't have done much for his morale, especially as his sixty-first birthday was only a month away! The letter continued:

> Bert [Illife, the Sales Manager] is running around like an excited pup, flinging his arms about and saying 'look at that table full of orders, what a trip and what business', smacking his lips and poor old Ritchie is sitting in his chair like a mournful collie dog and said 'I have to take my wife to Melbourne'. He looks very sad and sick and jealous—I just sympathised and laughed up my sleeve—old hypocrite. He feels as tho' he has been left out of things.

Eta's second letter mentioned that she was having shock treatment to help her recover from the trauma of Maurice's death.

'Old Dr Poet is very pleased and I very soon will have finished with him altogether, thank goodness.'

She also reported that she had taken the doctor a bottle of whisky and that he had patted her on the behind saying, 'Some man is missing out on very good woman'. 'Well after that,' Eta added, 'anything could have happened, but I just left.'

There are other letters which she wrote to Jack while he was away and each contain some jibe or allusion to him and other women or the odd taunt about how 'no one is sleeping in your bed—yet.' The game was obviously still in full swing even though Jack was on the other side of the continent.

During the same trip Jack and Colin Smith, the sales rep who did all the driving, ran into torrential rains. The Darling river was in flood, the billabongs were filling and running over, lake after lake was filling up. The two raced for Wilcannia to beat the rising water but were beaten by the flood. They had detoured out wide in an effort to skirt the flood water but were turned back by overflowing billabongs. Skirting wider again they were halted by the Tallawalka River which had been dry for many years. The two were ultimately forced to make a four-hundred-mile detour before finally crossing the bridge at Menindee.

Never one to waste a trip Jack kept detailed notes covering the Perth trip and in 1951 wrote *Across the Nullarbor*.

In the same year he finished writing *Outlaws of the Leopolds* from the material he gathered during his West Australian trip in 1934. He also began work on *The Red Chief* from material and notes which he must have briefly put together between 3 August and 4 September 1949 while travelling through the western districts of New South Wales, especially around Gunnedah, the Red Chief's tribal land. *The Red Chief* would be published in 1953.

The status quo at home seems to have been maintained throughout 1951—the disharmony continued. Jack had resumed his heavy drinking after returning from the Nullabor trip of the previous year. The more Jack drank the uglier he became, both phyisically and mentally. Each night Eta avoided or rejected his attemps to coerce or force her into his bed, which only served to frustrate him further. The more Jack drank the more Eta rejected him—the more she rejected him the more he drank. They were now locked into a desperate, repetitive pattern of action and reaction which neither was able to break. The girls, unhappy to find Eta very often in tears, formulated a plan to go to England. It was their hope that Eta, if relieved of the responsibility of maintaining a home for them, would find it easier to leave Jack. It was also their hope that

338

both Jack and Eta might find some relative peace and, I suspect, although it wasn't voiced, a measure of peace for themselves.

Both girls believed Jack to be their father by marriage; of course both he and Eta knew otherwise They also knew that the girls required birth certificates to obtain passports and that they would have to disclose the facts of their association for them to do so. This should have been the time to set the record straight but instead they chose to avoid revealing that he and Eta were living in a de facto relationship by having Jack legally adopt both girls without their knowledge.

Once again there is a conflicting story. Years later Val Pepper told me that Eta had told her in confidence that Jack had adopted the girls so that she would have no further legal claim to them. This would patently not be legal and Jack would have known this even if Eta did not. I don't doubt that it was said, for at that time each was committed to inflicting pain and distress.

The year ended with Jack making his usual Christmas promotional trip, this time from Sydney to Brisbane and back via a different route. The object: 'a business trip of goodwill to promote the sale of Australian books during the Christmas period by Press, Radio, Personal Connections and Autographing.' Jack, the unpaid goodwill ambassador, was Angus and Robertson's greatest asset.

1952 brought change: Eta left Jack's bed, preferring to sleep on the open back verandah; Wendy and Judy sailed for England, Judy to return home in 1956, while Wendy did not come back home until 1958.

Moderate recognition of Jack and Angus and Robertson came from London in 1953 with a letter from Arnold Gyde, director of the publishers, William Heinemann, who wrote asking Jack if he recalled meeting him and his wife when they had visited Australia. The purpose of his letter was to congratulate A&R on the quality of the Idriess collection: 'The collected editions of Idriess works are the most impressive in design and manufacture, while you carry the spirit of Australia in your small frame and the soul of Australia in your books.'

Australian publishing was no longer just a passing vogue, thanks to Jack Idriess and the Firm, both of whom had endured to triumph over market resistance, tariffs, depression and wars!

Life in 1953 appears to have continued very much as in the past. He received an invitation to celebrate Mary Gilmore's DBE and her eighty-eighth birthday. Mary Gilmore was now Dame Mary Gilmore and a Sponsor of the Australian Convention On Peace and War.

Outlaws of the Leopolds was published and received the usual enthusiastic reviews.

Mid-year he was on the road again, this time to the Brisbane Exhibition to 'talk to a small group of folk interested in selling and writing books and Australian literature generally'.

He finished the year with the one of the most extensive promotional tours, apart from the Perth trip, that he had ever undertaken. His papers show that he broke the trip into three phases:

Phase One commenced and concluded at Sydney visiting eighteen Towns in between, including all towns to Newcastle, to Tamworth, Gunnedah, Quirindi, Scone, Gosford, then back to Sydney. Phase Two commenced in Sydney and took in fifty towns, among which were Gloucester, Port Macquarie, Bellingen, Grafton, Yamba, Lismore, Brisbane and on the return journey Goondiwindi, Glen Innes, Tamworth, Coonabarabran, Parkes, Orange, Bathurst, Katoomba, and once again Sydney. Phase Three also commenced in Sydney and encompassed twenty-nine towns which included Wollongong, Moss Vale, Canberra, Young, Albury, Wangaratta, Melbourne, Tarcutta, Gundagai, Goulburn and on to Sydney.

As Jack didn't drive, and there is no mention of a salesman accompanying him, I assume he travelled on public transport. No doubt this would have made the trip tiring for a sixty-four-year-old man.

At the same time as he was wearing his goodwill ambassador's hat he was writing The Nor'Westers and his numerous lengthy letters. In answer to one of those letters, he received a delightful note from Jim MacDougall, the columnist who wrote the 'Contact Column' for the now-defunct evening paper, the Sun. The note read: 'I treasure your letters like pieces of Dresden ware because I feel it an honour that our most prolific recorder of the Australian story should find time to write to me.'

Apart from the honour, Jim might have wondered, had he known Jack's hectic lifestyle, just how the hell he found time to write to anybody!

Chapter Thirty-three
YET ANOTHER CHANGE

THE only constant in life is change. 1954 brought Jack another dramatic change of lifestyle, one which he probably had only vaguely foreseen—Eta left him to live with Frank in the home Frank had built at Sylvania in Sydney's southern suburbs. This brought to an end nineteen years of living with Jack, eight of which she had spent in the company of both men.

The trauma which accompanied the break is not evident. Jack told his friends and Ion Morrison that Eta had bought the house at Sylvania. Obviously this was a face-saving statement on Jack's behalf.

Joe Bourke, who had remained in New Guinea and had started a successful brewery after the war, wrote to say that 'this is a great idea of Eta's to buy the house on the Georges River...but it's a long drag from A&R's after a session at the St James—it would be possible to get the trains mixed up and wind up at Katoomba'. Joe Bourke was a colourful character in every sense of that description. Amongst Jack's many papers I found a typed outline of Joe Bourke's life. It was, to say the least, remarkable:

> Son of Pioneers. His grandfather carried the first overland mail by packhorse between Sydney and Melbourne. Soldier, recruiter, police master, gold digger, explorer, plantation manager, seventeen years of wandering life in New Guinea and adjacent islands. Met numerous adventures while recruiting in the headhunters' country of the mysterious Sepik river. When the wild rush commenced to Eddie Creek he was sent there in charge of the Native Police. Saw stirring times when the cannibal raiders ambushed the carriers taking food to the miners. Large numbers of the native carriers could not stick it, many died of pneumonia and dysentery, they tried to save as many as they could by tying them to stretchers and lowering them down the precipitous mountain trails (over this country the Fuzzy-Wuzzies are doing the same with our wounded boys).
>
> It was at this time that the 'White Angel of Bulolo' Mrs Doris Booth did her grand work. She had walked into the mountains

with the long trains of toiling men, there was no other way but to walk.

On that dreadful trail where every yard meant a step in dread or hope or despair, the raiders brought the mountain camp to the verge of extinction. When the raiders declared full time war Bourke was one of the chief men in charge of the primitive expeditions that fought the cannibals back through the mountains finally into their heavily stockaded villages of Salinkora and Kaisinik. In the storming of Salinkora and Kaisinik it was Bourke's men who finally captured the notorious Luluai, Yabbi.

Resigning from the Police, Bourke entered wholeheartedly into the hectic life of this most isolated and romantic goldfield in the world. He pegged out the Alvaleigh Claim near the famous Big Six, saw Lucky Joe Sloane clean up 685 ozs. of gold, 2064 Pounds or $3256 dollars in one day.

Saw the Big Six in one day clean 11,000 ozs., one third of a ton of gold, then worth about 33,000 Pounds or $132,000. In these days it would be worth $330,000, a glittering return for one clean up.

Gambling for unbelievable stakes went on night and day far up in that jungle camp. Bourke played in one game of poker, where the maximum stakes rose to 512 Pounds ($2048) for cards. In the first twelve months where raw gold was lying around every camp, meat tins full, dishes full, heaps of it lying on hut and tent floors he saw many a fortune won and lost in one a day.

A few years later saw Joe with an exploring and prospecting party 11,000 feet up in the dreadful limestone country near the headwaters of the Fly river. Although it rained every day, although they could hear the subterranean roar of the river far below, they had difficulty in catching enough rain water to cook their rice. For the water went straight down into the porous limestone and churned its way deep into the channels below. The maze of crevices in this terrible country beat their carriers and isolated their party in bitter cold on mountain tops of mist. They were to be supplied by 'plane, but the terrible country made this impossible. It was Tabal of the Unikia people who saved them, Tabal who speaks with his eyes, a magnificent savage with the extraordinary power of making his thoughts known through marvellous expressions of his eyes, and those same eyes could understand the white men's talk.

Adventure, strange peoples, strange lands have been Joe Bourke's constant lot during seventeen years of wandering in New Guinea. On numbers of occasions he has been compelled to fight his way out of some particularly nasty spots, with casualties to both sides. Among many strange people he met was one whole tribe that lived in one giant house for mutual protection. This house is built in the almost impenetrable rain forest near the heads of the Fly. On boles of giant trees it is built forty feet above the ground, it is six hundred feet long by one hundred feet wide, is oval shaped with loopholes in the floor through which to shoot down arrows into the attackers. In this great gloomy hive the married men sleep down the centre, the single girls sleep along one side, the single men along the side opposite. They disembowel their dead, and smoke-dry them, then bind them in banana leaves mummy fashion and lash them to the underside of the house.

When war broke out Joe joined the New Guinea Volunteer Rifles, that hard-bitten little crowd that were so long isolated around Wau and Bulolo while the Japanese tried their invasion of New Guinea with their greatest objective Port Moresby. During all those months the New Guinea Rifles, dependent practically on themselves, harassed the Japanese forces occupying Salamaua and Lae.

Joe had seen busy little townships grow up out of the headhunters country in the Bulolo Valley during sixteen years past, now he was to see them blasted to the ground in less than sixteen hours.

The adventures of Joe Bourke would fill a dozen books. Bourke is very keen on the vast possibilities of development of this Island continent. Its teeming jungles of softwoods so eminently suited for paper pulp, its unlimited quantities of kunai grass for the same purpose, its enormous swamp lands so great they could grow rice sufficient for a great percentage of the world's population. And its sago swamps, already planted by Nature with the sago palm. Its magnificent soils are adapted for the growing of every tropical product and among these Bourke is very keen on rubber, coffee, cocoa, tobacco and a score of similar products which will be in world-wide demand after the war.

A lover of Nature, Bourke has inexhaustible stories of the magnificent bird life of the Great Island, and many creeping crawling things that inhabit its mountains and gloomy swamps.

♦

JOE Bourke and Jack's other friends must have believed writing to be a very profitable career for they seem to have accepted that it had put enough money into the Idriess coffers for Jack and Eta to maintain two houses.

During this time Jack and Eta reached a civilised workable agreement. Jack continued to give Eta 'housekeeping money'; in return, she came to the house at Isaac Smith Street each Wednesday and Saturday morning to clean, shop and cook for him. As well as being a civilised arrangement, it appears to have become a friendly one, for after Eta completed the morning chores Eta, Jack, and very often Frank, would go to the races. This extension of the ménage à trois continued over many years.

The Nor'Westers was published that same year. This book contained a selection of twenty-seven true, previously unpublished stories of north-western Australia which Jack had collected during his 1934 epic journey. Now he was busy at work on *The Vanished People*; his thirty-fourth book, it recorded the life of a mystical vanished race which had lived in the Leopold Range of Western Australia and a New Guinea tribe of mystery people.

Gems from Idriess, a reader used as an educational tool in schools, had been published in 1949. This small volume, which seems to have vanished, contained a selection of thirty-six stories from previous books. The work was divided into three sections: Action, containing eleven stories; Suspense and Mystery, containing twelve stories; and Description and Reflection, containing fifteen stories.

1954 also saw the publication of the 'Frontier Library Edition' of eighteen volumes of *True Adventure in the Development of Australian Land and Sea*. Jack had more than realised his own dream and that of Walter Cousins.

However, family trouble, this time from the Idriess side, burgeoned forth and caused a rift that was not to be healed for many years.

Amy Owen Idriess had died and left the four Idriess children the expensive piece of real estate by the Mosman wharf. Jack sold, perhaps in an ill-considered moment, his quarter-share to his sister, Ildyce. A terrible argument later developed between the two when Jack claimed that she had robbed him. Jack and the delightful Dycie were no longer speaking to each other and that silence would continue until 1965.

Now he was alone. Eta had left, the girls were in England, thirteen thousand miles away, and Dycie might just as well have been that far away. Everyone who had ever meant anything to him had withdrawn from him. If ever he was given to introspection it would have been at this time; he must have compared his present situation to his last months at Broken Hill and experienced that same terrible loss all over again.

Now, forty-six years after Julia's death, and forty-six years after leaving Broken Hill, Jack began to write *The Silver City*—the story of the fabulous but heart-breaking Broken Hill—a book that for him required no research, and one which could have rolled off his pen, without a thought, years earlier. The fact that Jack was now able to write about his repressed, distressing memories of Broken Hill indicates that at last he had reached a turning point.

In 1923, a young lady by the name of Eileen had written him a poetical love letter mildly lamenting the lack of reciprocation of her affection. The letter closed with 'As gold is tried by fire so the heart must be tried by pain—you allow nothing to pain you'.

Jack, now more alone than ever before, had applied not fire, but a blowtorch to his heart when he wrote *The Silver City*. This was his catharsis. *The Silver City* was published in 1956.

Judy returned to Australia in that same year to spend some time in north-western Australia and to live and work at Tennant Creek for a while. She urged Jack to buy a jeep, the forerunner of today's four-wheel drive, and go travelling the outback with her and Wendy, after Wendy returned home. Jack didn't oblige; for whatever reason, he denied himself an experience he no doubt would have enjoyed. Perhaps he simply was not physically up to undertaking the rigours of travelling and roughing it any longer, especially as the malaria continued to burn away his energy.

Despite the repeated malaria attacks, he managed to find the time and energy to continue going to the races where he was the scourge of the bookmakers. Whether he had developed a system, just as he had done to beat the Chinese at fan-tan, or successfully studied the form guide, or whether he was simply the embodiment of that old Australian colloquialism, a 'tin-arse', an expression meaning a lucky gambler, whichever way it went, Jack repeatedly and consistently won large sums of money each time he went to the track. Just as he kept records of everything else, he kept records of his gambling outlays and returns, dates, horse names and numbers. It was a bad day if Jack didn't walk away winning upward of five hundred pounds —sometimes more, but very rarely less.

Eta selected the horses she gambled on by their names or because she liked the look of them. Jack didn't subsidise her betting bank for her outlays were small and made on the Tote, neither did he record her failures or successes, but at least they shared the common enjoyment of an afternoon at the races.

Life over the next two years seems to have rolled on in comparative peace. Jack maintained his work schedule at Angus and Robertson.

Dycie's second husband, John Rena, had died suddenly early in 1951. Dycie, now alone and living in Grafton, continued to make regular trips to Sydney. Despite her rift with Jack, she and Esmé, who had been living in Sydney for some years, continued to call at Angus and Robertson to visit Ritchie where the three would indulge in their famous, impromptu, boisterous drinking sessions.

Jack no longer joined them; there are two possible reasons why he was no longer a participant. Perhaps he was aware of the pernicious personality fluctuations which the whisky produced, or he was simply avoiding Dycie.

On one of these occasions, the two Idriess sisters, who were said to have been very beautiful, charming, talented, well-educated women whom men found irresistible, and who 'lit up the room when they entered', descended on the inner sanctum of Ritchie's suite. The party which developed grew noisier by the minute until Jack, in a towering temper, burst into the room and roundly abused both women. Supported by Ritchie and Frank Clune, who was also visiting and contributing to the frivolity, Ildyce and Esmé took absolutely no notice of Jack. Still in a rage Jack left the room, but it was not long before he came back and, after an even greater show of anger, forced his sisters to leave.

It seems that Jack just may have become the worst, and most terrifying, of all wowsers—the reformed drinker and smoker, for he claimed to have given up smoking in 1951.

In 1957 he wrote and had published *Coral Sea Calling*, a historical adventure of the beautiful and treacherous Coral Sea. It told the true story of the adventurers who throughout the nineteenth century made perilous voyages into its waters in quest of bêche-de-mer and pearl shell, of savage chiefs who ruled its islands and of seamen who charted it, of the explorers who struggled up its mainland coast and of those people who took the responsibility of establishing and imposing law and order on its wild men, both black and white.

Then in 1958 came the wonderful *Back O' Cairns* which told of the great pathfinders, men like Atherton, Mulligan, Doyle and Palmerston; and the search to find the route to the hinterland; of the rivalry between the three ports of Cardwell, Port Douglas and Cairns; of the gold rushes to the Palmer and Hodgkison; of attacks by Aborigines; of the building of the astonishing railway up the Barron Gorge.

During this period, Wendy returned home. Over the preceding year she had begun to worry about Jack, who was now sixty-nine. While she had been away she had established a very successful restaurant in Paris. Although the decision to leave it behind was difficult, she returned, believing that she would ultimately have to care for Jack in his declining years.

1959 brought the publication of *The Tin Scratchers*. This is a fascinating exploration into Cape York with 'Cyclone Jack' himself and the times when he lived and worked with the hard-bitten pioneers of the tin fields. In *The Tin Scratchers* he recreates all the colour, humour and vitality of the frontier days of tin-mining.

Jack was also working on *The Wild North* in 1959, a collection of stories gathered from the primitive frontier where the women were as tough as the men. These are tales of the Cape York Peninsula and its wild west coast, of the Coral Sea, of gold and pearls, of land and cattle, sandalwood-getters and untamed men and women.

Before *The Wild North* could be published, the saga of the first and most dramatic takeover of the seventy-five year old publishing firm of Angus and Robertson began.

This bitter struggle began in 1959 when Walter Burns, an expatriate New Zealander, became a director of Angus and Robertson and subsequently the managing director in March 1960. There would be many assassinations in the corridors of power while the battle raged back and forth between the warring factions, a battle which would continue for almost a year before the dust appeared to settle in December 1960.

This great reshuffle is truly fascinating for anyone who, like myself, had cut their teeth on the great Australian books produced by the old Firm. If it had not been for Angus and Robertson and the magnificently brave publishing decisions of George Robertson, Walter Cousins, Albert Ritchie, George Ferguson and countless others, the face of Australian publishing would not be what it is today. The efforts of Ion L. Idriess, who not only wrote many long-term best-sellers, but tirelessly promoted and supported the Firm in the darkest days of the Depression and beyond, and who was largely instrumental in the establishment of the then two-hundred-thousand-strong mail-order and credit customer list, and all the other men and women dedicated to keeping the Firm's rich Australian blood pulsing, cannot be underestimated.

Would British publishers have published such authors as C. J. Dennis, Steele Rudd, Paterson, Lawson, Idriess? I think not. Even if they had, the financial return to the authors would have been so meagre that these writers would have given up the unequal struggle and generations of Australians would have been denied their heritage of unique Australian literature. Australians would have been divested of a knowledge of their history, which would have been lost in favour of a steady diet of British fiction.

It is also very probable that without Angus and Robertson writers such as Norman Lindsay, Katharine Susannah Prichard, Alec Chisholm, Frank Dalby Davison, Ruth Park, Frank Clune, E. V. Timms, Xavier Herbert, Olaf Ruhen, D'Arcy Niland, and others too numerous to name, might never have been published.

For many Australians, and many Angus and Robertson authors—Jack included—and its managers, the takeover in 1960 by Walter Burns was too galling to contemplate.

We were incensed! We had survived the Depression and two world wars, one of which touched on our own shores. We had thumped the hell out of the Japs and managed to ship most of those 'damn' Yankees back home. Menzies had his foot on the Communists, or had driven them under the bed, the Petrov Affair had slipped into history, and now a bloody upstart New Zealander had snatched our golden publishing icon from within!

Overnight Walter V. Burns, a New Zealander, and a brother Anzac, became the Firm's 'Cain' taking the life of A&R's 'Abel'. Hardly a day passed without a detailed report in the press on the battle for control of Angus and Robertson.

To add insult to injury Burns did not have a publishing background. Burns, had become managing director of Angus and Robertson by shrewdly and quietly purchasing a large number of shares and had no interest in publishing; he had his sights fixed firmly on realising high profits from Angus and Robertson's real estate assets. He saw great opportunities in the four-storey office block in the city centre and formulated a plan to turn the valuable site into a shopping complex, just as Gordon Barton was to do some several years later.

Burns came to publishing with the incisive marketing philosophy that books were merchandise, 'like soap to be manufactured and sold as quickly as possible; the profit motive should be the mainspring'. What else could be expected from a man who had successfully marketed such mundane items as textiles, garden seeds and slippers? Obviously he had no concept of the sophistication, perception and sheer guts required to publish and successfully market an intellectual property.

The result was a general furore in the Firm and the publishing industry in general. The *Observer* on 23 July 1960 observed:

> The marriage of a man of his temperament—shrewd, vital, likeable, bold—and an old firm of this kind—genteel, leisurely, cultured, as

much an institution as a commercial firm—was clearly not made in heaven...

To Mr Burns the publishing department did not make sense. It did not make enough profit, did not produce enough bestsellers and had too much power over the retail wing. It seemed obvious to him that salesmen should have the biggest say in publishing policy...The first to resign was the production manager, Mr P. Tracy. He was followed by a senior editor, Mr A. E. Bolton, Mr Pratt and Mr D. Moore. When the art director, Mr Q. Davis resigned, Mr Burns abolished the whole art department. The publishing staff dropped from thirty to eighteen—which Mr Burns considered big enough anyway.

After many rumours of the complete closure of the publishing arm of Angus and Robertson a compromise of sorts was obtained.

In December Mr Burns was said to have enquired of Sir Frank Packer whether Consolidated Press Holdings would be interested in making a takeover offer for the ordinary stock of A&R. There followed another flurry of accusations that Burns had evinced the desire that the company should cease to exist. Burns threw up his hands and roundly declared that the enquiry had come from Sir Frank.

The Australian Consolidated Press Holdings takeover offer was rejected by Angus and Robertson but not before the Federal Opposition Leader, Mr Calwell, leapt to his feet and into print to deplore the Packer offer as being 'cannibalism' which would result in a monopoly which would mean Australian authors would be restricted in their expression! At the same time the Minister for the Territories, Paul Hasluck, deplored the 'narrowing of the field', and William McMahon urged common sense, expressing his faith that those involved would 'win through to do the right thing'.

Then thirty-four of Angus and Robertson's authors signed a statement that they would all seek a release from their agreements which required them to make first submissions of their next literary work to A&R. Among those names were Ruth Park, Colin Simpson, Pixie O'Harris, Mary Gilmore, Kenneth Slessor, Emile Mercier, D'Arcy Niland, May Gibbs and Nancy Keesing. All thirty-four were opposed to the board nominees. Colin Simpson, the group's spokesman, said they were attempting to save Angus and Robertson as a publisher.

Jack was not a signatory. Oddly enough not one Idriess letter appeared in the press relating to the boardroom fight. However he did write to Burns addressing him as 'representing his publishers, Angus and Robertson'. The letter demanded of Burns his assurance that his works and those of his fellow Australian authors would be protected and continue to be published and that the film rights to those works would be protected and copyright maintained and enforced by Angus and Robertson. Otherwise he would be forced to take steps against him! Jack didn't elaborate on what steps he was intending to take.

I doubt if Burns was in any way concerned. While he had decimated the publishing department and ruined the Halstead Press trading profit (which fell from thirty-seven thousand pounds to five hundred and eighty pounds in the seven short months of his reign as managing director), Burns had, apart from creating the most dramatic and controversial period in the history of Angus and Robertson, produced a succession of takeovers in the retail sector which made the company the largest force the Australian book trade had ever known.

The old Firm was carved up into self-contained segments: there was A&R—the main firm—with subsidiaries, A&R Wholesale, A&R Properties, A&R Publishing, A&R Bookshops, Halstead Press and HEC Robinson. Each was charged with the responsibility of 'expanding'.

The final shareholders vote went against the Burns team although Burns stayed as a director. The direction of Angus and Robertson would never be the same again. There were many changes to executive positions while the new policy directed towards real estate remained, such that the shareholders experienced a distinct rise in the market price of Angus and Robertson shares.

The war between Burns and Angus and Robertson was over. A compromise had been established and what remained of the old publishing staff stayed with the Firm, but the Burns policy was incorporated into the previously existing system. Good books, which ought to be published but which would not make much profit, were still to be published and more popular books were to be added to the new list.

Throughout the ordeal Jack, it seems, still wielded his popular pen. In the midst of all the shouting and turmoil, *The Wild North* achieved publication. Perhaps Jack had managed to rattle Burns— just a little.

What is certain, however, is that Sir Frank Packer, who now entered the arena, managed a resounding rattle all of his own. A new war for control of Angus and Robertson was about to begin.

Chapter Thirty-four
A Spot and a Cake

B̲URNS continued to finger the publishing side of Angus and
Robertson and directed Jack to write to Aubrey Cousins, son of
Walter and director of Halstead Press, to tell him to sell Jack's
books in America. Why Burns would ask Jack to become involved
in the internal management of sales of books in A&R is not
explained; nonetheless Jack did write the letter, although I doubt he
took the project seriously. At that time he was working on *Tracks of
Destiny*—not destined to be one of Jack's greatest books.

His fan mail still poured in, generally addressed to him c/o
Angus and Robertson; Jack kept a lot of these letters and the
envelopes they came in. One of the most engaging and creative
was addressed 'Idriess—Greatest Writer—Defender of Aborigines
Rights, c/o Angus and Robertson Ltd. Australia's Greatest
Publishers'.

The previous year's disturbances at A&R had unsettled
many authors. The Australian Book Society mounted a campaign to
enlist public support for their work. To this end they came to Jack
asking him to add his signature, along with other authors, to a public appeal calling for greater support for Australian writers, which
he did willingly.

In 1960 Australians and Angus and Robertson lost a writer,
and Jack and Frank Clune lost a friend—Edward Vivian Timms.
Like Jack and Frank, Timms had fought at Gallipoli. Lieutenant
Timms AIF and his men were among the first to wade ashore on
that bloody beach and fight as far inland as the Australians were to
get before the campaign bogged down. An early casualty, Timms,
badly wounded in the head, was sent back home to be finally discharged in 1917.

On 20 June 1960, Frank Clune wrote a letter of condolence to
Alma Timms:

> We're all proud of Vivian Timms. He loved his country, he fought
> for it, and he wrote for it. We were there—Timms, Idriess and
> Clune, sharing the honour of best-sellers in Angus and Robertson's

catalogues for thirty years, and now the melody of the trio is broken. We played different instruments, but harmoniously, as we all received a baptism of fire on the beach named Anzac, and we took delight in each other's successes. Never jealous, and always generous in appreciation.

During an eventful life Timms had nineteen books published, seven hundred radio plays put to air, and wrote more than a hundred short stories. A film was made from his first book, *The Hills of Hate*. Apart from writing radio plays and short stories, Timms wrote serials and scenarios for films, including *The Squatter's Daughter*. Timms also ran the Digger's Radio session for the ABC from 1938 through to 1940. All this after Timms had been told by the army doctors to take life easy after his discharge from the army in 1917!

November 1961 and the independence of Angus and Robertson was under threat once again. Sir Frank Packer, who, according to the assistant managing director of Consolidated Press, Mr L. K. Martin, 'decides everything, does everything and runs everything on behalf of the company', had decided to take over Angus and Robertson. This statement was made in court during a hearing to establish the right of Wilson's Laundry, an associate company of Consolidated Press, to evict the tenants from 175–179 Castlereagh Street, Sydney. This statement and others were given to prove that whatever Packer wants, Packer gets.

At that time Australian Consolidated Press had bought the shares of Swain and Co. (a stationery and bookselling store which Burns had acquired in 1960) and additional shares, some eight hundred thousand in all, which gave ACP a holding of over twenty per cent in Angus and Robertson.

On 1 December the chairman of Angus and Robertson, Norman Cowper, sent 'vital information' to shareholders in a bid to stop further sales of shares to Sir Frank Packer.

This letter outlined the board's concerns relative to working with Packer: 'The Directors of Angus and Robertson re-examined the possibility of working with a newspaper organisation. Their earlier view was confirmed that doing so would destroy Angus and Robertson as an objective publisher.' They refuted the claims made by Sir Frank Packer in a letter to Angus and Robertson's shareholders, two days earlier, that Consolidated Press was not trying to get control of Angus and Robertson and cited five instances to prove their point.

These points as set out in the A&R director's letter to shareholders included Clyde Packer's trip to England in an attempt to persuade British publishers to sell their shares in Angus and Robertson to ACP or to refrain from voting on the takeover offer. The A&R directors advised that both proposals were 'rejected out of hand' by the British publishers. They pointed to the fact that ACP had also offered Australian shareholders a price for ordinary shares in excess of the figure advertised at that time. They showed that Packer had conducted an intense campaign to acquire the majority of the First Preference shares. Shares of this class, for which his published offer was 27/6, were bought during that week for prices of £3/10/0d and £5. These purchases were effected by high-pressure tactics, reported to have included visits at night to elderly ladies by directors of Consolidated Press armed with transfer forms and cheque books!

As a young executive, at around that same time I was paid a visit by the two very large Packer brothers in which it was suggested I should do business with them and was made an offer too good—as they saw it—to be refused. The two big young men who virtually filled my office that day suggested that refusal of their offer could—in the long term—be detrimental to the department store of which I was advertising manager at that time. I can sympathise with the 'elderly ladies'.

Both Angus and Robertson and Sir Frank Packer sent letters and proxy voting forms to the shareholders, each stating that the lodging of these proxy votes would cancel out any previous vote.

Sir Frank simply sent a copy of his proposal to the chairman, Norman Cowper, which on the face of it appeared to have been a reasonable approach, particularly if not read in conjunction with the A&R director's letter to shareholders as above. Sir Frank's letter closed with: 'I am sorry that you have rejected this proposal. It means we will now enter into an election battle and, of course, if we are defeated this year it will have to take place again next year—or sooner—in order to safeguard our big investment.'

Jack had sold the two hundred shares he held early in 1962—he didn't record the name of the buyer. On the back of the envelope he had scribbled: 'To Darwin. To Alice Springs. To Birdum.' The open space of the great North-West seems to have rated above the A&R in-fighting and no doubt would have been very appealing to him at that time.

The Angus and Robertson Interim Report to Shareholders 28 April 1962 under Section 9, General, reported: 'The Directors consider that the affairs of the company and its subsidiaries have settled down well after all the troubles of the last few years and that the management, financial and property problems arising from the acquisitions of 1960 are being resolved.'

Under Section 10—Board Changes: 'Mr Cowper resigned as director representing the holders of First Preference Shares on 26 January 1962, and on 30 January 1962 Sir Frank Packer was elected by the First Preference Shareholders to the vacancy.

On 26 January, Mr Gerald Packer resigned his office as Director of Angus and Robertson and the Board 'appointed Mr Cowper to the casual vacancy thus created and he was re-elected as Chairman of the Board.'

Burns, the man who had started all the commotion back in 1960, had resigned some weeks before due to 'ill health'. Jack, in his own words, 'stayed out of the bitter battle'.

Jack had a good reason not to be interested in the power struggles at Angus and Robertson; his own problems surmounted anything that was happening to the Firm. Over the preceding year and a half he had believed he was going blind. However, on 15 February he wrote a note in his taxation record:

> Haven't put any Xpenses in for a good while, pending final verdict by eye specialist. He'd warned me eighteen months ago I might have to face blindness. So latterly it did not seem to matter much whether I kept up expenses and tax etc. But now he tells me the eyes have improved so much I may be OK. So I suppose here's where I start off again.

During all the plotting and counter-plotting Jack continued on his way. The old days were over, the new guard had changed the Firm so much he didn't feel he was a part of it any more.

Despite all the internal problems the Angus and Robertson staff had maintained business as usual. *Tracks of Destiny* had been released in time for yet another Christmas in 1961. Beatrice Davis, then his editor, wrote to Jack asking him for an autographed copy. Beatrice also reminded Jack of how he and Timms had always exchanged inscribed copies of their books, at the same time asking him to inscribe a copy for Alma, so that her collection would be kept complete.

Jack continued to write, working on *My Mate Dick*. This book recounts his experiences with Dick Welch when the two, ever hopeful of finding the golden rainbow, tramped with their pack horses all over the Cape York Peninsula.

My Mate Dick was published in October 1962. The other Christmas books released on to the market that year included Joan

Lindsay's *Time Without Clocks,* Nino Culotta's (John O'Grady) *Gone Fishin'* and Harry Gordon's *The Embarrassing Australian.* All these books were recognised for their 'exceptional design', as quoted in a newspaper of the time.

My Mate Dick was reviewed by H. W. Ponder of the *Age* who was definitely a fan of Jack's! The review began with:

> It is safe to say that no other Australian writer's books are more assured of a welcome than those of Ion Idriess. And one cannot help wondering whether he may not indulge in a sly chuckle now and then over the ease with which his unpretentious yarns beat the more highly polished rivals of the past...Like its predecessors Mr Idriess's latest book makes a real contribution to the all-too-few first-hand records of a vanished phase of Australian development. No doubt many aspiring authors would give their ears to know his secret. Quite possibly he doesn't even know himself. At all event he delights to tell us, the literary pundits have proclaimed from the first that he can't write.

Also published that October was John Hetherington's *Forty-two Faces: Profiles of Australian Writers.* Jack was one of the forty-two and that same year he was listed in *Who's Who in Australia.*

October also saw Australian booksellers exhibiting, for the first time, a comprehensive show of four hundred titles from eighteen Australian publishers at the Frankfurt International Book Fair. At that fair sixty thousand new books were displayed by two thousand publishers from thirty-two countries.

Jack, now seventy-three, was still very popular. Letters of appreciation for *Back O' Cairns* poured in from all over Australia along with a massive amount of general fan mail. The pupils of Cleveland Street High School wrote to ask if he would write an article for their annual school journal the *Echo.* The article they requested was to be entitled 'Cleveland Street to the Quay—a Mile of History.'

At the same time that Jack was working on his new book, *Our Living Stone Age,* his inventive mind was busy on one or two life-saving inventions. In 1963, for example, Jack wrote to Alderman Jenson, Lord Mayor of Sydney, to ask him if he could assist in realising an idea Jack had for a personal oxygen container which heart patients and asthma sufferers could carry with them to obtain instant assistance in the event of an attack. He further suggested that the users could wear a badge which showed a small red flame signifying that a 'life-saver' was in their pocket. This was probably the forerunner, although not recognised, for the atomisers or 'puffers' used by asthma sufferers today. Jenson passed the suggestion on to W. F. Sheahan, MLA, Minister for Health, for consideration. Most likely that was the end of it.

Our Living Stone Age appeared in 1963. It was the first of two companion volumes written about the Aborigines, the people he knew and loved so well. Jack's daughter, Wendy, edited these two books. The first one concerned the life of the Aboriginal baby, child and teenager; it covered rituals, things sacred and the lore of the tribe right up until the time of marriage. Jack said:

> This book is meant to be the first of two books ...the first is to explain the life of the stone age man and woman from birth to marriage; the second book from marriage to death and beyond. I have tried to make it a human story as well as being correct, in order that you will understand our wild Aboriginal as a human being and an interesting one. I have also tried to write so that you will know the wild man's heart, and the heart of his woman and baby before they vanish way.

Our Stone Age Mystery, the companion volume, was published in 1964. In this volume Jack describes traditions and beliefs dealing with life after marriage. The witch doctor, the old women of the tribe and the Council Elders all make their appearance in this narrative, as does their belief in such abstractions as life after death, reincarnation, the spirit world and sacred ceremonies.

Both these books are written with the true insight that only comes from personal experience. They cannot be described as anthropological as Jack did not deliberately set out to study the Aborigines; rather these books are a loving record of what he experienced and observed during those times he lived and travelled with a number of different Aboriginal tribes in various parts of Australia. Neither can they be termed definitive works, for no doubt there were many tribes with whom Jack never made contact. However, his intimate knowledge of the day-to-day life, legends and beliefs, of those men and women whom he did come into contact with, was recorded in these volumes. Such knowledge was obtained at a time when most European whites were still fearful of the Aborigine and definitely not interested in preserving the culture for future generations.

Jack was still an inveterate gambler. In December 1964, as was his usual routine, he had taken a taxi to the TAB to place a bet. On that day, which Frank, Eta's companion, recalled as exceptionally hot, being around the forty-five degrees celsius mark, Frank had come to mow the lawn at Isaac Smith Street. After Jack had been away for a longer period of time than was usual Frank became worried that something may have happened to him on that very hot day. He left the mowing and went to look for him. When he eventually found Jack he had broken an arm, suffered during a fall.

Frank took him to the hospital, where, after waiting for some long time in the expectation of taking him back home, he was told that Jack had suffered a stroke.

While he was in hospital Allie Innes wrote him a letter which began: 'All dressed up in his best pie-jamies and the dear little nurses all a sittin' holding his hands (how I remember my nurse days, I had a devil a minute to hold, even a nice author's hands ... 1914—1918 was all pills and pain!)'

That same year Dycie also suffered a major stroke. There are several telegrams in Jack's files notifying him that Dycie was in hospital. Terry also told Jack and at that same time asked Jack if he would like him to bring his sister to visit him when she recovered. When they met again after all the years of estrangement the two got on well but Dycie, as a result of the stroke, had forgotten all about the argument between them.

Terry's impression of Jack at that time was of a frail elderly man, still rather eccentric, talking of the time when the world's population would be too great for its resources. In fact he said Jack had a plan to cope with this problem (he wouldn't have been Jack if he didn't have a plan). He envisaged an undersea city in a dome on the Barrier Reef which would take the population overflow.

Terry said: 'I think he was writing about it at that time. I recall him talking about smoking which he had given up fourteen years before and that sometimes he still got the craving to smoke even then. His solution was to put it out of his mind by concentrating on some other thing.'

Terry took Dycie to visit Jack a number of times. In reference to the drinking habits of both he said: 'I don't recall him drinking on those afternoon visits. Mum, incidentally, had given drink away after her stroke, so two people who seemed certain to become alcoholics were diverted from that fate one way and another.' Jack had given up hard liquor by this time but still enjoyed a bottle, or two, of beer a day.

Jack was still sending his off-beat tax returns and letters to the Taxation Department. The officer who received this one, if he had a sense of history and humour, should have framed it:

Dear Sir,

To save myself 365 entries per year I think it best to put home and weekend entertainment-business expenses at three Pound per week. It costs more but I don't like to think of it. This unavoidable expense and all in connection with the collection of material, and the production of books, I arrive at it this way.

Visitors, either on holiday or business or both, from all parts of Australia, from Tasmania, generally men of the land, prospectors, timber getters, drovers etc., quite a few from New Zealand, and miners, planters, officials, pearlers on holiday from the Coral Sea, New Guinea, Solomons and other South Pacific Islands. Even from New Caledonia. These folk, if they do not know my private address seek me out at the office. Quite a lot of them I'm obliged to bring home, week nights or weekends. They have done the same to me, will do so again if opportunity occurs, and naturally they expect the same courtesy. Then again, from a strictly business point of view they are my connections for materials for future books.

Apart from these outback and Island folk there are city business friends, and city businessmen. Writers, artists, several publishers, production men at printing works, and the distributing base. All mentioned, and others too ... such as an occasional shipping man for instance, and country booksellers, if not calling at my place on strict business invariably call on a part business, part return entertainment basis. They all naturally expect a bite to eat and a spot, and such stuff does not grow on trees.

It is rarely indeed that I spend a night, let alone a weekend away from home, unless I be absent on a trip.

Apart from the above folk, there are others who make it their business to find out my private address. These cost me but little except an awful waste of time. Though often enough I feel impelled to invite them inside and that inevitably means at least a spot and a cake, unless they invite themselves to stay on, which means two spots and two cakes.

These callers are aspiring writers to be, artists who want to be, fathers and mothers who believe their youngster a budding genius, inventors, people with some political or business or empire development scheme, religious and health people with out-of-the-way ideas. The aspiring writer and artist people want advice and I do the best I can. The others have some queer notion that I must get behind their schemes and 'push' them no matter how mad the idea, no matter the wasted time, organisation, work, money.

I have to listen to all of these. For the would-be writers

and artists, especially the parents I often feel sorry and invite them inside, which adds a mite to the expense account. All these folk appear to think that individually they are the only one in the world who is taking up my time. They never dream of what that time means to me—I easily could write another book a year with that time.

It can easily be realised then the trouble. I would be [hard] put to make a note of every person, their business, or worries, or hopes or enquiries, the dates and various expenses etc. etc. So I am simply claiming three Pound per week for home/business expenses all the year round. It actually costs me quite a lot more than this, as I feel sure can be realised.

Then, for some reason, he must have remembered that he had never claimed a tax allowance for the three children, adding the following in the hope that this consideration on his behalf would be returned in kind:

P.S. The above of course does not refer to ordinary family expenses, the upbringing and education of three children etc. for which, to the best of my memory I have received no allowance.

One gets the feeling everyone that Jack had ever known, or was likely to know, was burrowing up from the centre of the earth, issuing out of the woodwork or leaping down from the trees to demand a 'spot or two' and a 'cake or two' and that Jack was conducting a down-beat version of the Mad Hatter's Tea Party at Isaac Smith Street and all at not inconsiderable expense to himself.

The Royal Geographic Journal in London gave *Our Living Stone Age* an excellent review. Encouraged by this academic acknowledgement Jack turned his attention to the *National Geographic Magazine* in the hope of achieving world-wide readership. To this end he wrote to Gough Whitlam who was at that time Deputy Leader of the Labor Party and challenging Calwell for Leadership. It is not known why Jack would have specifically approached Whitlam for assistance. Whitlam in turn made contact with Alan Renouf at the Australian Embassy in Washington DC, asking him to do whatever he could for Jack. Alan Renouf replied on 15 January 1965:

The best method would be for Mr Idriess to send his two recent books on the Aborigines, as mentioned by you, to me at the Embassy. We will then have them brought to the attention of the Editorial Board of the *National Geographic* with the information that

Mr Idriess is available to supply articles and photographs on primitive and exotic places.

The *National Geographic* misinterpreted the situation and thought that Jack wanted to have them publish his *Our Living Stone Age* and *Our Stone Age Mystery*. Once again Jack wondered if he was communicating in English or a language foreign to both. The letter was signed by James Cerruti who stated, 'We are impressed with your writing, we would be very interested to hear from you in the event that you are going out on another research and writing tour.' And further he advised that the *National Geographic* already had on hand an article which dealt with the Australian Aborigines. Obviously they didn't know that they were writing to a seventy-four-year-old man who had recorded the life and customs of tribes which no contemporary writer could hope to duplicate.

Among his numerous birthday wishes for 20 September 1965 were two rather special notes: 'How richly rewarded in friendship is your life. Stout heart we salute Ion. Allie Innes.'

From Colin Simpson:

Long may he run, who's run so well,
Australian books' own harrier
Who led the way and won the day
The man who broke the barrier.

Jack's output had slowed down. There were no Idriess books published in 1965 or 1966, but he was working on two books, *Opals and Sapphires* and *Challenge of the North*.

Challenge of the North was the result of an approach by a group calling themselves the 'North Australia Society'. They had formed at the University of Sydney following a two-day 'Northern Development Symposium' held at the University of NSW in February 1966.

This group asked if he could advise them on National Development possibilities. This approach by a group of young people inspired him originally to write an article or two based on his personal knowledge of the north. Then, after dwelling on the society's idea, he enlarged the original thought into a series of concentrated articles written directly to the members of the group, dedicating each chapter for their use.

In a letter to Mr Timothy M. Gibson Esquire, the Hon. Secretary, North Australian Society, April 1966 he wrote:

I will write direct to you, a representative Body of this young, so enterprising Generation, somewhat alarming but so interesting to us 'Older Hands'—a bunch of young folk who have thought out, and are ready to spend their thought, time and work upon a vital National subject. I will be 'talking' to you all, and will put all, or rather the little I know into the chapters of this book and you can take whatever you can use for your work from the chapters.

Jack wrote again to the young Mr Gibson, on 3 April 1967, almost a year later:

Well the book is nearly finished. The idea of writing to your generation through your society appeals to me, and I hope you will be able to help make realities of at least some of the ideas I put forward. The future is in your hands, and I am positive your generation has the capacity to meet the challenge.

He wasn't prepared for the answer he received, on 10 April 1967, from Hon. Secretary, T.M. Gibson:

The student enthusiasm for Northern Development has slid down the scale somewhat since the controversy around the issues has largely died down, particularly among the students. The fact that around the University campus there are so many more important issues for the students to discuss—the more prominent political issues etc., Northern Development has been pushed down the list of priorities. Subsequently, the few of us left have decided to 'hibernate' for a while, at least until 'the North' hits the headlines once again. Then we will see if we can make use of the momentum to gain more support.

Nevertheless, please do not let the idiosyncrasies of University students stand in the way of your desire to get your book published.

Finally may I ask that you do not flatter us by mentioning us in your book—we are but a handful of Australia's youth, probably a very unrepresentative anonymous handful. It would embarrass us immensely were you to interpret our enthusiasm as the enthusiasm of Australia's youth.

There is an undated note written in his large, square hand attached to this correspondence and signed I. L. Idriess which bears testimony to his disappointment and bewilderment over the shelving of the project so close to his heart. This is the only note in all his papers where he was moved to write an explanation:

> Explanatory Note re early correspondence to Sydney and Kingsford University Groups re purpose of writing *Challenge of the North*. They agreed wholeheartedly, but to my surprise failed miserably when they saw it was to be a real job. They pulled out in a hurry when they saw it was not going to be what they called 'a stunt'—and for them I felt disgusted, and surprised too. Surely they were not representative of the whole 'mob' of student life.

It is somehow sad that now, at the end of Jack's writing life, the young men and women of Australia to whom he had written for over a period of almost forty years had changed. It is even sadder that he didn't recognise that these young students were the new, educated, politically aware generation. At that time these young men and women he was so 'disgusted' with were protesting and revolting against the right of the Liberal Menzies Government to send conscripts to war—to Vietnam...Anzac 1967.

Back in April 1965 Menzies had waited until Calwell, the Leader of the Labor Party, and the Deputy Leader, Whitlam, were away from Canberra before announcing to an almost empty House of Representatives that eight hundred troops had been committed to fight in Vietnam. This battalion had been drawn from the Compulsory Military Service Militia. Then in March 1966, not quite a year later, Menzies trebled Australia's ground forces in Vietnam to four thousand five hundred men.

This was the first time ever that Australian conscripts were sent on active overseas service. One of Whitlam's first acts as prime minister when the Labor Party took office in 1972 would be to put an end to conscription for military service.

It seems that Jack agreed with conscription, for in his files is a letter circulated by Charmian Clift, George Johnston, David Martin and others who were calling for support from other authors to protest against Australia's participation in Vietnam. The letter asked for authorisation to append Jack's name to the statement. Jack had scrawled 'I certainly do not !!!' in red across the letter.

I have pondered the meaning behind those four words; whether his disagreement was levelled at conscription or the concept of protesting, I cannot say. In view of his opposition to Australians fighting 'other people's wars', I cannot believe that he condoned conscription.

Chapter Thirty-five
WHERE ALL THE CREEKS
SHOW COLOUR

1 967 closed with the loss of Prime Minister Harold Holt. On 17 December Holt had gone spear fishing alone at Cheviot Beach, Portsea, on the Mornington Peninsula in Victoria. Holt had entered a high surf never to leave it. To add to the drama, Holt's body was never recovered. It was rumoured that Holt, who had gone 'all the way with LBJ', was intending to recall the troops from Vietnam that same week. As a result Holt's disappearance generated a number of wild rumours all connected with Vietnam. There were those who firmly believed that the 'Russians had got him' by literally snatching him out of the surf while he was swimming, and had taken him back to Russia in a submarine. Why anyone would imagine that Holt was so important to the Russians is quite difficult to understand. The other camp, the anti-Americans, were convinced the Americans had got wind of the fact that Holt intended to pull the Australian troops out of Vietnam and sent the CIA 'to do for him'. None of which solved anything; Holt was no longer Prime Minister. In his place, as caretaker prime minister, was the Country Party's Jack McEwen.

And 1967 closed as usual with the Queen's traditional Christmas Message to the Peoples of the Commonwealth. A few days later a number of prominent Australians received royal recognition with the release of Her Majesty's New Year's Honours List. Among those was a popular Australian author—one Ion L. Idriess—for his services to the Australian Publishing Industry.

Jack was awarded the Most Excellent Order of the British Empire (OBE). Congratulations flowed in from such people as Paul Hasluck, Jack's friend, who was later to become Sir Paul Hasluck and Governor-General of Australia; Roden Cutler, Governor of NSW, later to become Sir Roden Cutler; the Police Commissioner of NSW, Norman Allen; Colin Simpson, author and journalist; Charles Moses, later to become Sir Charles Moses and Chairman of the Australian Broadcasting Commission; W. G. Osmond, Secretary of New South Wales Branch of the Returned Services League; Jack's sister, Kate, and the inimitable Joe Bourke, who was at that time living at Nambour, Queensland.

Sir Charles McDonald, Chancellor of the University of Sydney, wrote offering his congratulations and those of the University of Sydney: 'On behalf of the Fellows of the Senate of the University of Sydney and on my own behalf as Chancellor I extend to you the warmest of congratulations on your being made an Officer of the Most Excellent Order of the British Empire. Your many and great tributes to literature have long since earned you a high place in our literary history, but it is nevertheless most pleasant that this high honour from the Queen has come to you.'

Premier Robert Askin wrote: 'Please accept my warmest congratulations on the honour conferred on you by Her Majesty in recognition of your outstanding service to literature'

Federal Treasurer William McMahon, later to become Sir William McMahon, wrote: 'Please accept my warm congratulations and those of my wife on your OBE. I am personally delighted and it goes without saying that this recognition will be welcomed with the widest of pleasure both at home and overseas.'

An interesting note of congratulations arrived from Sir Roy McKerihan CBE: 'Hearty congratulations on the honour of OBE bestowed on you, an honour very richly deserved. As one who was born in Bulmer Street, Tenterfield, it gives me pleasure to see another Tenterfieldite from the same street receiving recognition. May you live long to enjoy the fruits of this distinction.'

John Ferguson and the publishing staff of A&R wrote perhaps the most telling congratulatory note of all which concluded: 'We don't think you really know how much you have done for Australia.'

Colin Simpson wrote: 'I was delighted to hear your name in the Honours list this morning. Such recognition is your due, and all authors are honoured when one is. However, I'm not writing because I feel a bit of the rub-off, but because I'm gratified and want to say so. All the best for the New year, and I trust that old bastard time treats you with proper respect from here on!'

Alma Timms wrote: 'A short note to give you my heartfelt congratulations upon your recent honour OBE. And how you deserved it, and I know Timmy would have been delighted as I am. I hope you are in good health and keeping up the writing. May we meet someday at A&R's.'

'Black Jack' John McEwen, the formidable force in the Liberal-Country Party coalition government of the time and succeeding coalition governments, a man who is said to have been responsible for the slogan 'Australia Rides on the Sheep's Back', wrote as the then caretaker prime minister for the Liberal Government to salute another 'boy' from the bush.

In February 1968 Jack received a letter from the Royal Commonwealth Society in Sydney telling him how disappointed they were that he was 'unable to attend the Reception on 18 January for recipients of New Year's Honours bestowed by Her Majesty The Queen'. The letter went on to say they were delighted to have had the pleasure of the company of Mrs Idriess and daughter. Jack who was not impressed by the royalist fuss and fanfare had left Eta and Wendy to represent him. The letter then progressed to the real business of the day and extended to him an Honorary Membership of the NSW Branch of the Royal Commonwealth Society for a period of six months—the normal joining fee being waived until the beginning of November 1968. Jack declined their generous offer.

However Jack was not everyone's darling that January. In fact he was something of a irritation to R. W. Boswell, Secretary to Walden, who appears to have been Minister for National Development in Canberra. Boswell obviously had been instructed to investigate Jack's scheme to turn the Queensland rivers over the range into the inland, as contained in *The Great Boomerang*. The tone of Boswell's letter, while polite, explains that the concept had been thoroughly examined, but finished in controlled exasperation: 'It is not possible and if it were would only sufficiently irrigate five hundred sq. miles.' So that at that time, it seems, was that. This idea however did not die and has the habit of surfacing every so often.

In 1968 Jack received a remarkable letter from a entrepreneurial German residing in Australia, who wanted Jack to advise him on a suitable method for extracting gold from sewers. Maybe he expected to find earrings and other gold pieces that inadvertently or by misadventure had been lost forever down the sewer.

Frank Clune, that other 'Digger' writer and long-standing friend of Jack's, wrote to him after the publication of *Opals and Sapphires*. After congratulating him for achieving yet another publication he turned to their association in days gone by:

> It was all your fault! Your books gave me itchy feet, and an itchy pen, which resulted in about two million words scattered over sixty books and acres of articles in magazines. And all due to you Jack. Aren't you proud of your protégé? It was just a fluke that I got my 'Dig' story out of your *Cattle King*, otherwise I might never have written another thing. Thanks Jack for the inspiration. I sincerely

hope and trust that your two score or more books will inspire other Australians to pick up the pen—when you're too old to dream—and write.

Jack's lively mind was not entirely focused on writing books. Although eighty he was still busy with inventions; this time he turned his attention to attempting to reduce death and injury resulting from road accidents. He sent his life-saving proposal, complete with skecthes, to M. A. Morris MLA. His plan was to manufacture a spring device to attach to car bumpers to reduce the impact of crashes. Morris thanked him for his concern and told him that such technical plans were not inside his province and suggested that the idea would be better turned over to the car manufacturers.

August 1969 brought the news that Morry of Desert Column fame had died at the age of seventy-two. Another of the Section of Four had slipped away. The letter from Morry's daughter mentioned that Jack had spent some time recuperating at Morry's home in Hunchy, Queensland when Jack came back after the war.

The old 5th Light Horse Regiment men were slowly fading away. In Jack's files are many letters from Frank Byron who was the secretary for the 5th Light Horse Association. Frank was a tireless worker and dedicated to the 5th. He also wrote regularly to Jack to keep him up to date with all the news of the men, and after reunions he recounted on paper for Jack the stories told that night. The recurring theme contained in these letters was 'do you remember?' As the years passed his letters, with increasing frequency, told of the death of yet another man of the old 5th. I don't know if these letters depressed Jack but speaking for myself after reading those letters which spanned approximately fifty years I felt that I knew these men and couldn't help feeling a certain sadness each time I read of another death.

Every year the 5th Light Horse Association printed a Christmas card. The card for Christmas 1969 carries a particularly poignant poem written by Ireton 'Bill' Adams dedicated to those faithful horses of the mounted regiment:

And here's a toast to our Equine Friends
Of those days so long since past
They played their part to the very end
A long and arduous task.

So charge your glasses comrades of mine
And let your voices ring
As we wish them to Valhalla's halls
Midst Princes and midst Kings!

Jack kept most of his Christmas cards. The 1969 Christmas card from Eric Jolliffe had a reproduction of a Jolliffe pencil sketch of Albert Namatjira on the cover. Inside was an amusing note from Jolliffe:

What's happened to the beaut long type years we used to have in the tough old days? Wouldn't it? Just when you learn to live without anxiety or stress or a hungry gut they start making the bloody days shorter!

The only momentous event to occur in 1969 was the publication of Jack's last book, *The Challenge of the North*.

Alma Timms wrote in early January 1970. Jack, whom some—including Professor Colin Roderick—referred to as a mystic, had written to Alma to tell her that Timms had contacted him after his death. Jack believed it was possible for those who had died to make contact with those they had left behind. In this instance Timms had made the contact, perhaps even appeared, to tell Jack he should urge Alma to complete the unfinished manuscript of his last book, *Big Country*, and have the work published.

Alma wrote: 'Strange that you should have that affinity with the "Beyond" for I have that too. There IS something beyond. I can only do my best and trust to the Gods as to what will happen after that. In the meantime Ion give me a jolt sometimes and say "Get on with the job". I'll hear you.'

Alma Timms did complete the manuscript and *Big Country*, the last of the Timms *Colonial History* novels, was published five years later in 1974.

Pat Burgess from the *Daily Mirror* gave Jack a call in October 1970, just to check up on the 'old devil'. Jack, then eighty-one, must have been feeling his age for Burgess reported his conversation with him:

Jack sees death as a black hunter loping evenly through spinifex and along dry creek beds. 'Sometimes', Jack says, 'death has the face of Nemarluk before he died of a broken heart in Darwin's Fanny Bay Gaol. He isn't unfriendly but he just lets me know he is there. He lets me know he isn't extended yet, that he's getting ready to catch me up. To remind me, he makes one of the old wounds ache. Or he'll let me break an arm or a finger, like I did when I fell out of the taxi outside the TAB last week—just to let me know he's closing in.'

Jack hadn't fallen out of the taxi. He had closed the door on his coat and the taxi driver, unaware of this, had driven off, dragging Jack some distance along the roadway. Fortunately, this time, Jack had the jump on old Nemarluk and caught him napping before he could get into full stride, managing to out-run him for a few more years.

Following the accident Jack went to live for a short time with Eta and Frank at Sylvania so he could be taken care of. This didn't sit well with Jack, and his stay was very brief. The time had now come for Wendy to return to Isaac Smith Street to look after him, just as she had known she would have to one day.

Pat Burgess's article in the *Daily Mirror* began with a typical account of Jack:

> Some Queensland people who admire the writings of author Idriess wrote asking me if Jack Idriess (he wrote sixty-two [*sic*] books) is still alive. So I figured the best thing to do was to ring Jack and ask him.
>
> 'At eighty-one I'm doing pretty well,' said Jack, who lives at Kingsford. 'I go to the local every day and have a chat ... and I go to the TAB and have a bet. Despite a paralysis five years ago I can't complain. Mum says I can't get any rattier than I have always been, so everything is tickety boo really.'
>
> What we can't insert into this item is Jack's light rippling laughter. 'Anyway,' says Jack, 'it's a reasonable question—am I alive! I've been reported dead fourteen times and so far as I know they've all been wrong.'

As usual Jack had his age wrong—he was eighty-two.

♦

IN 1972 Angus and Robertson moved to 102 Glover Street, Cremorne, a very long way for a frail eighty-three year old man to travel to autograph books; however he continued to do this each second week.

McDenagh Pty Ltd in Gunnedah NSW, was the recipient of numbers of these autographed books. Since its publication in 1953 McDenagh had sold many hundreds of copies of *The Red Chief* which Jack autographed with pre-determined messages before the book left A&R. In the files there are fourteen pages of the various inscriptions he used as messages from the author.

By 1973 the old order had changed for ever for Angus and Robertson. Gordon Barton of IPEC and Call to Australia Party fame, whose company Tjuringa Securities had earlier bought the old Firm, had moved the A&R publishing offices to Cremorne, sold the old shop at Castlereagh Street and bought new premises to establish the A&R bookshop and head office at 209 Pitt Street, with a view to its real estate potential. Burns would have approved!

Jack wrote to Beatrice Davis, the woman who had edited many of his works:

> Sorry about selling the Firm. What of the Future? *The Diamond Book* is going well. [It had been reprinted in 1965.] But then so is *Lasseter*, after all these years, sold as well as the lot of them put together, relatively speaking. Good looking reprints, these last *Fortunes in Minerals, Prospecting, Cattle King*. Don't feel happy about them being printed in Hong Kong though. How will this affect Halstead? At Canberra Copyright Library, only twelve Idriesses in sight, Librarian swears that he has great difficulty in getting books for copyright from A&R in particular. Surely there must be some mistake here. Cousins was so keen, and I thought—George was. That Library was built especially for Australian Copyright by Govt. years ago. Am very worried about it.

The year when the Public Lending Right scheme, instituted by the arts-conscious Whitlam government, came into operation, 1974, was a good year for Jack for he was the scheme's top beneficiary. The wheel had turned full circle almost at the end of his life; now eighty-five, he would at last benefit financially from those forty-seven titles which were still in circulation through public libraries.

It would be impossible to calculate the financial return had lending rights been payable right from the beginning of his writing career or even from the first publication of the best-selling *Lasseter's Last Ride* and onwards.

Jack finally sold the house at Isaac Smith Street in Kensington, the house Eta had pushed him to buy in preference to paying rent. Very frail and unable to read he spent the closing days of his life being cared for by Wendy by the sea at Mona Vale on Sydney's northern beaches.

Wendy cared for him for as long as she was able. After discussing the need to seek professional help when Wendy could no longer physically lift him or care for him adequately, they came to the mutual decision that the time had come for Jack to enter a nursing home.

On 6 June 1979 Ion L. Idriess, 'Cyclone Jack' or just plain 'Jack' to most who knew him, and to thousands who didn't, and 'Pop' to Wendy, Judy and Eta, died in the Mona Vale nursing home where he had spent the last few months of his life.

Despite the fact that Jack and Eta had experienced what appears to have been a friendly association for the twenty-five years prior to his death she refused to attend his funeral. The reason? The adoption of the girls—she still maintained that he had done this to rob her of their custody!

Jack's long-time friend, Colin Simpson, spoke at his funeral service, while the ode 'Age Shall Not Weary Them' was recited by Sir Anthony Trollope, great-great-grandson of the English novelist. Relatives and friends placed red poppies on his casket, but perhaps the most appropriate wreath was one of bottle-brush flowers, which bore a card wishing him well at the place 'where all the creeks show colour'.

Just for the record Jack—in case you're reading over my shoulder, as I know you are—how about we get your age right? Something you never could do, a remarkable piece of nonsense for someone like you. However, I know for a fact that you missed your ninetieth birthday by three months; I am prepared, nevertheless, to draw the long bow of truth just a little and drink a spot or two—to hell with the cake—to the most eventful and fruitful ninety years— give or take three months—one man ever lived!

Major books published by Ion L. Idriess

1927	Madman's Island
1931	Prospecting for Gold
1931	Lasseter's Last Ride
1932	Flynn of the Inland
1932	The Desert Column
1932	Men of the Jungle
1933	Drums of Mer
1933	Gold Dust and Ashes
1934	The Yellow Joss
1935	Man Tracks
1936	The Cattle King
1937	Over the Range
1938	How Must Australia Fight?
1939	Forty Fathoms Deep
1939	Cyaniding for Gold
1940	Lightning Ridge
1940	Headhunters of the Coral Sea
1940	The Great Trek
1941	Fortunes in Minerals
1941	Nemarluk: King of the Wilds
1942	The Guerrilla Series:

            Shoot to Kill

            Sniping

            Guerrilla Tactics

            Trapping the Jap

            Lurking Death

            Scouting

Index

Nemarluk

by

Ion Idriess

Nemarluk, one of the most feared Aboriginal renegades in the north of Australia, had vowed to rid his land of all intruders. This is the story of the last three years of his life, and his extraordinary battle with the tracker, Bul-Bul, brought in by the Northern Territory police in a final desperate attempt to put an end to Nemarluk's fight.

Ion L. Idriess had already brought Lasseter and Flynn to the public's attention with his action-packed stories. He had first-hand knowledge of the courage of Nemarluk and wanted to immortalise the man he called the King of the Wilds.

One of the classic tales of outback history brought to life by the Boswell of the Bush, Jack Idriess.

IMPRINT LIVES

$14.95 rrp

ISBN 1-875892-10-9

flynn

of the

Inland

by

Ion Idriess

Almost single-handedly John Flynn of the Australian Inland Mission brought to the outback the Flying Doctor Service and the Bush Hospitals. His magnificent vision, formed as he travelled on the back of a camel across the vast space of Australia's outback, took a lifetime of courageous commitment to bring to reality.

'It's impossible to read this book and remain untouched by the greatness of John Flynn's inspiration.'
Morning Post, London

IMPRINT LIVES
$14.95 rrp
ISBN 1-875892-11-7

Prospecting for
Gold

by
Ion Idriess

'I felt certain there must be gold in those hills, Jack', wrote a prospector to Ion L. Idriess, 'but I knew very little about the game.' And so Jack Idriess wrote *Prospecting for Gold*. After many editions and over 300,000 copies sold, it is now the classic self-help manual for would-be prospectors.

'This book is written to help the new hand who ventures into the bush seeking gold... The "towny" prospector, with this book as a guide, will soon master methods of prospecting and the working of his find.'

In an easy conversational tone, the author of *Lasseter's Last Ride* and *Flynn of the Inland* sets many a hopeful prospector on the road to discovering gold.

IMPRINT
$16.95 rrp
ISBN 1-875892-12-5